Broadway Yearbook, 2000–2001

The Broadway Yearbook Series
by Steven Suskin

Previous Titles

Broadway Yearbook, 1999–2000

2000 2001 BROADWAY YEARBOOK

Steven Suskin

OXFORD

UNIVERSITY PRESS

2002

OXFORD
UNIVERSITY PRESS

Oxford   New York
Auckland   Bangkok   Buenos Aires   Cape Town   Chennai
Dar es Salaam   Delhi   Hong Kong   Istanbul   Karachi   Kolkata
Kuala Lumpur   Madrid   Melbourne   Mexico City   Mumbai   Nairobi
São Paulo   Shanghai   Singapore   Taipei   Tokyo   Toronto

and an associated company in Berlin

Copyright © 2002 by Steven Suskin

Published by Oxford University Press, Inc.
198 Madison Avenue, New York, New York 10016

www.oup.com

Oxford is a registered trademark of Oxford University Press

ISBN 0-19-514882-7; ISBN 0-19-515637-4 (pbk.)
ISSN 1473-933X

1 3 5 7 9 8 6 4 2
Printed in the United States of America
on acid-free paper

For

Helen, Johanna,

and Charlie

Contents

Curtain Calls

Broadway Yearbook, 2000–2001

The Curtain Rises

The 2000–2001 season was in several ways remarkable. Item one: Most remarkable of all, needless to say, was the arrival of *The Producers*. Broadway typically has a supersmash hit or two every decade. The 1940s had *Oklahoma!* and *South Pacific*; the 1950s had *My Fair Lady*; the 1960s had *Hello, Dolly!* and *Fiddler on the Roof*; the 1970s had *A Chorus Line* and *Annie*; the 1980s had *Cats* and *Les Misérables* and *Phantom of the Opera*; the 1990s had *Rent* and *The Lion King*. But *The Producers*, in terms of immediate impact, was bigger than them all. That is, the show itself became a news event, setting off its own media frenzy. Nathan Lane and Matthew Broderick and Mel Brooks were suddenly all over the place; front pages, feature stories, magazine covers, cartoons. There were even stories in newspapers in China, a country not heretofore noted for its affinity for American musical comedy.

This was a mammoth hit; even people in the theatre, who have connections, simply couldn't get tickets. I've been around since before *A Chorus Line*. While house seats on these earlier blockbusters were not easy to come by, it was usually possible for people in the business to get at least a pair for themselves. *The Producers* was such a tight ticket that many people working in the theatre—including some on fairly high levels—were simply unable to get seats during the first six months. I'll make an educated guess that *The Producers* was the hottest ticket in at least fifty years; from what I've heard, *South Pacific*—in 1949—might have been of comparable stature.

Will *The Producers* be the most successful musical in history? Will *The Producers* be the most lucrative show in history? The $100 top (thanks to a $10 price hike on the day the reviews hit) should help them outearn shows like *Dolly* (which opened at $9.40). But it is unlikely, in my view, for *The Producers* to approach the profit levels of *Cats* and *Les Misérables* and *Phantom of the Opera*; these imports were built for mass production in multiple languages, while *The Producers* calls for special talents and probably won't translate as well. But as for the effect of a show on its place and time, I don't suppose Broadway has ever seen anything like *The Producers*.

Item two: Let us look at the past ten seasons, specifically, the new American plays that made money. (This list includes new American plays only—no imports, revivals, solo shows, or attractions produced by nonprofit theatres.)

The 1990–1991 season had one, Neil Simon's *Lost in Yonkers*. The 1995–1996 season had one, Terrence McNally's *Master Class*. The 1996–1997 season had one, Alfred Uhry's *The Last Night of Ballyhoo*. The new play hits of 1997–1998 and 1998–1999 and 1999–2000 were all imports. (*Dirty Blonde*, the final play of 1999–2000, reported a profit in *Variety* but appears to have ended its Broadway engagement in the red.)

That gives us only three moneymaking new American plays in ten full years. In 2000–2001, in a two-week stretch alone, there were three—count 'em—three. And they did not merely break even: Neil Simon's *The Dinner Party*, David Auburn's *Proof*, and Charles Busch's *The Tale of the Allergist's Wife* garnered sizable profits, with recoupment coming in each case in less than twelve weeks. Three in ten years; three in two weeks. Remarkable.

I have not included revivals in this equation; it should be pointed out that two profitable revivals were also simultaneously on the boards, *Gore Vidal's The Best Man* and Lily Tomlin and Jane Wagner's *The Search for Signs of Intelligent Life in the Universe*. (*The Best Man*, like *Dirty Blonde*, reported a profit in *Variety* but apparently closed with a small deficit.) All five shows opened within two months. There is only a limited audience for nonmusical shows on Broadway; at least, that's what they've always told us. Suddenly, enough cash-bearing theatregoers materialized to patronize them all.

Item three: The Shuberts are Broadway's most productive producers ever, with something like 650 productions since the firm's founders came to town in 1901. Lee Shubert, the most powerful of the brothers, died on Christmas Day 1953. Three weeks later, the final Shubert-produced show of the era opened at the Royale (and closed the same day). It wasn't until 1976 that the Shubert Organization—as we now know it—picked up the gauntlet, starting with shows like *Sly Fox*, *Amadeus*, *Ain't Misbehavin'*, and *Cats*. The 2000–2001 season marked the first season in twenty-four years in which the Shuberts did not produce a single Broadway show. (They did produce two in 1999–2000 and planned at least one for 2001–2002.)

Item four: The 1999–2000 season was remarkable for a three-day stretch—April 14 through 16—when for the only time in memory each and every Broadway theatre had a show on the boards. This record was almost, but not quite, surpassed in 2000–2001. Thirty-seven houses—including Broadway's newest, the American Airlines Theatre—were lit for a full four weeks, from April 16 through May 13. One was dark, though; the Winter Garden, which was undergoing a full-scale renovation (and fumigation) in preparation for its fall 2001 booking, *Mamma Mia*. Perhaps this lack of empty theatres to fill helps explain the Shubert Organization's absence from the producing ranks in 2000–2001. Or was it simply a reaction to the Patrick Stewart affair, in which the actor publicly attacked the Shuberts from the stage of *The Ride Down Mt. Morgan* in April 2000?

Item five: *The Producers*, again. Broadway musicals are a life-and-death matter to die-hard theatre fans; but a Broadway musical making worldwide news? In the twenty-first century, when you're unlikely to hear a new show tune on the radio, ever? Hard to believe, and remarkable.

Broadway Yearbook, 2000–2001 presents an analytical discussion of each show that opened on Broadway between May 29, 2000, and May 27, 2001. I have also deemed it fitting to include certain non-Broadway productions of importance, namely, the City Center Encores! series. The shows are discussed in chronological order; an alphabetical arrangement might make it easier to browse through to find a specific show, but it seems pertinent to have the reader discover each show in the same order as the critics and theatregoers. Timing—that is, the competition on the date of opening—was a significant factor in the reception and fate of some of this season's offerings.

The opening night credits and cast list are accompanied by a discussion of the production. I neither ask nor expect the reader to necessarily agree with my opinions. You will no doubt concur with some and not others—hopefully more of the former than the latter. Taste is individual, or at least it should be. I have tried to be consistent in my opinions and to support my arguments (in the nonargumentative sense of the word). It is one thing to turn thumbs up or thumbs down; it is another thing to explain *why* the thumb is nudged toward the heavens or the opposite. Or someplace in between.

My aim has been to keep things informative and instructive; hence, the discussion is laced with examples from general Broadway history (and my checkered twenty-five years on and around Forty-fourth Street). What were the shows like? How were they received, by both the critics and the audiences? What other factors contributed to their success or failure?

The discussion of each show is followed by a section of related data, starting with dates and length of run. Performance and preview totals have been compiled using information from the League of American Theatres and Producers. In some cases these differ from the "official" counts distributed by press agents; I consider the League tabulation—reported week by week, along with the grosses—to be more accurate. Profit-and-loss information comes from a variety of sources, including the invaluable *Variety*. Shows from nonprofit organizations have been similarly classified where applicable, based on an estimate of surplus income generated by the production. It should be understood that a show that ends its Broadway run with a loss might well make up the difference from post-Broadway income. Conversely, it is not unknown for a show to have recouped its costs but—due to an overextended run or unforeseen touring costs—to slip back into a deficit.

Shows that were still running on May 28, 2001—the first day of the 2001–2002 season—are so indicated. (For the sake of completeness, closing dates and performance totals are included for shows that ran into 2001–2002 but closed before this book went to print.) Next comes the critical scorecard, which gives the reader a general idea of the critical reception of each production. The scorecards are based on the opinions of seven to ten critics from major newspapers and magazines. The number of reviews varies; not all attractions were covered by all the critics. (In a few "special" cases, productions discussed herein were reviewed by only a handful of reviewers.) The scorecards reflect the opinions of the critics from the *New York Times*, the *Daily News*, the *New York Post*, *Newsday*, the Associated Press, *Variety*, the *Village Voice*, and *New York Magazine*. Weekly magazines that offer occasional reviews, such as *Newsweek*, *Time*, and the *New Yorker*, were also included in some of the tabulation.

Reviews have been rated in five categories:

Rave   Overwhelmingly positive, enthusiastically indicating that the show should be seen

Favorable	Positive, indicating that the show is good though not outstanding, or that the show is good despite minor flaws
Mixed	Positive and negative aspects are presented, with no overall recommendation; sometimes the reviewer is simply unclear
Unfavorable	Negative, indicating that the show doesn't work— often despite positive elements or good intentions
Pan	Overwhelmingly negative, indicating—often with a hint of annoyance—that the show was downright bad

Quite a few of the reviews fall somewhere between two categories. I have called 'em like I see 'em, although a pollster would probably say that there is a two-point margin of error.

A brief financial section gives the reader an idea of the show's economic performance. Figures, again, have been compiled using information from the League of American Theatres and Producers. Finally, Tony Awards (and nominations) received by the show and its personnel are listed, along with other major awards.

Following the main body of the book are six appendixes that, it is hoped, will prove a useful supplement to the discussion of the season.

And so the curtain rises, as they say, on *Broadway Yearbook, 2000– 2001.*

See you at the theatre.

The Shows

Macbeth

Word from Boston spread around town on the afternoon of May 31 that Kelsey Grammer's *Macbeth*—the first new Broadway show of the season—was about to disband its band of witches and shutter four days later, on Tony Award Sunday. This in the face of the worst pre-Broadway reviews in—well, nine weeks, when Elaine May's *Taller Than a Dwarf* met similar resistance from the same critics at the same theatre in the same town.

Terry Byrne of the *Boston Herald* noted that the play—which "usually incites gut-wrenching terror, sadness and, finally, redemption"—in Grammer's hands "elicits only snickers and the kind of horror that comes from seeing a production go completely awry." Ed Siegel in the *Boston Globe* called it a "two-hour freight train of an adaptation." Markland Taylor of *Variety* called it "a reasonably competent, underlit staged reading," finding the star "a stolid, somewhat flat-footed middle-class, middle-aged man."

Here, you had a surefire crowd nonpleaser. But you also had a major television star in tow. A TV star who, presumably, was likely to sell a certain number of tickets on the basis of his name. What's a producer to do? It takes a certain amount of integrity to simply return that ticket money, to admit that the TV star was ill served and his fans would no doubt be bored silly. To say, in effect, "We're not going to stick you even though we've already got your money in our bank account."

It did not take three weird sisters, or a theatre-producing genius, to forecast that lousy reviews for the show—and condescending ones for the star—awaited on Broadway.

THE MUSIC BOX

THE ESTATE OF IRVING BERLIN AND THE SHUBERT ORGANIZATION, OWNERS

SFX Theatrical Group
and
Emanuel Azenberg
present

KELSEY GRAMMER
MACBETH
WITH DIANE VENORA

By William Shakespeare

Michael Gross   Stephen Markle
Kate Forbes   Peter Gerety   Peter Michael Goetz   Bruce A. Young

John Ahlin, Starla Benford, Ty Burrell, Parris Nicole Cisco, Kelly Hutchinson, Austin Lysy,
Mark Mineart, Jacob Pitts, Grant Rosenmeyer, Myra Lucretia Taylor, Sam Breslin Wright

Set and Costume Design   Lighting Design   Sound Design
Timothy O'Brien   Terry Hands   Tom Morse

Original Music   Special Effects Design   Casting
Colin Towns   Gregory Meeh   Jay Binder

Tech Supervision   Production Stage Manager   Public Relations
Unitech II, Corp   John M. Galo   Barlow • Hartman

General Manager   Executive Producer
Abbie M. Strassler   Lynn Landis
                                  SFX Theatrical Group

Fight Director
B.H. Barry

Directed by
TERRY HANDS

Cast (in order of appearance)

Seyton Peter Gerety
Witches Myra Lucretia Taylor, Starla Benford, Kelly Hutchinson
Duncan Peter Michael Goetz
Malcolm Sam Breslin Wright
Ross Michael Gross
Macbeth Kelsey Grammer
Banquo Stephen Markle
Lennox Ty Burrell
Lady Macbeth Diane Venora
Fleance Jacob Pitts
A Porter Peter Gerety
Macduff Bruce A. Young
Donalbain Austin Lysy
An Old Man Peter Michael Goetz
Murderers John Ahlin, Mark Mineart
Lady Macduff Kate Forbes
Her Son Grant Rosenmeyer
Her Daughter Parris Nicole Cisco
An English Doctor Peter Michael Goetz
A Scottish Doctor John Ahlin
Gentlewoman Kelly Hutchinson
A Servant Jacob Pitts
Young Siward Austin Lysy
Siward Peter Michael Goetz

Of course, the out-of-town reviewers might have been far, far, far off base; this has been known to happen. In this case, though, they weren't—and the producers presumably recognized the fact. Under the circumstances, what did *Macbeth* have to look forward to? It did not take three weird sisters, or a theatre-producing genius, to forecast that lousy reviews for the show—and condescending ones for the star—awaited on Broadway.

That *Macbeth* would decide to close was a bit of a surprise, unless one noticed producer Emanuel Azenberg's name above the title. Manny Azenberg has been at it for almost forty years, with a pretty good track record. He has produced some exceptional shows—like *Ain't Misbehavin'* and the 1998–1999 revival of *The Iceman Cometh*—and a very few failures along the way. (Does anyone remember the cannibalism drama *Devour the Snow?*) But Manny knows, generally speaking, what to expect once his shows leave the rehearsal hall and hit the stage. He has also produced some worthy but difficult shows, some of which have succeeded (like *Children of a Lesser God*) and others that have been heartbreakers (like *Side Show*, the Siamese twin musical). He has also produced all of Neil Simon's new work since 1972.

Azenberg's most recent play was the Donald Sutherland–John Rubinstein starrer *Enigma Variations*. It was scheduled to open in late April 2000 at the Brooks Atkinson, just six weeks prior to *Macbeth*'s Broadway opening. After seeing the reception of the show's Toronto tryout, Azenberg and his partners decided to cancel New York. (The show went to London instead—under the title *Enigmatic Variations*, without Azenberg's involvement—and received a hostile reception.) Faced with the same situation on *Macbeth*, it seemed that Azenberg had been wise enough and brave enough to simply pull the plug.

Then word came, on Friday, June 2, that it was all unfounded rumor and *Macbeth* was coming to the Music Box as scheduled. Buyer beware.

Macbeth marked a not-so-auspicious Broadway debut for SFX, the entertainment industry behemoth. In the last few years of the twentieth century, SFX bought or leased 120 "live entertainment venues" in the top fifty markets. "The world's leading promoter, producer, and presenter of diversified live entertainment, SFX is all about providing Spectacular, Fun, and X-citing live entertainment on a scale never before imagined." The plan, it appears, is to make it difficult for a show or an act or a rock band to successfully tour without having SFX as a landlord or—preferably—as a partner. (In July 2001, following the period covered by this book, SFX changed its name to Clear Channel Entertainment.)

SFX's first move into live theatre had come with its purchase of PACE Theatrical. PACE began in 1982, when a group of operators of theatres in secondary cities got tired of being cut off from the big-money touring shows. By banding together, they reduced costs and attracted better product by offering more playing dates than they could individually. PACE grew and grew, as they affiliated with more and more venues and accumulated an impressively large base of money-paid-in-advance subscribers. PACE eventually began to produce shows of their own to fill empty playing time, although their choices—geared toward their theatrically unsophisticated subscribers—were inevitably lowbrow by Broadway standards. Like a clunky 1988 touring production of *South Pacific* starring Robert Goulet, which did phenomenal business but skirted Broadway. The PACE formula was to find a "star," submit the name to their marketing department, and—once cleared—build some show or other around said star.

PACE began circling Broadway, providing investment money for "class" shows like Manny Azenberg's production of *Jerome Robbins' Broadway*. They realized that they were spending millions of dollars booking big hit musicals—namely *Cats*, *Les Misérables*, and *Phantom of the Opera* —into their theatres again and again. Why not try to produce their own? (Big hit musicals, that is.) Their first major attempt was the moderately successful *The Who's Tommy*, in 1993. They finally hit the big time, in

a manner of speaking, with the long-running *Jekyll & Hyde*. Despite scathing reviews, Frank Wildhorn's first Broadway musical opened in 1997 and ran into 2000–2001, closing after 1,543 performances. A three-year run, yes; but *Jekyll & Hyde* lost millions and millions of dollars. Anyone can keep a Broadway show running for a year or two or more if they don't mind pouring in millions; the trick is to generate enough money at the box office to turn a profit.

In 1997, PACE was purchased by SFX for $130 million. And then in June 1999, SFX purchased the bankrupt Livent as well. Livent's first big Broadway musical was *Kiss of the Spider Woman*, which bested *Tommy* in the Tonys and went on to become the longest-running musical ever to lose millions of dollars (until bested by *Jekyll & Hyde*, that is). SFX Theatrical—run by the former PACE staff—took over Livent's critically praised *Ragtime*, which also closed after two years with a hefty loss, and *Fosse*, which appears to have been the only Livent-originated musical to break even.

Other Livent assets included some prime real estate, such as Broadway's spanking new Ford Center, and several musicals in preparation. These included *Sweet Smell of Success*, a Marvin Hamlisch–Craig Carnelia–John Guare–Nicholas Hytner effort that at this writing is scheduled for the 2001–2002 season and—more immediately—the can't-miss blockbuster *Seussical*. The latter, from Stephen Flaherty, Lynn Ahrens, and Frank Galati of *Ragtime*, promised to be one of the important Broadway events of 2001. But before *Seussical* came to town, SFX tried its hand with *Macbeth*.

What happened, apparently, is that three-time Emmy Award winner Kelsey Grammer was unable to find a suitable movie to make during the hiatus between the sixth and seventh seasons of his sitcom, *Frasier*. Before heading to Hollywood, Grammer was a stage actor; he played Lennox in Sarah Caldwell's 1981 production of *Macbeth* at the Vivian Beaumont. When leading man Philip Anglim was raked over the coals by the *Times* critic, he became indisposed (as they say), and on went his understudy: Kelsey Grammer. Grammer long relished another crack at the role (as they say), and—with no suitable movie in the offing—his wife suggested that he just bite the bullet (as they say).

Lady Grammer—Camille Donatacci, that is—called a friend, concert promoter Ron Delsener. Delsener, a colorful throwback to the sixties who enthuses at an energetic clip, must have said something like "That's-great-babe-whatever-Kelsey-wants-hey-I've-got-a-partner-whatever-Kelsey-wants-babe." Delsener's company, Delsener/Slater, was the first of the major promoters bought by SFX. He called his partners—the PACE people at SFX Theatrical—and Broadway had its first show of the 2000–2001 season.

Broadway has long welcomed Hollywood stars looking for what they used to call a respite from Tinseltown. Many such luminaries have headed east during career lulls. In the old days, people like Katharine Hepburn and Henry Fonda consistently returned to the Broadway from which they sprang. Even nowadays, still-in-demand A-list stars like Dustin Hoffman, Al Pacino, Meryl Streep, Glenn Close, Kevin Kline—and newcomers like Liam Neeson and Ralph Fiennes—occasionally disappoint their agents and managers and money people by insisting on doing stagework.

Grammer is not, perhaps, in a class with these thespians; but he certainly had an immense following, a successful full-time job that paid him scads more than he could make on Broadway, and no need to subject himself to what turned out to be a scathing reception. There was no earthly reason for this *Macbeth*—except that Kelsey Grammer felt like doing it.

Kelsey Grammer wasn't bad, really; he was simply ill-starred. He seemed to be gingerly dancing about, carefully executing his remembered moves and crosses.

One of the advantages of SFX's across-the-board connections is that a project like this can become a fully funded reality with a snap of the fingers. One of the disadvantages, as *Macbeth* demonstrated, is that a project like this can become a fully funded reality regardless of artistic merit. As Dr. Einstein never theorized: S(tar)FX + money = profit.

SFX appears to have attempted to come up with as classy a production as possible. Azenberg—the highly visible lead producer of Kevin Spacey's *Iceman Cometh*—was invited in, apparently, to take care of the art stuff. Terry Hands, the former artistic director of the Royal Shakespeare Company, was hired to direct. Diane Venora, a frequent essayer of Shakespearean roles in America, was named Lady Macbeth. Venora had been an acting-scene partner of Grammer's at Juilliard, from which he was expelled.

So here you had a respectable-sounding package, although the package turned out to be empty. The director came up with a minimalist production—minimal in scenery, costumes, cast, and thought. Hands has done some interesting work as a director, including the notable *Cyrano de Bergerac/Much Ado About Nothing*, which Derek Jacobi played at the RSC in 1983 and on an American tour in 1984. I worked on the American leg, as it happens, and both productions were striking. What I found most remarkable about them, aside from Derek's performances, was the lighting. Hands—one of only two lighting designer–directors I've ever come across—sculpted the stage in darkness, showing us only precisely what he wanted us to see.

The two RSC shows were first-rate; but, then, Terry was working with Sir Derek and an acting company of Shakespearean veterans. Hands returned to America with a big Broadway musical: the infamous *Carrie*, which some of you might recall. His only subsequent local appearance has been with *Macbeth*, which had a company of non-Shakespearean veterans.

The lighting, anyway, was striking.

You knew you were in trouble right from the start, when you couldn't understand what the bag-lady witches were saying. (It sounded something like "When'll we three me again, thunder babble bab inrai.") Grammer's Macbeth entered wearing a mask, which was a good idea. When he got to Invernesse, he changed to a nice white T-shirt, displaying his muscles and hearty physique. All the other guys wore long sleeves, but it gets cold in those castles and over-air-conditioned Music Boxes.

The star wasn't bad, really; he was simply ill-starred. Grammer's grammar and diction were impeccable, he had his lines down, and he knew how to produce the sounds. But for a Juilliard graduate—or, rather, a Juilliard student—he was strangely uncomfortable onstage. In the premurder soliloquy ("Is this a dagger which I see before me . . ."), he seemed to be gingerly dancing about, carefully executing his remembered moves and crosses. Or maybe he was just remembering his Boston reviews? He turned out to be one of the neatest dagger murderers in memory, doused in blood from wrists to fingertips but otherwise clean as a whistle. Bruce A. Young's Macduff, though, was pretty good.

"Screw your courage to the sticking-place and we'll not fail," said Lady M just before Mr. M climbed the stairs to do the most foul deed. Grammer screwed his courage, as it were, in attempting *Macbeth*, and even more so in coming to town after being besieged in Boston. But screwed courage wasn't enough, not this time it wasn't.

Still, one must keep these things in perspective. In June 2001, it was announced that Grammer had re-signed with *Frasier* for $1.76 million per episode. If the man wishes to return to Broadway next season, or every season, I say—let him.

> "Screw your courage to the sticking-place and we'll not fail." Grammer screwed his courage, as it were, in coming to town after being besieged in Boston. But screwed courage wasn't enough.

The Man Who Came to Dinner

While preparing to go off to the 7:00 P.M. official opening of the new American Airlines Theatre and *The Man Who Came to Dinner*, I received an e-mail from the author of one of the most controversial musicals of the 1999–2000 season castigating me for a comment I had made on the Internet about his work. Not castigating me, exactly, but upset by a comparison I'd made between his show and a similar one.

The point of his e-mail, though, appeared not to have been what I had said. (He acknowledged that I at least *listened* to his music, while other critics make off-the-cuff comments—in this case blithely comparing his work to that of Frank Wildhorn and Igor Stravinsky—without any critical basis.) What upset him, mostly, was that his show did not receive a "respectful" review in the *New York Times*. The critic didn't actually address his score, the composer complained, because he (Ben Brantley) went on at length complaining about the director's prior Broadway musical. And he (the composer) expressed the popular—and reasonably accurate—assessment that a bad review in the all-powerful *Times* was fatal. Finally, he concluded that the treatment he received from the *Times* and its "incompetent critic"—his words, not mine—was an important topic for people like me to write about. But, of course, he didn't expect me or anyone to write anything critical of the *Times*.

Seeing as how the composer raised serious issues in his e-mail, I felt it proper to carefully address his questions. I made it clear that I respected his work (which I do). But certain portions of the show, simply and clearly, did not work for me while I was sitting in the theatre. I cited specifics, and in our continuing interchange of e-mails he indicated that he was quite aware of these specific weaknesses. The fact is, once you have fifty or sixty or eighty people acting and staging and designing and producing and operating the scenery, your work might not necessarily come across the footlights precisely the way you intended. And once $5 or $6 or $8 million have been spent, it ain't so easy to fix it. Anyway, we ended up with a clutch of mutually respectful e-mails.

Part of my response addressed the composer's complaint about "respectful notices" from the paper of record: "That's something I've grown not to expect. Ever since I've been in this business people have been complaining about the critic from the *New York Times*. The fact is, whoever they hire gets to say whatever he wants. I'd like to think that the opinions are well-founded, but the most you can hope for is that the critic is consistent and that he explains and supports his views. (I use the word 'he' because there hasn't been a first-string female drama critic in New York since 1943.) As for being respectful—well, it's much easier to write a bad review than a cautious review.

"The way to change the power of the *Times* is simple: Just have producers refuse to take ads (which of course is impossible). The way it works now, Brantley can give a show a really devastating pan—like he gave *Footloose* or *Saturday Night Fever*—and the producers will still spend, literally, hundreds and hundreds of thousands of dollars on full-page ads. So why should the *Times* try to restrain their critic?"

Oddly enough, something of the sort did occur back in 1915. The critic from the *Times* wrote a lousy review of a lousy play called *Taking Chances*. The producers—Lee and J. J. Shubert—banned the critic from their theatres and demanded that the *Times* replace him. The *Times* sided with their man and retaliated by banning all Shubert advertising from its pages. This was big-deal news, with columns full of coverage; freedom of the press and all that. (While they were fighting it out, another war started—the *Lusitania* was sunk the day that the courts ruled in favor of the critic.)

> Woollcott loomed large over the cultural scene of these United States until his death in 1943; imagine a combination of Larry King, Oprah Winfrey, and Liz Smith. For all his importance and self-importance, his books all but disappeared within a generation.

But getting back to the evening of July 27, I read the e-mail from the composer; walked over to the new Roundabout; and returned to answer the message. The next morning I combed all the reviews I could readily

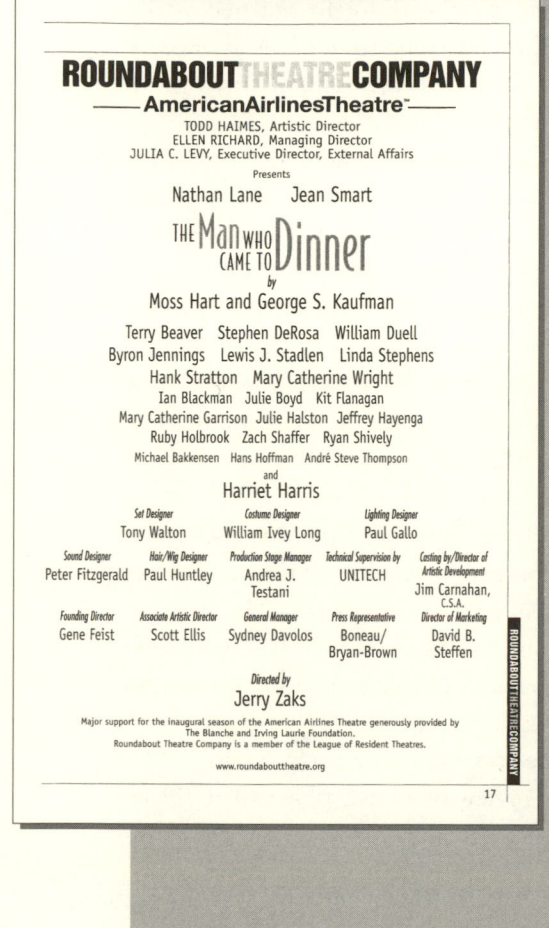

ROUNDABOUT THEATRE **COMPANY**
————— **AmericanAirlinesTheatre**™ —————
TODD HAIMES, Artistic Director
ELLEN RICHARD, Managing Director
JULIA C. LEVY, Executive Director, External Affairs

Presents

Nathan Lane   Jean Smart

THE Man WHO Dinner
CAME TO

by

Moss Hart and George S. Kaufman

Terry Beaver   Stephen DeRosa   William Duell
Byron Jennings   Lewis J. Stadlen   Linda Stephens
Hank Stratton   Mary Catherine Wright
Ian Blackman   Julie Boyd   Kit Flanagan
Mary Catherine Garrison   Julie Halston   Jeffrey Hayenga
Ruby Holbrook   Zach Shaffer   Ryan Shively
Michael Bakkensen   Hans Hoffman   André Steve Thompson

and

Harriet Harris

| *Set Designer* | *Costume Designer* | *Lighting Designer* |
| Tony Walton | William Ivey Long | Paul Gallo |

| *Sound Designer* | *Hair/Wig Designer* | *Production Stage Manager* | *Technical Supervision by* | *Casting by/Director of Artistic Development* |
| Peter Fitzgerald | Paul Huntley | Andrea J. Testani | UNITECH | Jim Carnahan, C.S.A. |

| *Founding Director* | *Associate Artistic Director* | *General Manager* | *Press Representative* | *Director of Marketing* |
| Gene Feist | Scott Ellis | Sydney Davolos | Boneau/Bryan-Brown | David B. Steffen |

Directed by

Jerry Zaks

Major support for the inaugural season of the American Airlines Theatre generously provided by
The Blanche and Irving Laurie Foundation.
Roundabout Theatre Company is a member of the League of Resident Theatres.

www.roundabouttheatre.org

17

ROUNDABOUT THEATRE COMPANY

Mrs. Stanley   Linda Stephens
Miss Preen   Mary Catherine Wright
Richard Stanley   Zach Shaffer
John   Jeffrey Hayenga
June Stanley   Mary Catherine Garrison
Sarah   Julie Boyd
Mrs. Dexter   Kit Flanagan
Mrs. McCutcheon   Julie Halston
Mr. Stanley   Terry Beaver
Maggie Cutler   Harriet Harris
Dr. Bradley   William Duell
Sheridan Whiteside   Nathan Lane
Harriet Stanley   Ruby Holbrook
Bert Jefferson   Hank Stratton
Professor Metz   Stephen DeRosa
Prison Guard   Hans Hoffman
Prisoners   Michael Bakkensen, Ian Blackman, André Steve Thompson
Expressmen (Act 2)   Michael Bakkensen, Ian Blackman
Sandy   Ryan Shively
Lorraine Sheldon   Jean Smart
Beverly Carlton   Byron Jennings
Mr. Westcott   Ian Blackman
Radio Technicians   Hans Hoffman, André Steve Thompson
Choir Boys   Jack Arendt, Zachary Eden Bernhard, Jozef Fahey, Brandon Perry, Matthew Salvatore, Ryan Torina
Banjo   Lewis J. Stadlen
Deputies   Michael Bakkensen, André Steve Thompson
Police Officer   Ian Blackman
Expressmen (Act 3)   Ian Blackman, André Steve Thompson

Setting: The home of Mr. and Mrs. Stanley, in a small town in Ohio

put my hands on. Raves from the *Daily News* and the *New York Post*. Favorable reviews—edging toward raves—from *Variety*, the Associated Press, and *Newsday*. And only one bad review, from the *Times*. A couple of other pans eventually turned up, but as of that Friday morning, it was Brantley against the world. There he was again, pounding away at a show that—in this case—everyone else seemed to like. He sat in the same theatre at the same performance as his colleagues—a laugh-filled performance, for whatever that's worth—and he just poked holes in virtually everything director Jerry Zaks and star comedian Nathan Lane and the rest of them did.

And everything Brantley said, in my opinion, was absolutely correct. Let other reviewers find the evening—or at least parts of it—funny; the play, as a whole, came across dated and leaden, buoyed by the sometimes funny gags grafted on by Mr. Zaks. But the minority view—that is, Mr. Brantley's and mine—was that Kaufman and Hart's well-written play succumbed to the fixing.

There is an odd coincidence in all of this. (There must be, or else why would I go on like this?) The old-time critic whose seat Mr. Brantley presently occupies—the one who gave the Shuberts a bad review and ended up going to court over his right to express his critical opinion—was an exceedingly odd fellow named Alexander Woollcott: the thinly veiled protagonist (or is it antagonist?) of *The Man Who Came to Dinner*. The Shubert affair made Woollcott famous along Broadway. Some years later he was stolen away from the *Times* by the tottering *New York Herald*. Not interested in moving to a second-rate paper, Alec made the ridiculous demand of $2,000 a month—he was earning $100 a week at the *Times*—and couldn't turn away when the *Herald*'s cash-rich new owner unblinkingly met his demand.

Woollcott loomed large—very large—over the cultural scene of these United States until his death in 1943. In 1929, he went on the airwaves and became one of the most famous personalities of the day. The Town Crier, he was called; he talked about anything and everything, three times a week (sponsored by Cream of Wheat, manufacturers of mush). Imagine, if you will, a combination of Larry King, Oprah Winfrey, and Liz Smith. That gives you some idea of the power Woollcott wielded in his day. He had no real competition, either, which made him quite the *enfant terrible*. That he was celebrated as a wit, raconteur, and arbiter of taste was odd, in that his taste appears to have been set in the 1890s and his writing style was floridly purplish. For all his importance and self-importance, his books and other work all but disappeared within a generation, and he is remembered today mostly—if at all—for his association with *The Man Who Came to Dinner*.

Woollcott was the center of two overlapping circles of celebrities of the twenties and thirties: the Algonquin Round Table of literary lights and quipping wits, and his own personal club of very important people. Alec was at their beck and call, serving as confidant and—not incidentally—boosting their careers in the newspapers, in magazines, and on the airwaves. He also had the power to take a floundering book and praise it onto the best-seller lists, as he did with James Hilton's sentimental novel *Goodbye, Mr. Chips*. The flip side to all this was Woollcott's dark underbelly. When crossed he turned waspish and vile, with his public platforms giving him multiple opportunities to be lethal. Woollcott was famously generous and magnanimous with his friends; they were expected to pay court, though, and when Woollcott wanted a favor, they had no recourse but to come through.

One of those favors resulted in *The Man Who Came to Dinner*. In 1938, playwright S. N. Behrman—a Woollcott pal—created a role for Alex in his

comedy *Wine of Choice*. (Burns Mantle of the *Daily News* called him "a third-rate actor in a fourth-rate play.") Woollcott was nevertheless enthused by the easy money he could earn appearing onstage and pleased by the public adulation he could receive from his numerous fans, so he asked the Pulitzer Prize–winning team of George S. Kaufman and Moss Hart to write a play he could star in. Kaufman knew Woollcott as well as, or better than, anyone. He had been drama editor at the *Times* when Woollcott was the critic; the pair had collaborated on two (minor) plays; and Kaufman's wife, Beatrice, was one of Woollcott's very closest friends. Bea and Alec would go touring Europe together, as a platonic couple. (Word has it that Woollcott was rendered impotent by a childhood case of measles, leaving him asexual.)

While Woollcott was playing *Wine of Choice* in Philadelphia, he spent one memorable Sunday night at Hart's farm in Bucks County. Woollcott not only demanded that Hart immediately get to work on "his" play but also insulted the other house guests, took over his host's bedroom, terrorized the staff, demanded chocolate milkshakes at midnight, and inscribed in the guest book: "I wish to say that on my first visit to Moss Hart's house I had one of the most unpleasant evenings I can ever recall having spent." Relaying the events to Kaufman, Hart looked on the bright side. "Wouldn't it have been horrible if he'd broken a leg or something, and been on my hands the rest of the summer?" The two comedic scribes looked at each other, and a hit was born.

The goal had been to come up with a play for Woollcott to act in, not a play about him. Hence, the notion to place the character in a wheelchair; the ungainly and unkempt Woollcott was terribly obese, and the authors foresaw that he would have trouble moving gracefully onstage. As they proceeded to work, they realized that the role would be far too demanding for an amateur actor like Woollcott to handle. Fortunately, Alec agreed that it would be immodest for him to appear more or less as himself. He suggested that they get the similarly rotund Robert Morley—a British actor who was just then the toast of Broadway—to play the role. With Morley disinterested, the part went to Monty Woolley, a buddy of Cole Porter who had directed several musicals. (Porter and Hart wrote their 1935 musical *Jubilee* while on a grand round-the-world cruise with Woolley, who directed.)

Woolley created Sheridan Whiteside on both stage and screen; Clifton Webb headed the national company. Woollcott himself starred in the second touring company, although he seemed somewhat too benevolent in the role of the monstrous guest. Kaufman knew Woollcott's warts all too well, and he couldn't help but write them into the play; the hero is described as "a selfish, petty egomaniac who would see his mother burned at the stake if that was the only way he could light his cigarette." The public Woollcott was lovable, and the man seemed incapable of publicly "acting" otherwise.

"Of course, this is a libelous caricature," Woollcott wrote a friend. "I should feel insulted, but, knowing me, you understand why I swallow the insult with relish."

Flash forward sixty years to Nathan Lane, one of the few present-day actors with the comic presence to undertake such a role. Nathan Lane as

> Woollcott insulted the other guests, took over his host's bedroom, terrorized the staff, and demanded chocolate milkshakes at midnight. Hart looked on the bright side. "Wouldn't it have been horrible if he'd broken a leg and been on my hands the rest of the summer?"

Sheridan Whiteside sounded like a pretty good idea, initially; but on examination one had to wonder. Under his sometimes cranky demeanor, Lane is immanently likable. Fussy, yes; infuriating, yes; even annoying, perhaps. But dangerous? Vicious? Monsterish? Nope, the audience just won't buy it. And that was one of the main problems with this *Man Who Came to Dinner*. Woolley and Webb both had tart-tongued, acidic, bitchy sides to their nature. One look at Nathan Lane in Sherry's wheelchair let you know that this Whiteside was, at heart, a puppy dog of a fellow. Lane's favorable public image worked against his performance in the role (as had been the case with Woollcott). So what the play ended up with was a genial observer of the festivities rather than a raging cyclone at its center.

The topical nature of the play also presented some tricky problems. Woollcott lived for his friends, and the authors obliged by cramming the script with name-dropping. A hundred or so 1930s celebrities and near celebrities clutter the discussion, many of whom are long forgotten (starting with Woollcott himself). Because the action is specific to the late 1930s, how to bridge the gap for the audience? Print a biographical glossary in the Playbill, perhaps?

There are at least two ways of handling this. One is to do the play as written, and hope that the material will take care of itself. Old Mr. Molière based some of his characters on living beings, we are told, who were instantly recognizable by the people in the loges. These celebs, whoever they were, are long forgotten, but the plays seem to have done all right in the long run. The other option is to try to update the outdated references, but it can be extremely tricky to update some while keeping others. This is what Zaks and the Roundabout halfheartedly tried to do, with unfortunate results.

> Under his sometimes cranky demeanor, Lane is immanently likable. Fussy, yes; infuriating, yes; even annoying. But dangerous? Vicious? Monsterish? What the play ended up with was a genial observer of the festivities rather than a raging cyclone at its center.

Most of these "fixes," by some unnamed somebody, were merely odd. A speech citing Maude Adams, Irving Berlin, Rembrandt, and El Greco was changed to Maude Adams, Irving Berlin, Raphael, and El Greco. Go figure. At least one change was especially jarring, a joke about the 1932 kidnapping of the Lindbergh baby. This was, at the time, the crime of the century. I was pretty much appalled that George S. Kaufman (whose work

I greatly admire) would allow such a joke. So much so that I made a note of it and vowed to check the script. Kaufman and Hart, needless to say, did *not* poke fun at the Lindbergh baby. Someone else put it in, and I'm rather surprised that Anne Kaufman Schneider—who is a careful and diligent guardian of her father's work—let it slip by.

The original joke was about the Charley Ross case; Ross was the first child kidnapped for ransom in the United States, back in 1874. Over the years, several impostors stepped forward claiming they were Charley Ross, much in the same way that people claimed to be Anastasia (daughter of Nicholas and Alexandra) or even the Dauphin (the child of Louis XVI and Marie Antoinette). This is all pretty obscure today, but audiences in 1939 were aware of Woollcott's fascination with unsolved crimes because he featured them on his broadcasts. As it happened, Woollcott grew up near the old Ross mansion in Germantown, New Jersey; as a child—a strange and unhappy child—Alec used to stand on the street corner where Charley was abducted and hope for something to happen.

Granted, few of today's theatregoers can be expected to laugh at the Charley Ross line. But the Lindbergh baby didn't get a laugh, either; more important, it was jarring enough to take at least some audience members away from the play. In a fast-paced comedy like *The Man Who Came to Dinner*, the last thing you can afford to do is get the audience to thinking logically (and missing the next series of lines).

What caused more puzzlement, perhaps, was the treatment of the real-life characters written into the play. The most effective portion of Zaks's production was the whirlwind scene in which a character named Beverly Carlton dropped by. Byron Jennings seems to have heard of Noël Coward and been encouraged to play him to the hilt. The evening—which had been meandering through an act and a half—suddenly picked up, briefly. (The delicious Cowardish pastiche, "What Am I to Do," was written by Porter, whose name does not appear anywhere in the Roundabout program.) A second real-life character, Dr. Gustav Eckstein—a then-renowned naturalist and pal of Woollcott's—was renamed Professor Metz and played more or less as written by Stephen DeRosa.

The other two "real" characters were problematic, though. Jean Smart swept in as Lorraine Sheldon, playing what seemed to be a full-scale Tallulah imitation. (How many in today's audience remember Tallulah, anyway?) Zaks and Smart proceeded to do anything for a laugh, but the laughs only hurt the texture of the play. Kaufman and Hart quite clearly patterned Lorraine after Gertrude Lawrence, the musical comedy star

The Man Who Came to Dinner
Opened: July 27, 2000
Closed: October 8, 2000
85 performances (and 32 previews)
Profit/Loss: Nonprofit [Profit]
The Man Who Came to Dinner ($65 top) was scaled to a
potential gross of $349,943 at the 740-seat American
Airlines Theatre. Weekly grosses averaged about $264,000,
settling in around $275,000 but topping $300,000 in the
show's final two weeks. Total gross for the run was
$3,854,225. Attendance was about 91 percent, with the
box office grossing about 75 percent of dollar-capacity.
(These figures are not indicative, as the potential was
calculated at the top ticket price, but subscribers paid
less.)

TONY AWARD NOMINATIONS
Best Performance by a Leading Actress: Jean Smart

Critical Scorecard

Rave	3
Favorable	4
Mixed	0
Unfavorable	0
Pan	3

who hobnobbed with royalty although she came from the slums of London. Kaufman and Hart drew Lorraine and Beverly like jealous siblings squabbling for the attention of their beloved mother, Whiteside—which was not far from fact. The dialogue specifically refers to Noël and Gertie's competitive onstage battles during the run of Coward's *Tonight at 8:30* (1936). With Lorraine portrayed as an American social climber with a somewhat southern accent, the sense of the piece goes out the window.

The treatment of Banjo, similarly, was oddly skewed. Lewis J. Stadlen came in like a whirlwind for the final section of the third act, chewing every piece of scenery that wasn't nailed down. It's a good thing, too, because by this point the production had totally run out of steam. Stadlen gave one of those performances fated to grab a Tony Award nomination, although what opens in July is often forgotten in May, as it was in this case. (Poor Stadlen was robbed of a Tony, for lack of a nomination, when he made his Broadway debut as a teenaged Groucho in *Minnie's Boys* in 1969.)

The trouble is, though, he wasn't playing the part that the authors wrote. Banjo is—or, rather, was—Harpo Marx. *Times* drama critic Woollcott embraced the brothers when they came to Broadway in a ragtag vaudeville show in 1924, hailing their act as a work of supreme art and citing the silent brother as "a great clown." Woollcott then passed the boys on to his pals Kaufman and Berlin, who wrote a first-class musical for them—*The Cocoanuts*—which launched their careers in both New York and Hollywood. One might expect Groucho to have become the darling of the wits of the Algonquin Round Table, but it was Harpo who was enshrined in Woollcott's circle.

Stadlen—no doubt at the behest of director Zaks—played him as a combination of Groucho, Chico, Harpo, and Jimmy Durante. He even went so far as to interpolate what seems to be an old Jimmy Durante song, with a title like "Didya Ever Have a Feeling That Ya Wanted ta Go and a Feeling That Ya Wanted ta Stay?" (Why didn't Roundabout credit Durante and Porter for their songs? Were audiences supposed to assume that Kaufman and Hart wrote them?) Instead of drawing a specific character, Stadlen was all over the place. The point of this was—I don't know. It worked extremely well while Stadlen was onstage and then left us deflated upon his exit.

The comic personas of Harpo and Durante are miles apart. Motion picture fans might recall that in the 1941 film version of *The Man Who Came to Dinner* the role of Banjo was played by, yes, Jimmy Durante. (Lorraine was played by American actress Ann Sheridan, who might have been closer to Tallulah than Gertie.) But what, I ask you, does the motion picture version have to do with the stage version? Changes are made for any number of reasons, which have nothing to do with the integrity of the script. (When Kaufman saw the changes wrought by Hollywood on his 1936 play *Stage Door*, he suggested that while they were at it they might as well have changed the title to *Screen Door*.)

A more detrimental failing, perhaps, was the handling of Whiteside's secretary, Maggie Cutler. She was not based on a real person; rather, she was pretty clearly modeled on the wisecracking, one-of-the-guys gal Friday who turns out to be a woman with feelings—the sort of role played by Rosalind Russell in countless Hollywood comedies. Maggie is the conscience of the play, enjoying and facilitating Whiteside's antics until he crosses over the line—and then putting him firmly in his place. (Hart wrote the role for Edie Atwater, his girlfriend at the time.) Harriet Harris gave a shrill and at times unattractive reading of the role, which did considerable damage to the heart of the play. But this seemed in keeping with Zaks's direction.

All in all, this *Man Who Came to Dinner* was intermittently comic but inconclusive, as if the plan had been to enhance the "funny" parts and rush through the others. Most of the play's references were lost on the audience; even the Lizzie Borden business fell flat. (Kaufman and Hart used the famous ax murderess to tie up the loose ends of their plot, and the people sitting around me clearly had no idea what they were talking about.) There is no way—and no need—to educate the audience on such matters. I would have to believe, though, that it would have helped if the actors at least knew whom they were supposed to be playing.

Gore Vidal's The Best Man

Gore Vidal's 1960 political drama *The Best Man*—or *Gore Vidal's The Best Man*, as it was officially retitled for the occasion—is a rather boxy, old-fashioned play. However, it is well crafted and well written, and in its best moments it makes for crackling entertainment. On the page, but not onstage. At least, not on the stage of the Virginia Theatre.

Vidal's point of departure was Henry James's novel *The Tragic Muse*, in which the main characters start at far extremities, cross, and end in opposite positions. "Take a man of exemplary private life, yet monstrous public life," explained Vidal back in 1960, "and contrast him to a man of 'immoral' private life and exemplary public life. . . . Make the two men politicians, perhaps fighting one another for the Presidency. Then demonstrate how, in our confused age, morality means, simply, sex found out."

Vidal was not exactly a novice in matters political. His grandfather was Thomas P. Gore, the influential (and blind) Democratic senator from Oklahoma. At the time Vidal wrote *The Best Man*, his cousin Albert Gore Sr. was a Democratic senator from Tennessee. Vidal also had a tangential relationship with the wife of the Democratic junior senator from Massachusetts. (Hugh Auchincloss divorced Vidal's mother to marry the mother of Jacqueline Bouvier, giving them a stepfather in common.) When Vidal was writing his play back in 1959, he couldn't have foreseen that Jackie's husband would be the Democratic nominee when *The Best Man* was produced in 1960. Nor could he have dreamed that Al Gore Jr. would be the nominee forty years later, when *The Best Man* returned to Broadway.

The revival plan, I suppose, was calculated to cash in on the 2000 election. Productions of *The Best Man* are rare, as is the case with most seventeen-character, multiset plays. Nonprofit theatres can handle such a large cast on occasion; the Roundabout's *Man Who Came to Dinner* had twenty-three. Actors (and their agents) typically accept the lower pay scales offered by nonprofits, but whisper the words "commercial theatre" and all bets are off. So the only practical way to mount one of these massive old plays is with stars, preferably a handful. You then offer them a "favored nations" contract: not as much money as they'd get in a play with only two stars, but a guarantee that nobody else in the cast was earning more.

Of course, until everything is signed and sealed you don't know exactly what kind of stars you will—or won't—end up with. The revival of *The Best Man* assembled six stars, or at least names familiar enough to reasonably merit star billing. Unfortunately, only two of the six proved suitable to their roles.

Now mind you, it is unfair to blame the actors for this; once offered a role, the only choice is whether or not to accept it. Nor

William Russell has spent fifteen or twenty years in the rough-and-tumble world of politics; he has also suffered a nervous breakdown. Spalding Gray looked, physically, like he'd spent the past fifteen or twenty years on the squash court.

should one put a black "X" beside the name of the casting directors; they simply round up possible suspects. It is the director who makes the choice, often in tandem with the producer (who might overrule a good but unknown actor in favor of an inferior actor who sells tickets). For the record, *The Best Man* had a top-rate casting director, Stuart Howard. To coin a new, old saying: You can lead an actor to a director, but you cannot make him think.

The Best Man takes place during a political convention, as two flawed candidates battle for the presidential nomination—"and may the best man win." Vidal pitted a noble, overly intellectual patrician (clearly patterned on Adlai Stevenson) against a sleazy politico known for smear-campaign tactics (patterned on Richard M. Nixon). Lest anyone miss the point, Vidal laced his play with allusions to Nixon's innuendo-based persecution of Alger Hiss, while RMN was serving on the House Committee on Un-American Activities.

Stevenson lost the 1956 race to the incumbent Dwight Eisenhower (and his running mate, Nixon). When *The Best Man* was written in 1959,

The Candidates

William Russell   Spalding Gray

Alice Russell, *his wife*   Michael Learned

Dick Jensen, *his campaign manager*   Mark Blum

Catherine, *a campaign aide*   Kate Hampton

Joseph Cantwell   Chris Noth

Mabel Cantwell, *his wife*   Christine Ebersole

Don Blades, *his campaign manager*   Jordan Lage

The Party

Ex-President Arthur Hockstader   Charles Durning

Mrs. Sue-Ellen Gammadge, *Chairman of the Women's Division*   Elizabeth Ashley

Senator Clyde Carlin   Ed Dixon

Delegates   Joseph Culliton, Joseph Costa, Patricia Hodges, C. J. Wilson, Lee Mark Nelson

The Visitors

Dr. Artinian, *a psychiatrist*   Michael Rudko

Sheldon Marcus   Jonathan Hadary

The Press

First Reporter   Joseph Culliton

Second Reporter   Joseph Costa

Third Reporter   Patricia Hodges

Fourth Reporter   C. J. Wilson

Fifth Reporter   Lee Mark Nelson

Additional Reporters and Hotel Staff   Kate Hampton, Michael Rudko

News Commentator   Walter Cronkite

Time: July 1960
Place: Philadelphia

Political conventions today are not what they used to be. There was a time when politics was played openly on the convention floor for the elucidation, delight, and occasionally dismay of the American people. This is the way it could have been in 1960, in Philadelphia, in a different world that, somehow, has not changed all that much.—Walter Cronkite and Gore Vidal

VIRGINIA THEATRE
A JUJAMCYN THEATRE

JAMES H. BINGER
CHAIRMAN

ROCCO LANDESMAN
PRESIDENT

PAUL LIBIN
PRODUCING DIRECTOR

JACK VIERTEL
CREATIVE DIRECTOR

JEFFREY RICHARDS / MICHAEL B. ROTHFELD   RAYMOND J. GREENWALD   JERRY FRANKEL   DARREN BAGERT
PRESENT

CHARLES DURNING   SPALDING GRAY   CHRIS NOTH

ELIZABETH ASHLEY   CHRISTINE EBERSOLE   MICHAEL LEARNED

GORE VIDAL'S THE BEST MAN

ALSO STARRING
MARK BLUM

WITH

ED DIXON   JORDAN LAGE   MICHAEL RUDKO

Joseph Costa   Joseph Culliton   Kate Hampton   Patricia Hodges   Lee Mark Nelson   C.J. Wilson

Walter Cronkite as the Voice of the Commentator

AND
JONATHAN HADARY

SCENIC DESIGN
JOHN ARNONE

COSTUME DESIGN
THEONI V. ALDREDGE

LIGHTING DESIGN
HOWELL BINKLEY

SOUND DESIGN/ORIGINAL MUSIC
DAVID VAN TIEGHEM

TECHNICAL SUPERVISION
NEIL A. MAZZELLA

HAIR DESIGN
BOBBY H. GRAYSON

MARKETING
THE NANCY RICHARDS GROUP

CASTING
STUART HOWARD, AMY SCHECTER & HOWARD MELTZER, CSA

GENERAL MANAGER
ALBERT POLAND

PRODUCTION STAGE MANAGER
JANE GREY

ASSOCIATE PRODUCERS
FRANCIS FINLAY NORMA LANGWORTHY LOUISE LEVATHES

DIRECTED BY
ETHAN McSWEENY

THE PRODUCERS WISH TO EXPRESS THEIR APPRECIATION TO THE THEATRE DEVELOPMENT FUND FOR ITS SUPPORT OF THIS PRODUCTION.

Nixon was the likely Republican choice for 1960, but few could have forecast that the Democratic contenders would be Hubert Humphrey and John F. Kennedy. The play opened on March 31, 1960, during the primary season, and closed July 8, 1961 after 521 performances.

While the author attempted to be more or less nonpartisan, he clearly regarded former secretary of state William Russell—the Stevenson stand-in—as the best man. And it is with the best man that this production most seriously faltered. Spalding Gray is a fascinating performer, best known for his eighteen autobiographical monologues (including the 1999–2000 season's *Morning, Noon and Night*). While he has filled in his career with occasional acting jobs (like Lincoln Center Theater's 1988 production of *Our Town*), he is one of those performers who don't exactly slip into a role. Gray and Russell (Stevenson) are both intellectuals with principles, but the actor's edgily contemplative persona worked against the character's character. And while I am not a proponent of typecasting, Gray simply looked all wrong for the part. Russell has served as a governor and a cabinet member, with perhaps fifteen or twenty years in the rough-and-tumble world of politics; he has also suffered a nervous breakdown. Gray looked, physically, like he'd spent the past fifteen or twenty years on the squash court. While he could easily pass for a contemporary politician, *The Best Man* is—and was mounted as—a period piece. (Let it be noted that Vidal once attempted an updated version of the play, complete with Carter and Reagan references. José Ferrer directed a cast headed by Buddy Ebsen, Mel Ferrer, Don Murray, and Hope Lange; it crash-landed at the Ahmanson in Los Angeles in 1987.)

Gray seemed *way* too young for this role. Stevenson—you remember that photo of him, with his shoe on his desk and a hole in his sole—was fifty-six when he ran for president. Humphrey was forty-nine when he battled Kennedy for the 1960 nomination. Gray, as it happens, was already fifty-nine when he took on the role, but I repeat: He looked way too young for an old-style politician, circa 1960. Dick Cheney—who like the fictional Russell spent many years in elected office, moved into the cabinet as secretary of state, and then spent several years in the private sector before receiving the vice presidential nomination on the 2000 Republican ticket—was at the time also fifty-nine. Cheney, with his three heart attacks, looked the role; Gray looked too damn healthy.

Mind you, it is unfair to blame Gray; he did what he was hired to do. (To quote the new old saying: You can lead an actor to a director, but you cannot make him think.) This central casting problem was compounded by the hiring of Michael Learned, a "star" by virtue of her three Emmy Awards for *The Waltons*. Ms. Learned—who has many years of stage experience—was good as Russell's estranged wife, doing especially well in the final scenes. Unfortunately, she looked like Gray's mother; they are more or less the same age, in fact but not in the mirror. Mind you, the plot hinges in part on Russell's roving eye (and what it says about his "character"). Presidential infidelities are nothing new; Roosevelt, Eisenhower, Kennedy, Bush Sr., and Clinton all faced these sorts of rumors. But without sounding sexist, you can make the case that there is a major motivational difference between a man who cheats on a wife who looks like Eleanor or Mamie or Barbara, and a man who cheats on Jackie or Hillary. From my reading of the text, it seems that Russell's marital baggage has more to do with his inner demons than with the bags under his wife's eyes.

Chris Noth, a "star" from the cable TV world, did marginally better than Gray as candidate Joe Cantwell. He managed to be weasily repugnant, but Noth also was somewhat too contemporary for the part. He seemed to step right out of the videotapes of the House Impeachment Committee, which was the right idea but the wrong generation. Christine Ebersole was the most effective of the "stars," with her portrayal of Cantwell's wife. Vidal seemed to write the character as a honey-dipped, cloth-coated Pat Nixon, and that's what Ms. Ebersole gave us. She'd end the season with a Tony Award, although not for *The Best Man*.

There were times when original star Melvyn Douglas seemed to be battling not the imaginary Cantwell but the real Nixon. This provided an added layer of relevance to the original production, along with a tension that was sorely missing in 2000.

Most suitable by type, perhaps, was Charles Durning, in the role of the kingmaker. Former president Hockstader is a crusty oldtimer fated to die in the last act, a self-proclaimed "hick" drawn along the lines of Harry S. Truman. The part called for Durning to shuffle around the stage with a twinkle in his eye; not much of a stretch, but something Durning was eminently capable of. (Durning had a problem remembering his lines in the early part of the run, which was duly noted by several critics. He was recovering from abdominal surgery when rehearsals began and didn't join the others until the final week. Once he caught up with the others, he was a delight.)

Rounding out the stars, in the smallest of the six roles, was the most accomplished of them all. Liz Ashley has been trodding the local boards since 1959; she starred opposite Robert Redford in 1963 in the Neil Simon and Mike Nichols superhit, *Barefoot in the Park*. Like many larger-than-life people in the public eye for forty years, she has had her share of bumps along the way; but she retains built-in stage presence and the ability to steal laughs by merely swiveling her head and glancing askance down her nose. She stole laughs here, all right, and picked up the proceedings every moment she was onstage; she also had a way of sitting with her legs crossed beneath her in a severely angled (and orthopedically impossible) "X." However, she, too, seemed way out of place at the 1960 Democratic National Convention. Vidal wrote an influence-rich old biddy, counseling the candidates and their wives on how to behave properly to win the female vote. (Don't do too much, like Eleanor; don't do too little, like Mamie.) Ashley's characterization had the smarts to out-Carville Carville—but again, this is supposed to be 1960. Watching Ashley on the stage of the Virginia, I couldn't help remembering her crackling performance on the same stage in the 1974 revival of *Cat on a Hot Tin Roof*. Liz seemed to want to crackle in *The Best Man*, but it's hard to crackle in a stale cracker barrel.

Billed down below the title with the featured players was Jonathan Hadary, who gave the best performance of the evening. As the fellow brought to town from Wilmington to expose the skeleton in the bad guy's closet, Hadary—who has played everything from *Torch Song Trilogy* to the Tyne Daly *Gypsy*—was like a panic-striken moth with singed wings, hopelessly trying to evade a super-duper never-miss flyswatter. In his big confrontation scene with Cantwell, Hadary blustered, turned tail, and seemed to visibly deflate.

A combination of indistinctly cast performers and ill-assembled performances points, usually, to an infirm directorial hand. Simply put, few

of the actors seemed to connect with one another. At all. There was one
long exchange between candidate Russell and ex-president Hockstader in
which Durning simply sat in his chair while Gray stood by the couch.
That's it; two stationary actors spouting memorized lines. Director Ethan
McSweeny came to *The Best Man* with no Broadway experience and only
one off-Broadway play on his résumé (*Never the Sinner: The Leopold and
Loeb Story*, which transferred from the Signature Theatre in Arlington,
Virginia). McSweeney did have something of a political pedigree, being
the son of a trusted Lyndon Johnson aide (and a present-day trustee of the
Kennedy Center and Ford's Theatre). Perhaps that helped earn Vidal's
approval.

Now, I'm the last person to suggest that you shouldn't give a bright
young director his or her chance at the big time. Under the circumstances, though—a big-budget Broadway shot with a difficult old play
and a first-time director—somebody needs to look at a run-through two
or three weeks into the process. If nothing is happening in the rehearsal
room, you either have to grit your teeth and do something about it—or
not. In this case, not. Every time playwright Vidal worked up steam, Mc-
Sweeny and his actors poured water on it. And not good, old-fashioned
Philadelphia tap water, either; designer water, in a green bottle. (There's
a good joke about Philadelphia tap water in the first act.)

The original production had an extratheatrical excitement to it. Russell was played by Melvyn Douglas. Douglas is best remembered today,

perhaps, as the fellow who made Garbo laugh in *Ninotchka.* Or maybe for his Oscar-winning performances as Paul Newman's father in *Hud,* or as the ailing millionaire in *Being There.* But back in 1960, the casting of Douglas was theatrical dynamite. Who better to play a character battling Nixon-like dirty tricks than the husband of Nixon's first and most famous victim?

"Helen Gahagan Douglas is pink right down to her underwear," claimed communist-hunter Nixon, knocking off the three-time congress-woman in the 1950 California senatorial race. Ms. Douglas responded by dubbing him "tricky Dick," a nickname he could never escape. This was still a fresh wound in 1960, and Mrs. Douglas remained a major celebrity; there were times when Melvyn Douglas seemed to be battling not the imaginary Cantwell but the real Nixon. This provided an added layer of relevance to the play, along with a tension that was sorely missing in 2000. Broadway's general sympathy for Mrs. Douglas—and antipathy for Mr. Nixon—might have helped Mr. Douglas take that season's Tony Award over equally fine performances by youngsters Jason Robards, George C. Scott, and Sidney Poitier. (The original *Best Man* was nominated for six Tony Awards, winning one.)

Sitting there biding my time through the second act, I continually found my eyes wandering upward from the characters to the immense, vaguely modernist lighting fixture over the stage. Consisting of numerous white globes in different sizes, it looked like so many Ping-Pong balls purposelessly strung together. After about two hours, I wondered—was the whole shebang defeated by the lack of a ceiling on the set? Not a solid ceiling, of course; you need to break the plane with pipes of lights and such. But any kind of ceiling—even a horizontal piece inside the proscenium arch—would serve as a picture frame, forcing our eyes down to remain on the actors. *The Best Man* is about tension and pressure, and how different individuals react to it. A low ceiling might reinforce that tension, especially with tall actors like Gray and Noth. At least, it would help glue our eyes to the playing area. Every time I gazed at the odd chandelier, the play lost steam; there was no tension, no pressure, and no ceiling.

Durning's character described how the oratory of William Jennings Bryan was like "thunder on a summer evening where everything is still." There was no thunder onstage at the Virginia, turning *The Best Man* into just another ordinary evening of old-time theatre.

During the final moments of the play, when the lights went down on the playing area and up on the far corners of the stage, the propmen let loose a cascade of balloons. This, presumably, was meant to be the payoff for the set—one last "punch" before the final curtain. Sight lines being what they were, though, I could barely see the balloons from my seat in the eighth row on the aisle. I imagine the effect was lost on more than half the house, while the harm of the noncompressed playing space was felt by all.

In a speech about old-time politics, Durning's character described attending a political rally as a child, in which the oratory of candidate William Jennings Bryan was like "thunder on a summer evening where everything is still." There was no thunder onstage at the Virginia, turning *The Best Man* into just another ordinary evening of old-time theatre.

The Dinner Party

Neil Simon's *The Dinner Party* opened December 2, 1999, at the Mark Taper Forum in Los Angeles, under somewhat unusual circumstances. For the first time since 1963, when something called *Nobody Loves Me* played a summer stock tryout in Bucks County, Pennsylvania, a new Simon play went into production without a Broadway booking. *Nobody Loves Me*—starring Robert Redford and Elizabeth Ashley, under the direction of first-time director Mike Nichols—ultimately made it to Broadway, under the title *Barefoot in the Park*. And so, as it turned out, did *The Dinner Party*, Simon's thirty-first Broadway offering.

The immense success of *Barefoot* and Simon's next play, *The Odd Couple*, turned the ex-TV writer into a one-man industry. Through good times and bad, there was always a new Simon comedy in the works—and for many years they were all golden, even the plays that weren't so hot. (Walter Kerr greeted Simon's 1966 hit, *The Star-Spangled Girl*, with "Neil Simon didn't have an idea for a play this year, but he wrote it anyway.")

But comic geniuses don't seem to want to be merely funny; they must bring life's meaning to their art. (See the dark films of Woody Allen, or better yet the Preston Sturges classic *Meet John Doe*.) Simon started exploring the dark side in 1970 with *The Gingerbread Lady*, a comedy-drama about a reformed alcoholic teetering on the brink of relapse. The play was rather good, but not what Simon's audience wanted. The once-infallible Simon began to teeter between funny hits and bittersweet failures, once again finding his stride with the *Brighton Beach* trilogy of the mid-1980s. Since then, though, everything has failed with the notable exception of the Pulitzer Prize–winning *Lost in Yonkers*.

Mind you, your average, everyday playwright would kill for only one

Cast (in order of appearance)

Claude Pichon   John Ritter
Albert Donay   Henry Winkler
André Bouville   Len Cariou
Mariette Levieux   Jan Maxwell
Yvonne Fouchet   Veanne Cox
Gabrielle Buonocelli   Penny Fuller

Place and Time: A private dining
   room in a first-rate restaurant in
   Paris. The present.

THE MUSIC BOX
THE ESTATE OF IRVING BERLIN AND THE SHUBERT ORGANIZATION, OWNERS

Emanuel Azenberg   Ira Pittelman   Eric Krebs
Scott Nederlander   ShowOnDemand.com
and
Center Theatre Group / Mark Taper Forum / Gordon Davidson

present

Neil Simon's
The Dinner Party

Henry Winkler   John Ritter   Len Cariou
Penny Fuller   Veanne Cox   Jan Maxwell

| Scenic Design | Costume Design | Lighting Design |
| John Lee Beatty | Jane Greenwood | Brian MacDevitt |

| Sound Design | Technical Supervision | Production Stage Manager |
| Jon Gottlieb | Unitech | David O'Brien |

| Casting | Press Representative |
| Jay Binder CSA & Amy Lieberman | Bill Evans & Associates |

| Marketing | Media Advisor |
| The Nancy Richards Group | Alan Bernhard |

| Associate Producers | General Manager |
| Ginger Montel   Marcia Roberts | Abbie M. Strassler |

Directed by
John Rando

Simon-caliber smash. A playwright with one major hit is brilliant; a playwright with two major hits is a genius; but a playwright with six major hits is sure to be attacked for the weaknesses of the seventh, eighth, and ninth.

An overview of Simon's career falls pretty evenly into three uneven segments. His first Broadway show was an inconsequential musical revue, *Catch a Star*, which played the Plymouth for twenty-three performances in 1955. (Simon seems to have obliterated this show from his record, and nobody else seems to recall it, so I suppose we might as well ignore it as well.) His first play was *Come Blow Your Horn*, a clumsy barrel of laughs that began a successful run in 1961. This was followed by the close-to-wonderful-but-stubbornly-unsuccessful musical comedy *Little Me*. Then came *Barefoot in the Park*, the first of nine-out-of-ten hits. This was followed by *The Odd Couple*; the musical *Sweet Charity*; *The Star-Spangled Girl*; *Plaza Suite*; the musical *Promises! Promises!*; *The Last of the Red Hot Lovers*; the aforementioned *Gingerbread Lady*; *The Prisoner of Second Avenue*; and *The Sunshine Boys*. Three of these, mind you, were merely adequate, but they were hits. Thus, from 1961 through 1972, Simon wrote ten hits—four of them significant moneymakers—and only two box office failures.

Things were different during Simon's middle period, from 1973 (when his work turned markedly darker) through 1986 (the end of his *Brighton Beach* trilogy). It should be noted that Simon's first wife, Ellen, died of cancer in 1973, an event that has had a tremendous impact on his work and subject matter. Simon turned to Chekhov for the gloomy *Good Doctor*, followed by *God's Favorite* (from that laugh-filled Book of Job)—his first two outright flops. He rebounded with the successful *California Suite*, *Chapter Two*, and the musical *They're Playing Our Song*. Simon then sank into what might be his poorest plays, *I Ought to Be in Pictures* and *The Curse of Kalenshikoff*. These presumably would have closed out of town, but Simon—as producer—opted to bring them in. (He changed the title of the latter at the last moment to *Fools*, which didn't affect *The Curse*.) These were followed by a rewritten version of *Little Me*, which pretty much accentuated the negative and failed more resoundingly than the original production. Simon once again rebounded with his hit trilogy of *Brighton Beach Memoirs*, *Biloxi Blues*, and *Broadway Bound*. Interspersed between the latter two was an ineffective female rewrite of *The Odd Couple*. Thus, from 1973 through 1986, Simon wrote six hits and six failures. Impressive enough for just about anyone, but not approaching his earlier pace.

The success of the trilogy seems to have wearied the indefatigable playwright Simon (who turned sixty in 1987). The inconsequential farce *Rumors* and the fractured psychodrama *Jake's Women* were followed by one of his strongest plays, *Lost in Yonkers*. But things went severely downhill with the stellar, can't-miss musical *The Goodbye Girl*, which proved to be a turmoil-racked fiasco. Simon returned to his old stomping grounds with *Laughter on the 23rd Floor*, a formulaic play built on a formula Simon knew so well. Despite what sounded like a

A playwright with one major hit is brilliant; a playwright with two major hits is a genius; but a playwright with six major hits is sure to be attacked for the weaknesses of the seventh, eighth, and ninth.

surefire teaming of Simon, director Jerry Zaks, and comedian Nathan Lane, *Laughter* was bafflingly unfunny. (Interviews for *The Dinner Party* mentioned that *Laughter* lost $800,000, an astonishingly high sum for a show that appeared to have done moderately well.)

Blaming failure on Broadway's ridiculously high costs, Simon and his producer Manny Azenberg rebelled—vociferously and publicly—by taking their next show off-Broadway. But *London Suite* was an even more tired retread of past glories (specifically *Plaza Suite* and *California Suite*), and it quickly faltered. Simon and Azenberg returned to Broadway with *Proposals*, yet another moody failure. (Like *The Gingerbread Lady*, *Proposals* might well have done better without the audience expectations raised by Neil Simon's name.) Thus, from 1987 through 1997, Simon wrote one hit and six failures. All in all, seventeen hits and fourteen failures. (I do not include two additional nonprofit failures mounted by the Roundabout: a third version of poor *Little Me* and the ill-assembled *Hotel Suite*.)

I can't think of any post–World War II American playwright who has had fourteen Broadway failures, for the simple reason that I can't think of anyone other than Simon who has had fourteen plays produced on Broadway. Folks like Tennessee Williams and Arthur Miller and Edward

Albee had somewhat similar career curves, with their early hits followed by strings of failure. This resulted in an increasing inability for these acknowledged masters to get their later work mounted on Broadway.

Simon never had any such problem, and for good reason: Beginning with *The Sunshine Boys*, he became the controlling producer of his work. Simon's producer for his early hits had been a character named Saint-Subber. (He was actually named Arnold, but that's another story.) When Simon realized that money was being skimmed, he turned to a fellow he played tennis with, the respected (and honest) general manager named Emanuel Azenberg. Simon thereafter financed and controlled the shows; Azenberg, initially with his then-partner Eugene V. Wolsk, managed the plays and received full producer billing. (Simon kept most of the producer's share of the profits, but a small share of a Neil Simon hit was worth far more than 50 percent of most other shows.)

Once Williams and Miller and Albee stopped writing hits, they had difficulty finding Broadway productions. Simon got through his spotty stretches by using his own checkbook; the losses from his failures were far outstripped by the royalties and profits and road companies and motion picture versions of his hits. So everything Neil Simon ever wrote over the course of thirty-six years—or, rather, everything he considered stageworthy—automatically came to town. Until *The Dinner Party*.

The word from Washington indicated that this was the old Neil Simon returned to his 1960s form, and that *The Dinner Party* was a satisfying laugh riot. As it turned out, it was not.

Several earlier Simon plays had tried out at regional theatres, resulting in substantial start-up savings, but always with preexisting Broadway plans. Not so *The Dinner Party*. "We didn't think it was right for Broadway," Azenberg explained to Mervyn Rothstein of the *New York Times*. So Simon offered it to producer Gordon Davidson, of the Center Theatre Group in Los Angeles. *The Dinner Party* opened at the Mark Taper Forum on December 2, 1999, to mixed reviews, and that might well have been the end of it.

Except something was up in Washington. The Eisenhower Theatre had a June 2000 booking of Oscar Wilde's *Lady Windermere's Fan*, from the Gate Theatre in Dublin. *Lady Windermere* suddenly fell out. Max Woodward, the director of theatre operations at the Kennedy Center, had just seen *The Dinner Party* and thought Washington audiences would love it, so he called the Taper. Davidson and Simon and Azenberg were all game, as were the show's two ticket-selling sitcom stars, John Ritter and Henry Winkler. So *The Dinner Party*—with three cast replacements—reconvened at the Eisenhower.

Simon and Azenberg might well have been skittish at the prospect, if only because of *Washington Post* critic Lloyd Rose. Back in her early days as first-string critic, she greeted the tryout of *Lost in Yonkers* with the comment that "Neil Simon has been writing plays for 30 years and he still can't handle the basic elements of dramaturgy." This elicited howls from Simon and Azenberg, with vows that they would never again try out a show in Rose's jurisdiction. But Ms. Rose, presumably older and wiser, found *The Dinner Party* "laugh-out-loud funny!" The other local reviews followed suit, and *The Dinner Party* was a smash, breaking long-standing box office records. This made a Broadway transfer inevitable, with backing from a consortium of six producers (plus the playwright). Simon and Azenberg prominently featured Ms. Rose's verdict in their advertising, resulting in a healthy Broadway advance in excess of $2 million.

The word from Washington indicated that this was the old Neil Simon returned to his 1960s form, and that *The Dinner Party* was a satisfying laugh riot. As it turned out, it was not. The Broadway reviews were especially negative, as indicated in the scorecard. Again, *The Dinner Party* might have fared better critically without Simon's name on it. Without Simon's name, though, it would not have built up a hardy advance; and without a hardy advance, the devastating reviews and cautious word of mouth might have ended the *Party* prematurely. As it was, the show paid off within three months.

One thing was for sure: Neil Simon's thirty-first play was funny. It was a strange kind of funny, though. The constant stream of jokes was hit-or-miss, and many of them were somewhat extraneous. And way too many of the jokes were apathetic. There were jokes about one of the characters who paints pictures of cars; plenty of jokes about this, none especially funny. (His painting is of the "Range Rover school," we're told.) This fellow also had an index finger injury from a bow tie accident, which was also mirthlessly milked. There were jokes about Zola and Dickens, whom the dullard mistook for living people. At one point, Simon compared "a figure of speech" with "a figure of dead silence." (Huh??) There were exchanges such as (1st Man:) "Do you have a cigarette?" (2nd Man:) "I don't smoke." (1st Man:) "Well, you should." Later on, 1st Man said to 2nd Man: "I wish you were a cigarette"—which elicited an enormous cascade of laughter from the audience. Parts of it, anyway. And there was a joke about Albert Einstein and his relatives. Relatives, relativity, get it? "Do you think that's where he got the idea?" asked one of the men. "Don't even go there," said the other. But how did any of this apply to the play or the characters?

There was also a gap in logic at the base of Simon's situation. Three unrelated divorced couples are mysteriously brought together. It turns out that Gabrielle—the eldest of the wives—has arranged the party in order to punish her ex-husband, André. But just who are the other characters? We know that the other couples—or, presumably, one member of each couple—were clients of Gabrielle's divorce lawyer. But did the lawyer have only two other divorce cases in his files? And did he simply open his records to Gabrielle and let her pick through the phone numbers? Mr. Simon has plenty of experience with divorce and divorce lawyers, as has been documented in the public press. Do

> Simon had his characters ask questions like "Wouldn't the world have cheered if the Elephant Man had met an elephant woman?" and you didn't know whether you should laugh or sputter or just shake the cobwebs out of your ears.

these guys let their clients pull up a chair and pick through the Rolodex? Simon built his boulevard farce around three exceedingly odd couples, but the truth of the underlying situation was a wee bit too contrived.

Nevertheless, I must report that the fellow seated to my left was positively sputtering throughout the first half of the play. Not laughing, but sputtering (moistly) at every joke and gag. Until about an hour into this intermissionless, one-hundred-minute evening. At that point, the jokes didn't stop; just the laughter. The dialogue between the spurned Gabrielle and the nasty André became so viciously ugly that even the laughers were dumbfounded. "I plunged everything into you, like an animal" he confessed. "If you're a maggot," she asked, "is it wrong to love another maggot?" Simon had his characters ask questions like "Wouldn't the world have cheered if the Elephant Man had met an elephant woman?" and you didn't know whether you should laugh or sputter or just shake the cobwebs out of your ears.

The eccentric comedienne Veanne Cox came off best. She looked—and acted—like a Charles Addams drawing of a Munch character, comporting herself in one memorable (if out-of-place) moment like James Thurber's drawing of Ophelia leaping through her mad scene. Veterans Len Cariou (André) and Penny Fuller (Gabrielle)—who had together supported Lauren Bacall in the 1970 musical hit *Applause*—gave commanding performances despite the unattractive material in their hands. (These roles were played in Los Angeles by Ed Herrman and Frances

Conroy.) Sitcom imports Ritter and Winkler had considerably less to do, other than pleasantly peddle weak jokes and sell tickets. Jan Maxwell was adequate as the other wife, but the lot of them appeared to get little assistance from director John Rando.

The laughter—and the sputtering—returned at 9:25, but way too late to help. At 9:30, Ms. Maxwell said, "It's over, thank God. Open the doors." Unfortunately, they didn't. Not just yet.

Proof

Manhattan Theatre Club has enjoyed a long and distinguished life since it began operations in 1970. Under the guidance of artistic director Lynne Meadow and executive producer Barry Grove, who arrived in 1972 and 1974, respectively, it has provided audiences with a steady stream of entertainment. Intimate plays have been its mainstay, with multiple offerings from playwrights such as Terrence McNally, A. R. Gurney, Athol Fugard, Beth Henley, Alan Ayckbourn, David Margulies, and Charles Busch. MTC's biggest "hit" was its early musical revue *Ain't Misbehavin'*, which enjoyed worldwide success when it transferred to Broadway in 1977.

For many years, MTC and Joseph Papp's New York Shakespeare Festival were leaders of New York's nonprofit theatre world. Three other companies eventually crept up on them, and for the last dozen years the spotlight has been focused more prominently on Playwrights Horizons, Lincoln Center Theater, and the Roundabout. Until the 2000–2001 season, that is.

MTC has continued to enjoy numerous commercial transfers, but most of its recent shows headed to the Lortel or other off-Broadway perches; the last to reach Broadway was McNally's *Love! Valour! Compassion!*, back in 1994. While MTC does not—and should not—see Broadway as a major goal, it has been impossible not to notice the parade of commercial transfers from the other nonprofits. The fact that Lincoln Center and Roundabout mount their mainstage

Proof proved to be pretty good for a "first" play. Or for a tenth play, for that matter. A compelling family drama built on gripping character study, with plenty of laughs.

WALTER KERR THEATRE
A JUJAMCYN THEATRE

JAMES H. BINGER
CHAIRMAN

ROCCO LANDESMAN
PRESIDENT

PAUL LIBIN
PRODUCING DIRECTOR

JACK VIERTEL
CREATIVE DIRECTOR

MANHATTAN THEATRE CLUB

artistic director LYNNE MEADOW   executive producer BARRY GROVE

ROGER
BERLIND

CAROLE
SHORENSTEIN
HAYS

JUJAMCYN
THEATERS

OSTAR
ENTERPRISES

DARYL
ROTH

STUART
THOMPSON

present

MARY-LOUISE PARKER
in

proof
by
DAVID AUBURN

with

LARRY BRYGGMAN

JOHANNA DAY   BEN SHENKMAN

set design
JOHN LEE BEATTY

costume design
JESS GOLDSTEIN

lighting design
PAT COLLINS

original music & sound design
JOHN GROMADA

technical supervisor
NEIL A. MAZZELLA

production stage manager
JAMES HARKER

casting
NANCY PICCIONE/
DAVID CAPARELLIOTIS

press representative
BONEAU/BRYAN-BROWN

mtc associate artistic director
MICHAEL BUSH

directed by
DANIEL SULLIVAN

productions in Broadway-eligible houses gives them a leg up, perhaps; but that hasn't stopped Playwrights and newcomers like New York Theatre Workshop from arranging multiple transfers. Let me reiterate that the purpose of a nonprofit theatre is not—or, at least, should not be—to send productions on to commercial afterlife. However, a sizable portion of the profits from such transfers go back into the nonprofit's coffers. This can make an enormous difference—one need only look at the increased output of the New York Shakespeare Festival's glory years, financially fueled by millions of *Chorus Line* dollars. (In November, MTC announced plans to purchase and renovate the derelict Biltmore Theatre on Forty-seventh Street, giving them their own Broadway-eligible mainstage.)

Many recent nonprofit-to-Broadway transfers have been musicals, which seems to have encouraged MTC to start a musical theatre program. After several mishaps—*Captains Courageous, The Green Heart,* and the curiously unpalatable 1993 version of Stephen Sondheim's *Putting It Together,* starring Julie Andrews—MTC poured its hopes and resources into the February 2000 production of *The Wild Party.* There were two competing versions of *The Wild Party,* as discussed in *Broadway Yearbook,*

1999–2000, and MTC's was the underdog. The New York Shakespeare Festival version had a score by the acclaimed Michael John LaChiusa; direction by the award-winning wizard George C. Wolfe; ticket-selling stars (at least nominally) like Mandy Patinkin and Eartha Kitt; and a princely $6 million Broadway mounting. MTC had a relatively unknown author and director and cast, with an off-Broadway-sized budget.

They also had a pretty good show, and one that under other circumstances might have seemed a sure bet for transfer. Not perfect, perhaps, but intriguing and worthwhile. MTC's fascinating-if-hazy *Wild Party* appeared far more viable to this viewer than the NYSF version, but circumstances seemed to conspire against both of them. Most dangerously, commercial producers—in the face of great word of mouth during previews —saw fit to announce a Broadway transfer before the opening, waving a red flag at critics who otherwise might have offered encouragement.

This was, presumably, a severe disappointment for the MTC folks; again, they hadn't had a Broadway presence since 1994. But what can you do, other than continue to do what you do? Which in MTC's case meant finishing the 1999–2000 subscription season with Charles Busch's *Tale of the Allergist's Wife* and David Auburn's *Proof*, both of which would end the year as bona fide Broadway hits (with investments speedily recouped).

Proof was a typical MTC offering: a somewhat eccentric, one-set, four-character character study examining ideas and relationships. But typical is perhaps an inaccurate description of David Auburn's provocative and arresting drama. The thirty-one-year-old playwright came to MTC out of nowhere; or, rather, MTC read the script and was perceptive enough to recognize its worth. Auburn, from Juilliard's playwriting program, had only a few minor credits at the time; but MTC latched onto Auburn and mounted his *Proof* as a reading in its "6@6: Discovering the New Generation Series" in April 1999. Someone thought to ask Mary-Louise Parker to do the reading, and *Proof* was in the pudding. MTC scheduled it as the final offering of its 1999–2000 season; critical raves made *Proof* a sellout; and Auburn's play (with Ms. Parker) was quickly booked into the Walter Kerr.

Proof proved to be pretty good for a "first" play. Or for a tenth play, for that matter. Auburn's plot centered on the arcane field of higher mathematics. Coming on the heels of Michael Frayn's 1999–2000 Tony Award–winning *Copenhagen*, this implied another rewarding-but-densely-theoretical evening in the theatre. As it turned out, this was not the case at all.

A mathematical genius dies, and a brilliant but unknown "proof" is discovered locked in his desk. Is it his—or is it the work of his untrained daughter, who knows only what she has picked up around the house? Auburn chose mathematical proofs for *Proof*, but the great man could just as easily have been a painter or sculptor or poet. This plot sounds vaguely familiar; I wouldn't be surprised if such plays exist somewhere in the annals of dead plays, although presumably not with mathematicians.

Auburn got his *Proof* off to a strong start and never looked back. The result: a compelling family drama built on gripping character study, with plenty of laughs. Much noted were two moments in the first act, both of which met with audible gasps from the audience. The play began with a long midnight chat between Catherine (the daughter) and Robert (the addled mathematician). Catherine is clearly in a depression; she is very much like her father, it is the dawn of her twenty-fifth birthday, and she is well aware that her father's slide into mental illness first manifested itself when he was twenty-five. They talk at length about being "crazy." ("Even your depression is mathematical," the father points out—and it is.)

Robert argues that his daughter can't be crazy, "because crazy people don't sit around wondering if they're nuts." Catherine attacks the logic of his position. (Logic is a major component of her being.) Robert says that she can't be crazy because a crazy person would never admit she was crazy, yet he himself is crazy and admits it; ergo, she wants to know how his theory (reassuring her that she is not crazy) can be true.

"Because I'm dead." And of course, he is; it has been apparent in just about everything he's said since curtain up, only we haven't caught on. Everything Auburn had laid out so far—which the audience bought, and absorbed—suddenly had a different meaning; Catherine had been talking to herself all along. But we were too absorbed in the ongoing plot to reassess what we'd heard. Auburn drew the pair so clearly and lucidly, and so idiosyncratically, that we were stunned by the revelation—and eager to see what happened next. And what happened next was that the audience sat forward in their chairs and put on what you might call their listening ears. Auburn won the evening, twelve minutes in; he had us with him, so long as he didn't muck things up down the line.

Auburn crafted a similar surprise at the end of the first act. Robert's former student Hal discovers an unknown proof hidden in the professor's desk—a proof of world-shattering importance (in the sciences, at least). In a whirlwind of a three-way discussion with Hal and Claire (Robert's other daughter), Catherine is maneuvered to reveal the truth of the proof: It is not something the mad professor painstakingly worked out in his brief moments of lucidity. "I didn't find it," she finally admits. "I wrote it." Quick curtain.

Once again, the reality of everything we had heard thus far was proven false. Auburn gave us fifteen minutes to work it out.

People tend to overlook the importance of a good curtain line. There's nothing like jolting your audience with a thunderclap and dropping the curtain before they have a chance to recover. This sends them out into the lobby talking about the play, as opposed to basketball scores or football scores or tech stock prices, and it brings them eagerly back into their seats. Bad or boring plays often lose patrons at intermission. It is not un-known for such attractions—like the 1999–2000 season's *Epic Proportions* and the NYSF *Wild Party* —to keep audience members in their seats by keeping the house lights off, thus removing the means of mass escape. When a show loses its intermission during previews, be wary—and try to get an aisle seat.

One could find a few little chinks in Auburn's work, if one were so disposed. Early in the first act Catherine tells us the story of one Sophie Germain, who spent the French Revolution locked up in her father's study, reading his math books. She came up with an important proof—the Germain primes—although she had to publish them under a man's name. This anecdote is rather baldly inserted, for obvious purposes. (While stumbling through the backstreets of the Left Bank shortly after seeing *Proof*, I came across an engraved tablet on a centuries-old building reading "Sophie Germain, philosophe et mathématicienne, née a Paris en 1776 est morte dans cet maison, le 27 Juin 1831.")

Another slight weakness: Auburn sees fit to have Catherine and Claire slug it out in the second act; it seems that Claire went off to New York to make her career, forcing Catherine to stay in Chicago and take care of

Robert and thereby sacrifice her chance at an education. This is not exactly new territory; Broadway audiences heard this very same exchange in the 1999 revival of Arthur Miller's *The Price*. (There are other parallels between the two plays, although *Proof* is infinitely stronger.)

But these are minor qualms, and—hey—this was a first-time playwright. And he did a masterful job. Auburn was greatly abetted by cast and director. Daniel Sullivan had an intensely busy 1999–2000, with, in quick succession, the Pulitzer Prize winner *Dinner with Friends* (which opened in November), the Cherry Jones revival of *Moon for the Misbegotten* (in March), and the MTC production of *Proof* in (in May). I was less than overwhelmed by *Misbegotten*, but Sullivan did incredibly well with *Dinner with Friends* and *Proof*. Performances and staging melded seamlessly with the text.

> **Mary-Louise Parker was mesmerizing. When her characters are riled—and Ms. Parker's characters often do seem to be riled—her forehead seems to sprout storm clouds. Let a smile break through, and the world and the theatre light up.**

The first scene ended with a big fight between Hal and Catherine over a stolen notebook. He was trying to do a good deed, but she wouldn't listen, so Hal stormed across the porch and exited through the screen door. End of scene, except that Hal—the actor Ben Shenkman—caught the door as it was about to slam shut; held it; and then closed it silently, almost tenderly. Was this business an authorial stage direction? It's not in the script that the press agent handed me at the theatre. Was it the actor's idea? Or was it the director who came up with it? We don't know, and that's all to the good.

Robert, the father, has a crucial speech in a second-act flashback. His character has been well for seven months, although we know that this will not last. Catherine tells him that she has enrolled in college and is moving out of the house. Auburn gives Robert a somewhat sentimental monologue—almost a last hurrah—in which he tells us how he loves Chicago in September. During this speech, Larry Bryggman lost control of his left hand; it simply went haywire. It rattled within his sleeve, he shoved it into his pocket and in his fury almost tore the pocket right out of his jacket—all the while delivering this overly calm speech about the sailboats on the water and the Cubs losing and college students in bookstores. Quite clearly, Robert's sanity was once again slipping away; by his actions—and by his worried glance at his hand cramming the pocket—it appeared that he already knew what was ahead. Again, this is not in the script, but it tells us so very much information we need to know—information that the dialogue will tell us later on, but it's so much more effective to have us discover it for ourselves. There were a number of moments like this in *Proof*, as there were in *Dinner with Friends*, which indicate Mr. Sullivan's invisible fingerprints.

And then there was the cast, led by an amazing portrayal by Mary-Louise Parker. Parker has always been highly distinctive. Some criticize her for her mannerisms, which are indeed often present. She is slightly reminiscent of Sandy Dennis, but Dennis was usually controlled by her mannerisms. Parker seems to use them, consciously, as part of her vocabulary. (I'd suspect that she also chooses her roles very carefully.) At any rate, she was quite good in *Prelude to a Kiss* and simply wonderful in both *How I Learned to Drive* and *Proof*. Mesmerizing, I thought. When her characters are riled—and Ms. Parker's characters often do seem to be riled—her forehead seems to sprout storm clouds. Let a smile break through, and the world and the theatre light up.

Parker was in especially fine company. Larry Bryggman is one of those character men whom you vaguely remember until you read his Playbill bio. ("Oh, yeah, he was the guy who played the Arthur O'Connell role in the 1994 Roundabout revival of *Picnic*.") Playing a ghost can be either very easy or very tough, depending on the circumstances. The ghost role here was very tough. Bryggman appeared all too alive in his first-act scene, when he was already dead. In his second-act scene he was still alive, but you could see the shadow of madness creeping over his features. In his final scene, when Robert's senses have permanently departed, there was an incredibly touching moment of such father-daughter solitude—Bryggman sitting on the couch, Parker comforting him as he appeared to be on the brink. Magical performances.

Watching *Proof* on that cold February night without Mary-Louise Parker and without Larry Bryggman and with only half a house, it was infinitely clear that Auburn's play was *that* good.

Ben Shenkman had a similarly complex chore as the "math nerd" Hal, come to protect his mentor Robert's legacy but finding himself more interested in protecting Robert's fragile daughter. In the end, he realizes that Catherine is the mathematical genius that he himself will never be; in a way, Catherine becomes the addled genius, and Hal becomes the protective Catherine. (Hence, he storms out after that first-act argument but instinctively prevents the door from slamming.) Shenkman does this all

Proof
Opened: October 24, 2000
Still playing May 28, 2001
248 performances (and 16 previews)
Profit/Loss: Profit
Proof ($69 top) was scaled to a potential gross of $427,309
    at the 924-seat Walter Kerr. Weekly grosses averaged
    about $314,000, building to a high of $414,000 for
    Christmas week. Total gross for the partial season was
    $10,361,991. Attendance was about 81 percent, with the
    box office grossing about 73 percent of dollar-capacity.

TONY AWARD NOMINATIONS
Best Play: David Auburn (WINNER)
Best Performance by a Leading Actress: Mary-Louise Parker
    (WINNER)
Best Performance by a Featured Actor: Larry Bryggman
Best Performance by a Featured Actor: Ben Shenkman
Best Performance by a Featured Actress: Johanna Day
Best Direction of a Play: Daniel Sullivan (WINNER)

PULITZER PRIZE
David Auburn (WINNER)

NEW YORK DRAMA CRITICS CIRCLE AWARD
Best American Play: David Auburn (WINNER)

DRAMA DESK AWARDS
Outstanding Play: David Auburn (WINNER)
Outstanding Actress: Mary-Louise Parker (WINNER)

*Critical
Scorecard*

Rave 7
Favorable 2
Mixed 1
Unfavorable 0
Pan 0

in such a way that you want him—and Hal—to get the girl. And he does.

Johanna Day was the odd man out, as it were. Her character is a rich and successful survivor, but she doesn't count because she can't count (mathematically speaking). Auburn gave the two sisters a delicious exchange wherein Claire brought Catherine—who looked like she hadn't showered in a week—a bottle of hair conditioner for "healthy hair." Catherine informs her that hair is dead tissue. What's a sister to do?? As Claire says later in the midst of a scientific argument, "I really don't know anything about this."

By the final scene, the whole situation has erupted. Hal returns, convinced that Catherine—and not her father—is the true author of the proof; Catherine, whose world has collapsed, is not prone to let him off the hook. Romantics in the audience were no doubt hoping that Hal would plead with her to stay in Chicago, or ask her to move in with him, or even just go over and kiss her. But Mr. Auburn simply has Hal ask Catherine to calm down and read through some of the proof with him. She does, somewhat warily. After two lines of $q$ns and nth primes and b positives, Parker's body transformed itself. Her spine straightened, she let her bag slide down her lap to the floor, and she was suddenly in control; no madness here, just a mathematical genius at work. I don't know who came up with that sliding bag—a gesture that frees Catherine of the various shackles suppressing her character—but what a perfect and lovely ending.

I left the theatre so overwhelmed by Ms. Parker's performance that I slightly overlooked Mr. Auburn; it took a day or two to realize how strong the play itself was. When Parker took a half-week vacation in February, I decided—with some apprehension—to go back and see how things fared without her. When dealing with such a brilliant performance, you can't reasonably expect much from an understudy. To my surprise, Caroline Bootle's performance was good enough that you wouldn't know you were seeing an understudy. Not up to Parker's level, naturally; but then, this was Bootle's very first performance in the play. (Understudies don't get previews; they are lucky if they even get to rehearse with the rest of the cast, as opposed to the other understudies.) As if to help me realize how well Bootle was doing, Bryggman's understudy was also on—and the poor man was merely adequate. Yes, he said his lines and got through the play, but the subtext was missing. It also became apparent just how much Bryggman's performance—as an observer—supported Parker and Shenkman.

Watching *Proof* on that cold February night without Mary-Louise Parker and without Larry Bryggman and with only half a house, it was infinitely clear that Auburn's play was *that* good. But I wouldn't have missed Ms. Parker's phenomenal performance for the world.

The Full Monty

Since the mid-1990s, we have been reading continually about Broadway's four promising young composers: Adam Guettel, Jason Robert Brown, Michael John LaChiusa, and Ricky Ian Gordon. Audra McDonald—the top new Broadway singer of her generation—made it official, in a way, by devoting her smashing 1998 debut album, *Way Back to Paradise,* solely to their work. The unquestioned promise of these fellows—all four of them—became so generally accepted that they were constantly hailed, in one breath, as the great hope of the American musical.

Brown was the first to reach Broadway. *Parade* (1998), from Lincoln Center Theater, was a serious, tragic musical that failed to enthuse critics or theatregoers; it quickly closed. LaChiusa soon followed, with two Broadway musicals within twenty weeks. *Marie Christine* (1999), from Lincoln Center Theater, was a serious, tragic musical that failed to enthuse critics or theatregoers; *it* quickly closed. *The Wild Party,* from the New York Shakespeare Festival, was a serious, tragic musical that—well, you get the idea. At this writing, neither Martin nor Guettel has yet to reach Broadway. Guettel, though, has done the most impressive work of the group thus far, with the off-Broadway *Floyd Collins* (1996) and his 1998 song cycle *Saturn Returns* (which was recorded under the title *Myths and Hymns*).

These guys, as I said, were generally acknowledged to be leaders of the pack. This made it all the more startling that the first good musical of the century—no, I don't count *Aida*—came not from one of the anointed few but from a guy with no theatre background whatsoever.

The Full Monty first passed through the hands of Guettel. The immensely talented composer, who happens to be the grandson of Richard Rodgers but holds his own very nicely, was initially approached to write the musicalization of the 1997 sleeper film hit. (When the Old Globe Theatre's artistic director Jack O'Brien and managing director Tom Hall started to hatch *Monty*, they were producing a regional theatre mini-tour of *Floyd Collins*.)

Guettel turned down the offer—he was too busy, he said—but steered them to a guy he knew from his rock band. David Yazbek had two non-blockbuster CDs to his name and absolutely no affinity for musical theatre. (According to his Playbill bio, he was "responsible for the unrelenting theme song to *Where in the World Is Carmen Sandiego?*") But Guettel said Yazbek was the right man for the job, the *Full Monty* people listened to Yazbek's work, and they were sufficiently impressed to gamble their millions. Which turned out to be Broadway's most successful gamble since Disney handed *The Lion King* to Julie Taymor. The show played a tryout at the Old

The first good musical of the century came not from one of the anointed few—Guettel, Brown, LaChiusa, or Gordon—but from a guy with no theatre background whatsoever.

Globe, in San Diego, and appeared to be an unstoppable hit from the first performance. (The only thing that put a damper on *The Full Monty*, it turned out, was *The Producers*, which opened late in the season, monopolizing audiences and awards.)

Yazbek started off in fine form, with a quartet that brought to mind Frank Loesser. Loesser opened his *Guys and Dolls* with three racetrack gamblers standing on a street corner, setting the stage with their folksy vernacular in "Fugue for Tinhorns" ("I Got the Horse Right Here"). That's pretty much what Yazbek did with four unemployed steelworkers, complaining that they are treated like "Scrap." ("What I want? That's easy asshole, I want a job," goes the opening song.)

Yazbek's score has a strong Loesserish influence, which was certainly a good choice. Frank once wrote a musical called *How to Succeed in Business without Really Trying* (1961). Few people consider *How to Succeed* a great score, and there's a reason for this: The show is a nonstop string of jokes, and Loesser consciously chose to let the songs supplement the jokes. That is to say, instead of interrupting the book with beautiful ballads and knockout character songs (as in *Guys and Dolls*), Loesser wrote songs about strung-out office workers on a coffee-less coffee break, and jealous executives plotting in the men's room, and irate secretaries wearing the

⌐EUGENE O'NEILL THEATRE
A JUJAMCYN THEATRE
JAMES H. BINGER   ROCCO LANDESMAN
CHAIRMAN   PRESIDENT

PAUL LIBIN   JACK VIERTEL
PRODUCING DIRECTOR   CREATIVE DIRECTOR

Fox Searchlight Pictures
Lindsay Law
Thomas Hall

present

THE FULL MONTY
THE BROADWAY MUSICAL

Book by   Music and Lyrics by
Terrence McNally   David Yazbek

John Ellison Conlee Nicholas Cutro Jason Danieley Lisa Datz
André De Shields Thomas Michael Fiss Kathleen Freeman Romain Frugé
Annie Golden Marcus Neville Emily Skinner Patrick Wilson

Jay Douglas Laura Marie Duncan Angelo Fraboni Denis Jones Jannie Jones
Liz McConahay Sue-Anne Morrow Jason Opsahl Patti Perkins
Jimmy Smagula C.E. Smith Matthew Stocke Todd Weeks Ronald Wyche

Scenic Design   Costume Design   Lighting Design   Sound Design
John Arnone   Robert Morgan   Howell Binkley   Tom Clark

Orchestrations by   Dance Music Arrangements by   Conductor
Harold Wheeler   Zane Mark   Kimberly Grigsby

Casting by   Production Supervisor   Production Stage Manager
Liz Woodman Casting, C.S.A.   Gene O'Donovan   Nancy Harrington

Press Representative   General Management
Barlow • Hartman public relations   The Charlotte Wilcox Company

Music Direction/Vocal and Incidental Music Arrangements by
Ted Sperling

Choreographed by
Jerry Mitchell

Directed by
Jack O'Brien

WORLD PREMIERE AT THE OLD GLOBE THEATRE, San Diego, CA
Original Cast Recording Coming Soon on RCA Victor.

Georgie Bukatinsky Annie Golden
Buddy "Keno" Walsh Denis Jones
Reg Willoughby Todd Weeks
Jerry Lukowski Patrick Wilson
Dave Bukatinsky John Ellison Conlee
Malcolm MacGregor Jason Danieley
Ethan Girard Romain Frugé
Nathan Lukowski Thomas Michael
Fiss *or* Nicholas Cutro
Susan Hershey Laura Marie Duncan
Joanie Lish Jannie Jones
Estelle Genovese Liz McConahay
Pam Lukowski Lisa Datz
Teddy Slaughter Angelo Fraboni
Molly MacGregor Patti Perkins
Harold Nichols Marcus Neville
Vicki Nichols Emily Skinner
Jeanette Burmeister Kathleen
Freeman
Noah "Horse" T. Simmons André De
Shields
Police Sergeant C. E. Smith
Minister Jay Douglas
Tony Giordano Jimmy Smagula
Swings Sue-Anne Morrow, Jason
Opsahl, Matthew Stocke, Ronald
Wyche

Location: Buffalo, New York
Time: The Present

Original Broadway Cast Album:
RCAVictor 09026-63739

same "one-of-a-kind" party dress, all of it topped off with an inspirational, hypocritical hallelujah chorus of hypocrisy. This left many thinking that the composer did a merely okay job, but nothing special; *How to Succeed* won seven Tony Awards—even the conductor won—but Loesser went home empty-handed. He got a Pulitzer Prize for his work, though.

Yazbek's *Monty* music was underappreciated in the theatre, and not without reason: He and librettist Terrence McNally settled on song slots that served comedy at the music's expense. Five of the show's thirteen musical numbers fall under the category of noisy, nontheatrical, heavy-rhythm songs. Three of these came early on, giving a faulty impression of

the overall quality of the score. No harm done; most of the traditional-
ists in the audiences had already decided they liked the show anyhow.
Those who kept listening closely, though, found that Yazbek actually did
some impressive work.

The composer was given only one quiet, contemplative slot, which he
filled with a lovely lullaby called "Breeze on the River." This is a tender
beauty with an impatiently insistent beat, sung by the hero to his son. (I
always thought Buffalo was on a lake, however.) "Big-Ass Rock" takes its
cue from Guettel's grandpa's "Pore Jud Is Daid," the mock dirge from *Oklahoma!* Here, two of the main characters try to talk a third out of suicide.
They do so, with wit, but the song is greatly enhanced by Yazbek's sweet
countermelody in which the formerly despondent Sad Sack sings: "I've
got a friend / Like Carole King, or was it Carly Simon, used to sing? / I always get those two confused / But anyway. . . ." This is true musical theatre
character writing; that's the hazy way this character thinks, and it is very
funny and genuine and real. Yazbek also showed his skill with "You Walk
with Me," a funeral anthem that turns into a tender love song between
two misfits (and gets some big laughs, too). Not easy to do, folks.

Capping it all was a song shoehorned into the plot, bluntly called
"Jeanette's Showbiz Number." This was sung by Kathleen Freeman, who
played one of those old-time rehearsal pianists (somewhat reminiscent of
the late Dorothea Freitag). This character was not in the original film, so
it was left for librettist Terrence McNally to create her out of thin air.
(When one of the men asks who she is, another answers, "She just
showed up—piano and all.") In this showstopping second-act opener,
Freeman—or Jeanette, rather—
spins her résumé out of Yazbek's **Yazbek's score has a strong**
imagination. "When I once in- **Loesserish influence, which was**
sulted Frank, I played with bro- **certainly a good choice.**
ken fingers," she tells us, and we
howl. (Sinatra, not Loesser.) Yazbek has clearly studied that *Guys and
Dolls* classic, "Adelaide's Lament." He doesn't copy it; he merely applies
Loesser's lesson, with panache.

If Yazbek was a stranger in a strange land, he was guided by top musical
theatre talents. Ted Sperling is one of the keenest music directors around,
his credits including important work with Bill Finn, Stephen Sondheim,
Stephen Flaherty, and Adam Guettel. Sperling also provided *Monty*'s
vocal and incidental arrangements, presumably helping Yazbek fill out
the evening. Harold Wheeler, of *Dreamgirls*, *Side Show*, and *Swing!*, pro-

The Full Monty
Opened: October 26, 2000
Still playing May 28, 2001
246 performances (and 35 previews)
Profit/Loss: To Be Determined
The Full Monty ($85 top) was scaled to a potential gross of
$628,547 at the 1,088-seat Eugene O'Neill. Weekly grosses
averaged about $514,000, with the show falling below
$500,000 in the spring (when the *Producers* came to
town). While business was usually strong, the show broke
the $600,000 mark only four times (in the first nine
weeks). Total gross for the partial season was
$18,041,851. Attendance was about 90 percent, with the
box office grossing about 81 percent of dollar-capacity.

TONY AWARD NOMINATIONS
Best Musical
Best Book of a Musical: Terrence McNally
Best Original Score: David Yazbek
Best Performance by a Leading Actor: Patrick Wilson
Best Performance by a Featured Actor: John Ellison Conlee
Best Performance by a Featured Actor: André De Shields
Best Performance by a Featured Actress: Kathleen Freeman
Best Direction of a Musical: Jack O'Brien
Best Choreography: Jerry Mitchell
Best Orchestrations: Harold Wheeler

DRAMA DESK AWARD
Outstanding Music: David Yazbek (WINNER)

Critical
Scorecard

Rave 1
Favorable 4
Mixed 2
Unfavorable 1
Pan 2

vided a swinging and witty set of orchestrations—I think I heard not
only an anvil but also a chain saw emanating from the pit—and Kimberly Grigsby was the dancingest conductor on Broadway since Joyce
Brown led *Purlie*. Grigsby wore a sleeveless dress, so the lights occasionally picked up flashes of bare flesh from the orchestra pit—which was not
unsuitable to the project. This made Grigsby more visible than your average conductor, leaving the audience with the impression of a high-pow-
ered young woman controlling the out-of-work men and more or less running things—which was also not unsuitable to the project.

Librettist Terrence McNally seamlessly transplanted the action from
Sheffield, England, to Buffalo, New York. While totally rewriting the dialogue, he skillfully retained the heart. (Director Jack O'Brien appears to
have called the shots on *Monty* from the beginning, but a good director's
hand is invisible.) McNally is best known for his comedies, which in re-

cent years have gotten stronger and stronger and include such winning works as *Lips Together, Teeth Apart* (1991), *Love! Valour! Compassion!* (1994), and *Master Class* (1995).

His musical theatre career is more checkered. *Kiss of the Spider Woman* (1993) had its champions, though I personally found it highly distasteful. I admired his work on *Ragtime* (1998), but the show was overstuffed and unfocused, and part of the blame must fall to the librettist. Granted, Mc-Nally won Tony Awards for these two musicals; still, they both lost millions of dollars. While there were many reasons for this—including the managerial ministrations of Garth Drabinsky—the fact remains that not enough people liked the shows, resulting in moderate to poor word of mouth and dwindling houses. (If *Ragtime* had the same word of mouth as *The Lion King*, it would still be running.) Mc-Nally's earlier musicals were both outright failures, *Here's Where I Belong* (1968)—a musicalization of Steinbeck's *East of Eden*, from which McNally removed his name before the opening—and *The Rink* (1984). But McNally sure did well by *Monty*, coming up with a suitably crowd-pleasing book. Things fell slightly to pieces in the second act, with some especially sketchy storytelling. The show was well-nigh into its third

hour by then, so McNally and O'Brien apparently decided to get on with it and push their way to the rousing finish.

The proceedings were buoyed by a fine and highly likable cast, with eight or so winning performances. Patrick Wilson exuded charm in the leading role (billing notwithstanding); John Ellison Conlee played second banana, sensitively handling the "fatman" business (*you* try singing a love song to your stomach); Jason Danieley—who always seems to be good—was effective as the suicidal mama's boy; André De Shields danced up a storm, as he typically does; and Ms. Freeman rode herd over them all. Audiences and castmates were stunned to learn, after the fact, that the expertly comic Freeman had been suffering from lung cancer throughout the run. She died on August 23, 2001.

It should be observed that *The Full Monty* was laced with what one might call "NC-17" words and phrases. The vocabulary is so right for the characters—like the street patois of *Guys and Dolls*—and so devoid of animosity, that the result was really rather sweet. And then there was the strip. The plot built toward the moment when the six heroes doffed their policeman's trousers and went "the full monty," which was quite harmless as these things go. (The climax of the strip was pretty much drowned out by the glare of a bank of lights spelling out the title.) Even so, the guys garnered such good-will throughout the evening that the audience was completely behind them.

McNally and O'Brien, however, saw fit to start the show with a "real" male stripper, who appeared to be as authentic as you can get (without actually going "the full monty"). While certain segments of the audience whooped and hollered, I can see how this scene might have been offensive to some. *The Full Monty* was otherwise perfectly and happily suitable for teenagers; I suppose that at least some of them must have felt uncomfortable during this blunt bump-and-grind exhibition. Or, at least, their parents. (Is this why *The Full Monty*—playing the relatively small Eugene O'Neill Theatre, and despite great word of mouth—never attained sellout status?) The 1959 musical *Gypsy* included this same type of scene, with professional strippers instructing an amateur. There it was played for outright comedy, far less graphically and ever so much more effectively (with the bravura trio "You Gotta Get a Gimmick"). *The Full Monty*'s first-act strip scene was presented so tactlessly that I was surprised they didn't have the stripper jump into the auditorium and shimmy up the aisle soliciting twenty-dollar bills. Is this what kept *Monty* a big hit but not a sellout smash? I wouldn't be surprised.

> During the funeral scene, two male misfits connected in a touching duet. One blue-collar steelworker turned to the other and said, "They're holding hands." The other simply said, "Good for them. Good for them."

But McNally more than made up for it, with a wonderful—and significant—exchange. During the aforementioned funeral scene, his two male misfits connected in that touching duet ("You Walk with Me"). One blue-collar steelworker turned to the other and said, "They're holding hands." The other blue-collar steelworker, the leading man of the show, simply said, "Good for them. Good for them."

The Tale of the Allergist's Wife

Two weeks after the opening of the new Neil Simon play came a new Neil Simon play. Well, really, more like a new, *old* Neil Simon play. *The Tale of the Allergist's Wife*, it was called, and it was written not by old Doc Simon but by a fellow named Charles Busch.

One might well refer to *The Allergist's Wife* as an old Neil Simon play, as it was as funny as Simon's plays of the 1960s. Rip-roaring laughter, cascading from the stage for two hours: big laughs, little laughs, belly laughs, time-delayed laughs. I suppose that a theatregoer seeing the two shows in two days without a Playbill in hand might well have wondered just which one was written by the real Simon. *The Allergist* devolved into a problematic and un-Simon-like sex play, yes; but *The Dinner Party*—with sexual degradation at its center—was even stranger.

Charles Busch is a familiar name to many New York theatregoers, with more than a dozen produced plays since 1985. But never on Broadway. While Busch has a large following and a good reputation, his work has always been out of the mainstream. Or perhaps ahead of the mainstream. His biggest hit—prior to *Tale of the Allergist's Wife*, that is—was *Vampire Lesbians of Sodom*, which opened at off-Broadway's Provincetown Playhouse in 1985 and ran five years. His other works include *Psycho Beach Party*, *The Lady in Question*, and *Red Scare on Sunset*,

> **Rip-roaring laughter, cascading from the stage for two hours: big laughs, little laughs, belly laughs, time-delayed laughs.**

all of which were showcases for himself (and his gowns). Some of these were supposed to be pretty good, mind you; but I confess that I never got around to seeing any of them. Because they were too far out of the main-

Mohammed Anil Kumar
Marjorie Linda Lavin
Ira Tony Roberts
Frieda Shirl Bernheim
Lee Michele Lee

Place: A two-bedroom apartment on Manhattan's Upper West Side

ETHEL BARRYMORE THEATRE
243 West 47th Street
Ⓢ A Shubert Organization Theatre
Gerald Schoenfeld, *Chairman*   Philip J. Smith, *President*
Robert E. Wankel, *Executive Vice President*

MANHATTAN THEATRE CLUB
LYNNE MEADOW-ARTISTIC DIRECTOR BARRY GROVE-EXECUTIVE PRODUCER

CAROLE SHORENSTEIN HAYS DARYL ROTH STUART THOMPSON AND DOUGLAS S. CRAMER

PRESENT

LINDA LAVIN
TONY ROBERTS MICHELE LEE

IN

THE TALE OF
THE ALLERGIST'S WIFE

BY **CHARLES BUSCH**

WITH

SHIRL BERNHEIM ANIL KUMAR

SET DESIGN   COSTUME DESIGN   LIGHTING DESIGN   SOUND DESIGN
SANTO LOQUASTO   ANN ROTH   CHRISTOPHER AKERLIND   BRUCE ELLMAN AND BRIAN RONAN

TECHNICAL SUPERVISOR   PRODUCTION STAGE MANAGER   CASTING
GENE O'DONOVAN   WILLIAM JOSEPH BARNES   NANCY PICCIONE
DAVID CAPARELLIOTIS

PRESS REPRESENTATIVE   MTC ASSOCIATE ARTISTIC DIRECTOR
BONEAU/BRYAN-BROWN   MICHAEL BUSH

DIRECTED BY
LYNNE MEADOW

THE PRODUCERS WISH TO EXPRESS THEIR APPRECIATION TO THEATRE DEVELOPMENT FUND FOR ITS SUPPORT OF THIS PRODUCTION

stream, or maybe *I* was too far out of the mainstream. At any rate, Busch came to Broadway with a good reputation and a significant fan base. He didn't have the same built-in audience that the real Neil Simon had a couple of blocks over at the Music Box, but he had far more—and far better—jokes.

While I had not seen Busch's plays, I'd come across him a decade earlier. In 1988, I instigated a revival of a Harold Arlen–Truman Capote musical called *House of Flowers*. My partners and I arranged a production at the Old Globe Theatre in San Diego, to be adapted and directed by Jack O'Brien. After a year of work, though, Jack threw up his hands and threw in the towel, unable to figure out how to make the piece work. (It has a decidedly brilliant score, saddled by a decidedly problematic book.) My partners rebounded with director-designer Geoffrey Holder, who had appeared as an eccentric voodoo man in the original production. Geoffrey is a grand and grandly entertaining fellow, but after listening to his ideas for "fixing" the piece, I decided to bail out.

The show—as adapted by Busch—was ultimately mounted in 1990 for a pre-Broadway tryout, under the sponsorship of a low-caliber, famously chintzy stock operation. The moneyman insisted on casting a pop singing star in the lead, whose presence made an impossible mess of it. I caught up with it in Westbury—the closest it got to New York City—and drove back one of my former partners, who asked if I could give Charles a lift. If the production was hopeless, I was impressed by Busch's explanation of his intentions. He seemed to have a good handle on what to do, but he was handcuffed by Holder's foggy vision and the star diva's demands.

In any event, it took Busch until the fall of 2000 to finally reach the big street, and he did it with what I figure to be the funniest new American play to hit Broadway since John Guare's *Six Degrees of Separation* opened ten years earlier. (Ten years and three days, actually.) Funny enough, even, to survive a scattershot second act. *The Allergist*—or his wife, anyway—was hysterical right out of the box. The curtain rose on Linda Lavin lethargically lounging in her Upper West Side living room. "Now, later, yesterday. Ce n'est pas la difference," she intoned, like a Riverside Drive Anna Kareninitsky.

The audience exploded, and that was that.

Lavin was made for the role of Marjorie Taub; or, rather, Marjorie Taub was made to order for Ms. Lavin. The character first appeared in a sketch in Busch's 1996 one-man show *Flipping My Wig*, under the name Miriam Passman. (Synopsis: "A suburban housewife finally gets her chance to perform her musical tribute to Edith Piaf in a Greenwich Village cabaret, but her pent-up neurotic frustrations threaten to overpower her act.") As Busch related to Don Shewey in a *New York Times* interview, something clicked when he happened to attend that year's Lincoln Center Theater revival of Edward Albee's *A Delicate Balance*. "Wouldn't it be funny," Busch wondered, "to take these Jewish characters and put them in a rather cryptic Albee or Pinter play?" Thus, an upper-middle-class, Upper West Side, Jewish take on something not unlike Pinter's *Old Times*, a tangled tale of two women and one man.

And Busch knew who he wanted to play the lead; not himself but Linda Lavin, who had impressed him with her performance in *Death Defying Acts*, a 1995 evening of short plays by Woody Allen, David Mamet, and Elaine May. Lavin has been on Broadway since 1962, when she arrived in a small but impossible-to-miss role in *A Family Affair*. (This quick failure was composer John Kander and director Harold Prince's first musical.) Lavin has garnered laugh after laugh after laugh over the years, with her most memorable appearances being as a wisecracking would-be adulteress in need of a cigarette in Neil Simon's *Last of the Red Hot Lovers*

(1969) and as Neil Simon's mother, more or less, in *Broadway Bound* (1986). Lavin knows every trick in the book, and she bound them all together for *The Allergist's Wife*. Here she was a Prisoner of Riverside Drive (*ref.* Simon's *Prisoner of Second Avenue*), searching for meaning in life. "We're Russian peasants from the shtetl," she cries, "we have no right to be attending art installations at the Whitney." Or, as Kafka would say, she is "a cage in search of a bird."

"*Perdu*," Lavin's Marjorie wailed, spreading malaise like mayonnaise. *Perdu* is French for loss, or utter damnation as Mr. Busch would have it; Ms. Lavin half made it sound like the guy who sells chicken breasts. Her character is recovering from a breakdown. She cracked up by "accidentally" cracking up six porcelain figurines at the Disney Store; Goofy alone was worth more than $250. The play began with Marjorie discussing Turgenev with her Iranian doorman, who was installing a lighting fixture. When he tested the light, Lavin gave such a shriek that poor Mohammed (Anil Kumar) seemed to literally crawl the wall. It was that kind of a play, and Busch's out-of-kilter sensibilities kept the audience roaring at unexpected laughs.

Ms. Lavin's Marjorie, no matter how distracted, couldn't pass a pillow without fluffing it up. Her rare moments of calm were belied by her feet, which jingled and jangled and threatened to break full-out into Saint Vitus' dance; at one point, when convinced she has gone totally bonkers, she lurched about the stage like a donkey in heat. I've never seen a donkey in heat, but you get the idea.

Tony Roberts soon came in as her husband, a clueless, retired allergist. "Hey there, Kemo Sabe," he greets the Iranian (*ref.* The Lone Ranger and his faithful Indian companion, Tonto). Roberts was very good here, more interesting than he has been in years and years. His Ira was an observer; he stood by watching the others converse as if he were viewing a Ping-

Pong game. Every once in a while playwright Busch gave him a zinger, after which Roberts went back to the sidelines. (I realized, watching Roberts watching, that this was precisely what Woody Allen had him do in all those early comedies.)

Comic relief—or I should say, additional comic relief—was provided by Frieda, Marjorie's "farbissineh" mother. ("You didn't even speak Yiddish until you were sixty-five," Marjorie complains.) Frieda talks about her bowel movements constantly, more often than not when Marjorie is eating. She has not had a satisfactory one in four years, and her favorite cry is "Call Dr. Kevorkian." Her favorite word seems to be the four-letter euphemism beginning with "f." (For unrestrained gaiety, write into your play an eighty-year-old broad punching out four-letter euphemisms.) Frieda also gives us a rollicking story about Rivkie Dubow—her neighbor at Schwab House, with six grandchildren and a hair net—putting the moves on her while they were folding the prune butter into *hamentaschen*. This met with a tidal wave of hysteria.

> **"Wouldn't it be funny," wondered Charles Busch, "to take these Jewish characters and put them in a rather cryptic Albee or Pinter play?" Thus, an upper-middle-class, Upper West Side, Jewish take on something not unlike Pinter's *Old Times*.**

The third side of the Pinteresque triangle was a mystery character named Lee Green, née Lillian Greenblatt. She was quite a conundrum, and this is where the playwright ultimately ran into trouble. She was too much of a conundrum by half, and things got messy when Mr. Busch tried to clean up after himself. Lee has "accidentally" planted herself in the Taub home; she is a professional fund-raiser for the Universal Human Rights Coalition, one of those groups that purportedly buys vaccines for babies but sounds suspiciously like a terrorist front. Presumably she thinks she can rook the Taubs out of part of their fortune—he's a New York City allergist living in a $900,000 co-op, after all—but she might be ill-advised. People like the Taubs give money to Israel, rarely to the competition.

Busch has Lee tell us that she was "the first person Pat called after the resignation." Nixon, that is. She had a little affair with Günter Grass, was an intimate of Fassbinder, and buddies with Kerouac, Jimmy Baldwin, and "Andy." (She used to cook cans of Campbell's tomato soup for the latter.) She was friends with Princesses Grace and Diana; the latter, seated to Lee's left at a dinner party, "overheard my conversation with Henry

Kissinger on the tragic situation of the land mines. I guess I helped plant that seed.") Busch laid it on thick, but you really need to have a payoff for this sort of thing. Lee gave Steven Spielberg the idea for *E.T.* and was a pal to Quincy Jones, Martin Luther King, Placido Domingo, Lenny Bruce, and Andy Griffith. (How old is this gal anyway?) After a while, Busch seemed to be dropping names solely for laughs. And the laughs quickly grew weak, except for Lee's nifty, off-the-cuff admission that "I always travel with a wok and three pairs of eyelashes."

Marjorie, Ira, and Frieda are wild caricatures, but they are more or less real. Busch's impossible eccentrics had a ring of truth for the typical audience member. (Or at least, the typical New York–Jewish audience member.) Lee, though, appeared to spring fully grown from the screen of Mr. Busch's word processor. Joke upon joke upon joke, but no basic truth beneath it all.

As act 2 progressed, things got stranger and stranger, with Busch leading his characters into a ménage à trois. I mean, Ms. Lavin and Mr. Roberts were already in their sixties; do we really want to see them being seduced, right in front of our eyes, by Ms. Lee? (Is this Noël Coward's revenge?) Michele, the terrorist: "I'd like to get the two of you in that absurd marble tub and bathe and perfume you and pamper you like spoiled courtesans in a seraglio." Tony, the allergist: "We both have allergic reactions to many floral scents." Despite the shaky ground, Busch retained his high-octane laugh ratio—what more priceless than Lavin exclaiming, wonderingly, "I was a daughter of Sappho"—but the whole thing went to dramaturgicalogical pieces.

Even so, I'm glad to settle for the laughs. I simply feel the need to go on the record with a slight sense of disappointment. At intermission, I thought, "This play is wonderful," and put it in a class with its Manhattan Theatre Club twin, *Proof*. After the final curtain, I merely thought, "This play is very funny," and that was that.

After a particularly riotous exchange in which Mohammed related how Lee's terrorists killed his friend's uncle's business partner by sprinkling chopped-up tiger's whiskers in his hummus, thereby perforating his bowels—a tale of immense interest to Marjorie's anally obsessed mother—Lavin remarked, "Well, you certainly know your audience."

Busch certainly knows his audience, at least in New York. How *The Allergist's Wife* will play in Dallas or Cincinnati remains to be seen, and I don't suppose it will prove a staple in high schools or dinner theatres or Midwestern church groups. But for the mainstream middle-class Broadway audience —people who laugh at the mere mention of Zabar's or Gracious Home— Busch's *Allergist* was a riotous treat and most welcome.

> At intermission, I thought, "This play is wonderful," and put it in a class with *Proof*. After the final curtain, I merely thought, "This play is very funny," and that was that.

And let a word be said for the ad campaign. Someone had the bright idea of assigning *New Yorker* cartoonist Roz Chast to provide the artwork, and she did a brilliant job of it. Not only the artwork—an allergist's wife trapped in a shopping bag, with stickers from the Herman Hesse Fan Club Local 283, "proud parents of lovely, smart children who, for some reason, are still finding themselves," and an "I ♥ Spinosa" button—but the hand-lettered logo as well. And the front-of-house quotes, too! As you walked by the Barrymore, the signs made you want to go in and see the show again.

Matters of the Heart

The curse of the Broadway theatre, real estate–wise, is that it is a limited-use facility. You get eight performances a week—when you've got a show running, that is—which means you're open to the public roughly twenty-four hours a week. The rest of the time, you pay your electricity and heating and mortgage and insurance and everything else without the possibility of collecting any income. Most Broadway attractions play a Tuesday through Sunday matinee schedule, which leaves them dark two nights a week—nights when you could otherwise fill some seats.

These empty times are rarely used other than for occasional benefits, as Broadway stagehand and front-of-house rates explode once you go past eight performances and six days. Lincoln Center Theater has a different set of union contracts, which makes it easier to fill those dark nights with special two-performance-a-week attractions.

> *Matters of the Heart* turned out to be little more than a concert. And not a theatrical concert, either; more like a cabaret show.

Of necessity, these must have small casts and limited production values. For example, Spalding Gray sitting at a desk with a pitcher of water, as he has in a series of monologues that have filled the Beaumont's dark nights over the years.

Morning, Noon and Night, Gray's 1999 offering, seemed to do exceptionally well, extending for a total of twenty performances and a cumulative gross of about half a million. Lincoln Center filled the 2000 slot with Patti LuPone's *Matters of the Heart*, which turned out to be little more than a concert. And not a theatrical concert, either; more like a cabaret show.

LuPone, a musical comedy star who hasn't appeared in a new Broadway musical since Lincoln Center's 1987 production of *Anything Goes*, made a CD called *Matters of the Heart* (released in September 1999). The star launched her disc—which she also produced—with an evening at Joe's Pub (at the New York Shakespeare Festival) on September 26, 1999. Her *Matters of the Heart* concert—made up largely of material on the CD—was subsequently performed at the Sydney Festival in Australia, at London's Donmar Warehouse, and elsewhere before heading back to New York.

Previous dark-night attractions at both the Beaumont and Lincoln Center's Mitzi Newhouse Theater have been, in their own way, theatrical; one could always sense the participation of LCT's André Bishop and Bernie Gersten. *Matters of the Heart*, despite the presence of "additional dialogue" by John Weidman (of LCT's *Anything Goes* and *Contact*), seemed to be little more than a touring show—or concert, rather—

booked in to fill the stage for a few weeks' worth of dark nights. The show was no doubt fun for LuPone's fans but not quite the sort of thought-provoking theatre you expect from the folks at Lincoln Center.

A singing star performing song hits on Broadway can be quite a grand theatrical affair—think of Lena Horne's *The Lady and Her Music* (1981) or even Liza Minnelli's misguided *Minnelli by Minnelli* (1999). What we got here was Ms. LuPone; pianist-arranger Dick Gallagher at the Steinway (with crystal vase), stage right; and four string players with music stands, stage left. Gallagher drove

the pace from his keyboard, LuPone roamed the thrust stage, and the string players played politely. (In some of the numbers they simply sat

Patti LuPone

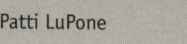

Original Studio Album: Varèse
Sarabande VSD-6058

LINCOLN CENTER THEATER
AT THE VIVIAN BEAUMONT

under the direction of

Andre Bishop and Bernard Gersten

presents

Patti LuPone
"matters of the heart"

musical direction and arrangements by Dick Gallagher

additional dialogue by John Weidman

conceived and directed by Scott Wittman

lighting by John Hastings
sound by Mark Fiore
production supervisor Richard Hester
hair and make-up by Danielle Vignjevich
Ms. LuPone's gowns designed by Oscar de la Renta

general manager Steven C. Callahan
production manager Jeff Hamlin
director of development Hattie K. Jutagir
director of marketing & special projects Thomas Cott

Sponsored by The Blanche and Irving Laurie Foundation

American Airlines is the official airline of Lincoln Center Theater
Kendall-Jackson is the preferred winery of Lincoln Center Theater

The CD of "Matters of the Heart" on LayZLay Records/Varese Sarabande,
is available in the theater lobby following the performance,
at your local record store or by visiting WWW.PATTILUPONE.NET

Piano provided by Steinway & Sons

---

there until the last refrain, when they finally picked up their bows to add some sweetening.)

LuPone made her grand entrance in a boat of a gown that looked like something Desirée Arnfeldt might have had her dresser whip up out of old drapes. She came down front and bowed, then said, "Good evening, ladies and gentlemen, I'm Loretta Young." (This got a laugh from LuPone's fans and people old enough to remember Young's dramatic-anthology TV series, which was canceled in 1961; otherwise, it was a wee bit obscure.) The dress was quite something, although it was hard to tell exactly what that something was. All one could be sure of was that it was a last-minute choice; the title page of the program bore the credit line "Ms. LuPone's gowns designed by Oscar de la Renta," but the opening night program was slip-sheeted with the info that the first-act gown was by Vicky Tiel and the second by Kleinfeld. What she wore the other nights, I can't tell you.

LuPone started the evening with a so-so rendition of Bob Merrill's "Love Makes the World Go 'Round" from *Carnival*, which was to be the theme song. That is, every once in a while they would plug in a few bars while transitioning to other, very different songs. LuPone then explained that the evening would feature songs of love—"first love . . . love lost . . . 'get the hell out of here before I kill you' love." This got a second laugh, and let me say—LuPone certainly knows how to play her audience. She then settled in to sing songs of first love, lost love, and more.

LuPone knows how to sing, which is all to the good; she also has a tendency to fall into her various mannerisms, which isn't. She is fully capable of avoiding said mannerisms, as she ably demonstrated in May 2000 when she essayed Mrs. Lovett in the New York Philharmonic's concert version of *Sweeney Todd*. But *Matters of the Heart* was aimed at LuPone's fans—not unreasonably, I suppose—and said fans seemed to want "their Patti." What made *Matters* interesting, mannerism-wise, was that we saw two different Pattis. One just sat there and sang "from the heart," as it were, and superbly so. The other played Patti LuPone.

The songs were a mixture of Broadway and pop, all more or less hanging on the hook of love making the world go round. The opening number was followed by that *South Pacific* favorite "A Wonderful Guy," in a gypsy violin arrangement. (Why??) After a pop song called "God Only Knows," she sang a rather effective rendition of "Easy to Be Hard" from *Hair*. I counted at least eight notes that she missed—or in some places misplaced, finding the notes a couple of beats later; but it didn't matter. LuPone reached out, made a veritable character study out of it, and got you.

And so it went. The evening settled down to a mélange of three types of songs: some that gave Patti the opportunity to leer and hint and be her public "self"; some that more or less supported the *Matters of the Heart* theme, which the star expressed little interest in; and some that demanded that she act. "Demand" is, perhaps, not the proper word. Rather, she simply chose to delve deeply into them, and showed us how very good a singing actress she can be. Her pairing of Joni Mitchell's "The Last Time I Saw Richard" and Jimmy Webb's "Where Love Resides," for example, the latter with a nice heart-tugging cello solo; or her second-act set of Judy Collins's "My Father" and Dillie Keane's "Look Mummy, No Hands." LuPone also worked her wiles on lighter-weight stuff like Gilbert O'Sullivan's "Alone Again (Naturally)," which was surprisingly moving. She gave us quite a few fine moments, but they were too

The show was no doubt fun for LuPone's fans but not quite the sort of thought-provoking theatre you expect from the folks at Lincoln Center.

isolated to make for an effective evening. LuPone did much better when Patti was off in her dressing room, overapplying lipstick.

For the record, Ms. LuPone sang no songs by Stephen Schwartz (who wrote her first two Broadway musicals) or Andrew Lloyd Webber (who wrote her two most important roles). However, she sang three songs by Stephen Sondheim, doing especially nicely on "Not a Day Goes By" and "Being Alive"; two songs by Rodgers and Hammerstein, getting quite an ovation on a rendition of "Hello, Young Lovers" that left me cold; and two by the up-and-coming John Buccino. One of these, "Playbill," was a clever but moving song about a woman sitting at a bar after a performance of Sondheim's 1994 musical *Passion*. There was also a finger-snapping, doo-wah version of Jerome Kern and Dorothy Fields's "The Way You Look Tonight." This last was not listed in the Playbill, but it's in my notes, and I couldn't have made it up; maybe it was just a dream, or an (unearned) encore. But why not just sing it the way they wrote it, Patti?

The evening settled down to a mélange of three types of songs: some that gave Patti the opportunity to be her public "self"; some that supported the theme; and some that demanded that she act, and showed us how very good a singing actress she can be.

Betrayal

I went to the 2000 revival of *Betrayal* as someone who had never quite connected with the work of Harold Pinter. His early plays were produced before I started attending serious drama. Three of them made quite a stir on Broadway: *The Birthday Party* (London, 1958; New York, 1967), *The Caretaker* (1960/1961), and *The Homecoming* (1965/1967). I read them, all three together, when I was about fifteen. Not the optimal introduction to Pinter, I suppose. Still, I found them absorbing, and I dutifully went to see the next Pinter play to make it across the pond. But *Old Times* (1970/1971) left me totally unengaged. I have duly attended the other two Pinter plays that have made it to Broadway, but I found *No Man's Land* (1974/1976) stodgy and *Betrayal* (1978/1980) just plain dull.

The only memorable part of any of them, so far as I am concerned, was the octogenarian sitting next to me in the second row

The 1980 Broadway production of *Betrayal* was so pallid that it made no impression on me whatsoever. The 2000 revival turned out to be extremely satisfying, revealing the play to be as intelligent and perceptive as any Pinter fan could ask.

of the Longacre for *No Man's Land*. This fellow was one of the most distinguished men I've ever seen. He was tall (though stooped), with a shock of white hair and marvelously intense eyes. It was instantly clear that he had to have been an actor, and a distinguished one; he looked like a handsome version of George Abbott.

He was presumably not there as a Pinter fan but as a colleague of John Gielgud or Ralph Richardson. (The two great English actors were starring in the sold-out limited engagement. The old actor and I were both sit-

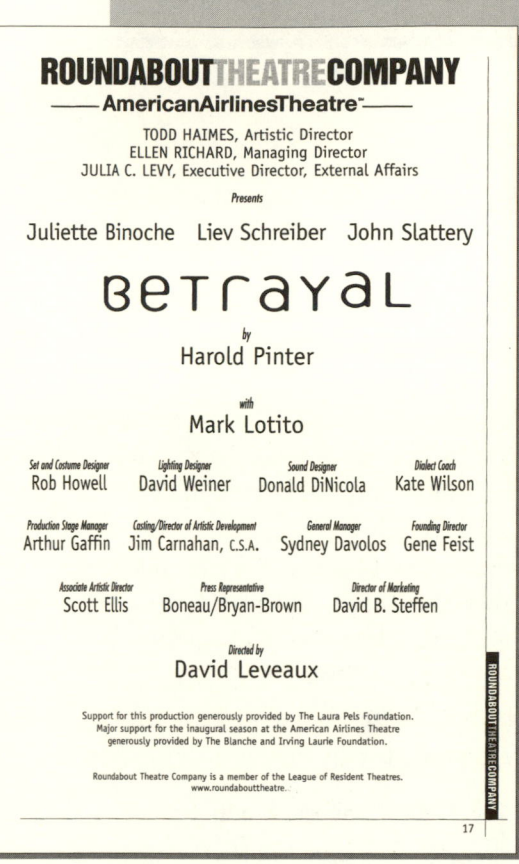

ROUNDABOUTTHEATRECOMPANY
——AmericanAirlinesTheatre™——

TODD HAIMES, Artistic Director
ELLEN RICHARD, Managing Director
JULIA C. LEVY, Executive Director, External Affairs

Presents

Juliette Binoche   Liev Schreiber   John Slattery

Betrayal

by
Harold Pinter

with
Mark Lotito

Set and Costume Designer	Lighting Designer	Sound Designer	Dialect Coach
Rob Howell	David Weiner	Donald DiNicola	Kate Wilson

Production Stage Manager	Casting/Director of Artistic Development	General Manager	Founding Director
Arthur Gaffin	Jim Carnahan, C.S.A.	Sydney Davolos	Gene Feist

Associate Artistic Director	Press Representative	Director of Marketing
Scott Ellis	Boneau/Bryan-Brown	David B. Steffen

Directed by
David Leveaux

Support for this production generously provided by The Laura Pels Foundation.
Major support for the inaugural season at the American Airlines Theatre
generously provided by The Blanche and Irving Laurie Foundation.

Roundabout Theatre Company is a member of the League of Resident Theatres.
www.roundabouttheatre.

17

ROUNDABOUT THEATRE COMPANY

Cast (in order of appearance)

Emma   Juliette Binoche
Jerry   Liev Schreiber
Robert   John Slattery
Waiter   Mark Lotito

Place: London and Venice
Time: Over the course of nine years

ting in house seats.) I thumbed through my memory trying to figure out who he could be; I knew it wasn't Alfred Lunt, who was ailing and unlikely to be in New York. As the play progressed —with Gielgud and Richardson sitting there talking and talking and talking—I found myself occasionally watching this old actor watching these two (younger) old actors.

I was in Sir John's dressing room after the show, when the fellow from the next seat clambered in, out of breath. (Gielgud was in the long, narrow closet of a room one flight up from the stage door, and he was somewhat embarrassed that this fellow had made the climb.) It turned out he was an actor named Glenn Anders, who starred in three Pulitzer Prize winners within five years (including Eugene O'Neill's *Strange Interlude*). I had done a project on one of the other plays, Sidney Howard's *They Knew What They Wanted*, so I instantly knew his name. This surprised both Gielgud and Anders. I later realized that I'd recognized Anders from a 1924 production photo in which he towered over Richard Bennett and Pauline Lord. Amazingly, the face and the frame were still the same.

This all has nothing to do with Harold Pinter. But what can I tell you?

It is my only memorable memory of Pinter's fourth, fifth, and final play (so far) to achieve a full Broadway production. More interesting than any of them, in my view, was a Claire Bloom–headed production of Henry James's *The Innocents* with direction (and apparently some script adaptation) by Pinter. This briefly played the Morosco in 1976, simultaneously with the American *No Man's Land*. Unfortunately, Pinter never saw *The Innocents* after it left the rehearsal hall. He fell seriously ill when the show headed to Boston, spending the tryout locked in his suite at the Ritz; he also missed the Philadelphia engagement. During New York previews, the cast went over to his hotel and did a read-through, but that was the extent of his presence. Nevertheless, this *Innocents* was wonderfully spooky and featured fine performances by Claire Bloom and a ghostly eleven year old named Sara Jessica Parker. (Parker, who now spells her name "Sarah," was hired as the understudy but took over the role when they fired another girl during rehearsals.) This *Innocents* also featured a wonderful manor house set, dominated by a grand, wooden staircase. It was by a new Broadway designer who immediately became one of my favorites, John Lee Beatty.

Most of the Pinter plays have been revived in New York over the years, including the Roundabout's 1994 *No Man's Land* with Jason Robards and Christopher Plummer. Still, I've remained resistant to Pinter's spell. The 1980 production of *Betrayal* was so pallid that it made no impression on me whatsoever; as the 2000 revival approached, I found myself racking my brain to remember who was in it. I eventually came up with Blythe Danner, who recalled the image of Raul Julia (miscast as Jerry, wearing Clark

> **How much of a contribution was made to this production by the director? David Leveaux didn't make the existing text any better, but he had me on the edge of my seat.**

Kent glasses), who eventually led me to an angry Roy Scheider (miscast as Robert). I couldn't remember anything else, save the fact that it was at the old Billy Rose Theatre, which was just then called the Trafalgar. (The Nederlanders bought the long-neglected jinx house and changed the name, hoping to attract a series of British imports. After *Betrayal* closed, they renamed it the Nederlander—which over the next two and a half years housed only one show, a one-night flop in 1981.)

At any rate, I traipsed to the American Airlines Theatre to see the first Broadway revival of *Betrayal* with an open mind, like all good little reviewers should. And what do you know? The production turned out to be

Betrayal
Opened: November 14, 2000
Closed: February 4, 2001
89 performances (and 28 previews)
Profit/Loss: Nonprofit [Profit]
Betrayal ($65 top) was scaled to a potential gross of
$349,943 at the 740-seat American Airlines Theatre
(although the show often played a seven-performance
week). Weekly grosses averaged about $267,000, hitting a
high of $315,000 in the final week. Total gross for the run
was $3,934,071. Attendance was about 89 percent, with
the box office grossing about 77 percent of dollar-
capacity. (These figures are not indicative, as the
potential was claculated at the top ticket price, but
subscribers paid less.)

TONY AWARD NOMINATIONS
Best Revival of a Play
Best Performance by a Leading Actress: Juliette Binoche

*Critical
Scorecard*

Rave 3
Favorable 2
Mixed 0
Unfavorable 3
Pan 2

extremely satisfying, revealing the play to be as intelligent and perceptive as any Pinter fan could ask.

Why the difference? It is generally agreed that the original Broadway production was weak, despite the fact that it was helmed by Pinter's original director (Peter Hall) and designer (John Bury). Hall and Bury did the London and American premieres of *Old Times* and *No Man's Land*, too. Whatever the problem was, the 1980 *Betrayal* did not begin to indicate the riches of the play. Pinter's language is typically cryptic, understated, and oblique. *Betrayal* is noted for being written backward. Not backward, entirely; the play takes place over the course of nine years, with most of the nine scenes stepping back (though three move forward). This was a novel effect, although certainly not original to Pinter. Pinter is also famous for his unspoken pauses, which indicate additional layers of meaning; "Pinteresque" has even entered the language. The information relayed by the actors during these pauses fills in the truth—or the nontruth —of the dialogue. It did, at least, in the 2000 revival.

Betrayal is purposely ambiguous. Emma (an art gallery owner) is guilty of betraying her husband, Robert (a publisher). Jerry (a literary agent) is guilty of betraying his best friend, Robert. Robert, it turns out, is also guilty of betraying Emma. And he has also betrayed Jerry, by not telling him that he knew all along that he was being betrayed. (The play has its roots in life; the real Emma was a journalist, her husband was a producer, and her lover was the playwright.) By spinning the tale backward, Pinter reveals these truths and half-truths according to his master plan, and the puzzle proves engrossing. Pinter also betrays the audience, for that matter, by allowing his characters to make false admissions to *us*. The play begins the day after Robert has learned of the long-ended affair, we are told and have every reason to believe; that's the foundation of the action, except that is turns out to be false. Right at the outset, Emma has betrayed Jerry —and the audience.

How much of a contribution was made to this production by the director? That's hard to say, especially since the director in question was David Leveaux. This is the same fellow who directed the startlingly good production of *The Real Thing*, a highlight of the 1999–2000 season. He also directed the startlingly intriguing production of *Electra* that visited Broadway in 1998. He also directed the startlingly vital 1993 Roundabout production of *Anna Christie*, which introduced Natasha Richardson and Liam Neeson to Broadway. And those are only his Broadway credits; who knows what he's done back home in England. He arrived for *Betrayal* rehearsals with an intimate knowledge of the play, having mounted productions in London, Paris, and Japan.

Leveaux didn't make the existing text any better, but he had me on the edge of my seat. Pockets of the audience were sleepy, I admit, but that is a hazard of playing to subscribers; you get some people who are not at all interested in the play but they've already paid for the ticket. Leveaux's production was spellbinding, with three far better than average performances and some remarkable collaboration with his designers.

Betrayal rises or falls, pretty much, on its triangle of actors. Juliette Binoche, Liev Schreiber, and John Slattery made an intriguing team (as had Stephen Dillane, Jennifer Ehle, and Sarah Woodward in Leveaux's *The Real Thing*). Ms. Binoche came to Broadway as a star, thanks to her Oscar for *The English Patient*. She made a stunning Emma, lovely and fragile on the surface but clearly turbulent beneath. Schreiber—also fairly well known, thanks to film, TV, and off-Broadway exposure—was also impressive. We could almost see his Jerry thinking feverishly beneath his facade, trying to appear in control while absorbing the truths and half-truths being flung at him by the other characters. Slattery was also wear-

> The large, boxy set was oddly masked—initially—by the house curtain at artificially low trim. As the evening progressed, and we learned more of the truth (as time worked backward), the trim became higher and higher until we finally saw the full stage picture.

ing a mask, but one of deception. His character is, presumably, the most betrayed; Slattery's Robert, though, seemed to be manipulating the others, the guiltiest of them all. The performance of this relatively little-known actor was a surprise to many, but as soon as he entered, I knew that we were in good hands; I remembered him as one of the few pleasures of Neil Simon's 1993 comedy *Laughter on the 23rd Floor*.

As with *Electra*, the design played an integral role in Leveaux's production. The large, boxy set was oddly masked—initially—by the house curtain at artificially low trim. As the evening progressed through its nine scenes, and we learned more of the truth (as time worked backward), the trim became higher and higher until we finally saw the full stage picture. Similarly, Ms. Binoche's costumes were passionately colorless at the beginning of the play (taking place two years after the end of the affair). At the end of the play, nine years earlier, Binoche was dressed in ravishing

scarlet. These choices were not written into Pinter's script; they were the work of director and designer. Scenery and costumes were designed by Englishman Rob Howell, who also did Leveaux's Paris *Betrayal*. Howell made his Broadway debut with the very different but equally effective 1999–2000 production of Sam Shepard's *True West*.

Leveaux, Howell, and lighting designer David Weiner collaborated on an especially stunning effect for the final scene. This is the beginning of it all, when Jerry first propositioned Emma (with the oblivious Robert walking in—in the middle of the seduction—chatting with them pleasantly, and departing). Pinter placed the scene in a bedroom, the third different bedroom in the play; Leveaux and associates chose to play it *in the dark*. That is, in the wedge of light provided by the opened bedroom door. We saw very little of what transpired, with the actors being mostly in the shadows; this only made us concentrate all the more on the hidden levels of the dialogue. It was a stunning and novel and gutsy way to stage the all-important final scene of the play.

Betrayal was a late replacement on the Roundabout schedule. Leveaux's production of Eugene O'Neill's *Desire Under the Elms* had been announced for the November slot at the American Airlines. (I suppose we'll get used to that theatre name in time, but it still seems a bit flighty.) Mary-Louise Parker was skedded to star, but *Proof*—which she was playing off-Broadway, at the Manhattan Theatre Club—turned into a hit, and she withdrew from the O'Neill to make the transfer to the Walter Kerr. A good thing, too, because this enabled the public at large to see her exceptional performance in David Auburn's exceptional play. But it also gave us Pinter and Binoche and a first-rate *Betrayal* as well. Thank you Ms. Parker, and Mr. Leveaux, and Mr. Pinter, and the people at the Roundabout.

The Rocky Horror Show

Broadway underwent a considerable change when *Hair* opened at the Biltmore Theatre on April 29, 1968. Here, in a bona fide Broadway playhouse, was an attraction very much unlike anything ever seen on Broadway before. Not simply because it was anti-war; or because it was rock-oriented; or because it featured—gasp!—full-frontal nudity; or because it advocated illegal drug use and intragender, interracial sexual freedom; or because it desecrated the American flag. Simply put, it was a show on Broadway—that most traditional of places—that specifically sought an audience of people who at the time wouldn't have been caught dead in a Broadway theatre.

The massive success of *Hair* slowly opened the formerly staid legitimate theatre to all sorts of new, unusual attractions. (Not coincidentally, Broadway entered a qualitative and quantitative nosedive at the time, resulting in more and more empty houses.) January 1969 saw two new, highly unusual musicals. One had a gold-label pedigree, coming from Tom Jones and Harvey Schmidt. They were the authors of *The Fantasticks*—which had been running off-Broadway for an unprecedented nine years—and the 1966 Broadway hit *I Do! I Do!* Cheryl Crawford, whose credits included *One Touch of Venus* and *Brigadoon* and other hits, was the producer. But *Celebration*—an experimental allegory, with masks—was the strangest musical Broadway had ever seen, and it lasted a mere 110 performances at the Ambassador. Three days after *Celebration* opened came a musical satire called *Red, White and Maddox*, an absurdist hatchet job on the segregationist governor Lester Maddox of Georgia. Not the sort of thing Broadway had seen before, it lasted 41 performances at the Cort (but it was very funny).

In November—just in time for Thanksgiving turkey—came the strangest musical Broadway had ever seen, a black militant diatribe called *Buck White*. This one starred that tap-dancing fool Muhammad Ali (billed, in extra-large type, aka Cassius Clay). Traditional Broadway audiences weren't interested in being called "whitey," and the nontraditional audience didn't come. (Did the producers expect the sporting crowd to plunk down $12.50 to see the former champ try to act?) That one lasted seven performances at the George Abbott, a jinx house on West Fifty-fourth Street that shuttered for good two years later.

Grin and Bare It was an old-fashioned (and fairly awful) sex comedy, which opened at the poor old Belasco in March 1970. However, it took place—you guessed it—in a living room full of nudists, including some memorably unattractive character actors. *Hair* had included incidental nudity; this was naked actors and actresses standing around delivering bad dialogue, trying to pretend that they weren't embarrassed for sixteen performances. A week later came the strangest musical Broadway had ever seen. (Well, maybe not as strange as *Buck White*.) *Blood Red Roses*, at the Golden, was an anti-war rock musical—the war in question being the Crimean War, go figure—for a single performance.

With theatre owners finding their less desirable houses harder and harder to book, the Shuberts threw in the towel—as it were—and allowed the long-running off-Broadway hit *Oh! Calcutta!!* to transfer to the once-hallowed Belasco in February 1971, for a year and a half of tourist business on twofers. Another vulgar, profane, and censorable attraction—the sort of thing that you'd never have seen on Broadway, before *Hair*—came to the Brooks Atkinson in May. But *Lenny* was an innovative, award-winning new play and ran for 453 performances. Times had changed.

Usherette	Daphne Rubin-Vega
Usherette	Joan Jett
Janet Weiss	Alice Ripley
Brad Majors	Jarrod Emick
Narrator	Dick Cavett
Riff Raff	Raúl Esparza
Magenta	Daphne Rubin-Vega
Columbia	Joan Jett
Frank 'N' Furter	Tom Hewitt
Rocky	Sebastian LaCause
Eddie	Lea DeLaria
Dr. Scott	Lea DeLaria
Phantoms	Kevin Cahoon, Deidre Goodwin, Aiko Nakasone, Mark Price, Jonathan Sharp, James Stovall

Time: Then and now
Place: Here and there

Original Broadway Revival Cast
Album: RCA Victor 09026-63801

CIRCLE IN THE SQUARE
UNDER THE DIRECTION OF THEODORE MANN and PAUL LIBIN

Jordan Roth
by arrangement with
Christopher Malcolm, Howard Panter, Richard O'Brien
for The Rocky Horror Company Ltd.
presents
Richard O'Brien's

THE ROCKY HORROR SHOW

Starring
Dick Cavett   Lea DeLaria   Jarrod Emick
Joan Jett   Alice Ripley   Daphne Rubin-Vega
and
Tom Hewitt
as "Frank 'N' Furter"
also starring
Raúl Esparza   Sebastian LaCause
with
Kevin Cahoon   Deidre Goodwin   Kristen Lee Kelly   John Jeffrey Martin
Aiko Nakasone   Mark Price   Jonathan Sharp   James Stovall

Book, Music & Lyrics
Richard O'Brien

Scenic Design	Costume Design	Lighting Design
David Rockwell	David C. Woolard	Paul Gallo

Sound Design	Video Design
T. Richard Fitzgerald/Domonic Sack	Batwin + Robin Productions

Musical Direction & Vocal Arrangements	New Orchestrations	Music Coordinator
Henry Aronson	Doug Katsaros	John Miller

Original Orchestrations	Original Costume Design
Richard Hartley	Sue Blane

Casting	Production Manager	Sets and Effects
Bernard Telsey Casting	Peter Fulbright	Showmotion Inc.

Assistant Director	Assistant Choreographer	Marketing/Promotions	Promotions
Jules Ochoa	Angie Schworer	TMG-The Marketing Group	Leanne Schanzer Promotions

Production Stage Manager	General Management	Press Representative
Brian Meister	Richard Frankel Productions	The Jacksina Company
	David W. Caldwell	

Choreographer
Jerry Mitchell
Director
Christopher Ashley

The Producers wish to express their appreciation to Theatre Development Fund for its support of this production.

Another musical unlike anything Broadway had ever seen came into the Hellinger—home of the great *My Fair Lady*—in October 1971. Like *Hair*, *Jesus Christ Superstar* effectively changed pop culture; it was also a big money-maker, running for 711 performances. Director Tom O'Horgan is pretty much forgotten nowadays, but he can very definitely be considered the man who changed Broadway, with his strong-visioned contributions to the simultaneous hits *Hair*, *Lenny*, and *Superstar*.

These strange-but-new attractions kept coming along at a clip of three or four a year, usually closing as quickly as they opened, and I needn't detail them all. Three occurrences raised eyebrows along the street, though. All of these shows—from *Hair* onward—had been restricted to secondary, out-of-demand theatres. In June 1972, the Shuberts desperately filled their highly prized Broadhurst Theatre with—egads!—a rock musical. This, more than anything, made it clear that we had entered a new era. *Grease* was the show, transferring from downtown; it moved again in the fall, around the corner to the similarly desirable Royale, and remained on

Broadway indefinitely. In October 1972, the Shuberts gave the Broadway Theatre to another rock musical, *Dude*—and allowed them to remove the seats and turn it into an environmental theatre-in-the-round. (Why? Because *Dude* was written by two of the three authors of *Hair*.) The musical, the strangest that Broadway had ever seen, lasted sixteen performances. The Broadway remained empty until March 1974, when Hal Prince's revival of *Candide* moved in with a similarly environmental production. The theatre wasn't restored until the summer of 1976, and it remained an undesirable house until 1987, when *Les Misérables* moved in.

The first new Broadway theatre constructed since the 1929 stock market crash opened in November 1972, with the not-so-melodious name Uris (now the Gershwin). In another sign that times had indeed changed, the show given this signal honor was, most surely, the strangest musical ever seen on Broadway. *Via Galactica*—a space-age musical with its leading man performing in a tin box (he was supposed to be a disembodied brain) and a stage full of trampolines—was appallingly bad. This despite—or because of?—the presence of world-renowned director Peter Hall. The publicity surrounding the opening of the theatre only accentuated the disaster at hand, which closed after seven performances.

Well, after all these exceedingly strange offerings came the strangest of all. You guessed it: *The Rocky Horror Show*, which opened at the egregiously assaulted Belasco on March 10, 1975. ("The Beautiful Belasco," they called it in the ads.) Since *Oh! Calcutta!!* closed in August 1972, the perenially underutilized Belasco had hosted only two shows, for a combined total of seventeen performances. Therefore, the Shuberts had little to lose in allowing the theatre to be reconfigured to a cabaret setup. The plan was for the renovation to be merely cos-

Fired from the London production of *Jesus Christ Superstar*, Richard O'Brien decided to write "a rock 'n' roll show that combined the unintentional humor of B movies with the portentous dialogue of schlock horror."

metic; in fact, though, they tore out David Belasco's old—and classy-looking—boxes. Following *Rocky Horror*'s demise after forty-five performances, the Shuberts reinstituted theatre seating, although it was a temporary setup. As I remember, there were a couple of rows of seats in the rear of the orchestra section that were laid out perpendicular to the stage. I don't suppose they ever sold these seats; the Belasco didn't have a hit until the limited engagement of Ralph Fiennes's *Hamlet* in 1995, by which time the house had been carefully and lavishly restored. But those glorious boxes were gone forever, wrenched out for *Rocky Horror*. (The scars, long hidden beneath drapes, were once more exposed for the Roundabout revival of *Follies*.)

The Rocky Horror Show was the handiwork of an actor named Richard O'Brien. Fired in 1972 from the London production of *Jesus Christ Superstar*, he decided to write what he recently described as "a rock 'n' roll show that combined the unintentional humor of B movies with the portentous dialogue of schlock horror." (He also described *Rocky Horror*, in an article for the opening of the Broadway revival, as a "joyous concoction of adolescent trash.")

The show was first mounted as a five-week special in the "theatre upstairs" at London's Royal Court Theatre, opening June 19, 1973. It reopened in November at the King's Road, a dilapidated old cinema roughly equivalent to our off-off Broadway, and became quite the rage. A natural for Broadway, the producers must have thought; but the New York *Rocky* did not attract the crowds that flocked to *Hair* and *Superstar* and *Grease*. It didn't attract any crowds at all and quickly shuttered. (The British have always been more accepting of things like "sweet transvestites from transsexual Transylvania.") A film version was released later in 1975—under the title *The Rocky Horror Picture Show*—and became an international cult favorite. Hence, the Broadway revival, twenty-six years after the production at the Belasco.

If every devoted fan of the film in the tristate metropolitan area bought a ticket to the revival—well, I suppose that every devoted fan of the film in the tristate metropolitan area *did* buy a ticket (or several) to the revival. But was that enough? Economics being what they are, *Rocky Horror* had to sell tickets to nonfans as well, and that seemed to be a tough challenge at $79.50 a seat (increased to $85 in April). They managed to survive the season, though, thanks to low operating costs; heavy discounting; and those $10 "participation bags" sold in the lobby, stuffed with confetti and newspaper and toilet paper and other goodies to throw at the actors on cue.

I didn't throw anything at anybody. I found the show moderately amusing (although this was certainly not a show that the producer wanted anyone to find merely "moderately amusing"). I enjoyed it far more than in 1975, when the only thing memorable was Tim Curry's commanding performance as Frank 'N' Furter, the transvestite in fishnet tights; but I still found it merely moderate.

Christopher Ashley did a clever job of directing, considering that the core audience knew the characterizations and blocking by heart (change it at your peril). There was little he could do other than reproduce the old moves, but he did it with great humor and spirit. Ashley has a wonderful comic sense, as demonstrated in the 1993 off-Broadway hit *Jeffrey*. He has yet to translate this to success on Broadway, but I expect he soon will.

There was also some impressive work from David Rockwell, a restaurant designer who built some wonderful gags into his set. He dressed the walls and lobby with shrouds encasing corpses, which not only added to the ambience but also got you in a suitable frame of mind before the show even started. The Circle in the Square has been an extremely difficult house, scenery-wise, since it opened in 1972. Its last three tenants, though—*Not About Nightingales* (1999), *True West* (2000), and now *Rocky Horror*—have had impressive and highly workable sets, which have used the oddities of the space to their advantage.

The revival cast included an array of popular musical theatre performers: Lea DeLaria, who graced the Gershwin Theatre—upstairs from Circle in the Square—with her take on the man-eating cabdriver in the 1998 revival of *On the Town*; Daphne Rubin-Vega, a Tony nominee for *Rent* (1996); Alice Ripley, a Tony nominee for *Side Show* (1997); and

> **I found the show moderately amusing (although this was certainly not a show that the producer wanted anyone to find merely "moderately amusing").**

Jarrod Emick, a Tony winner for the 1994 revival of *Damn Yankees*. Also onboard was rock singer Joan Jett, whose bio informed us that she is often called "the girl Elvis" and that she wrote and performed "I Love Rock 'n Roll," which "is the #28 song of all time." (I wonder where "Ol' Man River" falls on this list??)

Most of the actors merely played their stereotypical roles, adequately but with little extraspecial flair. Ms. Ripley was the exception, as the virginal ingenue. She did everything by the numbers, at first. As her character got caught up in the strange doings, though, the actress seemed to veer out of control; there was a wild look in her eye that told us that she was in on the joke, and all bets were off. By the end of the show she was truly possessed. This performance, combined with her brief stint as Daisy Mae in the 1998 City Center Encores! production of *Li'l Abner*, indicates that she's got a strong comic sense beneath that pretty facade. Look for an explosive Ripley performance somewhere down the line.

I was also exceedingly surprised—and pleased—by Dick Cavett, an overexposed talk show host of the 1970s. I've always found that a little Cavett went a long way. He walked into the world of *Rocky Horror* as the narrator and proceeded to have a capital time surveying the proceedings and wryly cracking bad jokes (presumably of his own creation). Like "This is *The Rocky Horror Show*. Not the one going on down in Florida." (Laugh) "This one is more rational." (For those of you reading this in 2017, this was a reference to the 2000 presidential election, the results of which were still in limbo at the time.) Or, "I just saw the author faint—he thought he heard one of his lines." As with designer Rockwell's corpses-in-the-walls, Cavett served to gently waft us from 2000 New York to author O'Brien's strange, old world.

> I couldn't help but feel that I was at a family reunion of someone else's family. I couldn't appreciate all those hilarious, fondly repeated punch lines, because I'd never heard the joke before.

But it was a world with two classes of citizens, the die-hard fans and the plain, old everyday theatregoers. Rabid audience members didn't only sing along with the actors; they delivered chunks of dialogue, too. After a while, I couldn't help but feel that I was at a family reunion of someone else's family. I couldn't appreciate all those hilarious, fondly repeated punch lines, because I'd never heard the joke before. And after a while, I didn't especially care to hear any more and wanted to slip away to the lemonade table.

The Search for Signs of Intelligent Life in the Universe

The phone rang on January 1, 1999. Lily had been approached to do a nationwide tour of auditoriums and large
arenas. Would I help figure it out? Thus began an adventure that wound
up, twenty-one months later, at the Booth Theatre on Shubert Alley, by
which time I was no longer involved with the project. Given the situation, it seems unsuitable to discuss *The Search* in the same precise manner
as I do the other shows in this book. But I can think of a thing or two to
say.

Back in the late twentieth century, I spent about fifteen years as a company manager and six years as a general manager–producer. One of the
shows I coproduced turned out to be a big enough hit—and, due to some
of the people involved, an unpleasant enough experience—that I was
able to, and impelled to, leave theatrical management altogether.

Lily Tomlin and Jane Wagner's *The Search for Signs of Intelligent Life in
the Universe* originally opened on Broadway at the Plymouth Theatre on
September 26, 1985. After 398
performances, it toured on and
off into 1991. Along the way, I
had the good fortune to take over
as general manager. Good for-
tune, I say, because Lily and Jane are two of the most remarkable people
around. Lily is an exceptional performer, as most people who've seen *The*

> **Lily and Jane are perfectionists; they
> simply won't settle on something duddy,
> as Lily would say.**

Lily
Trudy
Agnus Angst
Chrissy
Kate
Paul
Lud
Marie
Trudy
Tina
Brandy
Lyn
Edie
Margie

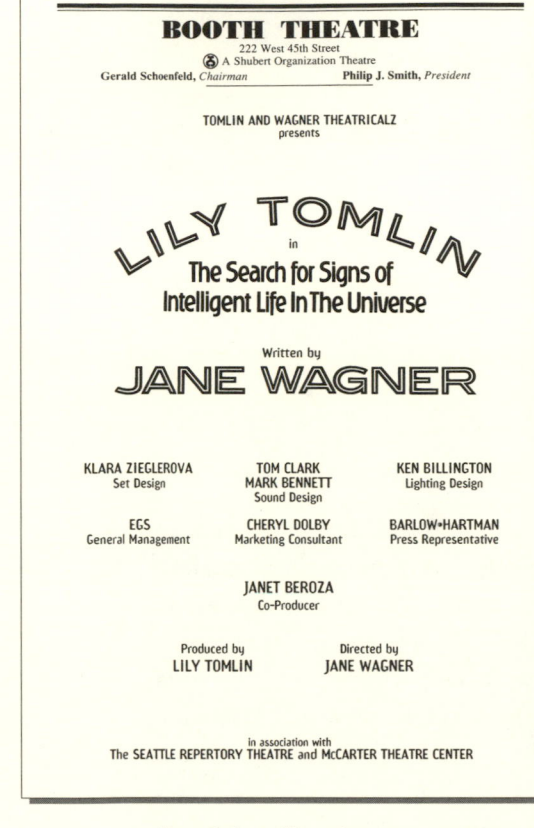

BOOTH THEATRE
222 West 45th Street
Ⓢ A Shubert Organization Theatre
Gerald Schoenfeld, *Chairman*   Philip J. Smith, *President*

TOMLIN AND WAGNER THEATRICALZ
presents

LILY TOMLIN
in
The Search for Signs of
Intelligent Life In The Universe

Written by
JANE WAGNER

KLARA ZIEGLEROVA   TOM CLARK   KEN BILLINGTON
Set Design   MARK BENNETT   Lighting Design
                          Sound Design

EGS   CHERYL DOLBY   BARLOW•HARTMAN
General Management   Marketing Consultant Press Representative

JANET BEROZA
Co-Producer

Produced by   Directed by
LILY TOMLIN   JANE WAGNER

in association with
The SEATTLE REPERTORY THEATRE and McCARTER THEATRE CENTER

Search would readily agree. Jane has, for many years, been Lily's writer and director; the characters are in many ways a collaboration, which is indicative of Jane's talents.

When I got the call for the new Lily project, I was happily out of the Broadway rat race (as they say, and not inaptly). But when Lily calls, what can a person do? I don't like to use the term genius, but it is an amazing and invigorating experience to work with someone like Lily. (Someone like Lily?? There aren't many.) So I told her that I had been away from the business for five years, but I'd be glad to help out.

The tour was proposed by a rock concert promoter who had produced Lily's first Broadway show, *Appearing Nightly* (1977). He wanted something that could play one- or two- or three-performance gigs in large auditoriums and small arenas. Something that could travel quickly and simply, without the full trappings of a touring theatrical show. As for what the show should be, he didn't especially care; he liked the idea of some kind of *Best of Lily Tomlin*, but he left it up to Lily and Jane.

The idea of the tour was attractive to them; the two- or three-performance engagements, usually with time off between cities, would allow time to refine, rehearse, and experiment with the material. (Lily loves to rehearse.) The tour was attractive to me, too, as general manager and associate producer; I envisioned an arrangement with the rock promoter whereby Tomlin and Wagner Theatricalz could produce the show with no financial exposure whatsoever. So, after much discussion, Lily and Jane decided to commit to the tour, and the booking process began. All we had to do was figure out what the show would be.

Lily and Jane and coproducer Janet Beroza began a long process of going through different ideas and material. While a *Best of Lily Tomlin* might seem surefire—and, I imagine, an "easy sell"—it wasn't workable. Lily is not a stand-up comedian, nor is she an impressionist. She does, for want of a better description, intensive (and extremely human) character studies. While her work generally elicits howls of laughter, the laughs are not the result of a cavalcade of jokes like you might get from an evening with Steve Martin or Bill Cosby. Lily's humor is contextual, and there is little context when you sit on a stool in a spotlight.

This intensive characterization is a large part of what made *The Search* so special. It presented fourteen characters, woven together into one grand tapestry. The play was built around Trudy, a bag lady with a shopping cart full of junk. ("You think I'm crazy for collecting all this junk. What do you call the people who buy it?") Over the course of two and a half hours, all roads led back to Trudy—making a suitable, and highly satisfactory, framework. Without props or wigs or costumes, Lily changed characters instantaneously; by the middle of the first act, a nod of the head or the sway of a shoulder was enough to inform the audience who was speaking.

I hope, and expect, we will one day see a new show from Tomlin and Wagner. They will need to find another just-as-perfect way to frame their material, though. Lily and Jane are perfectionists; they simply won't settle on something duddy (as Lily would say).

Back to the spring of 1999. In addition to deciding what to perform on tour, Lily had to get back in "playing shape" as it were. Lily hadn't been onstage, except for special benefits and speaking engagements, since 1991; the tour would include some weeks with as many as six performances. (You try jumping around on stage, alone, talking for two and a half hours straight, six or eight times a week.) And while Lily had and has more stamina than me or you or your average professional football player, she did turn sixty in 1999. In order to get back on her feet, Lily decided to work up the first act of *The Search* for an audience of college students.

And they loved it; they were astounded by it. This was a pretty rough performance, mind you, with primitive sound and lighting and half-remembered blocking; but this audience of kids in their early twenties was hanging on every word and every character. *The Search* was a product of its time; much of the material dealt with the women's movement and other aspects of the sixties and seventies. This might, indeed, have made *The Search* dated for 2000; and, yes, this was an issue with some audiences.

What we discovered, though, was that after more than a decade the material was in some ways stronger. During the original run, many of these topics still struck a nerve. A substantial segment of the audience,

inevitably, consisted of men and women who had been decidedly against the women's movement. (They thought, presumably, that they were going to a comedy hit with the gal from *Laugh-In*.) One of the reasons for the show's initial success—and one of the reasons for its enormous effect on audiences—is that Lily was able to win over many of the people who entered the theatre grudgingly. Entertain a chauvinist bigot while poking fun at his beliefs, and he just might leave the theatre questioning his viewpoints. For theatregoers who agreed with what Lily and Jane had to say, it was a liberating and emboldening event to hear such ideas publicly expressed.

That was in 1985. By 1999, a whole new generation of people (and theatregoers) existed who had more or less benefited from the struggles—to the point that they'd never even heard about the struggles. What was ERA? And who was Geraldine Ferraro, anyway? New audiences were fascinated by what Lily and Jane and Trudy and the rest of the characters had to say.

These early audiences convinced Lily and Jane that they should remount *The Search* for the tour. Part of the challenge was to do the show without scenery or specialized lighting; just plunk ourselves down in a new theatre and do a show that night. The old *Search* toured with two truckloads of equipment, which took two or three days to move and ship and reassemble. I said at the time, and often, that we were overcomplicated. What made the material work was Lily herself; she didn't need a set or any trappings, just enough lighting for the audience to see her and enough sound for them to hear her.

> **Lily was able to win over many of the people who entered the theatre grudingly. Entertain a chauvinist bigot while poking fun at his beliefs, and he just might leave the theatre questioning his viewpoints.**

The 1999 tour went especially well. Audiences loved Lily; business was usually quite good—in some cases restrained by poor local marketing—and reviews were almost always highly positive. The general tone: This is a remarkable performance; don't miss Lily in *The Search* (but we'd love to see her in a new play). And it *was* a remarkable performance; more remarkable, in some ways, than it had been in 1985.

This left us with another question: What next? After a significant amount of discussion—no decisions are rushed into with Tomlin and Wagner Theatricalz—we decided to bring *The Search* back to Broadway. (Long before we reached a decision, the Shuberts—who had hosted Lily in 1985—graciously offered a prime theatre.) As a manager-producer, I always liked the idea of mounting shows in conjunction with regional theatres. This can result in significant savings because they pay designer fees, construction costs, rehearsal costs, and the like. (While the play was not new, we would be working on a new set with a new design team.) Regionals are budgeted to produce a certain number of shows per season; if you can work within their budget (and supplement costs where necessary), then everyone is happy. The regional theatre and their subscribers get a (presumably) Broadway-caliber show with Broadway-caliber personnel, whatever that phrase might signify. The Broadway producers enjoy substantial savings.

Lily has a long-standing history of supporting regional theatres, which made it significantly easier to make those "Hello, have I got a play for you" calls to artistic directors. With our Broadway dates already penciled in—I determined that we had to open no earlier than mid-October but no later than the Thursday before Thanksgiving—it became a question of finding a regional theatre that could work around our schedule. Happily, we found two, the Seattle Repertory Theatre and the McCarter Theatre (in Princeton, New Jersey). This gave Lily fifty-odd performances and two distinct audiences before which to try out the play.

Everything was under way by the end of June, with tickets on sale for September in Seattle and October in Princeton. As we were setting our ad campaign for New York, I regretfully decided to withdraw from the production. I had been concerned, from the start, by my five-year absence from the field. Five years is not a lot, but many things had changed along Broadway (especially in the marketing area). I soon learned that there was nothing here that I couldn't handle; what I found, though, was that I didn't *want* to handle it.

The thought of doing one last show—and working with Lily and Jane again—was enough to get me involved in the project; and I was happy enough mounting the preliminary tour and arranging the regional tryout. But as I started dealing with agents and unions and what have you, I suddenly remembered why I had left the Broadway management business. I had been working at it since I was eighteen, and after so many years I had lost all enjoyment in it. As I began to set up a staff and an office, I realized that I didn't *want* a staff and an office. I also realized there were advantages to using an ongoing management operation; I certainly didn't want to overlook anything or make any decisions that might prove detrimental to Lily and Jane's interests. And so Tomlin and Wagner and I regretfully—but sensibly—parted ways.

The Search proceeded as scheduled. It arrived at the Booth, after stops in Seattle and Princeton, and opened November 16, 2000, for a ten-week limited engagement. Critical reaction was very good. The general tone: This is a remarkable performance; don't miss Lily in *The Search* (but we'd love to see her in a new play). Business was good as well, allowing the show to quickly recover its production costs. (This made me, as the person who set up the finances—and as friend to Tomlin and Wagner—*very* happy.) The show extended indefinitely, with business continuing at profitable levels until late April, when the slew of new shows fighting over the same ticket dollars indicated that it was time to go.

One night during the 1999 tour, I went up to the fourth balcony during a performance in one of our larger venues. These seats were high up, let me tell you. It was a plush, luxurious arts center with plenty of elevators, but the seats were so far from the stage that I—at least—could not see Lily's face at all. (My eyes are not what they were, but they're not *that* bad.) I turned away from the stage and looked toward the audience. The faces were rapt with attention. As Lily proceeded, I was stunned to see that the performance had the very same effect as it did on the folks in the "good" seats. The same laughs; the same delayed laughs; the same sitting-forward-in-the-seat anticipation. Much of the magic of *The Search* was in the pantomime; there were hundreds of props, but they were all invisible. Lily's motions and the accompanying sound effects made you think you were seeing what was not there,

She describes the awe of looking at "a group of strangers sitting together in the dark, laughing and crying about the same things." I stood inside the exit door and looked at the sea of faces: entranced; enchanted; laughing together, practically breathing en masse.

which worked fine in an 800-seat theatre like the Booth or an 1,100-seater like the Plymouth. But I was stunned to get this reaction in the fourth balcony of a 2,800-seat music hall. (This performance is what convinced me that *The Search* should go back to Broadway.)

Lily's character Trudy describes the awe of looking at "a group of strangers sitting together in the dark, laughing and crying about the same things." ("Awe infinitum," Trudy terms it.) That night, I stood inside the exit door and looked at the sea of faces in the dark. Entranced; enchanted; laughing together, practically breathing en masse. Trudy sums up the evening by saying: "The play was soup; the audience art." Even way up there in the fourth balcony, miles away from Lily's postage stamp–sized image, with the fast-approaching Hurricane Floyd whipping up the palm trees surrounding the theatre, the audience was art.

Seussical

Seussical, the big new musical "based on the works of Dr. Seuss," received raves from hard-boiled Broadway insiders invited to attend run-throughs of the developmental reading held in Toronto in August 1999. The tuneful, imaginative new musical was clearly destined to be a major hit. The only question was: Would it merely be a lucrative hit (like *Beauty and the Beast*) or a groundbreaking Broadway legend (like *The Lion King*)?

Things went downhill from there.

The idea of creating a musical peopled with characters created by the good Dr. originated with Garth Drabinsky, at that time still the chairman of what used to be Livent. *The Seussical*, as it was then called, was announced in April 1997 as a collaboration between songwriters Stephen Flaherty and Lynn Ahrens (of Livent's *Ragtime*) and playwright Ken Ludwig (of *Crazy for You*). By June 1998, Ludwig had been replaced by Eric Idle (of *Monty Python*).

The project went through a preliminary workshop in New York the following spring, culminating in run-throughs on May 14, 1999. Many of the principal cast members were to remain with the show through the Broadway opening (and most until the closing), including Kevin Chamberlin, Janine LaManna, Michelle Pawk, Erick Devine, Eddie Korbich, Alice Playten, Sharon Wilkins, and Stuart Zagnit. Other prominent actors who did not continue with the show included David Garrison, Ruth Williamson, Victor Trent Cook, and Eric Idle himself, who played the all-important role of the Cat in the Hat.

When the show went into rehearsals two months later in Toronto for the second, full workshop, Idle was gone as both author and star. Ahrens and Flaherty were now the official librettists, with Idle sharing credit with the pair for the concept. Andrea Martin came in to wear the Cat in the Hat's red-and-white stovepipe, and she apparently sparkplugged the event. (The inventive comedienne had won a Tony Award for her side-splitting performance as an Imogene Coca type in the 1992 Flaherty and Ahrens musical, My Favorite Year.)

Under the new title Seussical, the show was booked for an August 27 break-in at the Colonial Theatre in Boston, followed by a November 9, 2000, Broadway opening at the Richard Rodgers. As winter rolled into spring, cracks in the invincibility of the surefire hit of the fall started to appear.

Word leaked in April 2000 that Ms. Martin would not be part of the Broadway cast, which turned out to be the first public nail in Seussical's coffin. The official excuse was that she did not want to spend so much time away from her family in Los Angeles; or maybe she merely took a look at the rewrites? At any rate, Martin ankled, and thereafter seldom was heard an encouraging word.

The producers scrambled for a replacement, going through a long list of suitable "stars." (I told Lily Tomlin that she was cast in the role, according to a column item, which was news to her. Two days later she got a call from an SFX executive asking if she'd do it.) Finally, the Seussical folk wound up with that household name David Shiner. You know, David Shiner? The guy from Fool Moon. Not Bill Irwin, the other one. Strike two.

Word out of Boston—even before the first preview—was problematic, with Internet gossips spreading all sorts of dire dirt (most of it uncannily accurate, as it happens). The Boston reviews merely confirmed what theatre insiders already knew: Seussical was in trouble. ("How does a stage production that tries so hard to be the reincarnation of Dr. Seuss end up feeling like Mister Rogers' Neighborhood?" asked Ed Siegel in the Boston Globe.)

A musical trip through the world of Seuss sounded like a good idea, initially anyway. On consideration, though, it was fraught with peril. How do you combine characters from forty-four highly inventive but unrelated tales into an integrated plot? The concept that the Seussical people came up with was logical enough. Unfortunately, the words "logic" and "Seuss" belong in two different dictionaries.

RICHARD RODGERS THEATRE
UNDER THE DIRECTION OF THE MESSRS. NEDERLANDER

SFX THEATRICAL GROUP   BARRY & FRAN WEISSLER
and
UNIVERSAL STUDIOS
present

Book by
LYNN AHRENS and
STEPHEN FLAHERTY

Music by
STEPHEN FLAHERTY

Lyrics by
LYNN AHRENS

Conceived by
LYNN AHRENS, STEPHEN FLAHERTY
and
ERIC IDLE

BASED ON THE WORKS OF DR. SEUSS

Starring
KEVIN CHAMBERLIN

JANINE LaMANNA   MICHELE PAWK   ANTHONY BLAIR HALL

ERICK   EDDIE   ALICE   SHARON   STUART
DEVINE   KORBICH   PLAYTEN   WILKINS   ZAGNIT

ANDREW KEENAN-BOLGER

SHAUN AMYOT JOYCE CHITTICK JENNIFER CODY NATASCIA DIAZ DAVID ENGEL
SARA GETTELFINGER JUSTIN GREER ANN HARADA JENNY HILL CATRICE JOSEPH
MICHELLE KITTRELL MARY ANN LAMB DARREN LEE DAVID LOWENSTEIN MONIQUE L. MIDGETTE
CASEY NICHOLAW TOM PLOTKIN DEVIN RICHARDS WILLIAM RYALL
JEROME VIVONA ERIC JORDAN YOUNG

and
DAVID SHINER
as
THE CAT IN THE HAT

Scenery by
EUGENE LEE

Costumes by
WILLIAM IVEY LONG

Lighting by
NATASHA KATZ

Sound by
JONATHAN DEANS

Orchestrations
DOUG BESTERMAN

Music Director
DAVID HOLCENBERG

Dance Arranger
DAVID CHASE

Vocal Arranger
STEPHEN FLAHERTY

Casting
JAY BINDER
& SHERRY DAYTON

Music Coordinator
JOHN MILLER

Wig and Hair Design
PAUL HUNTLEY

Press Representative
BARLOW • HARTMAN
PUBLIC RELATIONS

Produced in association with
KARDANA/SWINSKY PRODUCTIONS
HAL LUFTIG & MICHAEL WATT

Associate Director
STAFFORD ARIMA

Scenic Design Coordinator
LARRY GRUBER

Associate Choreographers
ROB ASHFORD
JOEY PIZZI

Executive Producers
GARY GUNAS
ALECIA PARKER

Production Supervisor
BONNIE PANSON

Production Management
JUNIPER STREET
PRODUCTIONS

General Management
ALAN WASSER
ASSOCIATES

Choreographed by
KATHLEEN MARSHALL

Directed by
FRANK GALATI

Presented by
⊙ TARGET

The Cat in the Hat   David Shiner
Horton the Elephant   Kevin Chamberlin
Gertrude McFuzz   Janine LaManna
Mayzie LaBird   Michele Pawk
JoJo   Anthony Blair Hall
JoJo (Wed. evening and Sat. mat.)   Andrew Keenan-Bolger
Sour Kangaroo   Sharon Wilkins
The Mayor of Whoville   Stuart Zagnit
Mrs. Mayor   Alice Playten
Cat's Helpers   Joyce Chittick, Jennifer Cody, Justin Greer, Mary Ann Lamb, Darren Lee, Jerome Vivona
General Genghis Khan   Schmitz Erick Devine
Bird Girls   Natascia Diaz, Sara Gettelfinger, Catrice Joseph
Wickersham Brothers   David Engel, Tom Plotkin, Eric Jordan Young
The Grinch   William Ryall
Vlad Vladikoff   Darren Lee
Judge Yertle the Turtle   Devin Richards
Marshal of the Court   Ann Harada
Citizens of the Jungle of Nool, Whos, Mayor's Aides, Fish, Cadets, Hunters, Circus McGurkus Animals and Performers   Joyce Chittick, Jennifer Cody, Erick Devine, Natascia Diaz, David Engel, Sara Gettelfinger, Justin Greer, Ann Harada, Catrice Joseph, Eddie Korbich, Mary Ann Lamb, Darren Lee, Monique L. Midgette, Casey Nicholaw, Tom Plotkin, Devin Richards, William Ryall, Jerome Vivona, Sharon Wilkins, Eric Jordan Young
Swings   Shaun Amyot, Jenny Hill, Michelle Kittrell, David Lowenstein

Original Broadway Cast Album:
Decca Broadway 012 159 792

Horton Hatches the Egg (1940) was an early Seuss work—so early, in fact, that the reader might be surprised by the loose-lined quality of the artwork. (The characters are suitably Seuss, but the backgrounds are sketchy). Mayzie, "a lazy bird hatching an egg," is bored. She finds the perfect patsy in Horton the elephant, who agrees to egg-sit while she takes a vacation. Mayzie goes off to Palm Beach, never to return. Horton faithfully tends the egg in the tree—because "I meant what I said and I said what I meant, an elephant's faithful one hundred percent"—but the other animals taunt him. Big-game hunters come along and—never having seen an elephant on an egg in a tree—cart Horton and egg and tree off to New York and sell him to the circus. Horton is a star, and the circus finally hits Palm Beach. Just as the egg begins to hatch, Mayzie appears and demands it back (as the work is all done). Out pops an elephant-bird—that is, a bird with Horton's ears and tail and trunk—and Horton and offspring go back to the jungle, "happy, one hundred percent."

Seuss recycled Horton for a second, unrelated book called *Horton Hears a Who* (1954). Horton hears a small noise emanating from nowhere, which turns out to be the voice of the Mayor of Whoville, a town on a speck of dust. The other animals in the jungle can't hear the voice, so they taunt Horton, steal the speck, and toss it into a patch of clover one hundred miles wide. Horton goes through every clover one by one until he finds his Who friends, but once again the other animals take the speck and threaten to boil it in Beezle-Nut oil. Horton implores the Mayor of Who to have all his residents yell, to prove that they are there. It turns out that one little Who shirker is not yelling with the others, a boy named JoJo ("bouncing a yo-yo"). When JoJo adds his voice, the sound from the speck is finally heard by the animals, saving the residents of Who and proving that "a person's a person no matter how small."

Ahrens and Flaherty and Idle concocted their *Seussical* plot by fitting together the two *Horton* books. But the two *Horton* books, really, don't fit together. The musical started with Horton finding his speck, discovering the residents of Who, and being taunted by the other animals. (This number was led by a big-fat-loud black lady who looked unlike anyone else on stage, except her understudy. And I don't in any way mean to insult the performer; the role was apparently written, generically, for a big-fat-loud black lady.) Things continued until the clover was dispersed to the winds, at which point Horton ran into Mayzie and her egg. That is to say, with Whoville in desperately dire danger, Horton simply walks out on his Whos. He sits on Mayzie's egg, goes off to New York, and joins the circus. Will the Whos survive? Is a person, indeed, a person no matter how small?

While Horton hatched his egg, Ahrens and Flaherty drafted Gertrude McFuzz—from *Yertle the Turtle and Other Stories* (1958)—and had her take up where Horton left off. *Seussical* then entered a whole different (and weaker) story, with Horton on his egg until it was finally time to resolve it all and ring down the curtain.

While this poked a hole in Horton's dedication to his Whos, it proved a good idea entertainment-wise thanks to a pixieish charmer named Janine LaManna. Kevin Chamberlin—who was robbed of a Tony Award for *Dirty Blonde*—was quite good and immensely sympathetic as Horton, too; but all in all, he was pretty much up a tree. There was also a strong performance from a child actor named Anthony Blair Hall, who seemed more engaged in the proceedings than anyone onstage other than Chamberlin and LaManna.

The show, meanwhile, was laced with songs from Whoville. Dr. Seuss told us very little about the place; *Seussical* gave them scene after scene of stage time. The Mayor—the only Who character Seuss bothers with for more than two pages—is joined onstage by a wife, a son (named JoJo), and a whole community of Whos (all dressed in yellow). JoJo is sent off to military school, where he becomes involved in a war about a Butter Battle. This comes from Seuss's *The Butter Battle Book* (1984), an arms race

> How do you combine characters from forty-four highly inventive but unrelated tales into an integrated plot? Toss and mix the eccentric characters/ creatures together with no context, and you're left with a bunch of eccentric characters/creatures with no context.

allegory. Which is not addressed in *Seussical*, mind you; General Genghis Kahn Schmitz—from *I Had Trouble in Getting to Solla Sollew* (1965)— and his troops simply run around the stage in yellow short pants carrying on about butter side up and butter side down.

Did you need to read the collected works of Dr. Seuss to enjoy the musical? Did you need to know Seuss to understand the musical? Of course not; but as the old saying goes, it couldn't hurt. Part of the allure of Dr. Seuss was (and remains) his subversive messages; many of his books were allegorical pleas for equality, ecology, individuality, and other dangerous ideas. Toss and mix the eccentric character/creatures together with no context, though, and you're left with a bunch of eccentric character/creatures with no context.

Seuss's characters were the allure, but also the problem. Consider for a moment Charles M. Schulz's *Peanuts* gang. You have a half dozen, clearly definable core characters. Almost anyone who ever read the strip, whether in 1958 or 1993, knows most all those characters. Place an actor playing a dog playing a World War I flying ace atop a man-sized doghouse, and the audience will be right there with you. Pick a plot, any plot, insert the personalities, and there you have it; the characters dictate their behavior—just like in a long-running sitcom—and you can count on a sure quotient of audience familiarity. (This can viciously backfire if you mess it up, but that's another discussion.)

Try this with Seuss, and see what happens. The so-called Dr. was justly famous for his graphic style, and at least one of the characters—that bad Cat in the Hat—is iconic. But where do you go from there? Some theatregoers were no doubt familiar with Horton the Elephant, and others knew the Grinch (especially considering that Jim Carrey's *How the Grinch Stole Christmas* opened to record-breaking business two weeks before *Seussical* staggered into town). But who were these other characters/creatures? The *Peanuts* cast remained the same, more or less, over the decades. Most of Seuss's characters appeared in only one book, though, and there can't be too many people—other than Flaherty and Ahrens—who have read them all. We know the setup when Charlie Brown approaches psychoanalyst Lucy ("The Doctor Is In"); but who knows what happens when General Genghis Kahn Schmitz approaches Jo-Jo?

Nobody knows what happens when Schmitz approaches JoJo, because they existed in different universes. So here we have two characters with no history and no ground rules; Seuss, in fact, gave us only five lines of copy about JoJo, plus two drawings of less than an inch each. Seuss had a magical imagination, but he died in 1991; Ahrens and Flaherty forced themselves to build a world from his gibberish rhymes and line drawings. "Oh, the Thinks You Can Think!" goes their highly effective opening number. But it's hard to outthink Seuss, for two hours no less.

"Horton Hears a Who," the very next song, handily illustrated the problem. Here you had two dozen people telling us, interminably, what happened. Dr. Seuss did it in sixty words on seven lines on one page—and he told us everything he wanted us to know.

Seussical was best in its songs, though. Not surprising, in that Mr. Flaherty is one of the most melodic of the "new" composers working on Broadway; the only person under sixty-five who still writes in the Richard Rodgers–Jule Styne vein (and that's all to the good). Flaherty started off with a strong opening number, the aforementioned "Thinks" song (which, I'll admit, bears a passing resemblance to the title tune from *They're Playing Our Song*). He gave us a mysterioso little ditty called "A Day for the Cat in the Hat" (which sounded like a *Ragtime* leftover, but why not?) and a neat, skewed-rhythm theme for the seesaw "Here on Who." Flaherty and lyricist Ahrens offered hope to the world in "It's Possible" and soared to the stars in "Alone in the Universe." "How Lucky You Are" was a tuneful vaudeville turn, which was unfortunately repeated in the show twice too often. (During the reprise that ended the first act, I had the distinct feeling that the actors were telling the audience "how lucky you are" that you can leave at intermission, while we're stuck.) "Solla Sollew" is one of Flaherty's prettiest melodies ever. The playfully nonsensical Seuss was best captured in a nifty number called "Green Eggs and Ham." Significantly, Flaherty and Ahrens were unable to find a way to work this into the show. It wound up as the curtain call, and you know something is terribly wrong when the curtain call is one of the show's strongest spots. Throughout the evening, Flaherty facilely leapt from musical style to musical style, with first-rate support from orchestrator Doug Besterman and musical director David Holcenberg.

Flaherty and Ahrens did the best of the evening's work—as songwriters, that is. When the project seemed on the verge of collapsing along with Livent, they dug in to write the book as well. They became involved in just about every area of the production, not out of ego or pushiness but to keep the proverbial ball rolling. For this was a musical without a creative head. Garth Drabinsky had his pros and cons as a producer, certainly, which we needn't take up here; but Drabinsky was gone before

Seussical arrived. Creative input could not be expected from SFX The-atrical/PACE, whose expertise is in the operation of live entertainment venues. They have good management people, but the creative choices seem to be made by the marketing department. (These are the people who brought us *The Civil War* and *Jekyll & Hyde*. The latter ended its 1,543-performance run shortly after *Seussical* opened, the first Broadway show to break the thousand-performance mark and *still* lose money.)

SFX/PACE brought in coproducers Barry and Fran Weissler to con-centrate on marketing, apparently in the hope that they'd peddle the show as effectively as their revival of *Chicago* (which has proved to be one of Broadway's biggest gold mines ever). The Weisslers have what one might call a checkered reputation along Broadway. The authors had the right of approval of additional producers; my understanding is that Fla-herty and Ahrens accepted the Weisslers on the condition—*in writing*—that they didn't have to actually talk to them. (The third producer, Uni-versal Studios, was a simple investment-for-recording-rights deal.)

The Weisslers are famous along Broadway for their revivals. It takes skill to produce a revival, certainly; but there is another set of skills needed to produce a new show, and the Weisslers—who are also famous for their difficulty in deal-ing with artistic types—have so far been unable to crack that nut. Their highest-profile attempt so far was Tommy Tune's *Busker Al-ley*, with a score by the Sherman brothers (of *Mary Poppins* fame). This 1995 musical comedy was based on an old British film starring Vivien Leigh and Charles Laughton. (Tune played the Laughton role.) The show was scuttled during the pre-Broadway tryout, when Tommy buskered his ankle onstage in Tampa. (Rumors that Fran Weissler was spotted in the wings that night with a hockey stick are demonstrably untrue. As far as I can tell.) *Busker Alley* might well have been a fine evening of theatre, out-of-town reviews to the contrary. But the Weisslers didn't express belief in the show and wait for their star to mend; they simply took the insurance money and sent the show to the dump.

When *Seussical* reached Boston, Horton's egg—to borrow a metaphor—cracked. Faced with poor reviews, things grew excessively stormy, and the show came within an instant of being closed altogether. (The official

Everybody tried to doctor the Dr., but the doctor they needed—the only person with the proper Seussian imagination—was the one doctor who dreamed up the whole shebang in the first place.

closing notice was typed but never posted.) *Seussical* certainly needed a-fixin', but at what cost? A couple of million more dollars, it was determined, to pay for running losses in Boston, overtime costs for new sets and costumes, postponement costs for new rehearsal time, and more. Was it worth the salvage attempt?

At this point, Barry Weissler came to the fore with a plan for proceeding. The authors and the other producers—faced with the choice of handing control to Barry or just going home—chose to give it a go. It did not become a happy family; most of the communication was done through harried intermediaries. But everybody tried, in his or her own manner and often at cross-purposes, to doctor the Dr.

Bringing temporary "guest stars" into struggling shows only serves to weaken your long-term chances; you can't build a future on Band-Aids.

Changes there were aplenty. Rob Marshall, codirector of the successful revival of *Cabaret* and brother to choreographer Kathleen Marshall, came in (without credit) to replace director Frank Galati. Tony Walton—of dozens of hits and *Busker Alley*—came in (without credit) to revamp the scenery by Eugene Lee. William Ivey Long—of *Contact*, *Chicago*, *The Music Man*, *Annie Get Your Gun*, *Swing!*, and almost every other hit musical in town—came in (with credit) to replace Kathryn Zuber, who was fired even before the Boston opening.

For all the expensive fixing, little got fixed. If ever a show needed a show doctor, *Seussical* was it; but the doctor they needed—the only person with the proper Seussian imagination—was the one doctor who dreamed up the whole shebang in the first place. Seuss was apparently highly protective of his characters. One assumes he would have nixed any such project, kicking the nasty merchandisers—a bumpity dumpity clumpity shlump—down the dressing room stairs.

Complicating matters was the fact that there was no business. The enormous record-breaking advance sale, which was such a sure thing, never materialized. Ticket buyers, apparently, were concerned that it was only a kid's show and decided to wait until they heard something positive. Boston sales were so soft that they simply canceled the last weeks of the run. Tryout costs were so high (and sales so low) that it was far cheaper—though by no means inexpensive—to move to a rehearsal hall in New York.

The biggest change, as it turned out, did not change. David Shiner seemed to dangle like a thread from his role as the Cat in the Hat, with the producers acknowledging—in print and often—that he couldn't sing and he couldn't dance and he couldn't act. No suitable replacement could be found, so he stayed. With the producers acknowledging that he couldn't sing and he couldn't dance and he couldn't act. Now, there's a surefire way to increase your ticket sales.

No, Mr. Shiner wasn't especially good; he was, admittedly, a mime without singing, dancing, or acting experience. I'm not saying that the man was miscast in his role; but if that's the case, who—I ask you—was to blame? The actor, who seemed to have tried his best? Or the people who gave him the job?? The real problem, anyway, was the overall show, not the actor playing one of the roles.

The Cat in the Hat served as kind of a guide to the evening, stirring up trouble and keeping his paw in. The show's artwork featured the Cat malevolently peering out of a manhole cover in Hoboken. Publicity at the time of the photo shoot explained that this was meant to inform us that *Seussical* had an edge to it, that it wasn't just a kids' show. Other press releases targeted the show "at everyone from 7 to 77."

But who's Cat in the Hat was this, anyway? *The Cat in the Hat* (1957) and *The Cat in the Hat Comes Back* (1968) feature a very different scamp. Seuss's Cat isn't a bad fellow at all. He simply wants to entertain the boy and girl whose home he visits; "I know a lot of good tricks," he tells them. One trick leads to another, until the house is all "shook up." The Cat has all sorts of helpful ideas, which only make matters worse; but he is not evil, malicious, or dangerous.

The Cat in the Hat in *Seussical* seemed to hail not from the world of Seuss but from the world of musical comedy; think of El Gallo (Jerry Orbach) in *The Fantasticks* or the Emcee (Joel Grey) in *Cabaret*. From the beginning, there was a concern that this family musical would be perceived as children's theatre. In order to make the show adult-suitable, the creators decided to take the Cat in the Hat—a relatively minor character—and build him into an edgy, audience-savvy guide. The role seems to have been directly modeled on Ben Vereen in *Pippin*; the Leading Player, as he was called, was not even a character in the plot. Under Bob Fosse's guidance, and over the objections of the authors, Vereen became the "Magic to Do" star of *Pippin*. The Cat in the Hat was given material not unlike what we saw in *Pippin*, but he certainly didn't add magic to *Seussical*.

Shiner was not chosen for the role because he was best equipped to play it. Other actors—including some highly familiar and respected

Seussical

Opened: November 30, 2000

Closed: May 20, 2001

198 performances (and 34 previews)

Profit/Loss: Loss

Seussical ($85 top) was scaled to a potential gross of
$755,427 at the 1,339-seat Richard Rodgers. Weekly
grosses averaged about $446,000, peaking at $664,000
the week before the opening. Rosie O'Donnell averaged
$570,000 during her four-week visit, after which receipts
plummeted below $300,000. Neither Cathy Rigby nor
Aaron Carter had the same effect as O'Donnell, and when
the gross fell back below $300,000, the closing notice
went up. Total gross for the run was $12,927,734.
Attendance was about 73 percent, with the box office
grossing about 61 percent of dollar-capacity.

TONY AWARD NOMINATIONS

Best Performance by a Leading Actor: Kevin Chamberlin

*Critical
Scorecard*

Rave 0

Favorable 1

Mixed 0

Unfavorable 0

Pan 9

names—auditioned well. (Roger Bart, I'm told, was wonderful.) But
Shiner had a certain edge, a certain menace, which the others didn't.
After the Boston debacle, the producers scrambled to solve the problem,
but they couldn't find anyone they liked better. Oddly enough, they could
have gotten Andrea Martin; after the Boston closing, she agreed to come
back on the condition that they wait two weeks for her. With time and
money wasting away, the producers decided they couldn't wait. They felt
it was imperative for them to open before Jim Carrey's *Grinch* movie, although they ended up delaying their opening anyway—by three weeks.
Seussical finally opened, to bad reviews, bad word of mouth (except from
a small core of die-hard fans), and inevitable failure.

Within two months, Rosie O'Donnell—a showbiz booster and Weissler
partisan—stepped in as the Cat in the Hat, amid great publicity about
how she was going to save a failing show. Business grew worse and worse
until she got there, skyrocketed for her four-week engagement, then hit
bottom again when Shiner returned from his so-called vacation. At this
point, *Seussical* began advertising discounts in their *New York Times* display ads. They offered $85 orchestra seats for $49.50; when that didn't
work, they offered them for $30. ("It's Dr. Seuss' Birthday!" exclaimed the
ad.) To me, this seemed like a pretty good way of telling the public that
the show wasn't very good.

The producers finally sent Shiner packing a month later—with a
healthy buyout of his contract, hopefully—and in came Cathy Rigby to

play the Cat in the Hat. They later brought in a teen pop star, Aaron Carter, to play JoJo. But bringing temporary "guest stars" into struggling shows only serves to weaken your long-term chances; you can't build a future on Band-Aids, not when you need almost half a million dollars a week merely to stay afloat. Carter left on May 13. With Rigby slated to leave on May 20, and no phenomenal ticket seller itching to take her place, *Seussical* finally slipped off to "Solla Sollew."

I feel compelled to mention that my friend Catherine Egan—aged six and highly discriminating—loved *Seussical*, returned four times (on discounts and comps), and will always remember *Seussical* as "her" show. Surely it was a severe disappointment to its authors and creators and cast, and a financial bust to its producers; but to one little girl, at least, it will remain a highly treasured Broadway memory.

The concession stand in the lobby of *Seussical* carried the Cat in the Hat's red-and-white striped hat, at twenty dollars a head. From the looks of things, the hats sold briskly; but it takes a lot of hats to recover $11 million, at $20 a hop on pop.

Jane Eyre

I f the Broadway-bound *Seussical* led a charmed existence—until it hit a paying audience, anyway—poor *Jane Eyre* was forced to endure a tempest-tossed route to opening night. The musicalization of Charlotte Brontë's 1847 novel had one "star" name attached, the man who codirected the fabled *Adventures of Nicholas Nickelby* and the record-breaking box office hit *Les Misérables*.

No, not Trevor Nunn; the other one. John Caird is his name, and his involvement with those two shows is indicative of his talent. But Nunn has the name and acclaim. Caird's pedigree no doubt helped get *Jane Eyre* her two full-scale pre–New York tryouts, but his name apparently meant nothing in the Broadway booking wars.

In these days of the corporate behemoths, a number of independent producers can still get a theatre with a phone call or three, people like Robert Whitehead, Manny Azenberg, Roger Berlind, and even Cameron Mackintosh. For the most part, though, it has become a shuffle in which you sit around and hope for a theatre, never mind whether it's especially suitable. A quick survey of the contents of this book will demonstrate that many of the attractions discussed have names of theatre owners (Nederlander or Jujamcyn) or institutional producers (like Manhattan Theatre Club, Roundabout, or Lincoln Center Theater) or corporate producers with pull (like SFX or Dodger Theatricals) listed above the title.

Shows with no lofty attachments fall into two categories: the classy, likely hit—like *The Full Monty* or the 1999 *Kiss Me, Kate* revival; and the underdog with few prospects. One assumes that Caird had easy access to the Shubert Organization, which coproduced *Nickelby* and has been sheltering *Les Miz* since 1987. But Caird's only new musical since *Les Miz* was

Children of Eden, a high-profile West End disaster in 1991. The fact that the Shuberts were not interested in *Jane Eyre* clearly boded ill.

Jane Eyre's producers were a unique bunch: seven producers and associate producers, all women. Female producers are not a novelty; Irene Mayer Selznick produced *A Streetcar Named Desire* in 1947, and Anne Nichols produced her gold mine of a blockbuster *Abie's Irish Rose*—the first show to break the two-thousand-performance mark—back in 1922. Still, a coproduction by seven women was indicative of something. Were there no men who wanted involvement? *Jane Eyre* was initially produced in 1996, in Toronto, by two men—David and Ed Mirvish, in association with Pamela Koslow and Janet Robinson—and the early lineup of announced Broadway producers included at least one man. *Jane Eyre* is famously classified as "a woman's novel"—but still, the all-female lineup seemed curious enough to take note.

Without the sponsorship of—or a long-standing relationship with—one of the Broadway landlords, a show is forced to wait around like an unwanted orphan until something becomes available (i.e., another show folds). *Jane Eyre* hoped to come into New York following its California break-in at the La Jolla Playhouse (July–September 1999). A February 2000 Broadway opening was announced, but

I found myself rooting for *Jane*, despite it all. Every time they shot themselves in the proverbial foot, I looked around at the audience and hoped that they didn't lose too many people. Which they did.

with no theatre in sight the producers were eventually forced to cancel. They finally got a booking: the Brooks Atkinson, a small-capacity "dramatic" house that is not especially conducive to big-budget musicals. The Atkinson was unavailable to *Jane Eyre* in the spring of 2000 because it had been promised to *Enigma Variations*, a Manny Azenberg production, starring Donald Sutherland. When that show's Toronto tryout drew bad reviews and decided not to come in, it was already March—too late for *Jane* to unpack her bags in time for the Tonys. The Roundabout's limited engagement of *Uncle Vanya* took the Atkinson's summer slot, and John Caird's orphan-of-a-show prepared for a late fall opening.

Charlotte Brontë's first novel was a whirlwind success on its publication in 1847. *Jane Eyre* was originally labeled an autobiography, without Brontë's name. (The title page reads "edited by Currer Bell," this being the pseudonym Brontë used when she had a book of poems privately published in 1846.) *Jane Eyre* was clearly a work of fiction, but Brontë in-

≳N≲ BROOKS ATKINSON THEATRE
UNDER THE DIRECTION OF THE MESSRS. NEDERLANDER

ANNETTE NIEMTZOW   JANET ROBINSON   PAMELA KOSLOW and   MARGARET McFEELEY GOLDEN
in association with JENNIFER MANOCHERIAN and CAROLYN KIM McCARTHY

present

JANE EYRE

based on the novel by
CHARLOTTE BRONTE

book and
additional lyrics by
JOHN CAIRD

music and lyrics by
PAUL GORDON

starring

MARLA SCHAFFEL   JAMES BARBOUR

NELL BALABAN   SANDY BINION   ANDREA BOWEN   STEPHEN R. BUNTROCK   BRADLEY DEAN
ELIZABETH DeGRAZIA   BRUCE DOW   GINA FERRALL   BONNIE GLEICHER   RITA GLYNN
GINA LAMPARELLA   MARGUERITE MacINTYRE   LISA MUSSER   BILL NOLTE   JAYNE PATERSON
DON RICHARD   ERICA SCHROEDER   LEE ZARRETT
and
MARY STOUT

scenic design
JOHN NAPIER

costume design
ANDREANE NEOFITOU

lighting design
JULES FISHER & PEGGY EISENHAUER

sound design
MARK MENARD
& TOM CLARK

associate scenic design
KEITH GONZALES

associate direction
JAYNE PATERSON

projections design
JOHN NAPIER, LISA PODGUR CUSCUNA,
JULES FISHER & PEGGY EISENHAUER

casting
JOHNSON-LIFF
ASSOCIATES CSA
TARA RUBIN

music contractor
EUGENE BIANCO

computerized scenic effects
SMI/SHOWMOTION, INC.

production stage manager
LORI M. DOYLE

marketing consultant
MARGERY SINGER

press representative
THE PUBLICITY OFFICE

associate producers
ALISON FARQUHAR
REBECCA J. WANGNER

general management
RICHARDS/CLIMAN, INC.

music director, vocal and
incidental music arrangements
STEVEN TYLER

orchestration
LARRY HOCHMAN

directed by
JOHN CAIRD & SCOTT SCHWARTZ

AMERICAN PREMIERE OF JANE EYRE PRODUCED BY LA JOLLA PLAYHOUSE, LA JOLLA, CA.
MICHAEL GREIF   TERRENCE DWYER
artistic director   managing director
NEEL KELLER, ASSOCIATE ARTISTIC DIRECTOR/DES McANUFF, DIRECTOR IN RESIDENCE
THE PRODUCERS AND CREATIVE TEAM OF JANE EYRE WOULD LIKE TO THANK
LA JOLLA PLAYHOUSE FOR ITS CONTRIBUTION TO THE DEVELOPMENT AND PRODUCTION OF THE SHOW.

Jane Eyre   Marla Schaffel
Young Jane   Lisa Musser
Young John Reed   Lee Zarrett
Mrs. Reed   Gina Ferrall
Mr. Brocklehurst   Don Richard
Miss Scatcherd   Marguerite MacIntyre
Marigold   Mary Stout
Helen Burns   Jayne Paterson
Schoolgirls   Nell Balaban, Andrea
   Bowen, Elizabeth DeGrazia, Bonnie
   Gleicher, Rita Glynn, Gina Lamparella
Mrs. Fairfax   Mary Stout
Robert   Bruce Dow
Adele   Andrea Bowen
Grace Poole   Nell Balaban
Edward Fairfax Rochester   James
   Barbour
Bertha   Marguerite MacIntyre
Blanche Ingram   Elizabeth DeGrazia
Lady Ingram   Gina Ferrall
Mary Ingram   Jayne Paterson
Young Lord Ingram   Lee Zarrett
Mr. Eshton   Stephen R. Buntrock
Amy Eshton   Nell Balaban
Louisa Eshton   Gina Lamparella
Colonel Dent   Don Richard
Mrs. Dent   Marguerite MacIntyre
Richard Mason   Bill Nolte
The Gypsy   Marje Bubrosa [James
   Barbour]
Vicar   Don Richard
St. John Rivers   Stephen R. Buntrock
Swings   Sandy Binion, Bradley Dean,
   Erica Schroeder

Setting: The action is set in England
   in the 1840s at Gateshead Hall,
   Lowood School, Thornfield Hall, and
   the surrounding Yorkshire moors.

Original Broadway Cast Album:
Sony Classical SK 89482

cluded several autobiographical features. Most important, she spent a year as a student at the Clergy Daughters' School in Lancashire—an institution very much like Lowood. While there, an epidemic wiped out a large portion of the inmates, including two of Brontë's beloved sisters. Brontë returned to the school as a teacher, but she did not become a governess; did not fall in love with a wealthy landowner who kept his first wife locked up in the attic; and did not marry him after he'd been blinded and crippled. Brontë's brother, Branwell—an alcoholic drug addict—did indeed become a tutor and was fired for having an affair with his charge's mother, but that's another story.

The musical started its journey in the early 1990s when pop composer Paul Gordon—who has written songs for Bette Midler, Smokey Robinson, and Patti LaBelle—decided that he was going to write a Broadway musical and *Jane Eyre* was going to be it. Actor Anthony Crivello (of *Kiss of the Spider Woman*) became attached to the project as Rochester. He was then touring in *Les Miz*, providing Gordon with a conduit to Caird. There was a reading of an early draft on June 9, 1995, at the Manhattan Theatre Club, with Crivello, Marla Schaffel, and Mary Stout in the main roles. *Jane Eyre* was then produced out of town—way, way out of town—in Kansas, on December 1, 1995, at the Center Theatre of the Wichita Center for the Arts. (The Center had mounted the first major production of *Children of Eden* following its London debacle.) After revisions, the show received a full production at Toronto's Royal Alexandra Theatre on November 22, 1996—produced in direct competition with Garth Drabinsky's *Ragtime*, which opened across town two weeks later. *Ragtime* got the reviews and the quick Broadway transfer; *Jane Eyre* went back to the drawing board.

After more revisions, a second tryout was mounted in July 1999 at La Jolla. (At this point James Barbour replaced Crivello, who instead went directly to Broadway with *Marie Christine*.) Reaction, as before, was mixed. After even more revisions, *Eyre* finally opened on Broadway on December 10, 2000. (The show's complicated scenic scheme caused the opening to be postponed a week, resulting in "opening night" Playbills dated December 3.)

A month before previews, I decided it was time to read the novel (an engrossing work, by the way). I began to worry when a six-sided, full-color, glossy discount brochure arrived in the mail. Here was the hazy, daguerreotype-like photo of a hazy Jane Eyre, and an even hazier Rochester, with a not-so-hazy horse in the background. Inside, though, was an all-too-clear studio shot of Jane and Rochester in costume. She looked pretty enough to pose for Ingres, he looked handsome enough to play the title role in a summer stock production of *Tom Jones*. The brochure included headshots of the two stars: Schaffel in a glamorous pose with a big smile, and a brooding Barbour with strategically placed lighting and bedroom eyes. (Also included were headshots of Caird, who looks somewhat like James Lapine, except they cut the head off so you couldn't tell if he was bald; and Gordon, who looks—I guess—like a Hollywood composer, with a wispy mustache and goatee, wearing a T-shirt.)

Now, I know that appearances aren't everything, and you can't judge a musical by its cover art, but Jane and Rochester are supposed to be lacking in physical attributes. The heroine, according to Brontë, is decidedly *not* beautiful; as Jane narrates the novel, she constantly mentions her plain looks. Others agree, sometimes going out of their way to make cruel remarks in her hearing. Jane draws twin portraits, one of an idealized beauty—which looks just like the character Blanche Ingram—and the other of her oh-so-plain self. (The drawing of the portraits provided Gordon with his best song, the haunting "Painting Her Portrait.") Brontë also specified that Rochester was not "heroic-looking" or "handsome." Rather, "he had a dark face, with stern features and a heavy brow . . . his eyes and gathered eyebrows looked ireful and thwarted." For the third edition of the novel—issued within seven months, as the book was the *Gone with the Wind* of its day—Brontë refused to allow illustrations, explaining that "my personages are mostly unattractive in look, and therefore ill-adapted to figure in ideal portraits."

Merely cosmetic, you say, and irrelevant to placing the story on the musical stage? Maybe so, but the novelist uses the unattractiveness of her central characters as a major theme of the book. She introduces us to two outright beauties. One is Blanche Ingram, Rochester's fiancée, who is clearly not good enough—intellectually or at heart—for the master of Thornfield Hall. The other paragon of physical perfection is St. John Rivers, Jane's Adonis-like cousin who wants to take her off as his missionary wife. This godly, beautiful creature pleads for Jane to marry him, which is obviously not what Brontë wants the reader to want to happen. (This section of the novel is highly abridged in the musical.)

Thus, the two physically beautiful characters are not good enough prospects for our heroine and hero. The author plots the action so that both Blanche and St. John are thrown over by Rochester and Jane—so severely that one wonders if Ms. Brontë was herself a plain girl, and this was her revenge. None of this makes sense if Rochester is a typical modern-day leading man and Jane is a pretty little thing who's merely in need of some makeup tips. Let it be added that Ms. Brontë repeatedly makes the point that Jane is nineteen and Rochester just about double that. So even without the class distinctions, this would be a most unsuitable match. But, hey, this is musical comedy. Or, at least, musical theatre. So what if Jane and Rochester looked more like *Robert and Elizabeth* (*ref.* The tuneful 1964 British operetta about the Brownings)?

I was impressed with Caird's point of attack; rather than boiling down the overlong novel, he went right at it. I was concerned how it would all work out, though. His opening minutes took us from Jane's little attic at Gateshead Hall through her abuse by her cousin, to her banishment from the house and her entrance into Lowood, where all the children lined up to be lectured by Mr. Brocklehurst in a scene lifted out of Lionel Bart's *Oliver!* But in *Oliver!* we followed our hero through the workhouse slowly enough so that we could get to like him. Here, Jane's pre-Thornwood days were presented as if in a movie montage set to music; the plot highlights were all there, but we flew from peak to peak.

Once Jane met Rochester, things slowed down. (I'll say!) The many twists and turns of the courtship—or, rather, noncourtship—in the novel seem to have disappeared. Brontë's Jane did not seem necessarily preordained to find happiness in Rochester's arms; the very thought, in those class-conscious days, was unthinkable. In the musical, though, it was a given from Rochester's entrance that the pair was fated to be mated.

Jane and Rochester, onstage, spent hours and hours and hours singing songs. Then Caird did a quick dash through the final third of the novel, cutting to the famous final speech just in time to avert overtime for the stagehands. "And then, dear reader, I married him" was altered to the

Jane Eyre
Opened: December 10, 2000
Closed: June 10, 2001
209 performances (and 36 previews)
Profit/Loss: Loss
Jane Eyre ($86 top) was scaled to a potential gross of
$595,549 at the 1,022-seat Brooks Atkinson. Weekly
grosses averaged about $264,000, breaking $375,000 in
the opening week but quickly falling beneath $300,000
and—in May—beneath $200,000. Total gross for the run
was $8,083,185. Attendance was about 68 percent, with
the box office grossing about 45 percent of dollar-
capacity.

TONY AWARD NOMINATIONS
Best Musical
Best Book of a Musical: John Caird
Best Original Score: Paul Gordon (Music), Paul Gordon and
   John Caird (Lyrics)
Best Performance by a Leading Actress: Marla Schaffel
Best Lighting Design: Jules Fisher and Peggy Eisenhauer

DRAMA DESK AWARDS
Outstanding Actress: Marla Schaffel (WINNER)

*Critical
Scorecard*

Rave 0
Favorable 2
Mixed 0
Unfavorable 2
Pan 6

slightly clunky "And then, dear audience, I married him." (The harrow-
ing section in which poor Jane literally crawls through the gutter—while
the good people of England look on, without offering even a crust—was
omitted, as were the Rogers siblings and most of the St. John–missionary
plot.)

   Jane Eyre was pretty much savaged by the reviewers, to my view out of
proportion to its flaws. From its opening moments, the show drew me in;
I was on their side, despite various weaknesses, and hoped for the best.
This is not common; if it's bad, usually, I roll my eyes and give up on it.
But I found myself kind of rooting for *Jane*, despite it all; and every time
they shot themselves in the proverbial foot, I looked around at the audience and hoped that they didn't lose too many people. Which they did. In
this, I was reminded of Lucy Simon and Marsha Norman's *The Secret Garden* (1991), another impressive musical that never quite broke through
the cloudy cobwebs. I was very much intrigued by much of *Jane Eyre*—
especially the staging and design—but I was rarely able to enjoy it.

   The prime offender was the composer-lyricist, who did an impressive
job in spots. But spots aren't enough, not for a Broadway musical. In some
sections Gordon's music was emotionally gripping, but it eventually be-

came too repetitive for comfort. The root of the problem, perhaps, was the lack of singing characters. Jane took part in eighteen of the twenty-six songs listed in the program. Rochester, who didn't come onstage until midway through the first act, sang twelve. There is a point of diminishing returns for a singer; Fanny Brice has twelve songs in *Funny Girl*, and that's too many unless your name is Barbra Streisand. Schaffel and Barbour were both good, mind you, especially Ms. Schaffel; but the same voices, singing the same-sounding songs over and over again, eventually leads to a sense of sameness. Even so, I'd place Gordon's music considerably above recent scores like *Jekyll & Hyde* or *The Scarlet Pimpernel*.

No other character sang more than a couple of songs except Mrs. Fairfax, the hardworking comedy relief (who had two plus a reprise). Making quite a splash in the part was Mary Stout, who has played this same role—more or less—on numerous occasions, including the 1981 one-week flop *Copperfield* and the original 1994 production of Alan Menken and Lynn Ahrens's *A Christmas Carol*. Stout is generally an asset to any show in which she appears. She was especially effective in *Jane Eyre*, providing the only bright spots—despite some not particularly good "comic" material—in a somber evening.

The score was well outfitted by orchestrator Larry Hochman and music director-arranger Steven Tyler, and generally well performed by the hardworking ensemble. But oh, those lyrics. Caird was billed for additional lyrics, indicating that he must have fixed up some of the bigger clinkers. But not enough. This was the sort of show in which the hero keeps singing, "Why must I have eyes?" until he finally loses his eyesight at 10:35. Gordon's idea of comedy lyrics ran along the lines of "I would beg you to purge your un-virginal urge." And can you really expect an audience to listen to a song when it starts off with the baritone singing "I am no better than the old chestnut"? Above all, I can't help but wonder what is a "Secret Soul"? Is there such a thing as a nonsecret soul? Or is it something like an innersole?

Meanwhile, Caird's staging and the work of his fine design team—John Napier on the sets, Jules Fisher and Peggy Eisenhauer on the lights—created an impressive, new look for Broadway. The central device was something they called a carousel, fifty-three thousand pounds worth, which was suspended above the stage. This allowed them to have revolving scenery not only on the stage floor but above it as well. Caird described this as "the visual equivalent of a Chagall painting," with elements moving on and off (from the wings) and in and out (from the flies), as well as twirling into the stage space. The effect was rather spellbinding, especially with the addition of extensive projections. I suppose, though, that the full impact might have depended on where you were sitting. If the fifty-three-thousand-pound carousel flew effortlessly above the stage without a hitch, the show itself continually crash-landed until it just lay there, broken, upon the deck of the Atkinson.

Jane Eyre underwent an even stormier set of setbacks on its way to the Tony Awards, holding on despite weekly losses in the hundreds of thousands. The show, finally, was nominated for five awards, but money ran out, so on May 15 they announced a May 20 closing. Pop singer Alanis Morissette—a friend of composer Gordon—pledged $150,000 to cover losses, allowing the show to keep running. Upon announcement of the closing, the producers of the upcoming Tony Awards show decided to cut the *Jane Eyre* excerpt out of the overlong schedule.

> **This was the sort of show in which the hero keeps singing, "Why must I have eyes?" until he finally loses his eyesight at 10:35.**

(More time for Bialystock and Bloom.) When *Eyre* reversed course, the Tony producers decided not to restore *Eyre's* airtime. This created an immediate uproar, at least from the producers and fans of the show. They managed to get back at least some airtime, but I ask you—did they expect that they would win Best Musical over *The Producers?* Or did they expect that an unlikely but theoretically possible Best Actress win by Marla Schaffel would turn six months of bad word of mouth into landslide ticket sales? At any rate, *Jane Eyre* lost all her Tonys on June 3 and closed June 10, having run through an estimated $9.5 million.

A Connecticut Yankee

Richard Rodgers and Lorenz Hart made their name in May 1925 with the fresh-as-spring revue *The Garrick Gaities*, which introduced their first song hit, "Manhattan." The boys quickly got to work, writing nine full scores in only two and a half years. Times, methinks, have changed.

The early work of Rodgers and Hart—most of it in collaboration with longtime friend Herbert Fields as librettist—was typically breezy, lighthearted fun; "collegiate" is how the shows were often described. The ninth show, which opened in November 1927, was their biggest hit to date: a rollicking musicalization of Mark Twain's 1889 novel *A Connecticut Yankee in King Arthur's Court*. (While Mark Twain sounds ancient to us, at that time the novel was only thirty-eight years old. That's only a little more ancient than the source material for this season's *The Producers*.)

A Connecticut Yankee: The Musical, as they would no doubt call it today, was not great art; but audiences in 1927 didn't expect great art from Broadway musical comedies. Rollicking fun was more than enough. (As for the climate of the time, George and Ira Gershwin's *Funny Face*—starring Fred and Adele Astaire—opened three weeks later. Jerome Kern and Oscar Hammerstein's *Show Boat* came four weeks after that.)

A Connecticut Yankee was not great art, but audiences in 1927 didn't expect great art from Broadway musical comedies. Rollicking fun was more than enough.

Musical comedies in those days were buoyed by song hits, and *Connecticut Yankee* contained Rodgers and Hart's first blockbuster ballad. "My Heart Stood Still" was not written specifically for the show; it was first

Arthur Pendragon / later King Arthur
Henry Gibson

Gerald Gareth / Sir Galahad   Seán
Martin Hingston

Martin Barrett (The Yankee)   Steven
Sutcliffe

Albert Kay / Sir Kay   Mark Lotito

Fay Morgan / Morgan Le Fay
Christine Ebersole

Evelyn Lane / Dame Evelyn   Nancy
Lemenager

Alice Carter / Alisande (Sandy)
Judith Blazer

Angela / Maid Angela   Megan Sikora

Henry Merle / Merlin   Peter Bartlett

Sir Launcelot   Ron Leibman

Guinevere   Jessica Walter

Dancers   Robert M. Armitage, Vance
Avery, David Eggers, Anika Ellis, Matt
Lashey, Elizabeth Mills, Aixa M.
Rosario Medina, Megan Sikorka

Singers   Anne Allgood, Kate Baldwin,
Tony Capone, Julie Connors, John
Halmi, Chris Hoch, Robert Osborne,
Frank Ream, Keith Spencer, Rebecca
Spencer, J. D. Webster, Mimi Wyche

Locale: Hartford, Connecticut, 1927,
and Camelot, A.D. 528

CITY CENTER
Judith E. Daykin, President & Executive Director

CITY CENTER ENCORES!

ARTISTIC DIRECTOR	MUSICAL DIRECTOR
Jack Viertel	Rob Fisher

DIRECTOR-IN-RESIDENCE
Kathleen Marshall

A CONNECTICUT YANKEE

MUSIC BY	LYRICS BY	BOOK BY
Richard Rodgers	Lorenz Hart	Herbert Fields

Adapted from *A Connecticut Yankee in King Arthur's Court* by Mark Twain

STARRING
Judith Blazer   Christine Ebersole   Steven Sutcliffe
AND
Henry Gibson

ALSO STARRING
Peter Bartlett   Seán Martin Hingston   Nancy Lemenager   Mark Lotito

WITH SPECIAL GUEST APPEARANCES BY
Ron Leibman   Jessica Walter

Anne Allgood   Robert M. Armitage   Vance Avery   Kate Baldwin   Tony Capone
Julie Connors   David Eggers   Anika Ellis   John Halmi   Chris Hoch
Matt Lashey   Elizabeth Mills   Robert Osborne   Frank Ream   Aixa M. Rosario Medina
Megan Sikora   Keith Spencer   Rebecca Spencer   J.D. Webster   Mimi Wyche

The Coffee Club Orchestra
Rob Fisher, MUSICAL DIRECTOR

SCENIC CONSULTANT	COSTUME CONSULTANT	LIGHTING	SOUND
John Lee Beatty	Toni-Leslie James	Natasha Katz	Scott Lehrer
CONCERT ADAPTATION	PRODUCTION STAGE MANAGER	ORIGINAL ORCHESTRATION	MUSICAL COORDINATOR
David Ives	Bonnie L. Becker	Don Walker	Seymour Red Press

CHOREOGRAPHER	CASTING
Rob Ashford	Jay Binder

DIRECTED BY
Susan H. Schulman

Major sponsorship for *City Center Encores!* is provided by a grant from
AOL Time Warner, Inc.

The development of *Encores!* is assisted by seed support from The New York Times Company Foundation

A Connecticut Yankee is presented through special arrangement with
The Rodgers & Hammerstein Theatre Library, 1065 Avenue of the Americas, Suite 2400, New York, New York 10018
City Center 55th Street Theater Foundation, Inc. gratefully acknowledges the significant support it receives from the
New York City Department of Cultural Affairs including support through the Cultural Challenge Program

Baldwin Piano, Official Piano of City Center

---

used six months earlier in the London revue *One Dam Thing After Another*. At the time there was a world-famous fellow named the Prince of Wales. He would became Edward VIII in 1936, but within a year he abdicated the throne to marry American divorcée Wallis Simpson (at which point he became the Duke of Windsor). Without this melodramatic-but-chivalrous act, Queen Elizabeth would have merely been the king's niece, and we would never have heard of Prince Charles and Princess Di and Dodi and Camilla and the rest.

Anyway, this fellow was more famous than Frank Sinatra and Nancy Reagan combined. Shortly after the opening, the Prince of Wales went to a dance at the Royal Western Yacht Club in Plymouth. The bandleader asked what he wanted to hear, and the Prince requested "My Heart Stood Still." Neither the bandleader not the band knew it, so Edward got up on the bandstand—in front of the cream of British society and the press— and sang the song to the band, over and over, until they could play it. With the Prince of Wales as songplugger, and the resulting press coverage throughout the English-speaking world, "My Heart Stood Still" became one of the biggest song hits of its time. Comedienne Beatrice Lillie, who was signed for the Rodgers and Hart show after *Connecticut Yankee*, wanted the song for herself; the boys—who wanted it sung by real singers —said it was already taken.

So *Connecticut Yankee* opened with an already famous song hit. Rodgers and Hart added another, the anachronistic and wildly slangy "Thou Swell." ("Hear me holler / I choose a / Sweet lolla- / Palooza / In thee.") The score also contained a pair of delectable comedy duets; a stunning waltz that was cut after the opening (and remains lost to this day); and a few other interesting songs.

Rodgers and Hart followed *Connecticut Yankee* with seven Broadway musical flops—oops!—which were somewhat compounded by a Depression and a depressing interlude in Hollywood. The boys returned to Forty-fifth Street in 1936, with the first in a series of influential shows that changed the course of musical comedy. Having broken with Herb Fields, they chose to work with a top playwright-director who had never written a musical. George Abbott was already an old man—he was forty-seven, Rodgers was thirty-two—but he brought craftsmanship and discipline to the form. So much so that over the next two decades he developed what we still call the "Abbott musical." Rodgers and Hart, for their part, provided intelligent, laugh-filled, and increasingly well integrated scores.

"Why," Rodgers wanted to know, "would anybody want to do *Connecticut Yankee*?"

The highpoints of the Abbott/Rodgers and Hart collaboration were *On Your Toes*, *The Boys from Syracuse*, and *Pal Joey*, the latter two produced by Abbott himself. But *Pal Joey*—which opened on Christmas Day, 1940—marked the turning point for Hart. An intensely unhappy personal life finally began to affect his work, making him irresponsible and unresponsive. "Glad to Be Unhappy" was the rueful title of one of his 1936 song hits, but by 1940 the facade had smashed. The team wrote two additional musicals, *Higher and Higher* (1941) and *By Jupiter* (1942), but Hart was disappearing on binges more and more (leaving Rodgers to ghostwrite lyrics for his missing partner). When the pair were approached to write a cowboy operetta, Hart was in no mood to accept and in no condition to work. He passed, so Rodgers enlisted Oscar Hammerstein as his collaborator on what became *Oklahoma!*

The new show opened on March 31, 1943, and became an immediate break-the-bank success. Hart appears to have recognized that Rodgers was better off with Hammerstein; at forty-eight, he was suddenly redundant. This, accompanied by the death of his mother two weeks after *Oklahoma!* opened, put Hart in a tailspin. (Hart had one of those mother-son relationships that are the stuff of psychiatric casebooks.) Rodgers and Fields, trying to rescue Hart from his malaise, decided to prepare a revised version of their old hit *Connecticut Yankee*. As bait for Hart, they suggested that a minor role in the 1927 version be upgraded to a star turn for Vivienne Segal.

> The 1927 version, performed in as intact a condition as possible, would have seemed terribly quaint. But, at least, we might have been able to look at it and say, "I understand why this was a hit."

Segal sprang to stardom in 1915 as an eighteen-year-old soprano in Sigmund Romberg's *The Blue Paradise*; she was also the leading lady in Hammerstein's 1926 operetta *The Desert Song*. Her career had all but dried up when Rodgers and Hart put her in a featured role in their 1938 musical *I Married an Angel*. She turned out to have a flair for musical comedy, impelling Rodgers and Hart to write *Pal Joey* for her. (Vera Simpson = Vivienne Segal.) Hart also, apparently, fixated on the unlikely proposition that he marry Segal. Back to the old psychiatric casebook, I guess.

The presence of Segal got Hart on the wagon and back to work. Rodgers—acting as producer—booked a theatre and hired a cast; Fields prepared a new libretto, moving the action from 1927 to 1943; and Hart and Rodgers wrote nine new songs (only six of which were used). These included one of Hart's finest comedy lyrics, a macabre song in which Segal's character described how she murdered fifteen husbands in order "To Keep My Love Alive."

This showstopper for Ms. Segal was apparently the last song Hart completed. He proposed to her once more during the Philadelphia tryout, she turned him down once more, and he departed on one last binge. He reappeared on opening night in New York. Rodgers left word that Hart should be ejected from the theatre if he was drunk; he was. Hart stormed off through the snowy streets toward the bars of Eighth Avenue, without his topcoat. When he was found, drunk in the gutter, he had developed pneumonia. Larry Hart died on November 22, 1943, five nights after the opening of the *Connecticut Yankee* production that was supposed to bring him back to life.

The revival was pretty uneven. The "modern" sections of the book were updated to 1943. Martin, the Yankee, became a navy lieutenant; Sandy, the love interest, was a Wac; and Segal—playing Queen Morgan Le Fay in the flashback—was a Wave. But the show was terribly creaky, and indifferently received, and closed after a disappointing four months.

I once asked Rodgers about the rights to *Connecticut Yankee*, back in 1976 or so. He had Bob Baumgart, his right-hand man, take me to lunch (at Reubens, around the corner from the old Rodgers office at 598 Madison). "Why," Rodgers wanted to know, "would anybody want to do *Connecticut Yankee?*" I mumbled something about how good—and refreshing—the score was. "Rodgers says you should do *On Your Toes*. Much better show." Nothing came of this, but that was a direct Rodgers response to his then-forty-nine-year-old *Yankee*.

Flash forward to 2001. *Connecticut Yankee* had become the least familiar of the old Rodgers and Hart hits, making it a logical selection for treatment by the folks at City Center Encores! But which *Connecticut Yankee?* The smashingly successful, if ragtag, 1927 version? Or the failed 1943 rewrite? This question was addressed in a program note by new artistic director Jack Viertel and musical director Rob Fisher. They decided to keep the 1943 score, in part because of the new songs  (especially "To Keep My Love Alive") and in part because of the intact orchestrations by Don Walker. (Walker had done the prior Rodgers and Hart collaboration, *By Jupiter*, and was to do the next Rodgers musical, *Carousel*. In the early 1950s, Rodgers had Walker reorchestrate both *Pal Joey* and *On Your Toes*, although recent productions have returned to the Hans Spialek originals.) The concert version incorporated the new starring role devised for Vivienne Segal but "tried to retain the flavor of the

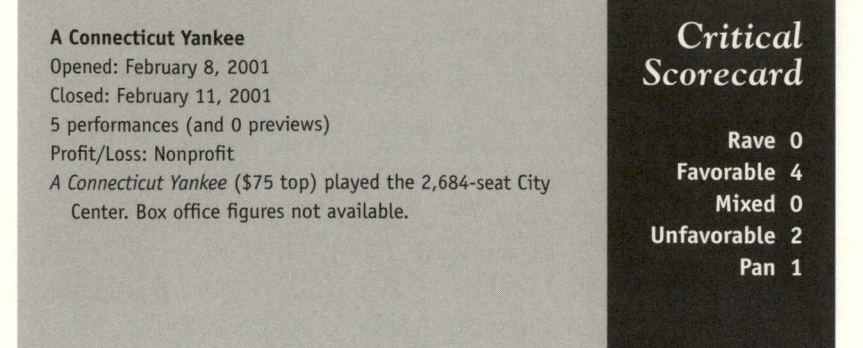

A Connecticut Yankee
Opened: February 8, 2001
Closed: February 11, 2001
5 performances (and 0 previews)
Profit/Loss: Nonprofit
A Connecticut Yankee ($75 top) played the 2,684-seat City
  Center. Box office figures not available.

*Critical
Scorecard*

Rave   0
Favorable 4
Mixed   0
Unfavorable 2
Pan   1

original 1927 script, with its pre-war, pre-depression dedication to pure hi-jinks."

All of this made a certain amount of sense. Still, the great value of Encores! is as a living museum; what we got here was an enhanced yet watered-down version of the property. I suppose that the 1927 version, performed in as intact a condition as possible, would have seemed terribly quaint on the City Center stage. But, at least, we might have been able to look at it and say, "I understand why this was a hit." What we got, instead, was something that made little sense altogether. It didn't work in 1943, and it certainly didn't in 2001. They called it the 1943 version, at least in the press releases; Encores! audiences—who had recently enjoyed Rodgers and Hart's infinitely more advanced *Babes in Arms* (1937) and *Boys from Syracuse* (1938)—might well have been puzzled by the apparent regression.

Unlike typical Encores! presentations, the proceedings were not especially enhanced by the cast. Steven Sutcliffe—best known as the younger brother in *Ragtime*—undertook the title role without much success. He sang passably well; but he wasn't a manipulative operator, which robbed the show of much of its comedy. The Segal role was played by Christine Ebersole, an Encores! favorite (with *Yankee* marking her fourth visit). I must confess that Ms. Ebersole rarely impresses me, although she did pretty well in this season's revival of *The Best Man* (and would give a first-rate performance in the season-ending *42nd Street*). But she didn't move me in Encores! productions of *Allegro*, *Lady in the Dark*, or *The Ziegfeld Follies of 1936*, and she didn't here.

Fortunately, Judith Blazer was on hand to play what had been the leading lady role in the 1927 version. Much of her part was cut to make room for Segal in 1943, but Blazer scored heavily with "Thou Swell," and her comic sense helped to keep the show alive (or at least tried to). Blazer's Broadway career is somewhat baffling. Her first break was as replacement for the female lead in *Me and My Girl*, in which she was rather scrumptious. Over the years she has brightened numerous studio cast albums of old musicals like *Girl Crazy* and *Babes in Arms*, but somehow she has never found a breakthrough role. The only other bright spot in the evening was Seán Martin Hingston, playing the dim-witted Sir Galahad. Hingston was instantly recognizable from the still-running *Contact*, where he played the man on the swing in the opener "Swinging," and was one of the most prominent dancers opposite "The Girl in the Yellow Dress." (Few people realized that he also played the Jerry Lewis–like busboy in "Did You Move?") Hingston proved to have a fine singing voice and good comic sense, which he mixed with some top-notch traditional Broadway show dancing.

Otherwise, though, things were pretty dreary. Even the music—which is traditionally the saving grace at Encores!—lacked the expected sparkle. I'm a big fan of orchestrator Don Walker, but his 1943 charts didn't excite me whatsoever. Music director Rob Fisher, who is usually jumping around the Encores! podium like a firefly, seemed to be merely excited by his chores. Still, you can't fault Encores! for trying *Connecticut Yankee*. It is historically important, as these things go, and it at least sounded good on paper. (One of the hazards of these concert versions is that you really don't know what you have until you get to the end of the first week of rehearsal, by which point you're two days away from an audience.) Using their typically expert and meticulous methods, they opened up a vintage treasure chest and found it only half full. But who could fault them for that?

A Class Act

The Manhattan Theatre Club's last Broadway hit prior to the 2000–2001 season, as previously related on these pages, had been *Love! Valour! Compassion!* Terrence McNally's 1994 play, in fact, had been their only Broadway success of the decade. Things changed —and how—with the start of the 2000–2001 season.

David Auburn's *Proof* opened on October 24, 2000, followed by Charles Busch's *The Tale of the Allergist's Wife* on November 2. These two transfers from MTC's spring 2000 season got the Broadway year off to a happy and healthy start, with both of them recouping their costs within three months (on the way to substantial profits). A third MTC offering, *A Class Act*, transferred to the Ambassador on March 11, 2001, with a fourth— their coproduction of August Wilson's *King Hedley II*— en route to a May 1 opening.

Has a nonprofit theatre ever had four shows running simultaneously on Broadway? I don't think so, although by season's end the Roundabout had three (revivals of *Cabaret*, *Design for Living*, and *Follies*), and Lincoln Center had two (*Contact* and *Invention of Love*).

A Class Act arrived with an especially curious history. Edward Kleban was one of Broadway's one-hit wonders. These fellows—they have all been men—turn up out of the blue, with a landmark musical, one of those shows that make you set for life. But that's it. Some of them never write anything again, like Sherman Edwards of *1776* fame. Others write show after show after show, all of which fail and none of which indicate the talent that went into their one hit. (Among the latter group: Mitch Leigh, who followed *Man of La Mancha* with such horrors as *Home Sweet Homer*, *Saravá*, and *Ain't Broadway Grand*; Joe Darion, who followed *La*

Mancha with *Illya, Darling*; and Martin Charnin, who followed *Annie* with *I Remember Mama, The First, Annie 2*, and others.)

Kleban was a special case. He was known along Broadway as a staffer at Columbia Records, producing albums that the great Goddard Lieberson was too busy to deal with. (These include two that I constantly listen to, *Jacques Brel Is Alive and Well and Living in Paris* and Styne, Comden, and Green's *Hallelujah, Baby!*) When Michael Bennett started developing his "dancer" project, Kleban—an aspiring composer—got the job on what would become the 1975 megamusical *A Chorus Line*. As lyricist, only; as composer, Bennett chose Marvin Hamlisch, dance music arranger for Bennett's negligible 1967 musical *Henry, Sweet Henry*. Hamlisch had just won three awards at the 1974 Oscars for his work on the films *The Sting* and *The Way We Were*.

A Chorus Line earned Kleban a Tony and a Pulitzer and millions of dollars. Everything, apparently, but respect and self-confidence. All the fellow wanted, it seems, was to write music for a Broadway show. He wrote and wrote and wrote and wrote. Incredibly enough, he was unable to get *anything* produced. (Other than *A Chorus Line*, for which he did not write the music.) Compare this with the aforementioned Mitch Leigh and Martin Charnin, both of whom were able to parlay their one superhit into more than a half dozen Broadway flops.

Kleban died of cancer in 1987, at the age of forty-eight, leaving behind a trunkful of scores and partial scores. These included adaptations of the novel *Scaramouche*; the plays *A Thousand Clowns* and *Merton of the Movies*; and the films *The Americanization of Emily* and *The Heartbreak Kid*. He also wrote several relatively personal musicals, which ultimately made possible the semiautobiographical *A Class Act*. These included *Musical Comedy*, about the BMI Workshop; *Subject to Change*, about divorce; *Gallery*, about famous paintings, with which Kleban (in *A Class Act*) is preoccupied; and *Light on My Feet*, an autobiographical musical that Kleban fashioned out of his trunk songs (and apparently presaged *A Class Act*). Promotional material and projections in

> **A Chorus Line earned Kleban a Tony and a Pulitzer and millions of dollars. Everything, apparently, but respect and self-confidence. All the fellow wanted, it seems, was to write music for a Broadway show.**

the second act of *A Class Act* also mention Kleban's work on *Scandal*, Michael Bennett's "orgy" project that died in workshop. (Kleban was not actually part of this project, although he wrote some material on spec, in-

Lucy   Donna Bullock
Bobby et al.   David Hibbard
Ed   Lonny Price
Felicia   Sara Ramirez
Lehman   Patrick Quinn
Charley et al.   Jeff Blumenkrantz
Mona   Nancy Anderson
Sophie   Randy Graff

Time: 1958–1988
Place: The stage of the Shubert
Theatre and other locations

Original Off-Broadway Cast Album:
RCAVictor 09026-63757

AMBASSADOR THEATRE

MARTY BELL   CHASE MISHKIN   ARIELLE TEPPER
present

The MANHATTAN THEATRE CLUB Production of

LONNY PRICE
NANCY ANDERSON   JEFF BLUMENKRANTZ   DONNA BULLOCK
DAVID HIBBARD   PATRICK QUINN   SARA RAMIREZ
and
RANDY GRAFF

in

A CLASS ACT

Music and Lyrics by
EDWARD KLEBAN

Book by
LINDA KLINE and LONNY PRICE

Scenic Design	Costume Design	Lighting Design
JAMES NOONE	CARRIE ROBBINS	KEVIN ADAMS

Sound Design   Orchestrations
ACME SOUND PARTNERS   LARRY HOCHMAN

Music Direction/
Additional Arrangements   Music Coordinator   Incidental Music
DAVID LOUD   JOHN MILLER   TODD ELLISON

Casting   Production Stage Manager   Technical Director
JAY BINDER   JEFFREY M. MARKOWITZ   DAVID BENKEN

General Management   Associate Director   Press Representative
DONALD FRANTZ   STAFFORD ARIMA   RICHARD KORNBERG & ASSOCIATES

Executive Producer   Associate Producers
EAST EGG ENTERTAINMENT   ROBYN GOODMAN
                        TOKYO BROADCASTING SYSTEM/KUMIKO YOSHII

Choreographed by
MARGUERITE DERRICKS

Directed by
LONNY PRICE

"A Class Act" was originally produced by the MANHATTAN THEATRE CLUB on November 9, 2000
and previously developed by MUSICAL THEATRE WORKS.

ORIGINAL CAST RECORDING AVAILABLE ON RCA VICTOR.

THE PRODUCERS WISH TO EXPRESS THEIR APPRECIATION TO THEATRE DEVELOPMENT FUND FOR ITS SUPPORT OF THIS PRODUCTION

---

cluding the song "Next Best Thing to Love.")

Why were none of these Kleban projects produced? The neurotic Kleban was apparently difficult to work with, as is clearly demonstrated in A Class Act. But it's an odd thing. When somebody successful in show business is impossible, word tends to spread rapidly. When A Chorus Line was produced, I was managing another Broadway musical. This was a small world; everybody knew somebody who knew everybody else. I had worked on earlier shows with a number of Chorus Line people, and I had friends who worked in high levels on Chorus Line. When A Class Act was first announced, I realized that I had never—in the twenty-five years since Chorus Line opened—heard a word about Kleban. I had never even heard anybody mention his name. When someone in this business is successful, stories—true or not—always spread. Especially if the person is impossible. But Ed Kleban? Not a word.

When Kleban died, he left the unsung songs to his friends. "It is my wish that my friends will arrange for the songs to be performed, preferably in a large building, in a central part of town, in a dark room, as part of a play, with a lot of people listening who have all paid a great deal to get in." This from his will, or at least his will as rewritten by the librettists of *A Class Act*. Fourteen years later, the songs were indeed being performed on Broadway, although few of the people listening paid a great deal of money to get in. That is to say, the show was heavily discounted for its forced three-month run.

Kleban left the rights to the autobiographical *Light on My Feet* to two friends, with the proviso that if the show wasn't staged within five years, the rights would go to Linda Kline. Kline, who is in some ways the model for the character Lucy in *A Class Act*, lived with Kleban for the last eight years of his life. She took the material to actor-turned-director Lonny Price, who turned the songs into a musical. It is not easy to write the book of a musical; it is not easy to direct a musical; and it is unheard of to write and direct a musical while starring in it. George M. Cohan used to do it; he'd write the songs and produce, too, but that's another story.

Price began his Broadway career as a gofer in the Hal Prince office. When Prince produced Stephen Sondheim's *Merrily We Roll Along*, Price got himself an audition—and one of the three main roles. He played Charley Kringas, a successful lyri-cist overshadowed by his compos-ing partner. Price's main number was "Franklin Shepherd, Inc.," in which his songwriter character teetered on the brink of a mental breakdown. (This would have fit right into *A Class Act*.) Price moved into directing with a series of cut-down off-Broadway reviv-als of musicals, including an ac-claimed version of Bock and Har-nick's *The Rothschilds*. His New York directing credits also include the long-running off-Broadway comedy *Visiting Mr. Green* and the short-running Broadway com-edy *Sally Marr and Her Escorts*. This was a biographical play about the mother of comedian Lenny Bruce; Price collaborated with Joan Rivers, who played the lead. Linda Kline saw *Sally Marr* and decided that Price was her man.

A Class Act
Opened: March 11, 2001
Closed: June 10, 2001
105 performances (and 30 previews)
Profit/Loss: Loss
A Class Act ($80 top) was scaled to a potential gross of
$587,587 at the 1,097-seat Ambassador. (These figures
include the post-opening price increase from $75.) Weekly
grosses averaged about $152,000, with only one week—
in late March—above the $200,000 mark. (Two weeks
later, they had a starvation-level $88,000 week.) Total
gross for the run was $2,558,362. Attendance was about
46 percent, with the box office grossing about 27 percent
of dollar-capacity.

TONY AWARD NOMINATIONS
Best Musical
Best Book of a Musical: Linda Kline and Lonny Price
Best Original Score: Edward Kleban
Best Performance by a Leading Actress: Randy Graff
Best Orchestrations: Larry Hochman

Critical
Scorecard

Rave 1
Favorable 5
Mixed 2
Unfavorable 0
Pan 2

It took seven years for Kline and Price to get their Kleban project on
the boards. During this time, Price became artistic director of the nonprofit Musical Theatre Works and gave up acting permanently (or so he
thought). Four days before going into rehearsal for the Manhattan Theatre Club production, Peter Jacobson—the actor cast in the role of Kleban—left to accept a role in a TV series. (Off-Broadway actors' salaries
are so low that Equity contracts provide an automatic out for a better-
paying job.) Now, who do you think they got to play the role of the neurotic, short, nervy Kleban?

Price, of course, and probably over strong objections from himself. A
writer-director is a sitting duck when things go wrong, especially for a musical previewing in New York. The purpose of extended previews is to
allow the creators to gauge audience reaction and react to it. This is hard
for the director to do if he's busy rewriting the script. Put the guy onstage
as well, and he really doesn't have time to observe or react or alter. If
you're the director-author-star and everything isn't smooth and perfect,
just watch the lances come out. Which they did, during the rocky preview period.

The off-Broadway *Class Act* apparently wasn't a happy family. Four of
the eight cast members chose not to make the transfer to the Ambassador. Jonathan Freeman went into a featured role in *42nd Street*; Ray

Wills went into the surefire hit *The Producers* and by Tony time was sub-
bing for the ailing Nathan Lane; Julia Murney went into a major role in
the short-lived MTC musical *Time and Again*; and Carolee Carmello had
a baby the week that *Class Act* opened on Broadway. Musical director
Todd Ellison, too, opted to shuffle off to *42nd Street*. This is, all in all, not
a great show of undying belief in the project. Choreographer Scott Wise
was similarly gone, although he was apparently replaced early on. The
show improved over the course of time, so that it was considerably better
when it arrived on Broadway.

As for Price-the-actor, he was very good in the role (and I say this in
spite of generally less than admiring reviews). Yes, he had a raspy singing
voice and gave a pushy, neurotic performance; but that's precisely what
the role called for: a pushy, neurotic, short, impossible fellow who sang
like a songwriter. But Price inhabited the role like a sprite. There was
something endearing about him; within fifteen minutes of his entrance—
when he was discovered lounging in one of the boxes, house left—he had
totally won me over. You got the impression of someone enjoying himself
as his own work unfolded in front of him, but there was never a sense of
ego; it was more a sense of wonder. Watching Lonny singing and dancing
and loping about the stage, I felt sorry that I had missed his performance
in *Durante*. This was a musical comedy that was shuttered by an earthquake, no less. They were trying out in San Francisco when the 1989
Loma Prieta earthquake inter-
vened, and the show's finances
weren't strong enough to with-
stand the lost performance rev-
enues, necessary repairs, ongoing
rehearsal salaries, and other costs.

**A writer-director is a sitting duck
when things go wrong. Put the guy
onstage as well, and just watch the
lances come out.**

I have been told that Price was pretty good, and I imagine there were
glimpses of his Jimmy Durante in his Ed Kleban.

The rest of the cast was admirable, with a rock-solid performance by
Randy Graff, a likable one from Donna Bullock (as the Kline character),
and highly effective stabs at Michael Bennett (by David Hibbard) and
Marvin Hamlisch (by the ever-resourceful Jeff Blumenkrantz). These
were only brief sketches, brightening up the second act. The characters
(other than Kleban) were a curious mixture of imaginary, actual, and
nonfactual; the only "real" character present throughout the show, other
than Kleban, was Lehman Engel (well played by Patrick Quinn). Engel
started the BMI Workshop in 1961, but he could not have been present

at Kleban's memorial; he died in 1982. The service in the musical is held
at the 1,500-seat Shubert Theatre, indicating that Kleban was an important personage indeed. In fact, it was Engel's memorial that was held at
the Shubert. Kleban's memorial was at the Anspacher, one of the smaller
spaces at the New York Shakespeare Festival; 275 seats were more than
enough. Why quibble? Things like this don't really matter; this was musical comedy, after all. But some of us take biography as fact. When you
find two or three things that you know are inaccurate, you wonder what
else might have been fudged.

And what of the score, anyway? After Kleban—the character—sings
"Paris Through the Window," his first submission to the BMI Workshop,
the only response from his peers is "It's . . . interesting." That's pretty
much how I felt about the score. There were some nice things; but Sondheim he wasn't, as hard as he tried. (This was typical of many of the aspiring songwriters of the seven-
ties and eighties.) In other places
the neurotic Kleban sounds like
the neurotic Billy Finn, who appeared with the astounding *March
of the Falsettos* in 1981. Consider
composer-lyricists Sondheim, Finn, and Maury Yeston, who arrived on
Broadway with *Nine* in 1982. Kleban, although "interesting," cannot
begin to compare to any of them. Not in my book, anyway.

Consider composer-lyricists Sondheim, Finn, and Maury Yeston. Kleban, although interesting, cannot begin to compare to any of them.

Does a new musical need to have a brilliant score to be effective? Of
course not. Look at *The Full Monty*; look at *The Producers*. But the whole
premise of *A Class Act* is based on the claim that Kleban was a great composer. The show entertained, but it didn't convince—which I suppose
the friends of Ed Kleban would see as failure.

A Class Act did fail, inevitably; they waited around, at starvation levels, until they won no Tony Awards. Their failure was not difficult to fore-
see. Go ahead and plunk down your credit card. What do you pick? *The
Full Monty? The Producers? Follies?* Or *A Class Act?*

Design for Living

Noël Coward's 1933 comedy *Design for Living* is famously about a ménage à trois. Or is it, exactly?

Act 1: Gilda lives with Otto, a bohemian painter, in squalor in Paris. Leo, their best friend, is a playwright who has just begun to achieve success. While Otto's away, Leo unexpectedly turns up and immediately lands in Gilda's bed. Otto is immensely pleased by Leo's return, until he realizes what has happened. Gilda runs off with Leo.

Act 2: Gilda lives with the now-famous Leo, in splendor in London. While Leo's away, Otto unexpectedly turns up and immediately lands in Gilda's bed. Leo is immensely pleased by Otto's return, until he realizes what has happened. Gilda runs off with Ernest, Otto's priggish art dealer. Leo and Otto, helped along by a bottle of brandy, commiserate over their lost Gilda. Otto puts his arm around Leo, and the pair break down in (alcoholic) tears.

Act 3: Gilda lives with her new husband, Ernest, in a dazzling New York penthouse. While Ernest is away, Leo and Otto unexpectedly turn up, but *don't* immediately land in Gilda's bed. She soon realizes, though, that she must be with Leo and Otto, and the three decide to run off together.

That's what the script says, anyway.

Director Joe Mantello's take on the play was somewhat altered. (The play was written in three acts but was performed at the Roundabout in two.) When Otto returned to his studio in act 1, he didn't simply greet his friend Leo. Coward's original stage direction: Leo takes both of Otto's hands and stands looking at

> One only wonders what on earth Otto and Leo wanted Gilda for. To carry their bags?

Gilda   Jennifer Ehle
Ernest   John Cunningham
Otto   Alan Cumming
Leo   Dominic West
Miss Hodge   Jenny Sterlin
Mr. Birbeck   Saxon Palmer
Grace   Marisa Berenson
Henry   T. Scott Cunningham
Helen   Jessica Stone

The action takes place in Otto's studio in Paris, Leo's flat in London, and Ernest's apartment in New York over the course of three and a half years.

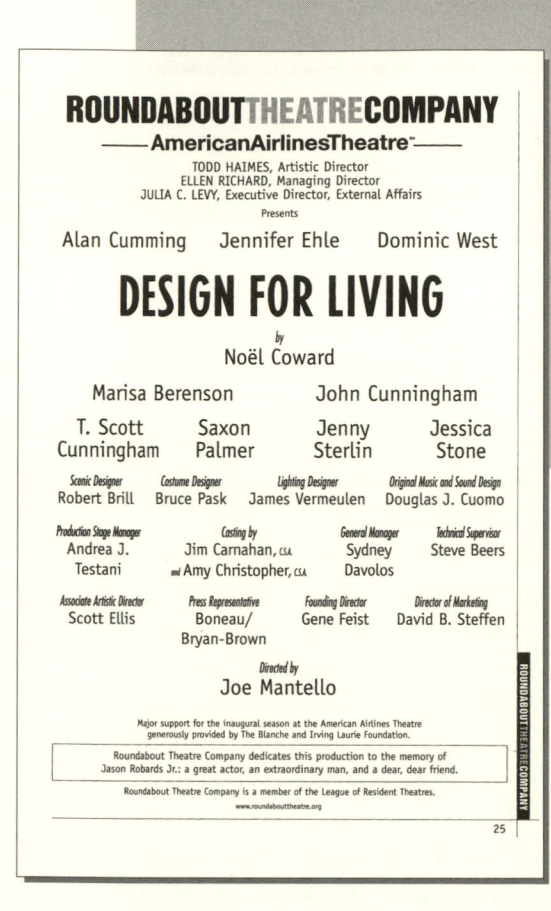

ROUNDABOUTTHEATRECOMPANY
——AmericanAirlinesTheatre——
TODD HAIMES, Artistic Director
ELLEN RICHARD, Managing Director
JULIA C. LEVY, Executive Director, External Affairs
Presents

Alan Cumming   Jennifer Ehle   Dominic West

DESIGN FOR LIVING
by
Noël Coward

Marisa Berenson   John Cunningham

T. Scott   Saxon   Jenny   Jessica
Cunningham   Palmer   Sterlin   Stone

Scenic Designer	Costume Designer	Lighting Designer	Original Music and Sound Design
Robert Brill	Bruce Pask	James Vermeulen	Douglas J. Cuomo

Production Stage Manager	Casting by	General Manager	Technical Supervisor
Andrea J. Testani	Jim Carnahan, CSA and Amy Christopher, CSA	Sydney Davolos	Steve Beers

Associate Artistic Director	Press Representative	Founding Director	Director of Marketing
Scott Ellis	Boneau/ Bryan-Brown	Gene Feist	David B. Steffen

Directed by
Joe Mantello

Major support for the inaugural season at the American Airlines Theatre generously provided by The Blanche and Irving Laurie Foundation.

Roundabout Theatre Company dedicates this production to the memory of Jason Robards Jr.: a great actor, an extraordinary man, and a dear, dear friend.

Roundabout Theatre Company is a member of the League of Resident Theatres.
www.roundabouttheatre.org

25

ROUNDABOUTTHEATRECOMPANY

him. Mantello's new stage direction: Otto catapults across the stage and lands literally wrapped around Leo, like two comrades who haven't seen each other since last Sunday afternoon on Fire Island. Later, in the second-act drunk scene on the couch after Gilda's desertion, Otto and Leo kissed and hugged and—well, comported themselves in such a way that would have made Coward blush. (He might well have enjoyed it offstage, but not in public.) When the boys arrived in New York in act 3, they were quite a sight; they'd fit right in at a midnight party after a Halloween parade in Greenwich Village. One only wonders what on earth this pair wanted Gilda for. To carry their bags?

Mr. Mantello was no doubt looking for a way to make the play relevant. Still, his methods seemed somewhat at odds with the text. Let us suppose, for a moment, that Leo and Otto *were* a couple in the modern sense of the word. What *would* they need Gilda for? Yes, they were friends before Gilda came along. But why, at the beginning of the play, is Otto living with Gilda? Why, when Leo appears in Paris, does he run off with Gilda (as opposed to Otto)? In explaining his attraction to Gilda, Leo mentions that he was jealous when Gilda first appeared on the scene; not mad at Gilda for coming between him and Otto but jealous because Gilda chose Otto instead of him. When Otto turns up in London, he is clearly itching not for Otto but Gilda. "I want to make love to you very badly indeed, please! I've been lonely for a long time without you, and I'm not going to be lonely any more." This production's Otto was far more impassioned when Mr. Mantello placed him in Leo's arms, in their underwear, despite the clarity of Mr. Coward's text.

In act 3, Coward says—that is, Leo says: "King Solomon had a hundred wives and was thought very highly of. I can't see why Gilda shouldn't be allowed a couple of gentlemen friends." He did not say anything about Otto having gentlemen friends, or about King Solomon and David. This type of speech, of course, might have gotten Coward hauled off to Reading Gaol in 1933.

Mantello retained the play's thirties style in the three sets, stylishly designed by Robert Brill (of the Roundabout's 1998 revival of *Cabaret*). They were overly grand, perhaps, but that was fine with me. But Mantello simultaneously bombarded our ears with modernistic music, at least some of which turned out to be rock versions of Coward tunes. Quick, where are we? The wardrobe, too, was stylishly in period—except for Otto, who started outlandish and went on from there. Most of the nine characters comported themselves in the style of the times, except for Otto (and—to a much lesser extent—Leo). Mantello obviously tried to give us a decidedly modern take on some of the play, but what—precisely—was the point?

There is no rule that a play must be cast and performed as originally intended; more often than not, that type of treatment leaves us with sterile theatre. But *Design for Living* is a special case. Imagine three of the greatest, most famous, most capable, and most stylish actors in the English-speaking world. People who, individually, can galvanize an audience simply by tapping a cigarette on a silver cigarette case. Long before any of them were famous, Coward, Alfred Lunt, and Lynn Fontanne used to sit around planning how one day they would star on Broadway together. And imagine them meeting over the course of eleven years, plotting and planning, "knowing that it was something that we wanted to do very much indeed, and searching wildly through our minds for suitable characters." This from Coward, who before he could take the stage had to write the thing.

Design for Living
Opened: March 15, 2001
Closed: May 13, 2001
69 performances (and 30 previews)
Profit/Loss: Nonprofit [Loss]
Design for Living ($65 top) was scaled to a potential gross of
$349,943 at the 740-seat American Airlines Theatre.
Weekly grosses averaged about $241,000, building to a
high of $265,000 in the final week. Total gross for the
season was $2,887,430. Attendance was about 83
percent, with the box office grossing about 69 percent of
dollar-capacity. (These figures are not indicative, as the
potential was calculated at the top ticket price, but
subscribers paid less.)

*Critical
Scorecard*

Rave 1
Favorable 4
Mixed 0
Unfavorable 0
Pan 5

"At one moment we were to be three foreigners, Lynn, Eurasian; Alfred, German; and I, Chinese. At another we were to be three acrobats, rapping out 'Allez Oops' and flipping handkerchiefs at each other."

It was tricky. How do you come up with three absolutely equal starring roles, for three absolutely equal stars? By 1933, Lynn Fontanne and Alfred Lunt were long married and typically playing couples onstage; audiences would naturally assume they were a couple. How could the Coward character fit it, not as a bystander but as an equal? The Lunts enjoyed an enormous success with their 1924 production of Ferenc Molnár's *The Guardsman*, which also had three central roles, a married couple and their "friend." Coward's challenge was to create a third character who would not just be the couple's friend; neither inferior, nor superior, nor observer. The triangle in *Design for Living* was created specifically to give the three actors juicy roles in which they could frolic. As

It is perhaps inadvisable to invite busloads of fourteen-year-olds to a press performance of a Noël Coward play about a ménage à trois.

Coward reported, "It has been liked and disliked, and hated and admired, but never, I think, sufficiently loved by any but its three leading actors."

The Roundabout's three leading actors gave interesting performances, seeing as how they were somewhat trapped between the text and the direction. Alan Cumming had a hard time of it in the Alfred Lunt part. There is a hazard in giving an unforgettable performance, like Cumming's turn in the Roundabout *Cabaret*; your next audience won't forget. Cumming's waiflike Otto, in a yellow punk haircut, had the likability of a puppy dog; he played the role like a young Peter Lorre, before Hollywood and morphine turned him into a caricature. Jennifer Ehle, who was so good in the 2000 revival of *The Real Thing*, also had a problematic assignment. Gilda is lighter than air, the ebullient center of the play; but Mantello's Gilda seemed overwhelmed by neuroses (or, perhaps, merely "Weary of It All"). How do you do both at once? Beats me. The London section of the play seemed more Cowardish than the other acts; at least until Gilda escaped and left Otto and Leo alone grappling on the couch. Ehle was very good in this section; Cumming was, too, in the Norwegian seduction scene the night before Leo's return. Perhaps there was a better *Design for Living* hidden within the Roundabout's production?

Dominic West, as the playwright, seemed to better fit the proceedings, probably because we had never seen him onstage before. John Cunningham, who has given memorable performances ranging from *Zorbá* to *Six Degrees of Separation* to *Sylvia*, was wasted in the role of Ernest. I didn't even realize it was him until I checked the program during intermission. On the plus side, Coward wrote in one of those eccentric housemaids who chew up the scenery. Mantello let her alone—he didn't change her name from Miss Hodge to Ms. Hodge, or anything like that—and Jenny Sterlin happily provided some low-comedy laughs.

Let it also be reported that I saw the play under extreme conditions. The performance I attended was the Wednesday matinee before a Thursday opening. It can be difficult to sell tickets to an intellectual show for a Wednesday matinee, so producers—with critics to worry about—have been known to paper the house. Unfortunately, the press preview of *Design for Living* was papered with the wrong audience. What they got was inner-city students who looked to be fourteen or fifteen, about 150 of them (of some 500 in attendance). What do you imagine happened when Otto leapt forcefully into Leo's arms? What do you imagine happened when the boys started rolling around in their underwear? And when Otto and Leo became passionately entwined—well, you can imagine. The theatre is celebrated for its ability to introduce new ideas and thoughts to its audiences, but I don't think this is what the education staff of the Roundabout had in mind.

As for the critics, they are far too professional to be thrown by catcalls and swoons and audience members yelling "gross" at inopportune moments. Still, it is perhaps inadvisable to invite busloads of fourteen-year-olds to a press performance of a Noël Coward play about a ménage à trois.

Bloomer Girl

When the 1944 musical comedy *Bloomer Girl* began its pre-Broadway tour in Philadelphia, it was hailed as the new *Oklahoma!* But a new *Oklahoma!* it wasn't, despite the presence of six stalwarts from the 1943 Rodgers and Hammerstein classic (choreographer Agnes de Mille; set designer Lemuel Ayres; costume designer Miles White; orchestrator Russell Bennett; and leading players Celeste Holm and Joan McCracken). *Bloomer Girl* came into town with a strong advance sale, received strong but not ecstatic reviews, and enjoyed a then-impressive 654-performance run.

Just after *Oklahoma!* settled in at the St. James, an agent named Nat Goldstone came across an unproduced play by Dan and Lillith James. Sensing that it had musical potential, he gave it to his client Harold Arlen, who agreed and sent it on to Yip Harburg. Harburg and Arlen had been collaborating on and off since 1932, with the hit-filled score of the 1939 film *The Wizard of Oz* among their credits.

Harburg had misgivings but eventually signed on. He typi-cally exerted control over as many aspects of his shows as he could get away with; in the case of *Bloomer Girl*, he received "Production Staged by" credit (although there was also a book director billed in smaller print). Harburg enlisted Hollywood screenwriter Sig Herzig to write the book. Herzig had a string of (mostly innocuous) credits, including work with Harburg on the films *Moonlight and Pretzels* (1933) and *Meet the Peo-*

> The book was the weak link, whimpering out when things grew serious in the second act. While 1944 audiences could and did sit through this sort of thing, it was hard going on 2001 audiences.

BLOOMER GIRL

BOOK BY
Sig Herzig and Fred Saidy
Based on a play by Dan and Lilith James

MUSIC BY	LYRICS BY
Harold Arlen	E. Y. Harburg

STARRING
Kate Jennings Grant Philip Bosco Kathleen Chalfant
Michael Park Anita Gillette Everett Bradley

AND
Jubilant Sykes

ALSO STARRING
Donna Lynne Champlin Herndon Lackey Ned Eisenberg
Merwin Goldsmith Mike Hartman Todd Hunter
Karine Plantadit-Bageot Nina Goldman Robert Wersinger

Deborah Allton Kate Baldwin Joe Cassidy Carson Church David de Jong Susan Derry
Roger DeWitt Donna Dunmire John Halmi Teri Hansen Joy Hermalyn
Cherylyn Jones Ann Kittredge Eddie Korbich Jason Lacayo Mary Kate Law
Lori MacPherson Michele Ragusa Vale Rideout Tim Salamandyk Gay Willis

The Coffee Club Orchestra
Rob Fisher, MUSICAL DIRECTOR

SCENIC CONSULTANT	COSTUME CONSULTANT	LIGHTING	SOUND
John Lee Beatty	Toni-Leslie James	Ken Billington	Scott Lehrer

CONCERT ADAPTATION	PRODUCTION STAGE MANAGER	ORIGINAL ORCHESTRATION	MUSICAL COORDINATOR
David Ives	Bonnie L. Becker	Robert Russell Bennett	Seymour Red Press

CASTING
Jay Binder

CHOREOGRAPHER
Rob Ashford

DIRECTED BY
Brad Rouse

Major sponsorship for *City Center Encores!* is provided by a grant from
AOL Time Warner, Inc.

The development of *Encores!* is assisted by seed support from The New York Times Company Foundation

Bloomer Girl is presented by arrangements with Tams-Witmark Music Library, Inc.
560 Lexington Avenue, New York, New York 10022

City Center 55th Street Theater Foundation, Inc. gratefully acknowledges the significant support it receives from the
New York City Department of Cultural Affairs including support through the Cultural Challenge Program

Baldwin Piano, Official Piano of City Center

Cast (in order of appearance)

Serena Applegate   Anita Gillette
Octavia   Michele Ragusa
Lydia   Joy Hermalyn
Julia   Ann Kittredge
Phoebe   Teri Hansen
Delia   Gay Willis
Daisy   Donna Lynne Champlin
Horatio Applegate   Philip Bosco
Gus   Ned Eisenberg
Evelina Applegate   Kate Jennings Grant
Joshua Dingle   Joe Cassidy
Herman Brasher   David de Jong
Ebenezer Mimms   Eddie Korbich
Wilfred Thrush   Tim Salamandyk
Hiram Crump   Roger DeWitt
Dolly Bloomer   Kathleen Chalfant
Jeff Calhoun   Michael Park
Pompey   Jubilant Sykes
Sheriff Quimby   Mike Hartman
Hamilton Calhoun   Herndon Lackey
Augustus   Todd Hunter
Alexander   Everett Bradley
Governor's Aide   Carson Church
Governor Newton   Merwin Goldsmith
Ballet soloists   Karine Plantadit-Bageot, Nina Goldman, Robert Wersinger, Todd Hunter
Suffragettes, sheriff's deputies, parade followers, and citizens of Cicero Falls   Deborah Allton, Kate Baldwin, Joe Cassidy, Carson Church, David de Jong, Susan Derry, Roger DeWitt, Donna Dunmire, John Halmi, Teri Hansen, Joy Hermalyn, Cherylyn Jones, Ann Kittredge, Eddie Korbich, Jason Lacayo, Mary Kate Law, Lori MacPherson, Michele Ragusa, Vale Rideout, Tim Salamandyk, Gay Willis

Place: Cicero Falls, New York
Time: The spring of 1861

*City Center Dedicates This Performance
to William Hammerstein*

ple (1944). Herzig brought along Fred Saidy, his collaborator on the latter. Saidy quickly became Harburg's theatrical partner, collaborating on the books for most of Harburg's subsequent musicals (beginning in 1947 with *Finian's Rainbow*).

The *Bloomer Girl* book was the weak link in the project, ranging from slight to creaky, and whimpering out when things grew serious in the second act. While 1944 audiences could and did sit through this sort of thing, it was hard going on 2001 audiences at City Center.

Things started off pleasantly enough, as a quintet of sisters awaited their traveling salesmen husbands with the quaint "When the Boys Come Home." (Quaint to us but substantially more relevant to audiences in the middle of World War II. By the final curtain, the husbands have enlisted in the Union Army—it's 1862—and the girls are singing "When the Boys Come Home" for real.) There then followed "Evelina," a lilting ballad of courtship. (Evelina is the sixth sister and obviously the sharpest of the lot.) In context, this ballad is decidedly satirical; Jeff Calhoun—not the choreographer of *Bells Are Ringing*, the Kentucky gentleman who sings it—thinks he's flirting with a housemaid when in fact he is being egged on by the heroine. Arlen set this to a deliciously tripping melody, with Harburg asking, "What's the use o' smellin' / Watermelon / Clingin' to another fella's vine?" This number played extremely well, but then came a concerted number in which the assembled characters "welcomed" the Kentucky gentleman into the family circle. This song was called "Welcome Hinges," as in "There'll be welcome hinges on the door," which leads to the question: Just what are welcome hinges? There'll also be welcome memories at the door, we're told, as well as welcome faces; all fell flat with the Encores! audience.

This was followed by a scene in "The Smoking Room." The five husbands of the five sisters sat around singing about life on the road. They didn't sit, actually; they stood on their marks, ranged across the stage apron, and haplessly paced in place. This to a song called "The Farmer's Daughter," in which the men confess their infidelities and discuss their methods of "seeking virgin territory." Yes, "farmer's daughter" jokes were a staple in the days of burlesque; but did Broadway audiences in 1944 just sit back and think, well of course those good old boys are naturally out cheating on their wives at every possible moment? Is this the good old American way? *Bloomer Girl* was a family musical, no less; did people think nothing of subjecting their wives and daughters to this? Maybe "It Was Good Enough for Grandma," to quote the title of the song that followed "The Farmer's Daughter," but it sure wasn't good enough for today's audience. Neither was the "Grandma" choreography, with the gals dancing around in circles as if they were churning pancake batter.

As if this all wasn't unfortunate enough, the next scene took place on the premises of a former bordello. Inevitably, each of the husbands of each of the daughters made an entrance, looking for the establishment's former residents. ("What are you doing here?") For a show that in its time made a stand for women's rights, this all seems somewhat backward from today's vantage point. After the one-two punch of "Welcome Hinges" and "The Farmer's Daughter," the audience pretty much gave up on the dialogue and sat back to listen to the music—which was the only reason to mount *Bloomer Girl* in the first place.

And something worthwhile immediately happened. Jubilant Sykes, an escaped slave, jumped out of the trunk in which he had been smuggled

from the South. That's the actor's name, Jubilant Sykes; the character was called Pompey. Pompey, it turned out, was owned by—guess who?—the man from Kentucky, who happened to be standing in the upstate New York ex-bordello when Sykes jumped out of the trunk. Talk about convenient dramaturgy.

Now, if you have a name like Jubilant Sykes, you'd better be pretty good. I first came across this fellow in May 1999 at a memorable Adam Guettel concert at Town Hall. Guettel did half of the singing himself—he's quite a performer—and he invited along a few folks to help.

People like Audra McDonald, Kristen Chenoweth, Jason Danieley, Annie Golden, and Billy Porter. Sitting on a stool among all these "theatre" people was Mr. Sykes, quietly minding his own business. Then Ms. McDonald started to sing Guettel's amazing "Come to Jesus." This is a very personal song—drawn from life, apparently—about a couple that breaks up after an abortion. Audra sang it with Guettel on her solo album

Way Back to Paradise, and Theresa McCarthy—who was also on the Town Hall stage that night—sang it with Guettel on the *Myths and Hymns* cast album. When it came time for Guettel to sing his part of "Come to Jesus" at Town Hall, Jubilant Sykes stood up instead, and he was positively mesmerizing. He also sang "Saturn Returns," in a deep, rich baritone unlike anything we've heard on Broadway.

Standing outside City Center before the start of *Bloomer Girl*, I ran into Frank Rich. We compared notes on what to expect of the evening, with talk coming around to "The Eagle and Me." This is a song about freedom, and it's a knockout. Arlen wrote a simple and jubilant banjo song, with the flavor of something you might have heard, at double speed, on the levee one hundred years earlier. Harburg followed suit, in a picturesque, freedom-lovin' mood. "Ever since that day / When the world was an onion / 'Twas natch'ral for the spirit to soar and play / The way the Lawd'a wanted it." "The Eagle and Me" is a favorite song of Frank's, and mine, and Stephen Sondheim's.

Back on the sidewalk before Encores!, we were talking about how much we liked "The Eagle and Me."

> Me: Wait until you hear this guy.
> Frank: Who's doing it?
> Me: A guy called Jubilant Sykes.
> Frank: Jubilant Sykes?
> Me: What a voice! You know that Adam Guettel concert at Town Hall a couple of years ago?
> Frank: I saw that.
> Me: Well, they had people like Audra and Chenoweth, and there was this guy with an amazing voice . . .
> Frank: . . . Who sang "Come to Jesus"? What a voice!

Right after all those bordello jokes, Sykes jumped out of his trunk, and it turned out that he can talk and act, too. He has an arresting stage presence; when he's onstage, you sit and watch and listen. He stopped the show cold with "The Eagle and Me." You didn't even mind that the choreographer had two chorus boys lift Sykes up and place him on a table downstage center in a spotlight for his final note. (Did the choreographer think that Sykes needed help to make the song work?)

> **Jubilant Sykes stopped the show cold with "The Eagle and Me." Listening to him sing about the bumblebee and the river and the eagle, I thought – Arlen would love this voice.**

Bloomer Girl
Opened: March 22, 2001
Closed: March 25, 2001
5 performances (and 0 previews)
Profit/Loss: Nonprofit
Bloomer Girl ($75 top) played the 2,684-seat City Center.
Box office figures not available.

*Critical
Scorecard*

Rave 0
Favorable 2
Mixed 1
Unfavorable 0
Pan 2

Listening to Sykes sing about the bumblebee and the river and the eagle, I thought—Arlen would love this voice. Late in the second act, someone—musical director Rob Fisher, I guess—had the radical idea of giving Sykes "Man for Sale," a number intended to be sung by a slave trader. This was perfect, in several ways. Sykes sang the song impeccably, as was to be expected. But having the slave sing the auctioneer's song added a layer of social commentary, accentuated by Sykes's diction; he used Harburg's trenchant words like a knife.

Arlen had written distinctive music since he came up with "Get Happy" ("Sing hallelujah, come on, get happy") in 1930. His early songs included "Stormy Weather," "I Gotta Right to Sing the Blues," "I've Got the World on a String," and—with Harburg—"It's Only a Paper Moon" and the *Wizard of Oz* score (including "Over the Rainbow"). As impressive as these songs are, his work became even richer when he started writing with Johnny Mercer in 1941, with a burst of creativity bringing forth "Blues in the Night," "One for My Baby (And One for the Road)," "Accent-u-ate the Positive," and "That Old Black Magic." He reunited with Harburg in 1944 for *Bloomer Girl*—Arlen's most successful show ever—but his music was somewhat less adventurous. The bluesy Arlen was evident only briefly; there's an exquisite sixteen-bar interlude in the "Liza Crossing the Ice" sequence that ranks with his most glorious work. (If you have a cast album on your shelf, it begins with "Oh, Lord, dis baby mus' be strong.")

Bloomer Girl proved an up-and-down sort of evening. The score is an entertaining one, with such minor treasures as "Evelina" and the ballad "Right as the Rain" (with intriguing "holds" written in) and "I Got a Song." There are a few too many ordinary songs, though, like "Welcome Hinges" and "Farmer's Daughter" and "Grandma" and "The Rakish

Young Man with the Whiskahs." As the evening wore on, these became hard to sit through—but there was always something worthwhile coming along.

Someone—director Brad Rouse? adapter David Ives?—came up with the idea of using placards alongside the proscenium to set the scenes. These were operated by a tired- and uninvolved-looking woman named Karine Plantadit-Bageot. After a while, it became clear that she was meant to be an oppressed slave—an intelligent and helpful decision. This paid off remarkably when the second act built to the climactic *Civil War Ballet*. As the number started with a distant, mournful bugle call, Ms. Plantadit-Bageot rose from her hard wooden stool and—with a swoop of her shoulders—brought the ballet to life. And the evening, too. The *Ballet*, which had not been heard in its full version in a half century, turned out to be quite marvelous. It was arranged by Trude Rittman, de Mille's rehearsal pianist, and meshed Arlen's music into a Coplandish terrain. (De Mille first gained prominence in 1942, with her choreography of Aaron Copland's *Rodeo*.)

Apart from Ms. Plantadit-Bageot and Mr. Sykes, the performances were somewhat muted. Michael Park did fairly well as the Kentucky suitor, and Everett Bradley (of the 1999 musical *Swing!*) turned up in the second act to do a knockout job on one song in one scene. (*Bloomer Girl* was the sort of creakily old-fashioned musical comedy where a character you'd never seen before could turn up late in the show, sing a showstopper like "I Got a Song," and go back to his dressing room.) But the main "stars" of the evening, Philip Bosco and Anita Gillette, were playing decidedly subsidiary roles; the actors playing their parts in the original production received seventh and sixth featured billing.

Back in 1944, Celeste Holm (as Evelina) was apparently charming enough to win over the most stony-faced theatregoer. She couldn't sing, especially; one opening-night critic suggested that Arlen "go after her with a machine gun." Holm was replaced by Nanette Fabray, who they say was magical in the role. This was one of those rare cases where a cast replacement job turned a performer into a star. Fabray was the biggest thing since Mary Martin, starring in four successive musical comedies. The final three failed, though, so Fabray left for Hollywood and was supplanted by the next big thing—a redhead named Gwen Verdon.

Encores! cast the part with Kate Jennings Grant, whose major musical roles had been in ill-fated revivals that never made it to town, a 1996 version of *Applause* and a 1999 version of Harburg's *Finian's Rainbow*. Grant was proficient as Evelina and under other circumstances might have proved capable; but she certainly didn't wrap the Encores! audience around her finger. Donna Lynne Champlin had the task of undertaking Joan McCracken's role of the chambermaid-turned-suffragette Daisy. This was apparently hysterical in 1944, in the hands of eccentric dancer-comedienne McCracken. Today, though, the material was mirthlessly un-funny, and poor Ms. Champlin had no option but to say the words and sing the lines.

Concert versions exist—and have proved unexpectedly popular—for a simple reason: they give musical theatre fans the chance to hear scores they are unlikely to hear otherwise. The trick is not only to do them well but also to select shows that audiences want to hear (or, upon hearing them, will be glad for the introduction). In that, the Encores! production of *Bloomer Girl* was totally successful. I, for one, would willingly travel miles and miles (or walk fourteen city blocks) to hear a full reconstruc-tion of any Harold Arlen score.

Judgment at Nuremberg

Abby Mann's *Judgment at Nuremberg* first appeared in 1959 as a television play, with a stellar cast (including Austrian actor Maximilian Schell). Producer-director Stanley Kramer brought *Judgment at Nuremberg* to the big screen in 1961, with Mann adapting his teleplay into a screenplay. (Mann won an Oscar for his efforts, as did Schell.) In 2001, Mann brought *Nuremberg* to Broadway, with Schell once more heading the cast. No awards, this time, and little acclaim. Why? Several reasons leap to mind. The medium; the stars; the time; and the times.

The Medium. The TV version was presented on the small screen, back in the days when the screen was still small. No HDTV; a close-up on a thirteen-inch screen was far from life-sized. Still, when the director wanted to make a point, he simply needed to instruct his cameraman. The film version, on the other hand, could magnify anyone or anything to the size of a barn wall. Do you want a bead of sweat rolling down someone's brow? Simple. But on the stage, in a boxy set, there's only so much you can do to direct the audience's attention where you want it to go. This is all the more relevant in a courtroom play, short on action and long on speeches.

A single actor standing on a Broadway stage can grab an audience and rivet their attention. Maximilian Schell simply seemed to turn on an inner spotlight, and we couldn't take our eyes off him.

That's not to say that a single, small actor standing on a Broadway stage can't grab an audience and rivet their attention. Mary-Louise Parker did it handily, at key moments, in *Proof*. The amazing Lily Tomlin did it

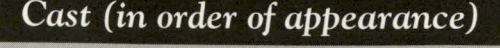

for two and a half hours in *The Search for Signs of Intelligent Life in the Universe.* Maximilian Schell, who spent most of the time during the stage production of *Nuremberg* sitting motionlessly in a courtroom chair downstage right, did it too; when his character had something to relate, Schell simply seemed to turn on an inner spotlight, and we couldn't take our eyes off him. But most of the other actors onstage with him didn't, or couldn't. They were just actors talking, which brings us to:

The Stars. The original *Nuremberg* had Claude Rains as the judge; Melvyn Douglas as the prosecutor; Paul Lukas as the main defendant; and the up-and-coming Schell as the defense attorney. The film version had Spencer Tracy as the judge; Richard Widmark as the prosecutor; Burt Lancaster as the main defendant; and Schell, again, as the defense attorney. (Schell beat out Tracy for the Best Actor Oscar.) Joining them in smaller roles were people with names like Dietrich and Garland and Clift, attracted by the importance of the project, the reputation of the director, and the ability to film their brief scenes, go home, and—in the case of Garland and Clift—pick up quick, confidence-boosting Oscar nominations.

The stage version had George Grizzard as the judge; Robert Foxworth as the prosecutor; Schell as the main defendant; and Michael Hayden as the defense attorney—nobody whom the average person in the food court of the shopping mall would recognize. The National Actors Theatre, with its low salaries and low profile (compared with, say, the Roundabout or Lincoln Center Theater), attracted little star power; Schell, who hadn't been on the Broadway stage since starring in John Osborne's A Patriot for Me in 1969, came along for sentimental reasons. Admittedly, a property like Judgment at Nuremberg shouldn't need stars to draw an audience. Would the film have been made, though, without bankable names like Kramer and Tracy and Laurence Olivier (who was replaced at the last minute by Lancaster)? Not too likely. It was a personal statement, and an act of courage, for a major star like Tracy to sign on to Judgment at Nuremberg in 1961; somewhat akin to Tom Hanks appearing in Philadelphia in 1993. In 2001, Nuremberg is no longer an act of courage; it's simply another retelling of the same old, horrible story. Diminished by the passing of:

Time. A controversial television play, two years later, can easily remain controversial. Wait another forty years, and the impact may well be diminished. Since Mann's story was first told in 1959 and 1961, the subject has been recycled in hundreds of other films and plays and TV shows. Yes, there are still new revelations and accusations and lawsuits stemming from the Nazi regime, with frequent new books and exposés. The subject is still newsworthy, but it no longer has the emotional pull it did when the conversation first began.

Images of murder have become standard fare on the front page and the evening newscast, and the morning newscast as well. With crimes against humanity commonplace, how could *Judgment at Nuremberg* be expected to raise many hackles?

And there's the question of the audience. Just about everyone who saw Nuremberg in 1959 or 1961 had lived through World War II. (This was not a movie for kids.) At some point—when the concentration camps were liberated, during the Nuremberg trials, or maybe not until they sat down to watch Stanley Kramer's film—they learned the truth of what happened in the concentration camps. One can only imagine the initial impact, on people who lived through this period, of the realization that civilized man was capable of such inhumanity.

As for the sensitivity of the subject at the time, it seems trivial to report that the phrase "gas ovens" was bleeped out of the 1959 broadcast. (The telecast was sponsored by the American Gas Association, who found this misleading; the Nazis used cyanide gas, they explained, not cooking gas.) In 2001, the stage *Nuremberg* had virtually no shock value. How could it? Not only because of the passing of time, but because of:

The Times. The changing times, that is. Two years after the release of the film, a ladies dress manufacturer named Zapruder turned his home movie camera on a motorcade in Dallas. Since then, images of death— images of murder—have become standard fare on the front page and the evening newscast, and the morning newscast as well. Now you can see the latest atrocity every half hour—complete with special graphics and spooky music—as well as made-for-TV specials glorifying the latest atrocity in order to peddle soap and soda. There is still a shock value to each of these horrible events, but it wears off after a week or so and leaves the mass market ready for the next event (that is, unless a relative or friend is among the dead, in which case you live with it forever and may well become cynical about the public reaction to the next such tragedy).

The happenings at Aushwitz and Dachau were special cases, of course, unparalleled for their inhumanity. But since 1993, there has been a new set of Nuremberg trials before the International Criminal Tribunal for the Former Yugoslavia at the Hague, and how many people have been paying attention? As the National Actors Theatre production rehearsed and previewed and opened, former Yugoslav president Slobodan Milosevic was hunkered down in his fortified compound doing his best to stay out of jail free. Was there a clamoring for him to be brought to justice, as if he was a Goering or a Goebbels or an Eichmann? No. To many Americans, it all seemed like some sort of faraway political struggle, with dictatorial leaders and stolen millions in Swiss banks. With crimes against humanity commonplace, how could *Judgment at Nuremberg* be expected to raise many hackles?

> "The audience that goes to see *Judgment at Nuremberg* already knows [what happened]. The ones who need to know don't go to see *Judgment at Nuremberg*."

When I expressed the lack of impact of this production, my father-in-law—who escaped from Vienna in 1935, when he was thirteen—asked,

"But don't you think that audiences today need to know such things?" He immediately answered his own question. "But the audience that goes to see *Judgment at Nuremberg* already knows. The ones who need to know don't go to see *Judgment at Nuremberg*."

If the play was—from the first—pretty much uninvolving, there was some first-rate work on the stage of the Longacre. Schell is a marvelous actor, and he gave a marvelous performance. As a respected jurist who served in a Nazi-era post equivalent to the U.S. attorney general, he looked somewhat pained by the accusations and the trial and—ultimately—the truth: "If we didn't know—it's because we didn't want to know." (Did Schell also look pained because he underwent an emergency appendectomy on March 10, during previews?)

George Grizzard, too, was excellent. An actor of great charm, he seems to have improved over the years. Here, and in his Tony Award–winning performance in the 1996 revival of *A Delicate Balance*, he seems to be doing the best work he has ever done. In an early scene, Grizzard—as Judge Haywood—was touring downtown Nuremberg. "Hard to believe it really happened," he says to his military guide (Ty Jones). "Not for me. I grew up in Texas," is the reply. "Can I imagine that the people there would have done things like this if there wasn't a government to stop them and they might be punished? I guess a day doesn't pass when I don't wonder about that." Grizzard gave a pained, almost horrified look here, saying more in his silence than he possibly could in words. And his character was never quite the same again; he seemed to carry that moment with him for the rest of the evening.

Most surprising, perhaps, was Michael Hayden in the role originally created by Schell. Hayden is best known hereabouts for his problematic Billy Bigelow in the Nicholas Hytner production of *Carousel* (London, 1993; New York, 1994). Problematic in that he acted the role admirably

Judgment at Nuremberg
Opened: March 26, 2001
Closed: May 13, 2001
56 performances (and 45 previews)
Profit/Loss: Nonprofit [Loss]
Judgment at Nuremberg ($75 top) was scaled to a potential
    gross of $487,042 at the 1,079-seat Longacre. Weekly
    grosses averaged about $160,000, hitting $179,000 in the
    first full week of previews but falling into the $150,000
    range after the opening. Total gross for the run was
    $2,025,590. Attendance was about 53 percent, with the
    box office grossing about 33 percent of dollar-capacity.
    (These figures are not indicative, as the potential was
    calculated at the top ticket price, but subscribers paid
    less.)

TONY AWARD NOMINATIONS
Best Performance by a Featured Actor: Michael Hayden
Best Performance by a Featured Actress: Marthe Keller

*Critical
Scorecard*

Rave 1
Favorable 3
Mixed 0
Unfavorable 1
Pan 5

but was ill suited to sing the songs. Hayden more than redeemed himself, though, as a replacement in the 1998 revival of *Cabaret*. He took on the role of Cliff Bradshaw, the American protagonist of the story, and is the only actor I've ever seen who has been able to make sense of the role. There was actually a real relationship between his Cliff and Susan Egan's Sally Bowles, which helped the show immeasurably. Hayden gave a fine performance in *Nuremberg*, looking and acting uncannily like a young Schell. There was also an especially affecting performance by Michael Mastro, in Montgomery Clift's role as the baker's assistant who underwent a forced sterilization.

The Playbill contained, in large bold-faced letters, "A Note from the Playwright." *Nuremberg* is long closed, but I think it fitting that the words be preserved:

On December 31, 2000, President Clinton signed the Rome Treaty for an International Criminal Court. "In taking this action, we join more than 130 other countries to reaffirm our strong support for international accountability and for bringing to justice perpetrators of genocide, war crimes, crimes against humanity. The United States has a long history of commitment to the principle of accountability based on our involvement in the Nuremberg tribunals that brought Nazi war criminals to justice."

Senator Jesse Helms of North Carolina called Mr. Clinton's decision "as outrageous as it is inexplicable. I have a message for the outgoing President. This decision will not stand."

General George Lee Butler, Jack Kirk, Admirals Eugene Carol and Stansford Turner and former Defense Secretary Robert McNamara support the treaty, saying it could serve to seek a more humane world and offer the hope of justice to millions and would make a profound contribution in deterring egregious human rights abuses worldwide.

—Abby Mann, 2001

The Invention of Love

William Goldman, in his 1969 book *The Season*, defined what he called the "Snob Hit." More or less, it is a sophisticated play that gets great reviews on Broadway and sells a lot of tickets (for a sophisticated play). Only a few people like it, and even fewer understand it. The play must be British, Goldman tells us; it must be at least partially unintelligible; and "the audience that goes to the Snob Hit must be convinced that the 'average' theatregoer wouldn't understand it." Goldman was not writing about Tom Stoppard's *The Invention of Love*, not back in 1969. (He did point out, though, that most Snob Hits incorporate "poets, clerics, historical figures from various ages"). Goldman was discussing Stoppard's *Rosencrantz and Guildenstern Are Dead*.

Before we proceed, let me say two things. First, the determination that a play is a Snob Hit does not necessarily signify that it isn't also a good play. *Rosencrantz*, in retrospect, is pretty good. Second, *The Invention of Love* had plenty to offer, even if it was a Snob Hit.

In a way, *Rosencrantz*—Stoppard's first play to reach London—upended the British theatre. John Osborne emerged in 1956 with *Look Back in Anger*, Harold Pinter in 1958 with *The Birthday Party*. With the appearance of Stoppard's *Rosencrantz* in 1967, this made quite a heady eleven years. If Osborne's work was angry and Pinter's cryptic, Stoppard seemed more interested in words and ideas and comedy. Born in Czechoslovakia in 1937 as Tomáš Straussler, Stoppard moved to Singapore with his family when he was two. When the Japanese invaded Singapore, he fled with his mother to India; his father was killed in the invasion. In 1945, his mother married a major in the British army named Stoppard, and Tom first moved to England the following year, when he was nine.

All of which is to say: English was a second language to Stoppard, the most verbally pyrotechnical English-language playwright since Shaw. (Stoppard grew up—and was schooled—in English-speaking countries, however.) Choosing not to go to university, Stoppard became a reporter at the age of seventeen. By 1958 he was a theatre critic, and in 1960 he started to write plays.

Rosencrantz—which started out as something called *Rosencrantz and Guildenstern Meet King Lear*—was first performed by students of the Oxford Theatre Group in 1966. The National Theatre produced it in London in April 1967, and it was an instant hit. ("The most important event in the British professional theatre of the last nine years," per London's *Sunday Times*.) American producer David Merrick scooped it up and imported it to New York in October 1967, where it became an even greater success. *Rosencrantz* won the Tony Award and the Drama Critics Circle Award and became the biggest Snob Hit in years.

Stoppard's next major full-length play was *Jumpers*, a tale of academic acrobatics, which opened in London in 1972. The February 1974 American premiere at Kennedy Center was perceived to be so important that it received nationwide coverage. A Broadway transfer that April, though, created not a whimper and suffered a quick and undeserving failure. (I was peripherally involved with the American *Jumpers*, which might explain why it is among my very favorite Stoppard plays. Brian Bedford gave a remarkable performance, which remains a golden memory.) The producers sabotaged themselves; they didn't commit to the move to New York until much too late, as a result of which they opened at the tail end of the season with virtually no advertising, publicity, or advance sale.

The determination that a play is a Snob Hit does not necessarily signify that it isn't also a good play.

I have been continually reminded of *Jumpers* over the last two years, thanks to an ongoing story in the *New York Times* about the ongoing battle between the New Jersey Division of Fish, Game and Wildlife and an eccentric lady who runs her very own tiger preserve in Princeton. It seems that a 431-pound tiger was found roaming on Route 537. Not my tiger, said the Tiger Lady of New Jersey, who had twenty-two other Bengals roaming her property. The state inspected and has been trying to shut her down ever since. What, you may ask, has this to do with *Jumpers*? The cast included a girl on a flying trapeze, hanging by her teeth, twirling like a top, stark naked. The role was played, in Washington and New York, by

LYCEUM THEATRE

Ⓢ A Shubert Organization Theatre

Gerald Schoenfeld, Chairman   Philip J. Smith, President

Robert E. Wankel, Executive Vice President

LINCOLN CENTER THEATER

under the direction of

ANDRÉ BISHOP and BERNARD GERSTEN

presents

THE INVENTION OF LOVE

A new play by TOM STOPPARD

with *(in alphabetical order)*

DANIEL DAVIS	ANDREW McGINN
NEAL DODSON	PETER McROBBIE
RICHARD EASTON	MATTHEW FLOYD MILLER
MIREILLE ENOS	CAITLIN MUELDER
JULIAN GAMBLE	MARK NELSON
DAVID HARBOUR	GUY PAUL
PAUL HECHT	MARTIN RAYNER
BRIAN HUTCHISON	PETER A. SMITH
BYRON JENNINGS	MICHAEL STUHLBARG
AARON KROHN	DAVID TURNER
ROBERT SEAN LEONARD	JEFF WEISS

Sets and Costumes BOB CROWLEY

Lighting BRIAN MacDEVITT   Sound SCOTT LEHRER

Original Music BOB JAMES   Hair/Wigs DAVID BRIAN BROWN

Stage Manager SUSIE CORDON   Casting DANIEL SWEE

Director of Development HATTIE K. JUTAGIR   Director of Marketing & Special Projects THOMAS COTT

General Manager STEVEN C. CALLAHAN   Production Manager JEFF HAMLIN

Directed by JACK O'BRIEN

The scenic design for *The Invention of Love* is made possible in part by a generous grant from the Henry Nias Foundation.
Thanks to the Theatre Development Fund for its support of this production.

AMERICAN AIRLINES is the official airline of Lincoln Center Theater.
KENDALL-JACKSON is the preferred winery of Lincoln Center Theater.

The producers and theater management are members of the League of American Theatres and Producers, Inc.

The Invention of Love issue of Lincoln Center Theater Review
is available at stands located throughout the theater.

Cast (in order of appearance)

A. E. Housman, aged 77   Richard Easton

Charon   Jeff Weiss

A. E. Housman, aged 18–26   Robert Sean Leonard

Alfred William Pollard   Michael Stuhlbarg

Moses John Jackson   David Harbour

Mark Pattison/W. T. Stead   Peter McRobbie

Walter Pater/Frank Harris   Martin Rayner

John Ruskin/Jerome K. Jerome   Paul Hecht

Benjamin Jowett/Henry Labouchère   Byron Jennings

Robinson Ellis/John Percival Postgate   Guy Paul

Katharine Housman   Mireille Enos

Chamberlain   Mark Nelson

Chairman of Selection Committee   Andrew McGinn

Oscar Wilde/Bunthorne   Daniel Davis

Ensemble   Neal Dodson, Brian Hutchison, Matthew Floyd Miller, Peter A. Smith, David Turner

this very same Tiger Lady (who even then had a "cat" or two). Joan Byron was her stage name; at the time she was married to Jan Marasek, one of Broadway's finest prop men. Was she a little strange? Well, let's just say that when the tiger story first appeared in 1999, I wasn't at all surprised.

Stoppard's next play, *Travesties*, was one of his most successful. It opened in London in June 1974—right after the Broadway *Jumpers* closed—and came to Broadway that October, where it won the Tony Award and the Drama Critics Circle Award and became the biggest Snob Hit since *Rosencrantz*. (In this, William Goldman was slightly mistaken. He decreed that there could be only one Snob Hit per author, on the theory that audiences baffled by the first would boycott the second.) *Night and Day* (London, 1978; New York, 1979) was far less successful, despite the presence of Maggie Smith. *The Real Thing* (London, 1982; New York, 1984), though, was Stoppard's first accessible Broadway play. Yes, he once again won the Tony and Drama Critics Awards, but it was no Snob Hit. American audiences enjoyed *The Real Thing*, rather than simply being impressed by it.

Stoppard then began to cool off, stateside. His 1988 play *Artist Descending a Staircase* was produced at the Helen Hayes with negligible results in 1989. He did not have another major New York appearance until the 1994–1995 season, when Lincoln Center Theater mounted both his 1988 play *Hapgood* (at their off-Broadway venue, the Mitzi Newhouse) and his 1993 play *Arcadia* (at the Vivian Beaumont). These were especially well received and probably could have successfully transferred to open-ended runs had schedules permitted. *Indian Ink*, which opened in London in 1995, has still not made it to Broadway. It is an unlikely prospect, dealing as it does with the end of British colonial rule in India.

And then came *The Invention of Love*, which opened in London in 1997. Lincoln Center Theater had the good sense to place this study of poet-classicist A. E. Housman in the hands of Jack O'Brien, who had directed their production of *Hapgood*. O'Brien, artistic director of the Old Globe Theatre in San Diego since 1981, has proven himself highly capable in all fields, doing intelligent work on new plays, classics, and musicals. He started his career on Broadway in 1972, with a failure so devastating that he hightailed it out of town (and eventually landed in San Diego). O'Brien was a protégé of Ellis Rabb, the actor-director who ran the APA repertory company. Rabb chose O'Brien to write the lyrics for an exceedingly odd musical called *The Selling of the President*. After Rabb departed and book problems developed, O'Brien was drafted as colibrettist. After the director was fired, O'Brien—who had no Broadway experience—ended up directing it, too. So simply by standing around and trying to help out, O'Brien found himself credited as lyricist-librettist-director of a five-performance turkey at the Shubert. As it happened, few people even noticed *The Selling of the President*, and it was quickly forgotten—except, I suppose, by Jack.

It's one thing to keep up with a playwright who stays two steps ahead of you. It's quite another to follow a brilliant lecturer when you neglected to read your homework.

O'Brien made occasional Broadway visits over the years—the 1976 revival of *Porgy and Bess*, the 1994 revival of *Damn Yankees*—but it took *The Full Monty* to establish him as a Broadway "name." Five months later, *The Invention of Love* came along and further impressed the folks on

The Invention of Love
Opened: March 29, 2001
Closed: June 30, 2001
108 performances (and 31 previews)
Profit/Loss: Nonprofit [Profit]
The Invention of Love ($60 top) was scaled to a potential
gross of $404,321 at the 906-seat Lyceum. Weekly grosses
averaged about $226,000, building to $250,000 at Tony
time and hitting a high of $299,000 in the final week.
Total gross for the run was $3,918,862. Attendance was
about 83 percent, with the box office grossing about 56
percent of dollar-capacity. (These figures are not
indicative, as the potential was calculated at the top
ticket price, but subscribers paid less.)

*Critical
Scorecard*

Rave 7
Favorable 1
Mixed 0
Unfavorable 2
Pan 0

TONY AWARD NOMINATIONS
Best Play: Tom Stoppard
Best Performance by a Leading Actor: Richard Easton
(WINNER)
Best Performance by a Featured Actor: Robert Sean Leonard
(WINNER)
Best Direction of a Play: Jack O'Brien
Best Scenic Design: Bob Crowley

NEW YORK DRAMA CRITICS CIRCLE AWARD
Best Play: Tom Stoppard (WINNER)

DRAMA DESK AWARDS
Outstanding Actor: Richard Easton (WINNER)
Outstanding Director of a Play: Jack O'Brien (WINNER)
Outstanding Set Design of a Play: Bob Crowley (WINNER)

Forty-fifth Street. O'Brien was the first person to receive twin Tony nominations as director of a play and a musical since—well, since 1999–
2000, when Michael Blakemore did it. Blakemore won both awards,
O'Brien won neither; but his work, especially on *Invention of Love*, was
wonderfully creative.

The critics, almost unanimously, loved this play (another hallmark of
the Snob Hit). Ben Brantley in the *Times* offered high praise, calling it a
"time-traveling fantasia about art, history, memory and homosexuality"
while adding the "the play has a breadth of historical and cultural allusion
to make Mr. Stoppard's *Travesties* (the one with James Joyce and Tristan
Tzara) seem like *Sesame Street*." Clive Barnes in the *Post* called it "a
magnificently funny play, but as fleshily layered as an onion, ideas wrap-
ping around ideas, thoughts jousting at thoughts, all jigging into place
like a crazy-quilt collage to offer a picture of English life at the beginning

of the 20th century." Linda Winer in *Newsday* called it "an enchanting, achingly articulate conundrum about the sexual repression that split one 19th century British soul into equal parts devastating reason and lyric melancholy," with Howard Kissel in the *Daily News* adding that "the calisthenics Stoppard provides for the cerebrum leave you giddy and exhilarated."

Did somebody say "Snob Hit"?

That's a good line from Mr. Brantley about *Sesame Street*, and particularly apt. The Playbill included eight dense pages about Housman and Wilde and Ruskin and Pater and Jowett and Pattison and Jerome and Harris and Labouchère and Postgate and Hardinge and Milner and Waugh—some of these guys weren't even mentioned in the play—and Richards and Robinson and Lucan and de la Mare and Plato and D'Oyly Carte (who was in the film *Topsy-Turvy*) and Stead, the editor of the *Pall Mall Gazette* who died on the *Titanic*. The boat, not the musical.

I, for one, don't mind "calisthenics for the cerebrum." I like to be challenged, actually; there's nothing so invigorating as a theatrical evening that keeps you on your toes. But it's one thing to keep up with a playwright who stays two steps ahead of you. It's quite another to follow a brilliant lecturer when you neglected to read your homework. *The Invention of Love* was like a brilliant lecture, where the lecturer neglected to assign the reading in the first place. And, mind you, I read *The Invention of Love* before seeing it.

Did you have to understand all the allusions to enjoy *The Invention of Love*? No, of course not. But would knowledge of the personalities and the history have made a difference? Absolutely. I found *The Invention of Love* to be memorable and engrossing. I thought that O'Brien's direction added layers of clarity, and I thought that Bob Crowley's set was a marvel. But I always felt like I was watching a play, listening and processing material; ob-

PLAYBILL

LYCEUM THEATRE

THE INVENTION OF LOVE

serving the experience of the play, never caught up in it—like I was at *Copenhagen* or *Proof* or the 2000 revival of *The Real Thing* or *Arcadia*.

Most of the critics wildly loved *The Invention of Love*, resulting in a clutch of "money reviews" capable of attracting a significantly substantial audience (although not the same audience that went to *The Producers* or even Neil Simon's *The Dinner Party*). Ten days later, the limited engagement (through May 27) was converted to an open-ended run. The show's five Tony Award nominations, oddly enough, caused the grosses to drop slightly. *The Invention of Love* won two Tony Awards on June 3—for Best Actor (Richard Easton) and Best Supporting Actor (Robert Sean Leonard)—but on June 13 it was announced that the show would close after all, on June 30. So much for the power of the Tony Awards, at least under these circumstances.

I would guess that LCT made a very wise decision to close when it did, facing what was surely a very lean July with little advance sale. While this would seem an obvious course of action, the 2000–2001 season saw at least seven shows that prolonged their runs (and their losses) past endurance. As for *The Invention of Love*, it was quite an achievement artistically, and passionately loved by many theatregoers, and all in all highly satisfying. So give it—and Lincoln Center Theatre and Jack O'Brien—a gold star.

> **I always felt like I was watching a play, listening and processing material; observing the experience of the play, never caught up in it—like I was at *Copenhagen* or *Proof*.**

Much of the action in the play involved three men in a boat—different sets of three men in a boat, actually—and one of the characters (and one of the men in one of the boats) was the nineteenth-century humorist Jerome K. Jerome. Stoppard has featured Jerome in the past, and I imagine he must have good reason. So if you'll excuse me, I'm finally off to read Jerome's *Three Men in a Boat*. Only a little too late to help with Housman and *The Invention of Love*.

Stones in His Pockets

The filming of a Hollywood blockbuster, as seen through the eyes of two extras on location in a provincial Irish village; fifteen characters performed by a cast of two. *Stones in His Pockets* sounded like it had to be pretty good, or pretty bad. The Irish actors were unknown in America, and the author was unknown, and the director was unknown (except to his wife, the author); still, the show managed to grab a Forty-fifth Street house in the midst of a severe booking jam. So *Stones in His Pockets* sounded like it had to be pretty good.

On top of which, look at this sampling of snappy one-word critical quotes from the London engagement: "Stunning!" "Spellbinding!" "Fascinating!" "Heartfelt!" "Hysterical!" "Irresistible!" And no, these weren't culled from little local giveaway journals; they were from the major critics in the major papers. *Stones in His Pockets* had to be pretty good, unless it was simply another example of the "what strange tastes these English have" syndrome.

It turned out that the advance word was pretty much on the mark. While I wouldn't suggest that other budding playwrights rush to their word processors and start processing multicharacter, two-actor plays set in provincial Irish villages, Marie Jones hit upon a wonderful idea, executed it delightfully, and found two performers who could handle it all impeccably.

Jake and Charlie are extras, satisfied to pick up forty quid a day (plus catered meals and desserts) as "background bog man." Simon is first assis-

Charlie Conlon   Conleth Hill
Jake Quinn   Seán Campion

GOLDEN THEATRE
Ⓢ A Shubert Organization Theatre
Gerald Schoenfeld, *Chairman*   Philip J. Smith, *President*

Robert E. Wankel, *Executive Vice President*

Paul Elliott, Adam Kenwright, Pat Moylan
Ed and David Mirvish, and Azenberg/Pittelman

Present

SEÁN CAMPION   **CONLETH HILL**

in

STONES IN HIS POCKETS

By
MARIE JONES

Design
Jack Kirwan

Lighting Design
James McFetridge

Production Manager
Patrick Molony

Technical Supervision
Unitech

Production Stage Manager
David O'Brien

Casting
Jay Binder, CSA

Associate Producer
Michael Fuchs

Press Representative
Boneau / Bryan-Brown

Executive Producers
**David Bownes
Ginger Montel**

General Manager
Abbie M. Strassler

Directed by
IAN McELHINNEY

The American production of STONES IN HIS POCKETS is sponsored in part by Allied Irish Bank and Aer Lingus.

tant director. Aisling is second assistant, and she apparently assists Simon after hours as well. Mickey is one of the few surviving extras from the filming of *The Quiet Man*, the 1952 Hollywood blockbuster starring John Wayne and Maureen O'Hara shot on location in the same provincial Irish village. Caroline Giovanni is the star of the present-day film—*Quiet Valley*—and apparently as big a Hollywood star as you can imagine. John is her dialect coach. Sean Harkin, Jake's young second cousin, is a drug addict. (All the locals seem to be cousins of Jake.) Finn is a childhood friend of Sean. Dave is a Cockney offering coke ("coke," not Coke). Jock is Caroline's security man. Clem is the director. Brother Gerard is Sean's former teacher. Mr. Harkin is Sean's father (and Jake's cousin). Kevin is an interviewer.

Ms. Jones's plot would handily serve as a soap opera. In fact, the whole thing *was* a soap opera, except for the theatrical tour de force of playing it with a two-man cast. Jake and Charlie were our hosts, as it were, and the only characters listed in the Playbill. Jake was just back from America, were he subsisted by tending bar and waiting tables. Unwilling to marry and settle down to a life of working three jobs at once to survive, he fled back home to his Ma. Charlie was in exile from Ballycastle, where the video store he owned went bust in face of opposition from the local equivalent of Blockbuster. (His girlfriend left him, too, for the manager of the new store.) Caroline, who has "a habit of going ethnic" on location, picks up Jake at the local bar and attempts to seduce him. ("I'm not just here to exploit the beauty of the land, I love it," she says, flouncing her curls.) Tragedy hits at the first-act curtain, as we learn that young Sean, the cousin-addict, has killed himself. When he didn't drown on his first attempt, he walked to the shore, put "stones in his pockets," and went back into the lake.

It turns out that Sean was rejected by everyone and everything—not only by Jake and Caroline but by life and the land as well. His funeral interrupts the filming schedule, leading to some philosophical discussion about the natives selling off their dignity and hopes in exchange for the money brought by on-location filming (and the resulting boost to tourism). But the whole thing acts as a bulletin board upon which to hang some juicy snapshots.

And juicy these snapshots were. The play began and ended with Jake (Seán Campion) and Charlie (Conleth Hill). Jake was the more likable of the two, no doubt by design. As the evening progressed, the pair instantaneously switched into various characters. Simon (Hill) and Aisling (Campion), the assistant director and his assistant, were in a world apart; I suppose Ms. Jones could next try a Simon and Aisling show if she pleased, although I'd hate to see anyone other than Mr. Campion play Ms. Aisling. Campion followed with Mickey, so stooped that he looked angular. (On the set of *The Quiet Man*, John Wayne always referred to him as "wee Mickey.")

By this point, you might easily guess which of the two actors won the 2001 Olivier Award for Best Actor, but you'd have guessed wrong. Caroline Giovanni, the Hollywood superstar, soon walked in. No, she didn't

Stones in His Pockets
Opened: April 1, 2001
Closed: September 23, 2001
198 performances (and 11 previews)
Profit/Loss: Profit

Stones in His Pockets ($70 top) was scaled to a potential
gross of $361,622 at the 804-seat Golden. (These figures
include the post-opening price increase from $65.) Weekly
grosses averaged about $197,000, building to almost
$280,000 in the weeks after the opening but falling to
the $160,000s by the end of the summer. Total gross for
the run was $5,141,100. Attendance was about 69
percent, with the box office grossing about 55 percent of
dollar-capacity.

TONY AWARD NOMINATIONS
Best Performance by a Leading Actor: Seán Campion
Best Performance by a Leading Actor: Conleth Hill
Best Direction of a Play: Ian McElhinney

DRAMA DESK AWARDS
Special Award for their performances: Seán Campion and
Conleth Hill (WINNERS)

*Critical
Scorecard*

Rave 3
Favorable 4
Mixed 0
Unfavorable 2
Pan 1

walk; she kind of floated, lazily rubbing her (invisible) curls against her shoulders like a kitten that had just learned to preen. This was Mr. Hill, wearing the same cloddish costume he wore throughout the evening. No wig, no dress, nothing but acting. During the seduction of Jake, she/he lounged on a couch (a trunk, actually) looking like one of those odalisques by Ingres. Later on she prepared a cup of coffee—lots of sugar, lots of cream—and served it to Jake, and I don't think we've seen anything like it since the banquet scene in *Tom Jones*. As you watched, you suddenly remembered—oh, yes, that *is* a man.

Hill's Caroline was priceless, as were two other of his mini-portraits. One was Jock, who looked less like a security man named Jock than a sailor man named Popeye, complete with the impossibly bulging chest and the swaggering strut. Where did Hill get that chest, anyway? Just arching his chest and pulling back his shoulders, I guess, but it sure looked like an overstuffed shirt. And he also created Clem Curtis, one of those overripe British film directors. Hill's Clem staggered around the set, belly first, looking like a combination of Charles Laughton and Herbert Marshall. Quite a card, he was.

Campion's Jake served as the center of the evening, but how could he possibly compete with Hill? There was a reason for this, it turns out. Ms.

Jones—a prolific playwright and actress—initially wrote *Stones in His Pocket* for Hill. Half the characters, anyway, with their lines and actions molded on Hill's voice and body. The play was first performed in Belfast in 1994, without Campion or director McElhinney. When Jones decided to rework the material four years later, she went back to Hill, who recommended Campion for the project. The new *Stones* opened in Belfast in May 1999 and worked its way to a fringe production at the hundred-seat Tricycle Theatre in London. The vast acclaim resulted in a quick transfer to the West End, followed by worldwide success.

Hill and Campion were well mated; I don't suppose you could find a better pair of actors for this play. They were so good that they—a pair of small-time Irish actors—could go all the way from Belfast to Dublin to the fringes of London to the West End to Broadway. They—and Jones— were helped along by the understated work of designer Jack Kirwan and director McElhinney. As you filed into the theatre, you saw an almost bare stage, with a sky blue cyc painted with overstuffed, fluffy white clouds. Along the upstage ledge were sixty-odd scruffy shoes, lined up in pairs. Also on stage were a trunk and a cube, suitable for use as furniture, props, and what have you. As the show progressed, they brought on the rest of the trappings: two folding camp stools, with canvas seats. Out of this, Jones and Campion and Hill and McElhinney built their own little universe, including two grandly exhilarating choreographic sequences. One came in the first act, during the "filming" of a scene in which the extras were instructed to follow nonexistent galloping horses with their eyes. (You had to be there, I guess.) Later, Campion and Hill put on a step-dancing exhibition with more laughs, in ninety seconds, than *Riverdance* managed in two hours.

In the end, Charlie and Jake concoct a screenplay of their own, "about a film being made and a young lad commits suicide. In other words, the stars become the extras and the extras become the stars." They pitch this to director Clem, who turns them down. "It's not commercial enough," he says, and he's probably right. Marie Jones, though, had the good sense to turn her idea into a play rather than a screenplay, and she surely raked in far more in royalties than she'd have gotten from a movie sale. She also left many **The story acts as a bulletin board upon which to hang some juicy snapshots. And juicy these snapshots were.** thousands of delighted theatregoers in her wake, and for this she well deserved her Olivier Award for Best Comedy. Which resulted, ultimately, in a movie sale for her cartoonish romp in which "the stars become the extras and the extras become the stars."

And then there were the cows. *Stones in His Pockets* was filled with cows, and not only in the artwork. Sean Harkin's father had to sell off his land—and lose his cows—to make ends meet. The cows herding in the field have been replaced by the extras herding in the same field, nodding their heads and rolling in the soil for forty quid a day. ("Just keep your head down and go where they put you," old-timer Mickey tells Charlie.) Sean, as a child, had written a veritable encomium to cows, which are "more useful than humans" because "you can get meat from them, then you can get milk and butter and they even make good school bags." The loss of the cows symbolized Sean's loss of life: "As he walked into the water to die the last thing he would have seen were the cows, the cows that should have been his future in the field looking at him." (Clem, the director of *Quiet Valley*, is not happy with the cows on location because "they're not Irish enough.") The opening shot of the screenplay that Jake and Charlie envision is "cows, every inch of screen, cows. Cows, just cows and in the middle of it all these trendy designer trailers, sinkin' into a big mound of steaming cow clap."

Hill and Campion were so good that they—a pair of small-time Irish actors—could go all the way from Belfast to Dublin to the fringes of London to the West End of Broadway.

All these cows, in the ads and in the play and staring at you from the cover of the Playbill, and *Stones in His Pockets* came to town at the height of an outbreak of mad cow disease. Hmmm.

Follies

All right. Thirty years ago, Ben was dating Phyllis. Ben was sleeping with Phyllis's roommate, Sally. Ben loved Sally. (This last is hazy, as love to Ben is a four-letter word). Ben married Phyllis. Sally, on the rebound, married Ben's buddy, Buddy. Thirty years later, they are all unhappily married. Meeting once more, Sally still wants Ben. Ben still wants Sally. (This is hazy, too.) Buddy is fed up with Sally; he knows she has always been in love with Ben. Phyllis is just plain fed up. Ben and Sally plan to run off together, but before they can get out the door, Ben has the mental breakdown he's been heading toward all evening.

Follies, the legendary Stephen Sondheim musical, is about Ben Stone. The road he took, and the road he didn't take, and his self-love/self-hate, and—all in all—about male menopause. (Harold Prince, director and producer of the original production, called the character "the perfect 1970s monolith approaching menopause on the cusp of a nervous breakdown." Prince also called the show "my autobiography.")

So why, I ask you, does this show about "the famous Benjamin Stone" take place at a reunion of Follies girls? Why is the show overstuffed with old-time chorus girls and old-time leading ladies and ghostly showgirls, and reminders of the passing of time and the ravages of aging beauty? Why bring on the girls if the show is not, really, about the girls?

Beats me.

All four main characters are having breakdowns, more or less; all are coping with the wrecks they've made of their lives. The "Loveland" section at the end of the evening gives them each a number illustrating their personal failures and follies. But Ben's folly comes last; the whole show

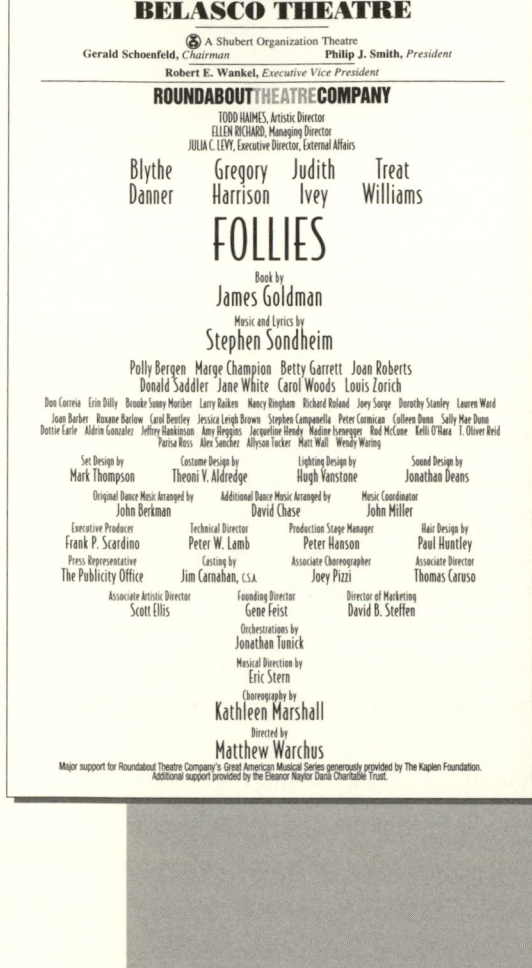

BELASCO THEATRE

Ⓢ A Shubert Organization Theatre

Gerald Schoenfeld, *Chairman*   Philip J. Smith, *President*

Robert E. Wankel, *Executive Vice President*

ROUNDABOUTTHEATRECOMPANY

TODD HAIMES, Artistic Director
ELLEN RICHARD, Managing Director
JULIA C. LEVY, Executive Director, External Affairs

Blythe   Gregory   Judith   Treat
Danner   Harrison   Ivey   Williams

FOLLIES

Book by
James Goldman

Music and Lyrics by
Stephen Sondheim

Polly Bergen   Marge Champion   Betty Garrett   Joan Roberts
Donald Saddler   Jane White   Carol Woods   Louis Zorich

Don Correia Erin Dilly Brooke Sunny Moriber Larry Raiken Nancy Ringham Richard Roland Joey Sorge Dorothy Stanley Lauren Ward
Joan Barber Roxane Barlow Carol Bentley Jessica Leigh Brown Stephen Campanella Peter Cormican Colleen Dunn Sally Mae Dunn
Dottie Earle Aldrin Gonzalez Jeffrey Hankinson Amy Heggins Jacqueline Hendy Nadine Isenegger Rod McCune Kelli O'Hara T. Oliver Reid
Parisa Ross Alex Sanchez Allyson Tucker Matt Wall Wendy Waring

Set Design by   Costume Design by   Lighting Design by   Sound Design by
Mark Thompson   Theoni V. Aldredge   Hugh Vanstone   Jonathan Deans

Original Dance Music Arranged by   Additional Dance Music Arranged by   Music Coordinator
John Berkman   David Chase   John Miller

Executive Producer   Technical Director   Production Stage Manager   Hair Design by
Frank P. Scardino   Peter W. Lamb   Peter Hanson   Paul Huntley

Press Representative   Casting by   Associate Choreographer   Associate Director
The Publicity Office   Jim Carnahan, C.S.A.   Joey Pizzi   Thomas Caruso

Associate Artistic Director   Founding Director   Director of Marketing
Scott Ellis   Gene Feist   David B. Steffen

Orchestrations by
Jonathan Tunick

Musical Direction by
Eric Stern

Choreography by
Kathleen Marshall

Directed by
Matthew Warchus

Major support for Roundabout Theatre Company's Great American Musical Series generously provided by The Kaplen Foundation.
Additional support provided by the Eleanor Naylor Dana Charitable Trust.

Dimitri Weissman   Louis Zorich
Showgirls   Jessica Leigh Brown, Colleen Dunn, Amy Heggins, Wendy Waring
Sally Durant Plummer   Judith Ivey
Sandra Crane   Nancy Ringham
Dee Dee West   Dorothy Stanley
Stella Deems   Carol Woods
Sam Deems   Peter Cormican
Solange La Fitte   Jane White
Roscoe   Larry Raiken
Heidi Schiller   Joan Roberts
Emily Whitman   Marge Champion
Theodore Whitman   Donald Saddler
Carlotta Campion   Polly Bergen
Hattie Walker   Betty Garrett
Phyllis Rogers Stone   Blythe Danner
Benjamin Stone   Gregory Harrison
Buddy Plummer   Treat Williams
Young Phyllis   Erin Dilly
Young Sally   Lauren Ward
Young Dee Dee   Roxane Barlow
Young Emily   Carol Bentley
Young Carlotta   Sally Mae Dunn
Young Sandra   Dottie Earle
Young Solange   Jacqueline Hendy
Young Heidi   Brooke Sunny Moriber
Young Hattie   Kelli O'Hara
Young Stella   Allyson Tucker
Young Roscoe   Aldrin Gonzalez
Young Ben   Richard Roland
Young Buddy   Joey Sorge
Young Theodore   Rod McCune
Kevin   Stephen Campanella
"Margie"   Roxane Barlow
"Sally"   Jessica Leigh Brown
Ladies and Gentlemen of the Ensemble   Roxane Barlow, Carol Bentley, Jessica Leigh Brown, Stephen Campanella, Colleen Dunn, Sally Mae Dunn, Dottie Earle, Aldrin Gonzalez, Amy Heggins, Jacqueline Hendy, Rod McCune, Kelli O'Hara, T. Oliver Reid, Alex Sanchez, Alyson Tucker, Matt Wall, Wendy Waring
Swings   Nadine Isenegger, Parissa Ross, Jeffrey Hankinson

builds to his sequence. Buddy has two girls in his number, Sally does hers alone, and in the 2001 Roundabout production Phyllis had six boys. Ben, on the other hand, forms a kickline with the entire chorus, and when he finally has his breakdown, the entire company is crossing and weaving through his nightmare. He winds up alone onstage in a stupor; in comes Phyllis, who comforts him and leads him off.

(This last sequence—singing; nightmare; breakdown; all alone on an "empty stage" set; consolation—is precisely what happens in the final scene of *Gypsy*, but let's not complicate matters.)

Take *Follies* and make the show about Phyllis and her conflicted life, and her affairs, and her sophistication hiding the emptiness inside; then, the follies of the *Follies* might make sense. Phyllis is the star of the show; at least, the actress playing Phyllis usually comes off as the star (and usually gets top billing). The show, you might say, is about Phyllis—but the *story* is about Ben. The two most important thematic songs of the evening, arguably, are "The Road You Didn't Take" and "Live, Laugh, Love." Ben's songs.

Perhaps this is the root cause of the perennial failure of *Follies*. At least some of this confusion stems from the show's long, twisting history. The story has been told before elsewhere, and not always consistently; I will only touch on it briefly. (Ted Chapin's highly anticipated book about the creation of *Follies* should give us a clear picture of what happened and why.)

The show that became *Follies* began life in 1965 as what has been described as a melodramatic murder mystery musical. Playwright James Goldman was a friend of Hal Prince. With his brother William Goldman, he had helped doctor Prince's unsuccessful 1960 musical *Tenderloin* (see *Broadway Yearbook, 1999–2000*). Without his brother, he wrote a play called *They Might Be Giants*, which Prince coproduced with Joan Little-wood in London in 1961 for an unsuccessful run. With his brother and John Kander, he wrote an unsuccessful 1962 musical called *A Family Affair*. When the latter ran into trouble during its tryout, Goldman's friend Prince was called in to take over—his first job as a director. Goldman also wrote the historical play *The Lion in Winter*, which had an unsuccessful run in 1966 (after work began on the musical that became *Follies*) and was later adapted into a successful motion picture.

The Girls Upstairs was optioned in 1967 by Leland Hayward and David Merrick, the producers of Sondheim's 1959 musical *Gypsy*. Hayward had been forced on Merrick; Merrick wanted Jerome Robbins to direct *Gypsy*, and Robbins insisted on Hayward's participation. As a trade-off, Merrick received the right to coproduce a future Hayward production. That deal obligated Hayward to raise the entire capitalization for the future show, which in the case of *The Girls Upstairs* he was unable to do. Merrick was lukewarm on the project; instead of helping raise funds, he let *The Girls* go.

Stuart Ostrow, who had not yet produced *1776* or *Pippin*, picked up *The Girls Upstairs* in 1969 and quickly dropped it. By this point Sondheim was already committed to write *Company* for Hal Prince. Sondheim asked Prince for a year's delay so he could find a new producer for the earlier show. Prince didn't want to delay *Company*, so he agreed that he would produce *Girls*—but after *Company*. While trying to figure out what to do

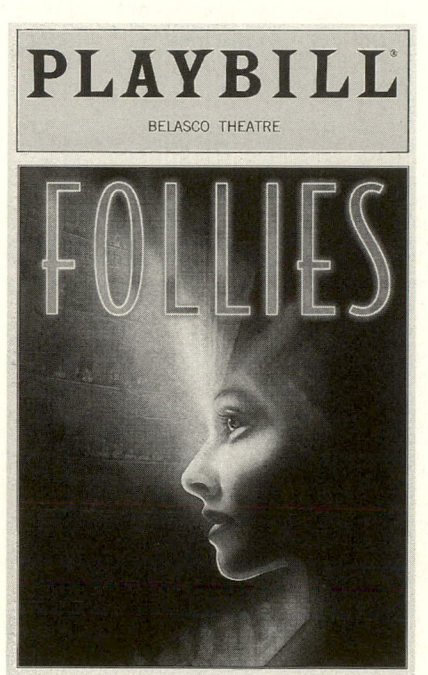

with *Girls*, Prince came across a photograph of Gloria Swanson standing in the rubble of the old Roxy Theatre. Thus began the transformation of Sondheim and Goldman's realistic book musical into the concept musical to end all concept musicals. Or was it the concept musical to begin all concept musicals?

Every time someone does *Follies*, people seem surprised to discover that the show is not very good. The score *is* very good; it was clearly the best score of the seventies when it opened, although it was tied in 1973 by Sondheim's *A Little Night Music* and surpassed in 1979 by Sondheim's *Sweeney Todd*. Strike that—let's just say they're each excellent. Anyway, Harold Prince and codirector-choreographer Michael Bennett and set designer Boris Aronson and costume designer Florence Klotz gave *Follies* a stunning production back in 1971, with some truly memorable performances. But the show doesn't work, and the problem lies in that book; or, perhaps, the pressures put on the book when it was stretched to fit the Prince-Bennett production concept. Walter Kerr, in the *Times*, called it "an extravaganza that becomes tedious for two simple reasons: its extravagances have nothing to do with its pebble of a plot; and the plot, which could be wrapped up in approximately two songs, dawdles through twenty-two before it declares itself done." Kerr is exaggerating, perhaps, but not all that much.

The original production had a small core of hard-core fans, certainly; but most theatregoers decidedly disliked it and did not support it, resulting in a disappointing run of 522 performances and a loss of almost its entire capitalization. That's not to say that *Follies* wasn't an important musical, and well worth doing, and perhaps even an earthshaking theatrical experience with far-reaching impact. I'm just saying, the show wasn't very good. The score was superb and kept me going back to the Winter Garden (on comps); but the drama was a muddle, and the whole ghostly aura smacked of artsy pretension. Sue me, throw brickbats if you will; but that's how it looked to me in 1971.

Follies was the concept musical to end all concept musicals. Or was it the concept musical to begin all concept musicals?

The "small core of hard-core fans" who loved the 1971 production has steadily expanded over the years to include many who couldn't possibly have seen it, but no matter. These people love to poke jabs at the fact that the show lost the Tony Award to the long-forgotten musicalization of Shakespeare's *Two Gentlemen of Verona*. This lark of a musical was concocted by director Melvin Shapiro and playwright John Guare; the latter wrote the nifty lyrics as well, to music by *Hair*'s Galt MacDermot. A decidedly antiwar musical glorifying interracial marriage and featuring a barrage of four-letter words, *Two Gentlemen of Verona* was nevertheless an enormous crowd-pleaser. Sondheim's *Follies* deservedly won the Tony for best score, but *Two Gents* won for best musical and best book (by Guare and Shapiro). And let me tell you, standing on the sidewalk outside the St. James after curtain calls of *Two Gents* you saw a sea of mostly ecstatic faces. Standing outside the Winter Garden, people didn't look too happy. Especially people over forty. And if you want to especially annoy your audience, keep them in their seats for 135 minutes without an intermission.

Watching the Roundabout revival of *Follies*, I found myself once more facing the same old frustrations. All four "stars" crossing swords, and all those ghosts—with helpfully color-coded costumes—expounding what the four stars said, and what they didn't say, and what they didn't say but meant. There was a scene with Ben and Sally talking about their lives today; a scene with Ben and Sally talking about their lives yesterday; a scene with Phyllis and Buddy talking about life with Sally and Ben; a scene with Phyllis and Sally talking about life with and without Ben. All of this was interspersed with songs from the old-time troupers, but the first half of *Follies*—which the Roundabout presented in two acts—was pretty much about Ben.

Look at the first act. After the prologue, the show begins with an opening number for the tenor. Then comes a "book scene" duet for Ben and Sally; an octet for the four leads and ghosts; three song pastiches for old-timers; a "book scene" soliloquy for Ben; a dance for the old-timers; a "book scene" song for Sally to sing to Ben; two more songs for the old-timers; and a "book scene" duet for Ben and Sally. That is to say, Phyllis—played by the "biggest" star in the original cast (Alexis Smith), the 1987 London cast (Diana Rigg), and here again (Blythe Danner)—has virtually nothing to sing for two-thirds of the evening. After the intermission, she has two knockout numbers "Could I Leave You?" and "The Story of Lucy and Jessie"—which somehow makes people think the show is about her.

Every time someone does *Follies*, people seem surprised to discover that the show is not very good. The score *is* very good, but the show doesn't work.

Phyllis originally did have a big duet with Buddy in the first act of *The Girls Upstairs*, to counter all those Ben and Sally songs: the title song, "The Girls Upstairs." Hence the lyric "Hi. Girls. Ben. Sally." Buddy and Phyllis were calling for the absent Ben and Sally, who presumably were coupled in a dark corner somewhere. In *Follies*, this number was sung by the four leads and their four ghosts—leaving Phyllis (and Buddy) without any big musical spots whatsoever until well after nine o'clock. While we're at it, let me mention that only five of the songs in my copy of *The Girls Upstairs* (dated July 1967) remained in *Follies*. Others song ideas were merely indicated or developed into different songs, like the sequence where Phyllis twangs a ukelele and sings "'I'm All Alone Tonight Because the Bastard's Gone and Left Me' Blues." Now there's a song I'd like to hear.

Getting back to *Follies*, all evening long you see ex-performer characters performing once more, either reprising old numbers (like "Broadway Baby" or "Who's That Woman?") or commenting from afar (like "I'm Still Here"). So what is Ben, a lawyer-turned-statesman, doing in a spotlight singing more songs than anybody?

If Ben is the key role, it is also the most difficult one. And difficult to cast. The 1971 production was stocked with old-time names, led by film star Alexis Smith, *Hit Parade* star Dorothy Collins, and movie musical semistar Gene Nelson. Also on hand was B-movie star Yvonne de Carlo and three long-ago musical comedy leading ladies, Mary McCarty, Fifi d'Orsay, and Ethel Shutta. For Ben, they cast—nobody. The original ad for the Boston tryout listed Smith, Nelson, and Collins only; the next generation added Jon Cypher as the fourth star. (Cypher had recently played the romantic lead in the musical *Sherry* and Katharine Hepburn's father, on tape, in the Bennett-choreographed *Coco*.) Finally, John McMartin was cast as Ben. McMartin had appeared in such musicals as the off-Broadway hit *Little Mary Sunshine* and as Gwen Verdon's milquetoast fiancé in *Sweet Charity*, and it turned out that he gave a fine performance in *Follies*. But in a show that was built around faded stars with still-familiar names, McMartin seemed to be from another world.

The marriage of *Follies* and the Roundabout seemed to be a mutually beneficial idea. The Roundabout had enjoyed a stunning and impressive success with their 1998 revival of *Cabaret*, which fixed several of the problems of that earlier Hal Prince show. (They had done less spectacularly with a tame 1995 revival of *Company* and an ineffective 1999 revival of Goldman's *The Lion in Winter*.) Under the guidance of Todd Haimes, the Roundabout had also demonstrated the ability to attract top talents, despite sub-Broadway budgets and pay scales. *Follies* was entrusted to British director Matthew Warchus, who had visited Broadway with two crowd-pleasers, Yasmina Reza's *Art* and the 2000 revival of Sam Shepard's *True West*.

Somehow, though, this *Follies* was out of step from the very beginning. *Follies* is about ghosts, Broadway ghosts in a Broadway theatre. The first thing we saw when we entered the Belasco was the curtain, bearing the name "Weismann Theater." Now, this is enough to drive a person crazy, especially a traditionalist. "Theatre" is the word; at least, that is the way it has been spelled along Broadway since forever. In 1962 or so, the *New York Times* decided to switch to "theater,"

In an unprecedented act, the *New York Times* ran five stories about the show on the Sunday before the opening. This, the same *Times* that gave the show two bad reviews in 1971 and pretty much scuttled its chances.

and since that time they have insisted on sticking to it. (While the *Times* insists on "theater," the paid ads in the *Times* use "theatre.")

In 2002, all the Broadway playhouses except one still used "theatre."

This might not seem all that important in the larger scheme of things. To me, though, "theatre" is magical; "theater" is just a building. And that's why we use "theatre," still; let them bring in electric lights and air-conditioning and sound amplification and even synthesized music, but we want our "theatre."

And there it was, "Weismann Theater" in block letters high enough to read from the second balcony. What matter that the Playbill and the marquee and the ads insisted that *Follies* was playing at the Belasco *Theatre*? What matter that David Belasco and Lee Shubert and Flo Ziegfeld and Roundabout and even the American Airlines Theatre use "theatre"? The published libretto, too, sets the action at the Weismann *Theatre*. Here was a show about the magic of the theatre; and here was a piece of scenery that, in the context of the show, was probably painted in 1927. The director and designer chose to call it "theater," and the spell was broken before they started.

This was indicative of the hit-or-miss nature of the venture. The physical production ranged from atmospheric to skimpy; you need a large budget to build and clothe the "folly" section of *Follies*, and Roundabout didn't have it. (This sequence, which is supposed to take us back to a dream of what the *Ziegfeld Follies* were, looked like it was constructed out of oversized Popsicle sticks dipped in Pepto-Bismol.) Even more damaging, perhaps, was the economic necessity of reducing the orchestration to a mere fourteen pieces. *Follies* is one of Sondheim's most expansive scores; I can imagine the composer and his ace orchestrator Jonathan Tunick weeping over all those lost, glorious colors. Conductor Eric Stern did a good job of compensating for the reduction and holding everyone together. Stern and Tunick were able to make *Follies* sound perfectly fine, if not as rich as it should. (Whoever was playing clarinet at the press performance I attended sounded like he was sight-reading underwater with molasses on his fingers. He absolutely butchered the solo parts in "The Girls Upstairs," and I do hope he was a one-night-only substitute.)

The casting, likewise, was iffy. Warchus appears to be an actor's director, and the leads seemed to have been selected without consideration of musical needs. Judith Ivey is a fine actress, and she brought some interesting touches to her portrayal of Sally. This character usually seems to be a victim of her dreams; Ivey made her a villain, with her obsession for Ben ruining the lives of everyone around her. Ivey's singing was harmful, though; her big number, Sondheim's breathtaking "Losing My Mind," had the feel of a suburban housewife auditioning for the PTA production of

Mame. (Yes, I know that the character Sally was merely a chorus girl; but in this show, in this spot, she needs to be able to make your heart weep.) Treat Williams was a stiff and wooden Buddy. "The Right Girl," his raging tantrum of a number, featured him loping around the stage as if he was playing musical chairs; whenever he got really mad and the percussionist hit his hi-hat, Williams (carefully) kicked one of the chairs over. (I don't blame the actor—he was simply doing as instructed.) Gregory Harrison got the problematic role of Ben, and he couldn't do much with it. Harrison, who first came to town with a hit TV series on his résumé, seems to want to be a musical comedy star. He is capable, I suppose, but there has been something off-putting in his three major performances so far: in the ill-formed *Paper Moon*, which closed out of town; in *Steel Pier*, which closed in town; and in this *Follies*.

> **Word-of-mouth was dismal; even Sondheim fans—thrilled to have the opportunity to see *Follies*—were sorry-grateful. One thing's for sure: It wasn't a wasted evening.**

Blythe Danner, as Phyllis, was the surprise. No, she couldn't sing; but what an acting performance! I've seen her onstage for years and years, since she first dangled from the edge of a loft-bed in her underwear in *Butterflies Are Free* in 1969, and she has always been pretty good. Her Phyllis, though, was razor sharp. Watching her watch Sally watching Ben, I thought: When did she get this good? Somebody write Ms. Danner a play, quick, Edward Albee or John Guare or David Auburn.

The subsidiary roles were filled with as many familiar names as possible, although not of the same starry caliber as past *Follies* productions. Polly Bergen came off best, as Carlotta. She did piercingly well with her solo, "I'm Still Here," despite puzzling staging—she sang it to the other characters, ringed around her at tables—and despite the fact that she lost the lyric twice the night I saw it. A mere glance from Bergen, though, told a thousand words. Betty Garrett walked around the stage with the same authority as Ethel Shutta, who created the role of "Broadway Baby" Hattie Walker—and that's a high compliment. Garrett gave the impression of being one of those Tenth Avenue gals who made it the hard way; she may be old and she may be tiny, but don't even think of trying to knock her down.

Jane White did well by Solange, finding jokes in "Ah, Paris!"; Donald Saddler and Marge Champion gracefully represented the frailty of passing time as the Whitmans (as well as taking over the dance specialty slot ini-

Follies

Opened: April 5, 2001

Closed: July 14, 2001

117 performances (and 31 previews)

Profit/Loss: Nonprofit [Loss]

Follies ($90 top) was scaled to a potential gross of $494,193
at the 995-seat Belasco. Weekly grosses averaged about
$383,000, remaining stubbornly below the $400,000 mark
except for the final full week of previews ($403,000) and
the closing week (when it hit $470,000). Total gross for
the run was $7,080,718. Attendance was about 88
percent, with the box office grossing about 77 percent of
dollar-capacity. (These figures are not indicative, as the
potential was calculated at the top ticket price, but
subscribers paid less.)

TONY AWARD NOMINATIONS

Best Revival of a Musical

Best Performance by a Leading Actress: Blythe Danner

Best Performance by a Featured Actress: Polly Bergen

Best Costume Design: Theoni V. Aldredge

Best Orchestrations: Jonathan Tunick

*Critical
Scorecard*

Rave 2

Favorable 1

Mixed 1

Unfavorable 2

Pan 4

tially performed by the cut characters Vincent and Vanessa); and Joan Roberts was highly effective as the oldest star of them all singing "One Last Kiss." Unlike the other veterans on hand, Roberts had an exceedingly minor career with only one important role to her credit—as the original heroine in *Oklahoma!* I would guess she got better reviews, and more press coverage, in this revival of *Follies* than she had in her entire career. (As far as I'm concerned, Roberts deserved a medal for agreeing to walk down the rickety *Follies* staircase with her cane.) The ghosts of the stars were all quite good, especially Richard Roland as Young Ben and Lauren Ward as Young Sally. Ward acted the situation better than anyone other than Danner. When Ben walked out on her, Ward's Sally looked like she'd been punched in the face.

From its initial announcement, the Roundabout *Follies* was embraced by Sondheim fans and the media. (In an unprecedented act, the *Times* ran five stories about the show on the Sunday before the opening. This, the same *Times* that gave the show two bad reviews in 1971 and pretty much scuttled its chances.) *Follies* was a shoo-in for the Best Revival Tony Award and numerous other nominations, at least until it started previewing on March 8. Word of mouth was dismal; even Sondheim fans—who were thrilled to have the opportunity to see *Follies* on Broadway—were, to borrow a phrase from the composer, sorry-grateful. By the time *Follies* opened, *42nd Street*—which had been previewing for two weeks to great word of mouth—was the show to beat.

A large advance sale enabled *Follies* to extend its originally announced run—as had always been the plan—moving the closing date from July 14 to September 30. Figures were deceptive, though. Like several of its sister houses, the Belasco is crippled by its second balcony. More than 200 of the 995 seats are up in the heavens, and you really can't see much from there. The sight lines for *Follies* from the second balcony, reportedly, were especially poor. The Roundabout priced the seats at $50 and $40, although they also publicized a day-of-sale price of $25. (By May, some of these were labeled obstructed and offered for a mere $15.) The orchestra and mezzanine were priced at a steep $90, but those seats were mostly filled with lower-priced subscribers (with a $45 price on the ticket).

The Roundabout operates on a lower-than-Broadway pay scale for their subscription runs, after which they must convert to the standard Broadway rates in order to continue. The Belasco, with fewer than eight hundred seats on the lower two floors, was far too small to support a show with forty-three actors and fourteen musicians and fourteen wardrobe people and who knows how many stagehands. Especially a show that got slammed by the *Times* and the *Post* and the *News* and most of the other local reviewers. Not to mention bad word of mouth—even from Sondheim fans.

Follies was shut out at the Tony Awards on June 3, and the televised excerpt—a severely truncated sliver of Polly Bergen singing her big solo—didn't translate into immediate ticket sales. On June 6, the Roundabout threw in the towel and canceled the extension, and *Follies* failed once more. But I'll take *Follies*, anytime. One thing's for sure: It wasn't a wasted evening.

One Flew over the Cuckoo's Nest

Steppenwolf and Gary Sinise and Terry Kinney and *One Flew over the Cuckoo's Nest*. What a perfect combination! After a three-month engagement in April 2000 at Steppenwolf's Chicago home, they paid a two-week London visit in July 2000. Advance reports confirmed that this *Cuckoo's Nest* was an electric evening of theatre. So why did it fizzle on Broadway?

"Fizzle" is not the word, perhaps. The reaction was wildly mixed and highly unusual. The Critical Scorecard on page 178 shows that four of the tabulated critics loved it (praising the theatricality and the performances) and five of them hated it (ruing the dramaturgy and the misogyny). Little middle ground, here. Business was reasonably good, but not quite good enough to recover the production costs (although income from post–Broadway engagements should allow the producers to turn a profit).

Cuckoo's Nest first appeared as a novel in 1962, written by a counterculture character named Ken Kesey. The novel soon became a cult classic. Even before it was published, screenwriter Dale Wasserman read the galleys and saw its movie potential. So did Kirk Douglas, who wanted to do it on Broadway first. Wasserman had written Douglas's 1958 film *The Vikings*. "That doesn't mean we liked each other," Wasserman said in an interview prior to the 2001 opening, "but we decided to work on the project together."

Douglas enlisted David Merrick to produce the play, which opened on November 13, 1963. Reaction was—oddly enough—wildly mixed, with some critics praising the theatricality and the performances and others ruing the dramaturgy and the misogyny. Opening on the heels of Neil Simon's *Barefoot in the Park* and Edward Albee's *The Ballad of the Sad Café*, *Cuckoo's Nest* closed in January after a mere ten weeks. (By this time, Merrick had his hands full with his new hit, *Hello, Dolly!*) The Kesey-Wasserman work went into flop-play limbo.

Kesey bought an old school bus, painted it in Day-Glo colors, and drove across the country with a bunch of friends, dispensing psychedelic drugs and spreading the creed of hippiedom. (This journey was memorialized in Tom Wolfe's 1968 *The Electric Kool-Aid Acid Test*.) Kesey died on November 10, 2001, at the age of sixty-six. Wasserman, meanwhile, occupied himself by adapting another unconventional novel. He had written a television play in 1958 called *I, Don Quixote*, which starred Lee J. Cobb, Colleen Dewhurst, and Eli Wallach. Wasserman turned it into the 1965 musical *Man of La Mancha*, which swept the world with its "Impossible Dream." This won Wasserman all sorts of awards and made him extremely wealthy. He then turned his attentions back to *Cuckoo's Nest*, preparing a revised version that surfaced off-Broadway in 1971. The show arrived at the height of the antiwar, antiestablishment era and enjoyed an impressive a 1,025-performance run; there was also a highly successful production in San Francisco.

While the Broadway *Cuckoo's Nest* was quickly forgotten, it apparently made a big impact on at least one person: Kirk Douglas's eighteen-year-old son, Michael. While starring in the early 1970s TV series *The Streets of San Francisco*, the younger Douglas started making short subjects. For his feature film debut, he bought *Cuckoo's Nest* from his dad (who still owned the screen rights). Using a non-Wasserman adaptation, *One Flew over the Cuckoo's Nest* (1975) became one of the biggest hits of its time. It won five Oscars, including Best Picture and Best Screenplay (by Bo Goldman and Lawrence Hauben). Best Actor was won by Jack Nicholson, whose performance turned him from a movie star into a movie legend.

Advance reports confirmed that this *Cuckoo's Nest* was an electric evening of theatre. So why did it fizzle on Broadway?

Steppenwolf has been known for vibrant, gutsy productions—"in-your-face Chicago theatre," they call it—and *Cuckoo's Nest* seemed a perfect vehicle for them. The Steppenwolf Theatre Company, as it's formally named, was formed in 1974 by Sinise, Kinney, and Jeff Perry. (The second Steppenwolf production, history relates, was a Chicago revival of

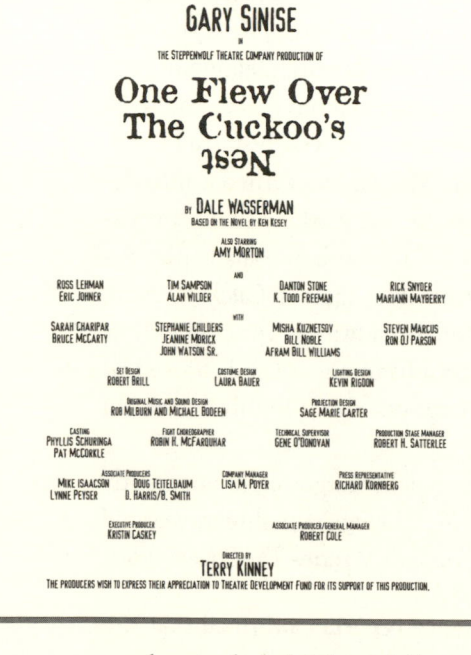

Grease!) Over several seasons, the company attracted a band of players that included John Malkovich, Joan Allen, John Mahoney, Laurie Metcalf, Glenne Headly, Kevin Anderson, and Frank Galati.

Their mission statement, and I quote: "Founded on a commitment to the principles of ensemble collaboration and artistic risk, the mission of Steppenwolf is to advance the vitality and diversity of American theatre, while maintaining the original impulses of the group. With the challenge of superior acting at the core of its theatrical endeavor, the acting ensemble continues to work toward a collective artistic vision not unlike great theater ensembles such as the Royal Shakespeare Company and the Moscow Art Theatre."

Steppenwolf first attracted national attention with a 1982 off-Broadway revival of Sam Shepard's *True West* (which had failed in its initial production). Kinney directed a cast headed by Malkovich and Sinise, with electric results. Steppenwolf began frequent off-Broadway visits, but the company's Broadway adventures have not been quite so happy. Their 1988 adaptation of John Steinbeck's *The Grapes of Wrath* reached Broadway in 1990, after engagements in Chicago, La Jolla, and London. Directed by Galati and with a cast headed by Sinise and Kinney, it won the Tony Award for Best Play but failed to sell many tickets. *The Song of Jacob Zulu* (1993), *The Rise and Fall of Little Voice* (1994), and a revival of Sam Shepard's *Buried Child* (1996)—directed by Sinise, starring Kinney—were all quick failures. And then came the heralded *Cuckoo's Nest*.

The play begins with Chief Bromden, the Indian inmate, in the midst of a hallucination. "Vague and milky light-patterns wreathe and intertwine across the stage," per the script, and Bromden goes into the first of several discussions with his dead father about "the Black Machine eighteen stories down below the ground." In the Steppenwolf production, the "vague and milky light-patterns" became a multimedia festival, with psychedelic lights, blasting sound, and what appeared to be bedded patients flying up through the windows to the sky.

Is this where this *Cuckoo's Nest* went wrong? The play is built upon the onstage fireworks that occur when the hero, McMurphy, moves into the ward—fireworks that, in the hands of Sinise, promised to be spectacular. But Kinney chose to make Bromden's hallucinations—which serve to bridge the scenes—so incendiary that a mere troop of twenty Steppenwolf thespians couldn't compete. I was also a bit thrown by the inclusion of hard rock music during some of these sequences. Now I realize that the proceedings don't necessarily take place back in 1960–1961, merely because that's when Kesey wrote his novel (which was published in 1962). But the play deals, distinctly, with society and power and protest. The student protests against Vietnam, which effected major changes in life in America, began long after Kesey sat down at his typewriter. In some ways, the novel can be said

One Flew over the Cuckoo's Nest
Opened: April 8, 2001
Closed: July 29, 2001
121 performances (and 24 previews)
Profit/Loss: Loss
One Flew over the Cuckoo's Nest ($75 top) was scaled to a
    potential gross of $509,780 at the 1,040-seat Royale
    (although the show often played a seven-performance
    week). Weekly grosses averaged about $357,000, peaking
    at $413,000 two weeks after the opening but otherwise
    remaining stubbornly around $350,000. Total gross for the
    run was $6,477,718. Attendance was about 81 percent,
    with the box office grossing about 69 percent of dollar-
    capacity.

TONY AWARD NOMINATIONS
Best Revival of a Play (WINNER)
Best Performance by a Leading Actor: Gary Sinise

Critical Scorecard

Rave 4
Favorable 0
Mixed 1
Unfavorable 0
Pan 5

to have influenced the social changes of the later sixties. But can this play, as written—with its themes, characters, and viewpoints—logically take place in the seventies? After the Kennedy assassination and the Vietnam War and the Nixon administration and Watergate?

The play itself offered some built-in problems. Wasserman described a world in which the bad guy—McMurphy—was good; the "good guy" in the white dress, Nurse Ratched, was bad; and the supposedly insane residents were the pure at heart. *Cuckoo's Nest* can be seen as a cowboy story. Here's Mr. Sinise, in an interview with Lance Gould in the *Daily News*: "The play is like a classic Western: You know, the town is completely controlled by the bad sheriff (in this case Nurse Ratched) and his bad men, and they're all submissive and scared to death. And in comes the lone rider who sees what's going on and sacrifices himself to liberate the townspeople."

McMurphy is so very coarse and dirty and vulgar that he can only be heroic. Ratched is the bad sheriff—although in a John Wayne movie she'd be run out of town in the final reel.

The problem is, Wasserman (and Kesey) paint the colors way too bold. McMurphy is so very coarse and dirty and vulgar that he can only be heroic. He even befriends the catatonic Indian. (Is McMurphy Jesus, come to rescue the weak and poor? He ends up, in the final scene, martyred.) Ratched, surely, is the bad sheriff—although in a John Wayne movie she'd be run out of town in the final reel. And if Ratched was the bad guy, her villainous band consisted of the women of the world.

All women were bad. Ratched and her mousey assistant, Flinn; the un-seen wife of Harding; the unseen mother of Billy; and just about any fe-male any of the characters mention. The exceptions, wouldn't you know, are McMurphy's two stripper friends, who come in to entertain the boys—although this slumber party directly results in the deaths of both Billy and McMurphy. Women (prostitutes excepted) are so bad, the au-thors seemed to be saying, that they need to be choked and throttled—which is what happened at the climax of the play, when McMur-phy levels Ratched to cheers from the multitudes.

With Sinise giving a surpris-ingly unengaging performance, the rest of the troupe fell flat. The exception was Ross Lehman as Harding, the intellectual "bull goose looney." Lehman's "Nurse Ratched is a veritable angel of mercy" speech in the first act was riveting; it was the one and only part of the evening that grabbed me (and everyone around me). Amy Morton, as the good nurse, was so martinet-like that I thought I was watching a puppet; but that's the way they wanted her to be, I sup-pose. Tim Sampson gave a sturdy, sympathetic performance as the Chief, although the combination of his diction and the sound effects made him impossible to understand during the hallucinations. K. Todd Freeman, who earned a Best Actor Tony nomination for Steppenwolf's *Jacob Zulu*, was directed to give an especially puzzling performance as Dr. Spivey, the resident psychiatrist. The character takes sides with McMurphy against Ratched more often than not, although he is ultimately too weak to keep the hero from his tragic end. As written, Spivey seems to be the voice of reason; as presented on the stage of the Royale, he was a bumbling clown and clearly a pushover. (In the group therapy scene, one of the loonies began jiggering his leg uncontrollably. Moments later, Freeman was di-rected to do the same.)

All in all, the surefire combination of *Cuckoo's Nest* and Steppenwolf turned out to be a dud firecracker. The most intriguing part of the evening was a comment I heard on the line to the men's room at inter-mission. "That's my mother," said one fellow to another. "Nurse Ratched. Just like her."

> Women (prostitutes excepted) are so bad, the author seemed to be saying, that they need to be choked and throttled— which is what happened at the climax of the play, to cheers from the multitudes.

Bells Are Ringing

The idea of producing Broadway revivals of Broadway musicals didn't come up much in the fifties or sixties. The potential Broadway audience was smaller in those days, when a two-year run was exceptional. How many people were likely to pay good money to see a show they had already seen? It was also problematic financially. The original producers and investors shared in a full slate of subsidiary rights, including motion picture rights and stock and amateur licensing; few of these income sources were available to backers of a revival. And then there was the theatre situation. With as many as fifteen new musicals on the boards in any given season, not to mention holdovers, theatre owners had their pick of new potential hits.

There were a handful of musical revivals in the early fifties. Only two of these were successful, *Pal Joey* in 1952 and a touring *Porgy and Bess* that played Broadway in 1953. Between 1954 (*On Your Toes*) and 1970 (*The Boy Friend*), there were *no* musical revivals on Broadway. Things changed with the unprecedented success of the revival of *No, No, Nanette* in 1971. There were two more musical revivals on Broadway in 1972, and three in 1973. By 1974, Broadway had five musical revivals—and only four new musicals!

Simply put, less new product—and less successful new product—created an opening for old product. With few new hits capable of touring, producers started assembling star package revivals for the road—and the successful ones treated Broadway as just another touring stop. (In 1977, Zero Mostel and Yul Brynner and Richard Kiley were all breaking box office records across the country, re-creating their original roles in *Fiddler* and *The King and I* and *La Mancha*.) The majority of revivals, let it be

said, lose money. But, then, the majority of new musicals lose money as
well. A revival flop generally loses less money than a new flop.

With the emergence of the rejuvenated road as a major force in the legitimate theatre industry, musical revivals have become more and more
important. (The Tony Award for Most Innovative Production of a Revival was first given in 1977. In 1995, the category was split into separate
awards for plays and musicals.) Two powerful Broadway producing organizations have provided a steady flow of revivals over the last decade. Fran
and Barry Weissler, who have garnered a reputation as Broadway's least
beloved producers, made their name and fame and fortune on revivals.
(As mentioned in the discussion on *Seussical*, they have been unsuccessful so far with new shows.) Dodger Theatricals, as well, have made revivals part of their steady diet. As the 2000–2001 season drew to a close,
the Weisslers and the Dodgers each had two revivals on Broadway. The
nonprofit Roundabout Theatre had two, as well, and there were an additional three playing under other auspices. Two more were on extended
pre-Broadway tours, *Fiddler on the Roof* (with Theodore Bikel) and *The
Best Little Whorehouse in Texas* (with Ann-Margret).

I have just done a highly unscientific survey of twentieth-century musicals and came up with about 140 that are potentially revivable. (More
than half have already been revived on Broadway, some on multiple occasions.) The pool is not likely to
increase, unless people start writing new hit musicals of the 1940s
and 1950s and 1960s. Thus, we
have already begun to see revivals
of musicals that might not necessarily be worth reviving.

The 1956 musical *Bells Are
Ringing* is an interesting case, in
that it has sterling credentials. A
fairly major hit in its day, it has
two still-familiar, all-time pop
hits, and it is fondly remembered.
(You'd have to be in your mid-
fifties or older to have seen the
original production, unless you
went when you were six).

Bells is built on as zany a foun-

PLYMOUTH THEATRE
236 West 45th Street
Ⓢ A Shubert Organization Theatre
Gerald Schoenfeld, *Chairman*   Philip J. Smith, *President*

Robert E. Wankel, *Executive Vice President*

MITCHELL MAXWELL   MARK BALSAM   VICTORIA MAXWELL
ROBERT BARANDES   MARK GOLDBERG   ANTHONY R. RUSSO   JAMES L. SIMON
IN ASSOCIATION WITH
FRED H. KRONES   ALLEN M. SHORE
AND
MOMENTUM PRODUCTIONS, INC.
PRESENT

FAITH PRINCE
MARC KUDISCH

Bells Are Ringing

BOOK AND LYRICS BY
BETTY COMDEN AND **ADOLPH GREEN**

MUSIC BY
JULE STYNE

FEATURING
**DAVID GARRISON   BETH FOWLER
MARTIN MORAN   ROBERT ARI   JEFFREY BEAN**

JULIO AGUSTIN
JOANNE BAUM   DAVID BRUMMEL   LAWRENCE CLAYTON
DARREN RITCHIE   ANGELA ROBINSON   LINDA ROMOFF

CAITLIN CARTER   JAMES HADLEY   ROY HARCOURT   STACEY HARRIS   JOAN HESS
EMILY HSU   SHANE KIRKPATRICK   MARC OKA   GREG REUTER   JOSH RHODES
ALICE RIETVELD   KELLY SULLIVAN

SCENIC DESIGN	COSTUME DESIGN	LIGHTING DESIGN	SOUND DESIGN
RICCARDO HERNANDEZ	DAVID C. WOOLARD	DONALD HOLDER	ACME SOUND PARTNERS

PRODUCTION STAGE MANAGER   CASTING   ASSOCIATE CHOREOGRAPHER   TECHNICAL SUPERVISION   VIDEO
ERICA SCHWARTZ   STEPHANIE KLAPPER, CSA   PATTI D'BECK   LARRY MORLEY   BATWIN & ROBIN PRODUCTIONS

MUSICAL DIRECTION AND   ORCHESTRATIONS   MUSICAL COORDINATOR   INCIDENTAL MUSIC   DANCE MUSIC ARRANGEMENTS
VOCAL ARRANGEMENTS   DON SEBESKY   SEYMOUR RED PRESS   DAVID EVANS/MARK HUMMEL   MARK HUMMEL
DAVID EVANS

PRESS REPRESENTATIVE   GENERAL MANAGEMENT   DIRECTOR OF MARKETING   MARKETING/ PROMOTIONS   ASSOCIATE PRODUCERS
BARLOW HARTMAN   ROBERT V. STRAUS PRODUCTIONS INC.   TRACEY   LEANNE SCHANZER   ALAN S. KOPIT
PUBLIC RELATIONS   ROBERT V. STRAUS/ELLEN RUSCONI   MENDELSOHN   PROMOTIONS, INC.   RICHARD BERGER

CHOREOGRAPHY BY
JEFF CALHOUN

DIRECTED BY
TINA LANDAU

The producers wish to express their appreciation to Theatre Development Fund for its support of this production.

TV Announcer   Shane Kirkpatrick
Telephone Girls   Caitlin Carter, Joan Hess, Emily Hsu, Alice Rietveld
Sue   Beth Fowler
Gwynne   Angela Robinson
Ella Peterson   Faith Prince
Carl   Julio Agustin
Inspector Barnes   Robert Ari
Francis   Jeffrey Bean
Sandor   David Garrison
Jeff Moss   Marc Kudisch
Larry Hastings   David Brummel
Louie   Greg Reuter
Ludwig Smiley   Lawrence Clayton
Dr. Kitchell   Martin Moran
Blake Barton   Darren Ritchie
Joey   Shane Kirkpatrick
Paddy, the Street Sweeper   Roy Harcourt
Mrs. Simms   Joan Hess
Olga   Caitlin Carter
Corvello Mob Men   David Brummel, Greg Reuter
Maid   Linda Romoff
Paul Arnold   Lawrence Clayton
Bridgette   Joan Hess
Man on Street   Josh Rhodes
Ensemble   Julio Agustin, Joanne Baum, David Brummel, Caitlin Carter, Lawrence Clayton, Roy Harcourt, Joan Hess, Emily Hsu, Shane Kirkpatrick, Greg Reuter, Josh Rhodes, Alice Rietveld, Darren Ritchie, Angela Robinson, Linda Romoff
Dancers   Caitlin Carter, Roy Harcourt, Joan Hess, Emily Hsu, Shane Kirkpatrick, Greg Reuter, Josh Rhodes
Swings   James Hadley, Stacey Harris, Marc Oka, Kelly Sullivan

The Time: Spring, the late 1950s
The Place: New York City

Original Broadway Cast Album:
Fynsworth Alley 302 062 115 2

dation as any musical ever. Ella Peterson, a lovably plain operator at a telephone answering service, acts as surrogate friend to her favorite clients: a broken-down playwright, a dentist who composes songs on his air hose, a Brando-ish actor with rocks in his mouth. The plot hinges on a bookie operation in which racetracks are coded as composers' names, with symphony numbers signifying races. All hell breaks loose when the heroine intercepts orders for Beethoven's Tenth Symphony—the tenth race at Belmont—and changes the bets to the ninth race. Beethoven wrote only nine symphonies; everybody knows that. Did Comden or Green come up with this nifty supposition? Or was it composer Jule Styne, who was perennially up to his neck in gambling debts? Whoever it was, it's a delicious conceit.

However—and it's a big however—the whole thing bogs down in the book, in a way that might well have surprised fans of the score. Take the dentist and the actor, for example. Ella pays a visit to Dr. Kitchell in a rather funny "doctor's office sketch," convinces him that he really is a very good songwriter, and steers him to an audition for new songs. She next pays a visit to Blake Barton, who is sitting at a soda fountain with his other motorcycle-punk-type cronies. (Why are they at a soda fountain eating sundaes? Was this funny, once?) Ella tells him that he really is a very good actor, gives him a lead on an upcoming audition—in the play that her playwright client is writing—and slips him the address of Brooks Brothers (where he can buy a suit). This is another comedy sketch, longer and not as funny as the first but necessary, plotwise. The two scenes, back-to-back, point us to one of the major problems with *Bells Are Ringing*. Here

The majority of revivals lose money. But, then, the majority of new musicals lose money as well. A revival flop generally loses less money than a new flop.

we are late in the overlong first act of this musical comedy, just when the audience is bound to get a little restless, and what happens? Two comedy scenes—*nonmusical* comedy scenes. That's right, not a song in sight, and that's wrong.

Bells Are Ringing has two main characters, Ella and "her sleeping prince" Jeff Moss, the playwright. There are also two subsidiary leads, Sandor (the gambler) and Sue (Ella's cousin, who owns the answering service). Otherwise, there are seven "featured" roles. Barton and Kitchell and Larry Hastings, Jeff's producer (who is also a customer of the answering service); two musical comedy detectives, Inspector Barnes and Francis; Gwynne, an extra girl at the answering service; and Carl, a delivery boy who spills the beans on Beethoven's Tenth. The number of these supporting characters that sing is—get this—*one*. Carl has a single, highly extraneous song inserted simply to give the show a flashy dance specialty. (The number, "Mu-Cha-Cha," was a pale attempt at re-creating the excitement of the showstoppers "Steam Heat" and "Who's Got the Pain?" in choreographer Bob Fosse's two previous musicals.) In the *Bells* revival, Kitchell was also given a song that had been a chorus solo in the nightclub scene.

> George Abbott wasn't called for *Bells Are Ringing*, and I can't help but wonder if that doesn't account for the haphazard structure, too many lengthy nonmusical comedy scenes, and too few singing characters.

But the supporting characters, clearly, don't offer much support in this musical comedy. The subsidiary leads don't, either; Sandor sings two songs, Sue sings one.

Ella and Jeff sing twelve of the sixteen songs—a lot for the stars of a musical—and too many of the songs are extraneous. I can think of only one other traditional musical with this kind of song distribution: Jule Styne's *Funny Girl* (1964). There, of course, he had a singer called Streisand, so it didn't matter much what anyone else was doing.

Bells, in 2001, was a musical comedy with the two leads singing the music and the rest of the cast supplying the (somewhat creaky) comedy. Is it any wonder that the show dragged on and on and on? Judy Holliday had more than enough charisma to carry the show (and knock *My Fair Lady*'s Julie Andrews out of the Tony Award race). Was it her lovable persona and enormous personal following? Or maybe audiences were simply more willing to sit through poorly structured and extraneous material in 1956.

There was a full complement of songs threaded through the long stretches of plotting and joking. "Just in Time" and "The Party's Over" are justly memorable, and most welcome. I've always enjoyed the aforementioned racetrack rundown, "It's a Simple Little System," as being a swell idea creatively executed. ("Who is Handel?" asks the head bookie; "Hialeah! Hialeah!" responds his hallelujah chorus.) And the leading lady has a tip-top eleven o'clock song, so contrived that a Judy Holliday or Faith Prince can out-Jolson Jolson. "I'm going back," she sings, "to the Bonjour Tristesse Brassiere Company." (*Bonjour Tristesse* was a racy 1954 novel by a nineteen-year-old Frenchwoman; the joke was lost, presumably, on 2001 audiences.) The rest of the songs are pleasant enough, enjoyable enough; but songs about strangers on subways and name-dropping socialites—even amusing songs—simply serve as padding.

Comden and Green and Styne, and their original director-choreographer Jerry Robbins and cochoreographer Bob Fosse, all knew their way around musical comedy by 1956. There was a common denominator among the creators: good old George Abbott. The modern musical comedy had more or less sprung out of Mr. Abbott's forehead, in a progression that went from *On Your Toes* to *Pal Joey* to *On the Town* (Robbins, Comden, and Green) to *High Button Shoes* (Robbins and Styne) to *Call Me Madam* (Robbins) to *Wonderful Town* (Comden and Green, with doctoring by Robbins) to *The Pajama Game* (Robbins and Fosse) to *Damn Yankees* (Fosse). But Abbott wasn't called for *Bells Are Ringing*, and I can't help but wonder if that doesn't account for the haphazard structure, too many lengthy nonmusical comedy scenes, and too few singing characters.

Bells was especially odd "on its toes." Abbott built many of his best musicals around dances by people like Balanchine ("Slaughter on Tenth Avenue" in *On Your Toes*), Robbins (several ballets in *On the Town*), and Fosse ("Steam Heat" and a ballet in *The Pajama Game*). *Bells Are Ringing* had both Robbins and Fosse on hand, with director Robbins calling the shots. So why is it such a lame dance show? An early party scene with the dancers doing party stuff; a highly incidental subway dance, which went on at length even though there was only the flimsiest reason for the characters to be in the subway in the first place; an incidental cha-cha thrown in because the heroine is about to go to a party; and a nightclub scene. I might be wrong, but *Bells* had to be the dullest show—dancewise—that Robbins or Fosse was ever involved in. And Robbins had carte blanche here. Go figure.

Bells Are Ringing was just another dispensable revival, in a season full of them.

All in all, *Bells* seems to me to be a George Abbott show without George Abbott. More accurately, it looks like a class project by an immensely talented bunch of graduating seniors, who did a pretty good job but could have used the master's touch.

Tina Landau, a decidedly modernist director, clearly saw that the show needed some oomph. Her solution was to place it squarely in the fifties. The fifties as seen through the nineties, that is, and that might well have been a mistake, because *Bells* did not take place in the fifties. It was written in the fifties, yes, but it took place in Never-Never Land.

For *Bells Are Ringing* is a fairy tale. A plain working girl dreams about

Bells Are Ringing
Opened: April 12, 2001
Closed: June 10, 2001
68 performances (and 36 previews)
Profit/Loss: Loss
Bells Are Ringing ($85 top) was scaled to a potential gross of
  $609,868 at the 1,022-seat Plymouth. Weekly grosses
  averaged about $271,000, hitting $339,000 the week
  after the opening but falling as low as $187,000 at the
  end of May. Total gross for the run was $3,527,176.
  Attendance was about 67 percent, with the box office
  grossing about 44 percent of dollar-capacity.

TONY AWARD NOMINATIONS
Best Revival of a Musical
Best Performance by a Leading Actress: Faith Prince

Critical Scorecard

Rave 1
Favorable 2
Mixed 1
Unfavorable 0
Pan 6

the glamorous, unattainable world outside. She puts on a glass slipper—or, in this case, a gown from *Traviata*—and becomes a princess, handily capturing her prince. The clock strikes twelve, the bubble bursts, "The Party's Over," and poor Cinderella—or Ella, or Melisande—flees back to her subbasement with its pails and mops. She even puts a mop over her head, as a disguise. The prince bursts in, the loose ends get tied, the bookies go to jail, and everybody lives happily ever after.

This is not a landscape in which foibles and follies of the fifties will help much, I'm afraid. We need a magical fairy tale, and a fairy-tale prince. Sydney Chaplin, who originated the role, was just that: the dapper son of the king of celluloid, the great Charles. Syd wasn't much of a singer, but Green introduced him to Holliday; she was smitten; and that was that. (Things weren't so rosy after the romance was over, but that's show business. Chaplin went on to serve the very same functions in *Funny Girl*, too. *That's* show business.)

The point is, Chaplin was an unattainable prince to a working girl from the wrong side of the tracks. Marc Kudisch, who played the role in the revival, was an up-and-coming musical comedy type; he made strong contributions to Cole Porter's *High Society* and Michael John LaChiusa's *The Wild Party*. But Kudisch wasn't handsome and classy enough to make the jaw of every woman (and half the men) in the audience drop. *Bells* needs Robert Redford, if you will, to complete the cartoon of Ella's fantasy. (If the guy looks like Robert Redford, he doesn't have to sing or dance.) Had they originally cast someone like Jerry Orbach in Chaplin's role, they'd have probably gotten a wonderful, warm performance. He wouldn't have provided the fuel that Chaplin gave Holliday to play off of, though.

The troubles with the 2001 *Bells* began early on. A November 2000 tryout at the Pasadena Playhouse (in California) was hastily canceled due to lack of funding. *Bells* vowed to go ahead nevertheless, announcing a four-week Boston break-in but ultimately settling for one week in Stamford, Connecticut. An ominous cloud appeared even before the first performance, when the local papers were told that they would not be getting tickets to the opening night.

The simple act of telling a newspaper editor not to send a critic is, in itself, a story. *Bells* might not, in fact, have been ready for a Connecticut reporter; but they were, in fact, charging Connecticut audiences $60 a ticket. The negative stories about the critical disinvitation were followed by bad word of mouth, which, in turn, were followed by bad reviews from the jilted critics. Malcolm Johnson of the *Hartford Courant* called it a "charming but feeble fable," while *Variety*'s local man, Markland Taylor, called it a "coarse, comic-strip revival."

The show moved back to New York for fine-tuning, but none of this boded well. Nor did gossip column items (apparently true) that coauthor Adolph Green was audibly cursing at the actors during preview performances. Nor did gossip column items (demonstrably true) that *Bells Are Ringing* checks were bouncing.

The show's troubles were nowhere near as serious as those of *Seussical*, say; but *Seussical* was a fully exploitable new musical with deep-pocketed backers and unlimited resources. *Bells* was just another dispensable revival, in a season full of them.

Blast

You could say that *Blast*, the self-described "explosive musical celebration," hit Broadway with a blast when it came to town for a ten-week engagement in mid-April. You could also say, though, that it was blasted by half the critics. Two of the four major New York dailies loved it, while the others positively excoriated it.

Consider this: "Exhilarating! Extraordinary!"—Howard Kissel in the *Daily News*. "Beguiling!" "Blissed-out"—Clive Barnes in the *Post*. "An unrelenting, amazingly whitebread amateur show"—Linda Winer in *Newsday*. And from Bruce Weber, the second-string critic of the all-important *Times*: "*Blast* bored me cross-eyed." Not what we call a money review.

Blast clearly struck a chord with some reviewers (and theatregoers), while definitely striking a nerve with others. These latter reacted as if they were insulted that *Blast* was on Broadway; it was too nontheatrical, too unsophisticated, and altogether far too squeaky-clean. Everyone is entitled to their opinion, I guess, even when their opinion can turn off thousands of potential ticket buyers. The *Times* critic was apparently hit by a backlash; in his review of *The Adventures of Tom Sawyer* a week later, he admitted that he is "a finicky theatergoer, the kind who is often accused of being a spoilsport, too eager to find fault and unwilling to yield to simple delight." This gave the benefit of the doubt to *Tom Sawyer*—which he otherwise drubbed, and not without reason—but it didn't help repair his *Blast* blast.

When the touring production of *Blast* was first announced, word was that it consisted of a marching band–like ensemble performing the sort of routines you'd see at football halftime shows. This was enough to keep me from wondering how I'd get through more than fifteen minutes without becoming—in the words of Mr. Weber—"bored cross-eyed." This turned out not to be the case at all, at least in my vision.

I ran into a friend at the opening-night party. (I liked *Blast* enough at a preview to return four days later, as a civilian, for the opening.) I didn't get to discuss the show with him, because these events are too loud and too full of people and flying food to have philosophical discussions. I called him the next day. He first saw *Blast* in London a year before it reached New York. He had to be dragged there kicking and screaming, he said; a marching band performing two hours of football halftime routines?? But

Blast clearly struck a chord with some reviewers and theatregoers, while definitely striking a nerve with others. These latter reacted as if they were insulted that Blast was on Broadway.

he loved it, so much so that he had his organization—one of those big corporations in the theatre business—sign on. If *Blast* could win over his jaded self, he figured, then it should work in America.

"But what about that review?" I asked. It turns out that my friend had just gotten off the phone with James Mason, the director and creator of *Blast*. (The quotes below are approximate, as this was a retelling of a conversation I did not hear.)

"Wasn't that a great night last night?" Mason asked him. "Wasn't the performance wonderful? Wasn't the party fun? Didn't everybody have a wonderful time?"

My friend, finally, said: "But didn't you see the reviews?"

"Yes," was the response. "And I feel sorry for that poor Mr. Weber. He seemed to be in such pain, having to say such unpleasant things about the show, and the cast. Poor man."

I have been at many late-night opening-night producer meetings, with the reviews rolling in; and I have heard plenty of comments about critics from producers who've just had their proverbial horse shot out from under them. Never, though, have I heard a producer express pity for a critic who has just cost him hundreds and hundreds of thousands of dollars.

But that, apparently, was the philosophy of Mason and his sponsor, Bill Cook. Cook Group Incorporated is "a worldwide family of companies that designs, manufactures and markets a complex group of diagnostic and minimally invasive surgical devices and instruments." That is to say, catheters and stents. At some point in time, the highly successful company (founded in 1963) became involved in funding the Indiana Uni-

Cast

Trey Alligood III

Rachel J. Anderson

Nicholas E. Angelis

Matthew A. Bank

Kimberly Beth Baron

Wesley Bullock

Mark Burroughs

Jesus Cantu Jr.

Jodina Rosario Carey

Robert Carmical

Alan "Otto" Compton

Dayne Delahoussaye

Karen Duggan

John Elrod

Brandon J. Epperson

Kenneth Frisby

J. Derek Gipson

Trevor Lee Gooch

Casey Marshall Gooding

Bradley Kerr Green

Benjamin Taber Griffin

Benjamin Raymond Handel

Benjamin W. Harloff

Joe Haworth

Darren M. Hazlett

Tim Heasley

Freddy Hernandez Jr.

George Hester

Jeremiah Todd Huber

Martin A. Hughes

Naoki Ishikawa

Stacy J. Johnson

Sanford R. Jones

Anthony F. Leps

Ray Linkous

Jean Marie Mallicoat

Jack Mansager

Brian Mayle

Dave Millen

Jim Moore

Westley Morehead

David Nash

Jeffrey A. Queen

Douglas Raines

Chris Rasmussen

Joseph J. Reinhart

Jamie L. Roscoe

Jennifer Ross

Christopher Eric Rutt

Christopher J. Schletter

Andrew Schnieders

Jonathan L. Schwartz

Greg Seale

Andy Smart

Radiah Y. Stewart

Bryan Anthony Sutton

Sean Terrell

Andrew James Toth

Joni Paige Viertel

Kristin Whiting

Original Touring Cast Album:
RCAVictor 09026-63723

versity School of Music; this led Cook to establish the Star of Indiana Drum and Bugle Corps in 1984, which in turn led to *Blast*. "It is the company's belief that sponsorship of such activities has a dramatic impact on both the members of *Blast* and its audiences. The creation and execution of this performance should be a life-changing, positive experience for everyone involved."

This sort of mission statement is in some ways quite laudable; put it in your Playbill bio, though, and you open yourself to jabs from critics who don't buy into your philosophy. One man's "life-changing, positive experience" can easily draw venom from another man or woman. (The aforementioned Ms. Winer called it an "Indiana school assembly with delusions of Las Vegas.")

The *Blast* ensemble consisted of sixty young men and women. According to the program bios, one of the dancers was nineteen years old and another thirty-two; the other fifty-eight ranged from twenty-one to twenty-nine, and these didn't seem to be the sort of theatre folk who lie about their ages. The group consisted of three distinct components: the brass section, the percussionists, and a "visual ensemble" of twelve dancer-singers. (Many of the performers effortlessly switched between groups to suit the needs of the orchestrators and choreographers.) The brass section specialized in trumpet, trombone, French horn, and tuba; there were also cornets, bass trombones, tromboniums, euphoniums, mellophones, flügelhorns, and even wee little piccolo trumpets which the players tossed high in the air between notes. (Don't try this at home.) The percussion section consisted of anything you could shake a stick at.

There was a grain of truth to the suggestion that this was a "whitebread" male entertainment from the hinterlands. According to an unscientific tabulation—from my seat, at the second performance I attended—the sixty-member troop included a grand total of three African-Americans. (One of whom was the most striking performer of the evening, Jodina Rosario Carey, a dancer who comported herself like she'd trained with Alvin Ailey.) There also appeared to be one American Indian woman, and one or two Hispanics. The "visual ensemble" was evenly divided among the sexes; otherwise, I found just three women instrumentalists. I noted, however, that there were more than a couple of men with multiple earrings. There were also quite a few flesh-colored bandages in sight; could some of them have been hiding tattoos of the nonmusical variety? Oh, one more thing: Fifty-nine of the sixty cast members were *thin*. Maybe from all that running around?? The one fellow who wasn't, Ben

Handel—a chunky percussionist with dirty-blond hair and round-paned glasses—turned out to be the star comedian of the second act.

I suppose I'd have been as annoyed by *Blast* as Weber and Winer, except that I liked it. The thing is, this was not marching bands in synchronized formations; *Blast* was music in motion. The evening began with a lone snare drummer onstage, beating out the tattoo that underlies Ravel's "Bolero." As the music began, on came the brass: choreographed trumpets, aerobicized trombones, and tubas crawling across the floor. (Tuba players crawling across the floor and playing at the same time, that is.) "Bolero," famously, builds and builds and builds. *Blast's* orchestrators managed to do just that, with the piece finally exploding into an orgiastic cacophony. In this case, two drummers came on, with kettle drums on wheels; as it came time for the final frenzy, they leapt into the air, landing full force on their mallets with the low-register brass blaring away while the aforementioned piccolo trumpets were tossed in the air and a pair of cymbalists danced like satyrs. The stage went wild, and so did the audience. Except for certain critics, apparently.

This was followed by a couple of items of minor interest, including one with the "visual ensemble" waving banners and chanting colors; another five minutes of this and they might have lost me. But the fourth number was a dazzler, set to Maynard Ferguson's "Everybody Loves the Blues." Eleven horn players draped themselves on turquoise folding chairs. On came Andy Smart, a trumpet player wearing sunglasses and a black Fosse hat with a turquoise band. Smart began playing, and let me tell you—this guy could play, giving a new meaning to the word "blast." The ensemble of horns, meanwhile, moved around so stylishly (while playing) that I thought, hey, they ought to send this choreographer over to *Follies* to help out.

This was followed by another less effective trumpet solo by another trumpet soloist, standing midair on a turquoise folding chair suspended from the flies. (Why? I wondered.) But the *Blast* corps went right back on track with a selection from Copland's *Appalachian Spring*. The middle section, from the sounds of it, was accompanied solely by percussion —who knew you could get such "musical" sound from percussionists?—and the majestic final part had a stageful of brass moving down to the curtain line playing full out into the house. Majestic, it sounded.

This was *not* marching bands in synchronized formations; *Blast* was music in motion.

This was immediately topped by something they called "Battery Battle," the counterpart of a challenge dance for two drummer boys. One fellow (Jeffrey A. Queen) offered a pyrotechnically dazzling display; a second (Nicholas E. Angelis) tried, more or less, to top him; and then the two attempted to engage in one of those old Errol Flynn swordfights, only with drumsticks. Sparks flew; it appeared that the sticks were chipping and the instruments were veritably smoking. They then went into a black-light section, joined by ten other drummers. Standing upstage in a line, they would rap upon the next drum over with fluorescent sticks. Was it "theatre"? Well, no; but it was arresting, and I'd never seen anything quite like it.

The evening went on this way, with more interesting numbers than not; of the sixteen selections, I found seven extragood and only four ordinary. One of the highlights was, of all things, a Spike Jones–like rendition of Leonard Bernstein's "Gee, Officer Krupke" from *West Side Story*. The musical term "scherzo" signifies a sprightly, humorous instrumental. That's precisely what "Krupke" was, complete with a trombonist on a unicycle. He exited up the aisle into the auditorium, crashed, and returned playing with his slide turned perpendicular. There was also a number called "Tangerinamadidge," which scattered the brass players throughout the house, playing their horns over your head and shaking hands with audience members. (This is the sort of thing that can understandably turn a grumpy critic lethal.)

Blast was also notable as the first Broadway attraction in years to arrive with no performers under union jurisdiction. Neither Actors' Equity nor AGVA (the American Guild of Variety Artists) appears to have expressed concern about the visual ensemble, who looked like dancer–singer–baton twirlers to me. Local 802 of the American Federation of Musicians did attempt to horn in on *Blast*, claiming that the other forty-

Blast
Opened: April 17, 2001
Closed: September 23, 2001
180 performances (and 13 previews)
Profit/Loss: To Be Determined
Blast ($80 top) was scaled to a potential gross of $902,406
   at the 1,678-seat Broadway. Weekly grosses averaged
   about $339,000, building to $425,000 in May but
   dropping to $233,000 after Labor Day. Total gross for the
   run was $8,169,127. Attendance was about 62 percent,
   with the box office grossing about 38 percent of dollar-
   capacity.

TONY AWARD NOMINATIONS
Special Theatrical Event (WINNER)
Best Choreography: Jim Moore, George Pinney, and John
   Vanderkloff

Critical Scorecard

Rave 3
Favorable 1
Mixed 1
Unfavorable 0
Pan 5

eight performers were "playing musicians" and thus covered by the Broadway contract. Technically, the Local 802 contract was negotiated with the League of American Theatres and Producers, and thus binding on its members. Nonmembers, including miscellaneous small-fry producers and Disney Theatrical, typically agree to abide by the League contracts or negotiate their own. The Shubert Organization, owners of the Broadway Theatre, are League members; the producers of *Blast* weren't, and thus saw no need to abide by the Local 802 contract.

Now, I'm all for union musicians and union members in general, but there are limits. Here you had musicians who needed to play numerous instruments; one fellow, according to the program, played trombone, bass trombone, euphonium, trombonium, and didgerydoo. (On this last: don't ask.) I'm sure that 802 could have sent dozens of people capable of playing all these instruments. But the musicians of *Blast* also needed to play the complete score onstage without a single piece of music; 802 musicians aren't required to memorize their parts. What's more, the staging necessitated that the *Blast* cast dance, crawl, leap, and execute choreography while playing. Next time you're at a musical, walk down to the orchestra pit at two minutes to eight and take a look. These men and women are trained musicians, and many of them are very exceptional players; but few of them are up to executing a back flip while playing Copland.

If a union can provide people capable of doing the job, then fine—let's discuss it. If a union cannot staff the job from within its ranks, then it seems like it is simply trying to take advantage of someone else's success.

Complicating this is the fact that Local 802 work rules allow musicians to miss a certain number of performances per week, by calling in "subs." These subs, theoretically, are supposed to be familiar with the score. Theoretically. (If you attend a big musical some Saturday night and hear the trumpet butcher the high notes, the odds are that the first-chair trumpet is off playing a big-money bar mitzvah.) Can you imagine a performance of *Blast* with six or seven underrehearsed subs onstage, rolling around with their euphoniums and mellophones and no music?

Local 802 of late has sponsored an informational advertising campaign, which included quarter-page ads in the very Playbills handed out at *Blast*. The ad said, in capital letters—some bold-faced, some merely underlined—"Paying for a theatre ticket? Then you deserve the best. Live music is essential to great theatre."

Was it "theatre"? Well, no; but it was arresting, and I'd never seen anything quite like it.

Here, at *Blast*, you had forty-five live musicians on the stage of a Broadway theatre—the most, I imagine, since some long-ago spectacle in the 1940s. In fact, *Blast* pretty clearly demonstrated the power of live music; forty-five players, all of them with loud instruments, firing away straight at you made for an illustrious sound. But Local 802 was not amused. I supposed that what they really meant was not "support live musicians" but "support dues-paying musicians."

The Producers

In retrospect, *The Producers* sounded like a surefire can't-miss crowd-pleaser. Start with that brilliant, comic gem of a film; put the whole thing in the hands of comic genius Mel Brooks; and cast expert farceurs Nathan Lane and Matthew Broderick in the leading roles. What could possibly have gone wrong?

Plenty.

The first rule of adaptations is—or should be—if you can't enhance the experience of the original, don't do it. As, for instance, the 1966 musical *Breakfast at Tiffany's*. This highly anticipated blockbuster garnered a massive million-dollar advance (at an $11.90 top), thanks to the popularity of the 1961 film and the musical's stars Mary Tyler Moore and Richard Chamberlain. But the show was a mess; in a drastic salvage attempt, producer David Merrick threw out the book on the road, replacing it with a new one by Edward Albee (of all people). Merrick ultimately closed *Breakfast at Tiffany's* altogether during Broadway previews, "rather than subject the drama critics and the public to an excruciatingly boring evening." And then there was the musical version of *Gone with the Wind*, a big hit in Tokyo (under the title *Scarlett*); a moderate hit in London; and a quick tryout failure in America in 1973.

Broadway has its own graveyard of musical versions of great films: the mausoleum includes titles like *Nothing's Sacred*; *Destry Rides Again*; *Hail, the Conquering Hero*; *The Yearling*; *The Blue Angel*; *La Strada*; and *Some Like It Hot*. Musicalizations of memorable (though less-than-classic) films have failed as well: *The Quiet Man*; *Miracle on 34th Street*; *Never on Sunday*; *Zorbá the Greek*; *Georgy Girl*; *Lilies of the Field*; *The Baker's Wife*; *King of Hearts*; *Woman of the Year*; and *The Goodbye Girl*. Most recently, *Sun-*

set *Boulevard* and *Big*—thud!—failed to measure up to their cinematic predecessors.

There have been exceptions, including *Promises! Promises!*, the 1968 adaptation of Billy Wilder's *The Apartment*, which enhanced the screenplay by adding a Neil Simon jokebook and the contemporary pop melodies by Burt Bacharach; *Applause*, the 1970 adaptation of *All About Eve*, which had a bravura performance by Lauren Bacall; *A Little Night Music*, the 1973 adaptation of *Smiles of a Summer Night*, which Sondheimized Bergman with ravishing results; and the 2000 adaptation of *The Full Monty*, which transplanted the characters to America. But a whole lot of money has been lost on Broadway stabs at surefire film hits.

(Movie musicals are even more difficult to stage. *Gigi, Singin' in the Rain, Seven Brides for Seven Brothers, High Society, State Fair*, and *The Red Shoes* all failed on Broadway. Not to mention *Footloose* and *Saturday Night Fever*; and, as I write this, *Fame* and *Dirty Dancing* and *White Christmas* and *An American in Paris* are being bandied about. The primary exception—a movie musical that was actually enhanced for Broadway—has been *42nd Street*, as discussed later in these pages.)

As for *The Producers*, it should be added that while Brooks earned an Oscar for his 1968 screenplay, the film itself was commercially unsuccessful in its original release. Not that that fact dampens the film's brilliance.

By 1968, Brooks was already known—in relatively limited circles—as one of America's funniest funny men. He began his writing career in 1951 as one of a pack of hardworking gagmen toiling for TV's "King of Comedy," Sid Caesar, on *Your Show of Shows* (and related programs). It's hard to stand out in the pack when the pack is filled with folks like Neil Simon, Larry Gelbart, Carl Reiner, and—at the tail end of Caesar's reign—Michael Stewart and Woody Allen. Once Caesar was deposed, each of these guys did okay on their own.

What could possibly have gone wrong? Plenty. Broadway has its own graveyard of musical versions of great films.

Brooks first established himself as an extraordinary zany in 1960, when he teamed with Reiner for the instant classic comedy LP *The 2000 Year Old Man*. This was followed the following year by *2000 and One Years*; both were best-sellers. Brooks won his first Oscar for the 1963 animated short subject, *The Critic*. In 1965, he was cocreator (with Buck Henry) of the long-running sitcom *Get Smart*. Brooks didn't stick around, though; he came up with the basic setup, wrote the pilot and two other episodes,

St. JAMES THEATRE

A JUJAMCYN THEATRE

JAMES H. BINGER
CHAIRMAN

ROCCO LANDESMAN
PRESIDENT

PAUL LIBIN
PRODUCING DIRECTOR

JACK VIERTEL
CREATIVE DIRECTOR

Rocco Landesman SFX Theatrical Group The Frankel · Baruch · Viertel · Routh Group
Bob and Harvey Weinstein Rick Steiner Robert F.X. Sillerman Mel Brooks
In Association with James D. Stern/Douglas Meyer

present

Nathan Lane Matthew Broderick

in

THE PRODUCERS

the new

Mel Brooks

musical

Book by Mel Brooks and Thomas Meehan Music and Lyrics by Mel Brooks
and by Special Arrangement with StudioCanal

also starring

Roger Bart Gary Beach Cady Huffman Brad Oscar

With

Madeleine Doherty Kathy Fitzgerald Eric Gunhus
Peter Marinos Jennifer Smith Ray Wills

Jim Borstelmann Jeffry Denman Bryn Dowling Robert H. Fowler Adrienne Gibbons
Ida Gilliams Kimberly Hester Naomi Kakuk Jamie LaVerdiere Matt Loehr Brad Musgrove
Christina Marie Norrup Angie L. Schworer Abe Sylvia Tracy Terstriep

Scenery Designed by
Robin Wagner

Costumes Designed by
William Ivey Long

Lighting Designed by
Peter Kaczorowski

Sound Designed by
Steve C. Kennedy

Casting by
Johnson-Liff Associates

Associate Director
Steven Zweigbaum

Associate Choreographer
Warren Carlyle

Wigs & Hair Designed by
Paul Huntley

Music Direction and Vocal Arrangements by
Patrick S. Brady

Orchestrations by
Doug Besterman

Music Coordinator
John Miller

General Management
Richard Frankel Productions
Laura Green

Technical Supervisor
Juniper Street
Productions

Press Representative
Barlow · Hartman
public relations

Associate Producers
Frederic H. and Rhoda Mayerson
Lynn Landis

Musical Arrangements and Supervision by
Glen Kelly

Direction and Choreography by
Susan Stroman

Original Broadway Cast Recording Available On Sony Classical

Cast (in order of appearance)

The Usherettes Bryn Dowling, Jennifer Smith

Max Bialystock Nathan Lane

Leo Bloom Matthew Broderick

Hold-me Touch-me Madeleine Doherty

Mr. Marks Ray Wills

Franz Liebkind Brad Oscar

Carmen Ghia Roger Bart

Roger De Bris Gary Beach

Bryan Peter Marinos

Kevin Ray Wills

Scott Jeffry Denman

Shirley Kathy Fitzgerald

Ulla Cady Huffman

Lick-me Bite-me Jennifer Smith

Kiss-me Feel-me Kathy Fitzgerald

Jack Lepidus Peter Marinos

Donald Dinsmore Jeffry Denman

Jason Green Ray Wills

Lead Tenor Eric Gunhus

Sergeant Ray Wills

O'Rourke Abe Sylvia

O'Riley Matt Loehr

O'Houllihan Robert H. Fowler

Guard Jeffry Denman

Bailiff Abe Sylvia

Judge Peter Marinos

Foreman of Jury Kathy Fitzgerald

Trustee Ray Wills

Ensemble Jeffry Denman, Madeleine Doherty, Bryn Dowling, Kathy Fitzgerald, Robert H. Fowler, Ida Gilliams, Eric Gunhus, Kimberly Hester, Naomi Kakuk, Matt Loehr, Peter Marinos, Angie L. Schworer, Jennifer Smith, Abe Sylvia, Tracy Terstriep, Ray Wills

Swings Jim Borstelmann, Adrienne Gibbons, Jamie LaVerdiere, Brad Musgrove, Christina Marie Norrup

Time and Place: New York, 1959

Original Broadway Cast Album: Sony Classical SK 89646

then left to launch his feature film career with what was then called *Springtime for Hitler*.

Brooks followed *The Producers* with a similarly unsuccessful (but nowhere near as interesting) film, *The Twelve Chairs* (1970). He persevered, however, and had a very good year in 1974 with two box office blockbusters, *Blazing Saddles* and *Young Frankenstein*. These twin hits made Brooks famous on a large scale, and he has remained so for more than a quarter of a century.

However—and there is always a however, isn't there?—success didn't give Brooks a gold finger (as it were). *Frankenstein* was followed by *Silent Movie* (1976); *High Anxiety* (1977); *History of the World, Part I* (1981); *To Be or Not to Be* (1983); *Spaceballs* (1987); *Life Stinks* (1991); *Robin Hood: Men in Tights* (1993); and *Dracula: Dead and Loving It* (1995). I'm sure there must be a whole lot of people, somewhere, who loved all of these films. (Anne Bancroft, maybe?) I myself ceased to be amused after *Young Frankenstein* and have found some of them painful to sit through. All in all, Brooks—despite his genius—has had bumpy sledding since *Young Frankenstein*. (At the same time, he has produced a fine slate of "non–Mel Brooks" films—under the banner Brooksfilms—including *The Elephant Man* and *My Favorite Year*.)

The Producers—the film, that is—is for obvious reasons a great favorite of theatre folk, present company included. For years, people had been after Brooks to turn the film into a big, bouncy, Broadway musical. In the spring of 1998, Hollywood mogul David Geffen—who had coproduced a couple of little shows on Broadway called *Cats* and *Dreamgirls*—finally talked Brooks into it.

Geffen, who eventually withdrew from the project, sent Brooks over to Jerry Herman. Herman, composer-lyricist of *Hello, Dolly!* and *Mame* (but no new Broadway show since 1983), sensibly figured that this was no job for him. The "Springtime for Hitler" production number was the heart of the film and inevitably would be the high point of the musical. How do you do *The Producers* with a score that omits "Springtime for Hitler"? Audiences would stone you. (For the record, *Breakfast at Tiffany's* was produced without "Moon River," *Gone with the Wind* without "Tara's Theme.") Sure, Herman or Charles Strouse or Cy Coleman or Stephen Flaherty could write new songs for *The Producers* and interpolate "Springtime for Hitler." It would sound totally different than anything else in the score, though, and presumably make the new songs sound relatively colorless. Herman told Brooks to get the guy who wrote "Springtime for Hitler"—

Melvin J. Kaminsky Brooks himself. Which appears to have been the answer Brooks wanted to hear in the first place.

Brooks did have some pre-*Producers* Broadway experience, but nothing that might inspire confidence. He made his local debut with a gem of a revue sketch in Leonard Sillman's *New Faces of 1952*. "Of Fathers and Sons" was a spoof of *Death of a Salesman*, with the noble young son disappointing his father by refusing to go into the family trade. (Dad was a pickpocket.) Sillman was quite a character—I did a few budgets for him in the early seventies, for which I never got paid—and I can only guess that the bravura comedy scene in *The Producers*, set in "the living room of renowned theatrical director Roger Debris's elegant Upper East Side townhouse on a sunny Tuesday afternoon in June," was patterned on the dramatis personae of and goings-on at Leonard's overmortgaged mansion at 17 East Seventy-ninth (owned, at this writing, by New York mayor Michael R. Bloomberg).

Brooks wrote his first musical in 1957, while still in Caesar's forum. *Shinbone Alley* was an unlikely tale about a cockroach in love with an

alley cat, starring Eddie Bracken and Eartha Kitt; it lasted a mere six weeks. The songwriters were also Broadway novices, although Joe Darion would reappear in 1965 with *Man of La Mancha*.

The 1962 musical *All American*, on the other hand, had the makings of a blockbuster. Songwriters Charles Strouse and Lee Adams (and their producer) were coming off *Bye Bye Birdie*; director Joshua Logan was still one of Broadway's greats (although he was fated never to have another hit); Brooks was the 2000 *Year Old Man*; and beloved song-and-dance man Ray Bolger was returning to Broadway after a decade's absence. The show, though, was a ragtag stinker and ran through its sizable advance in just ten weeks.

Brooks briefly returned to Broadway as ghost-doctor for *Kelly*, the 1965 musical that stunned the industry by closing the very same night it opened. (This was to become a common occurrence, but at the time it was a shocker.) Brooks was not to be blamed for *Kelly*; he simply stepped in to help Daniel Melnick, for whom he was then developing *Get Smart*. (Melnick was one of the *Kelly* producers, and Richard Rodgers's son-in-law.) The out-of-town madness of *Kelly* is relevant, though, in that it might well have sharpened Brooks's insight into Bialystock and Bloom.

Flash forward to 1998. After five or six poor films, Brooks turned back to Broadway. (Those with long memories will recall that washed-up film geniuses Ben Hecht and Preston Sturges both ended their careers as librettists of bad Broadway musicals. Adapted from good films.) How likely was it for a man with this set of Broadway credits to come back thirty-six years later with the biggest hit in well over thirty-six years?

Brooks was joined on the book by Tom Meehan, his collaborator on *To Be or Not to Be* and *Spaceballs*. Meehan came to *The Producers* with an all-time super-smash hit in his pocket, the 1977 musical *Annie*. He seemed fated to be a one-hit wonder, though, having followed his first show with the excessively mirthless *I Remember Mama*, *Annie 2*, *Ain't Broadway Grand*, and *Annie Warbucks*. *The Producers*, suddenly, gave Meehan two of Broadway's biggest hits of all time. Not bad for a fellow who turned to musical comedy in his late forties.

Nathan Lane and Matthew Broderick are among Broadway's top clowns, with surefire box office appeal. But that only takes them so far. Lane had a sitcom disaster in 1998 so embarrassing that he didn't even mention it in his Playbill bio (which said he won "the People's Choice Award for Favorite Actor in a New TV Series" but didn't tell us that the series was named *Encore! Encore!*). As for Broderick, *The Producers* was his second Broadway show in fifty-one weeks; look up *Taller Than a Dwarf* in *Broadway Yearbook, 1999–2000* for the gory details.

So maybe *The Producers* wasn't as foolproof as one might have imagined. But, happily, everything worked brilliantly. Brooks is famous for his excesses, and his cohorts seemed to keep up with his every deranged whim. Starting at the top were those stars of his. Lane has long demonstrated himself to be larger than life. In *The Producers*, he was given a full plate of jokes and comedy business worthy of his art, plus all the scenery he could chew. He, too, was on Broadway earlier in the year, in the Roundabout revival of *The Man Who Came to Dinner*—a highly capable comic actor undertaking a bravura comedy role for which he was mismatched. Max Bialystock, though, was in Lane's blood. He probably could have walked through this role effortlessly, just by conjuring the memory of Zero Mostel. But Lane chose not to take the easy path. He seems to have conjured Jackie Gleason—a very different balloon of a buffoon than Mostel—and stuffed him alongside Zero in Bialystock's cardboard belt. (Choreographer Susan Stroman seems to have been in on the joke, sending out ersatz June Taylor dancers for the opening number.) Thus, instead of merely getting an expert re-creation of Mostel's performance, Lane wisely gave us a new and original Bialystock. The result: After ten minutes you didn't miss Zero; you were too busy laughing at Nathan.

Broderick had a somewhat harder assignment with the somewhat lesser role of Leo Bloom. Why "Leo Bloom?" I ask parenthetically. I don't know, but Mostel's most important role—prior to his emergence on Broadway with *A Funny Thing Happened on the Way to the Forum* and *Fiddler on the Roof*—was as a somewhat different Leo Bloom, in the 1958 James Joyce adaptation *Ulysses in Nighttown*. Bialystocker was a major Jewish city in nineteenth-century Poland, and the birthplace of that non-bagel, the bialy; Max was the name Brooks had already given both his *Get Smart* hero and his own son.

Gene Wilder was unforgettable as the film's second banana (billed below the title), but Brooks and Meehan saw fit to expand the role to costar status. Broderick demonstrated that he was every bit as much of a ham as Lane; Matthew was Smithfield, to Nathan's Westphalian. (Smith and West, it sounds like one of those turn-of-the-century comedy teams made up of a couple of immigrants named Skulnik and Vestenberger.) The stage Leo had an added dimension, thanks to a grafted-on romance with the expanded Ulla Inga Hansen Bensen Yonsen Tallen-Hallen Svaden-Svanson (played with flair by Cady Huffman). Broderick came up with a lovely performance as a clown with heart. Pretty crafty, actually; as the plot allowed Bloom to bloom, Broderick sang and danced with the grace of an actuarial Fred Astaire.

The leading hams were supported by four more, just as flavorful. Gary Beach stole the show—or would have, were it not for the company of the others—as director Roger De Bris. (I always assumed Brooks named him after garbage—debris—but wouldn't you know it, Mel was thinking of the Jewish ritual of circumcision.) Beach's role was expanded, too, plunging him into the show-within-the-show. This was a major change from the film, where a character named Lorenzo St. DuBois tripped his way through the part. (His friends called him LSD, if that gives you an idea.)

I was especially pleased by the excision of LSD and his NSG (not-so-good) song "Love Power," which I find the weakest stretch of the film.

The leggy Ms. Huffman made a splashy impression as a showgirl ("Ziegfeld's Favorite") in the 1991 musical *The Will Rogers Follies*, which I otherwise found charmless and pretty offensive. Huffman's Ulla was not a dumb Swedish blonde; she was a smart Swedish blonde who knew precisely how to play her hand. Brooks gave her a philosophical turn called "When You Got It, Flaunt It," which she certainly did. Got it and flaunt it, that is.

Brad Oscar got the biggest break in the show, when Ron Orbach broke his leg during rehearsals. (Injured his knee, rather.) On went his up-from-the-chorus understudy, a fellow whose most recent gig had been as Santa Claus in Branson, Missouri. Oscar filled in for the Chicago tryout, received reviews too good to ignore, and Orbach was history. (Which takes us once again—for the third time in this *Broadway Yearbook*—to Neil Simon's 1993 *Laughter on the 23rd Floor*, a fic-

> **Broderick demonstrated that he was every bit as much of a ham as Lane; Matthew was Smithfield, to Nathan's Westphalian.**

tionalized farcical visit to the writer's room at the old Sid Caesar show. Among the characters was a not too fondly drawn version of Mel Brooks. And who played Simon's Brooks? Ron Orbach.)

Rounding out the "also starring" players was Roger Bart as Beach's "common-law assistant," who outdid all the second bananas for my dollar. (Or my $100.) Bart simply slinked his way through the evening, swiveling from his hips with his arms wrapped around his torso. The other performers took advantage of their laugh lines; Bart took advantage of everybody else's laughs. Pure delight.

When you get six principal performers this good—and a handful of others in numerous small roles—you might well look through the Playbill for the names of the casting directors. Geoff Johnson and Vinny Liff—despite years and years with all those *Cats* and *Phantoms* and *misérable* Parisians and Vietnamese—sure knew how to assemble a gaggle of gagsters.

Brooks, for his part, selected an exceptional staff for his big Broadway adventure. That is, he picked the right door to knock on at the inception. Director Mike Ockrent had a way with broad musical comedy, as evidenced by his direction of *Me and My Girl* and *Crazy for You* (both revised versions of 1930s musicals). Ockrent selected Susan Stroman to choreo-

graph the latter show, and the two quickly teamed professionally and mat-
rimonially.

Ockrent and Stroman set to work with Brooks on *The Producers* in late
1998, with Ockrent reassembling his favored colleagues: set designer
Robin Wagner (of *Crazy for You* and *Big*); William Ivey Long (of *Crazy for
You*, *A Christmas Carol*, and *Big*); orchestrator Doug Besterman (of *A
Christmas Carol* and *Big*); musical supervisor Glen Kelly (dance arranger
of *A Christmas Carol* and Stroman's *Steel Pier*); and conductor Patrick S.
Brady (rehearsal pianist of *Crazy for You* and vocal arranger of *Big*).

Curiously missing from the mix was Paul Gemignani, musical director
of *Crazy for You*, *A Christmas Carol*, and *Big*. Gemignani was apparently in
line for both *The Producers* and *The Adventures of Tom Sawyer*, the latter
spearheaded by *Crazy for You* librettist Ken Ludwig. When the dates
conflicted, he chose *Tom Sawyer*. My guy in the orchestra pit says that
Gemignani's *Sawyer* deal included a piece of the profits, which is highly
unusual for a musical director. *Tom Sawyer* ran two weeks, *The Producers*
ran forever. Gemignani received a lifetime achievement award on Tony
night, but he might well have re-
gretted not being part of Broadway's biggest hit.

Brooks and Meehan and Ockrent and Stroman got down to
work, but within the year Ockrent
became ill with leukemia; he died
in December 1999. (During the
initial months of the run, the *Producers* Playbills included a quarter-
page notice stating, "Mike Ockrent inspired the team of *The
Producers* forward on their joyful
musical adventure. We dedicate
each laugh to his memory," with
the address of the Mike Ockrent
Memorial Fund at Memorial
Sloan-Kettering Cancer Center.)
At that point, Stroman had
never directed a Broadway musi-
cal (although *Contact* and the revival of *The Music Man* were slated to
open the following March and April). Brooks, nevertheless, asked Stro-

man to take over as director of *The Producers*. A very good decision, as it turned out.

What does a director do, anyway? Many things. In the case of a gag-stuffed musical like this, she controls traffic and collates jokes, keeping the audience on the crest of hilarity. You can't have too many jokes, but *The Producers* did—so many that they could sacrifice big laughs for bigger ones. This made theatregoers want to go back again, to catch the gags they were too busy laughing through the first time. (Under present-day Broadway economics, repeat customers are becoming indispensable—although it's difficult to go back if you can't get a ticket in the first place.) The trick, here, was to organize things to maximum effect, making the show build and build and build. With *The Producers*, it was a question of Stroman using the various production elements—actors, scenery, costumes, lights, and orchestra—to make sure the pandemonium hit when she (and Mel) wanted it to.

Stroman did this magnificently. Selecting and editing what to use; policing the line between too much and *much* too much too much; and keeping her comic geniuses from stepping on each other's laughs. And not just the actors; *The Producers* featured numerous gags from other departments. It was almost as if Mel (as producer) directed his troops to devise the show that set designer Oliver Smith and costume designer Raoul Pène duBois and orchestrator Irv Kostal and choreographer Gower Champion would have come up with in 1959—and then goose up the effects a couple of steps past the bounds of taste. Wagner and Long and Besterman and Stroman came through, with laughs galore.

Like the singing pigeon puppets, with their Nazi salutes and armbands. Like the little old lady dance number, using walkers fitted with taps. Like the show posters on the wall of Max's office: *The Breaking Wind*; *King Leer*; *100 Dollar Legs*; *The Kidney Stone* and its sequel, *This Too Shall Pass*; and *When Cousins Marry*, with a drawing of a happy bride and groom with big smiles and crossed eyes. Brooks and Stroman and Wagner reprised this joke in the final scene, with even bigger results. A full-stage drop spelled out Bialystock and Bloom's hits: *Katz*; *Maim*; *South Passaic*; *A Streetcar Named Murray*; *High Button Jews*; *Death of a Salesman on Ice!*; *47th Street*; and *She Stupps to Conquer*.

Costume designer William Ivey Long—who just might have the best sense of humor (in his work) of any Broadway designer—had Mel Brooks and a big budget and cross-dressing directors and tap-dancing Nazis and showgirls wearing bratwurst and no holds barred, resulting in one of the funniest sets of costumes ever seen on the Broadway stage. My personal favorite: the garb of Shirley Markowitz (Kathy Fitzgerald), Roger De Bris's lighting designer. Following five supremely overdressed theatrical types, Shirley bounced on wearing brown work pants and a purple-plaid flannel shirt, looking like she was just back from a month on the farm with Peggy Webster and Cheryl Crawford. Oh yes, there was an oversized coil of electric cable swinging from the front of her belt. I've never seen a Broadway lighting designer hefting a coil of cable; they're in the wrong union, don't you know. I suppose this must have been in some way symbolic.

You can't have too many jokes, but *The Producers* did—so many that they could sacrifice big laughs for bigger ones.

The designers were adding frosting to the cake, as it were. The music department, though, had a lot of heavy lifting. The first-time songwriter's music tended toward the simplistic and was not all that distinguished. (Brooks's raucous lyrics, on the other hand, were wildly undisciplined but perfect under the circumstances.) Sitting through songs like "I Want to Be a Producer" and "You Never Say 'Good Luck' on Opening Night," I noted that while the music was undistinguished, the *numbers*—as performed and staged and orchestrated—worked wonderfully well. So let's say the score was very good, in the context of the piece at least. And isn't that what you want in musical comedy? I don't suppose that Mel's melodies will outpace Lerner and Loewe's songs for *My Fair Lady*, but his royalties well may.

Composer Brooks publicly and repeatedly praised Glen Kelly for translating his melodies into a full-fledged score, so I suppose that the praise was warranted. (Kelly was billed for "Musical Arrangements and Supervision.") Brady did a great job conducting his first big Broadway musical, providing sterling vocal arrangements as well. The "Führer is creating a furor" section of the "Springtime for Hitler" number was a delicious throwback to the Kay Thompson–Hugh Martin sound, and there was some lovely chirruping for the old biddies in "'Til Him." Besterman's orchestrations were consistently over the top, buoying the sometimes pedestrian melodies with brass and blare. Besterman also did a fine job earlier in the season, on the very different *Seussical*. On the Tony telecast, both Besterman and Brooks credited Larry Blank for "ghosting" a significant portion of the show. This is a common practice on Broadway musicals, when time—and overtime—are at a premium. Blank orchestrated about one-quarter of the show, including "When You Got It, Flaunt It" and "Till Him."

This seems as good a place as any to mention one of the more curious aspects of the piece: the song that got away. Not a song, exactly; an interior chunk of "Betrayed," rather. Word circulated early in the Chicago tryout that the show contained a wicked takeoff on "Rose's Turn" from *Gypsy*. Word circulated just as quickly that Arthur Laurents, librettist of *Gypsy*, claimed that it would weaken the future value of his show and forced Brooks to remove it.

Now, perhaps there was more to the case. While performing rights to a show are generally controlled jointly by the authors, rights for outside use of the songs belong solely to the songwriters. I don't suppose that Stephen Sondheim or the Jule Styne estate objected to this affectionate borrowing. There is plenty of precedent in the annals of Broadway; Gershwin on occasion quoted Kern and Arthur Sullivan, Sondheim quoted Gershwin and Kern, and numerous Broadway songs quote Irving Berlin. At any rate, it seems odd that *The Producers* thought to ask Laurents. He prides himself on being arbitrary, and it is not surprising that he objected. (Otherwise, would we even be mentioning his name here in *Broadway Yearbook*?)

What was lost was a ninety-five second swath of hilarity. The first section of "Betrayed" ends with the line "I have no one who I can cry to, no one I can say goodbye to." At this point in the original, Max cried: "Everybody's got his big moment. When's it gonna be Max's turn?" The orchestra, naturally enough, swung into that clashing vamp immediately identifiable to show tune fans. "Max is getting angry, Max is getting mad," he started, continuing through "Max is feeling left out, Max is getting pissed" until he finally complains, "Max is in the s—house, Max is up the creek." At this point he says, "I'm drowning, I'm drowning here" and the number resumed as in the final version. The "Max's Turn" section also included two measures of "Babette" from *On the Twentieth Century*, although I don't suppose that Comden, Green, or Coleman would have registered a complaint.

Yes, this was incredibly funny, and it's a shame that it had to be excised. No harm done, though; the song, in its final version, worked per-

> Sitting through the second act, I realized that my three favorite moments from the film had been omitted. And I was laughing so much that I really didn't care in the least.

The Producers

Opened: April 19, 2001

Still playing May 28, 2001

46 performances (and 33 previews)

Profit/Loss: Profit

The Producers ($99 top) was scaled to a potential gross of
$1,022,031 at the 1,706-seat St. James. (These figures
include the opening-day price increase from $90 to $99,
which with the "restoration charge" made the show
Broadway's first $100 musical. The St. James also increased
capacity by forty seats over the first month.) Weekly
grosses averaged about $979,000, selling just about every
ticket—except press and Tony voter comps—and ultimately
climbing over $1,060,000. Total gross for the partial season
was $9,664,942. Attendance was about 97 percent, with
the box office grossing about 98 percent of dollar-capacity.

TONY AWARD NOMINATIONS

Best Musical (WINNER)

Best Book of a Musical: Mel Brooks and Thomas Meehan
(WINNER)

Best Original Score: Mel Brooks (WINNER)

Best Performance by a Leading Actor: Matthew Broderick

Best Performance by a Leading Actor: Nathan Lane (WINNER)

Best Performance by a Featured Actor: Roger Bart

Best Performance by a Featured Actor: Gary Beach (WINNER)

Best Performance by a Featured Actor: Brad Oscar

Best Performance by a Featured Actress: Cady Huffman
(WINNER)

Best Direction of a Musical: Susan Stroman (WINNER)

Best Choreography: Susan Stroman (WINNER)

Best Scenic Design: Robin Wagner (WINNER)

Best Costume Design: William Ivey Long (WINNER)

Best Lighting Design: Peter Kaczorowski (WINNER)

Best Orchestrations: Doug Besterman (WINNER)

NEW YORK DRAMA CRITICS CIRCLE AWARD

Best Musical (WINNER)

DRAMA DESK AWARDS

Outstanding Musical (WINNER)

Outstanding Actor: Nathan Lane (WINNER)

Outstanding Featured Actor: Gary Beach (WINNER)

Outstanding Featured Actress: Cady Huffman (WINNER)

Outstanding Director of a Musical: Susan Stroman (WINNER)

Outstanding Choreography: Susan Stroman (WINNER)

Outstanding Book of a Musical: Mel Brooks and Thomas
Meehan (WINNER)

Outstanding Lyrics: Mel Brooks (WINNER)

Outstanding Orchestrations: Doug Besterman (WINNER)

Outstanding Set Design of a Musical: Robin Wagner (WINNER)

Outstanding Costume Design: William Ivey Long (WINNER)

*Critical
Scorecard*

Rave	8
Favorable	2
Mixed	0
Unfavorable	0
Pan	0

fectly. Late in the number, Max does a mini-montage reprise of the evening's proceedings. When he reaches the intermission, he says "intermission"—and sits silently on his cot, while the theatre rocks with laughter. Would this moment be as funny if it was the second break in the "Betrayed" number? No, I suppose it would be weakened. Besides, Nathan Lane underwent severe vocal problems for at least the first nine months of the run. Imagine if he had an additional ninety-five seconds to belt out angrily, pushing his tour de force well over six minutes. So the loss of "Max's Turn" was unfortunate, but perhaps for the best.

And yes, *The Producers* sported a $100 top ticket price. A $99 price, actually, with a $1 "restoration fee" tacked on. (This money goes to the theatre, not the production, although royalty recipients are now rightfully getting their hands on a slice of it.) *The Producers* producers raised the ticket price from $90 the day after the opening. Such an event might normally cause grumbling, but ticket buyers were way too busy trying to buy tickets to let the extra sawbuck get in their way.

The Producers so overwhelmed the 2000–2001 season that the show has inevitably spilled over into this volume's introduction. For a discussion of where *The Producers* fits in the Broadway pantheon, turn back to page 3.

One of the problems of adapting a beloved film—especially in this day of VHS and DVD, with fast forward at the ready—is the hazard of outraging fans whose favorite moments have been scrapped. Three of my favorite moments in the film:

Number 1: "He keeps boids. Doity, disgusting, filthy, lice-ridden boids." This from Liebkind's landlady (or concierge, as she proudly points out).

Number 2: The following exchange, in the box office lobby at the opening of *Springtime for Hitler*. (The film used the about-to-be-demolished Playhouse Theatre, across the street from the Cort, for interior and exterior shots). Max slips a pair of tickets to the drama critic of the *Times*, a distinguished old fellow in a Vandyke, apparently meant to resemble Harrison Grey Fiske.

"There seems to be some mistake," says the *Times*, "there's a hundred-dollar bill wrapped around these tickets."

"That's no mistake," says Max, "enjoy the show."

"Mr. Bialystock—what do you think you're doing?"

"I'm bribing you."

Number 3: During the first flush of the "Springtime for Hitler" number, there's a wonderful reaction shot of the audience, mouths collectively agape. A couple storm up the aisle, and a tart-tongued first-nighter says, "Well, talk about bad taste."

Sitting through the second act of *The Producers: the new Mel Brooks musical* (as it is officially named), I realized that my three favorite moments had been omitted. And I was laughing so much that I really didn't care in the least.

The Gathering

Arje Shaw, the author of the Holocaust-themed drama *The Gathering*, "arrived in New York City in 1949 at the age of eight with his parents and sister from a displaced persons camp in Bergen Belsen, Germany." This from his Playbill bio, which concludes with "Mr. Shaw would like to dedicate this play to the martyrs and survivors who found the strength to pick up the pieces and rebuild their lives."

Mr. Shaw was very much in earnest, and one can only admire his intentions. But his play was clunky. You might get the benefit of the doubt at the West Coast Jewish Theatre in Los Angeles, where *The Gathering* had its first reading with a cast headed by Ed Asner, or even at New York's Jewish Repertory Theatre, where it was produced in 1999 with Theodore Bikel in the lead. But Broadway is a tough-hearted place, especially when you're one of seven shows opening within the final sixteen days of the season.

What *The Gathering* did have was two highly effective scenes:

> One can only admire the playwright's intentions. But Broadway is a tough-hearted place, especially when you're one of seven shows opening within the final sixteen days of the season.

an arresting one at the end of the first act, and an engrossing one at the end of the second. In fact, I wouldn't be all that surprised if Mr. Shaw worked backward. The second-act scene was the heart of *The Gathering*, its reason for being; the first-act scene provided the reason for getting us to the second. All good plays should build to the first-act curtain and, ultimately, to the final scene; that's only natural. In this case, though, it was as if the two scenes were on steep cliffs with no access stairs. It appears as if Shaw started with his two highly dramatic scenes, then patched to-

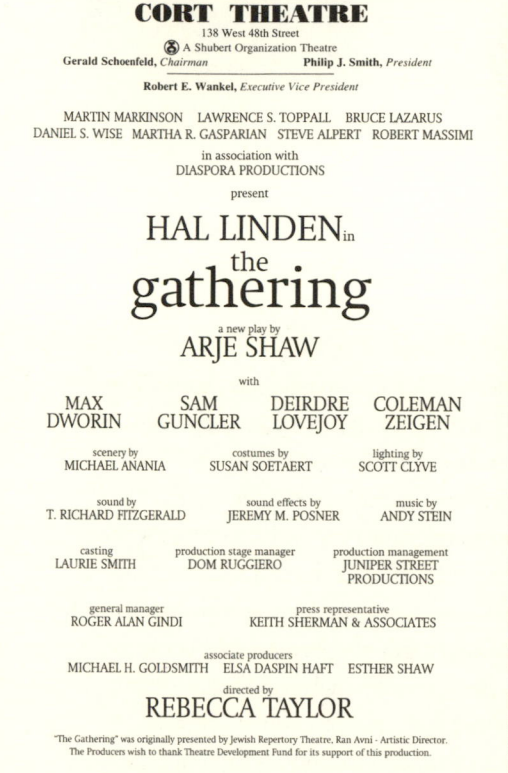

CORT THEATRE
138 West 48th Street
Ⓢ A Shubert Organization Theatre
Gerald Schoenfeld, *Chairman*   Philip J. Smith, *President*

Robert E. Wankel, *Executive Vice President*

MARTIN MARKINSON   LAWRENCE S. TOPPALL   BRUCE LAZARUS
DANIEL S. WISE   MARTHA R. GASPARIAN   STEVE ALPERT   ROBERT MASSIMI

in association with
DIASPORA PRODUCTIONS

present

HAL LINDEN in
the
gathering
a new play by
ARJE SHAW

with

| MAX | SAM | DEIRDRE | COLEMAN |
| DWORIN | GUNCLER | LOVEJOY | ZEIGEN |

scenery by   costumes by   lighting by
MICHAEL ANANIA   SUSAN SOETAERT   SCOTT CLYVE

sound by   sound effects by   music by
T. RICHARD FITZGERALD   JEREMY M. POSNER   ANDY STEIN

casting   production stage manager   production management
LAURIE SMITH   DOM RUGGIERO   JUNIPER STREET
PRODUCTIONS

general manager   press representative
ROGER ALAN GINDI   KEITH SHERMAN & ASSOCIATES

associate producers
MICHAEL H. GOLDSMITH   ELSA DASPIN HAFT   ESTHER SHAW
directed by
REBECCA TAYLOR

"The Gathering" was originally presented by Jewish Repertory Theatre, Ran Avni - Artistic Director.
The Producers wish to thank Theatre Development Fund for its support of this production.

Gabe   Hal Linden
Michael   Max Dworin
Diane   Deirdre Lovejoy
Stuart   Sam Guncler
Egon   Coleman Zeigen

Act 1
Scene 1:   Gabe's studio in New York
City, spring 1985
Scene 2:   Stuart and Diane's dining
room, later that day

Act 2
Bitburg, West Germany, one week later

gether the rest of it in sitcom fashion.

And, oh, what a patchwork we had to sit through in the course of this Holocaust drama.

Jewish joke after Jewish joke after Jewish joke. I counted four tuccus jokes in the first act, after which I stopped counting. And lots of food talk. Mr. Shaw had Diane, his housewife character, recite the menu for the Sabbath dinner for us: challah, salad, chopped liver, chicken soup, stuffed veal brisket, carrots, and rugelach. (Each course got knowing nods from the audience.) There she is, with her son and father-in-law who have Sabbath dinner with her every week and already know the menu. So why is she reciting it? To get a few minor laughs from the audience? And Mr. Shaw mined that chopped liver for all it was worth. "This will really plug me up," said Gabe, the grandfather. (Laughter.) "It's Jewish cement," said Gabe. (Laughter.) "It looks like doody," said the bar mitzvah boy.

Jokes about Gabe's *ferkahtah* apartment. Jokes about Eddie Fisher being confused with Bobby Fisher. Jokes about wontons being Chinese kreplach. Jokes about shiksas, jokes about Billy Graham, jokes about Uncle Schmucky. ("Every family has its own Uncle Schmucky," we're told. "They all have different names, but we know who they are.") And speaking of schmucks, jokes about Henry Kissinger: "Schmuck tries to do the right thing. . . . He just doesn't know what it is." When Diane came on carrying a Zabar's bag—good for a laugh—and we were simultaneously hit with another tuccus joke, I momentarily thought I was back at *The Tale of the Allergist's Wife*.

The Gathering takes place in the spring of 1985. Gabe is a Holocaust survivor who sits in his Upper West Side apartment sculpting a bust of Muhammad Ali. (Why Muhammad Ali? So Gabe can praise Ali for taking a stand as a conscientious objector during the Vietnam War?) Gabe's grandson Michael appears after school to practice for his bar mitzvah, although the pair toss quips like two little old men. ("Don't be so cynical," Gabe tells Michael, "not yet. You have time.") Michael is disturbed about his bar mitzvah, which is scheduled for the following week. (Gabe: "Think of the tuxedos! The diamonds! The facelifts!") What is it that makes him a man? Michael wants to know. Simply the calendar saying he has turned thirteen? Shouldn't he have to do something concrete to make him worthy? (That will come up again, in the second act.)

Diane—Michael's mother, Gabe's daughter-in-law—arrives to collect her son. She is a converted Jew, and very interested in cooking that Sabbath dinner (challah, salad, chopped liver, chicken soup, etc.). That night, they all sit around the table and await the late arrival of Stuart, Gabe's son and Michael's father. He finally arrives, and get this—he is President Reagan's speechwriter, and just about as non-Jewish as can be. (Diane is a converted Jew, Stuart is a converted WASP.) Dinner is finally served, at which point Stuart's boss Pat Buchanan calls. After some Pat Buchanan jokes, we learn that Reagan is off to West Germany. He has decided to visit Bitburg, a cemetery in which some Nazi war dead were buried.

Gabe is indignant, seeing this as an insult to the memory of the victims of the Nazis. (This visit, indeed, sparked a controversy at the time.) Gabe is also incensed that his own son is planning to write Reagan's speech. They get into a tense argument, at which point the play for the first time becomes interesting.

Act 2 takes place a week later. It opens with the voice of Gabe, leaving a message on Stuart and Diane's answering machine. He is at Bitburg, and he has taken Michael with him. (He charged the plane tickets on

> When Diane came on carrying a Zabar's bag, and we were simultaneously hit with another tuccus joke, I momentarily thought I was back at *The Tale of the Allergist's Wife.*

The Gathering
Opened: April 24, 2001
Closed: May 13, 2001
24 performances (and 12 previews)
Profit/Loss: Loss
The Gathering ($65 top) was scaled to a potential gross of
$429,063 at the 1,083-seat Cort. Weekly grosses averaged
about $80,000, with a low of $61,000 in the final week.
(They averaged 215 people per performance during closing
week, which—given the larger houses on weekends and
matinees—means that they were probably playing to
fewer than 100 people for some performances.) Total
gross for the run was $360,983. Attendance was about 28
percent, with the box office grossing about 19 percent of
dollar-capacity.

*Critical
Scorecard*

Rave   0
Favorable   1
Mixed   1
Unfavorable 3
Pan   5

Stuart's credit card.) He starts the call by asking why Stuart and Diane are not home, indicating that he knows them to be in New York. The lights come up on a cemetery consisting of three grave sites, apparently made of cardboard painted gray. Gabe and Michael can be seen hiding downstage of the cardboard (I mean, the graves). A German fellow walks on, leaves some flowers, and exits. A PA announcement tells us that the cemetery is closed for a private ceremony, everybody getten zee out.

Here we were, the second act had just begun, and the playwright had written himself into a box. (A cardboard box?) Gabe and Michael are hiding in Bitburg Cemetery. President Reagan and Willy Brandt are about to enter for a photo op. And we're watching a five-character play; we know that from the cast list in the Playbill and from the houseboards in front of the theatre. Gabe and Michael are onstage; Stuart and Diane are presumably in New York; and some German fellow in a raincoat has just made a crossover. Okay, Mr. Playwright, now what?

Gabe prompts Michael to say his bar mitzvah speech then and there, in Bitburg, as a protest against the world. (This ties in, all too neatly. By speaking out, the boy is worthy of becoming a man; and by standing on a cardboard grave, Michael draws a parallel with Muhammad Ali's anti-Vietnam stand.) Gabe and Michael hold up signs—made of cardboard that's supposed to look like cardboard—protesting Reagan's visit. They wave the signs around, as if waiting for CNN helicopter crews.

Gabe and Michael are there to protest Reagan's presence. But we're not going to see Brandt or Reagan or even Pat Buchanan; we're not going to see an army full of policemen or press photographers or anyone, unless they dress the actors playing Stuart and Diane in wigs and whiskers.

What's a playwright to do? As Leo Bloom said to Max Bialystock a few nights earlier, "no way out."

With the whole world waiting, and who knows how many people in the Reagan-Brandt entourage theoretically standing outside the gates, Shaw brings on—who? A young German soldier. (He was played by the only other cast member, the guy who did the walkover at the top of the act, only this time without his raincoat). He asks Gabe and Michael to leave; they refuse. He demands that Gabe and Michael leave; they refuse. We're six minutes past intermission, at least thirty minutes before the play can possibly end.

The German, named Egon, makes a few calls on his walkie-talkie, but does he bring in reinforcements? How can he? There are no other Equity members in the Cort, except for out-of-work actors dozing in their seats on comps. Do Gabe and Michael address the media? How can they? What can possibly happen, unless Nancy Reagan turns up and offers them jelly beans?

Needless to say, Mr. Shaw brought back Stuart and Diane. At the opening of this scene, in real time, Gabe left a phone message for them in New York. Before you can say Ed Koch, here they are—running on as if they'd just taxied over from West Eighty-seventh Street. And with the leaders of the free world cooling their heels offstage, the five actors stood amid the cardboard and talked till ten o'clock.

Preposterous, yes. Finally, Mr. Shaw went into his second big scene, serious and decently written. But how could he expect us to listen? It turns out that Gabe had a wrenching secret hidden away all these years. In the first act he had recited the oft-told tale of how he had bravely told off a Nazi, and how his mother

and sister had urged him into hiding. He escaped, leaving them behind to perish in the concentration camps. (Question: Why does he tell this story? His family has heard it before, so many times that Michael repeats full sentences as Gabe talks. So why does Gabe recite it again? Why does Diane recite the Sabbath dinner menu? Lazy playwriting?) In Gabe's big second-act speech, we learn that it wasn't his mother and sister he left behind when he escaped; it was his wife and infant daughter. Gabe is all broken up about it, his family is in shock to learn that he had another, earlier family, and the audience is in tears.

Effective writing, and precisely what Mr. Shaw had been working around to all evening. But one or two good scenes do not make a play, especially one that is clumsily stuffed with sitcom jokes. Shaw was a Broadway novice, as was his director, Rebecca Taylor. *The Gathering* was very much in earnest, as previously stated. But it was all pretty hopeless.

Hal Linden, as it turned out, did surprisingly well as Gabe. Linden started his career as a musical comedy character man; he achieved stardom with his Tony Award–winning performance in Bock and Harnick's *The Rothschilds*; and he wafted off to fame with the sitcom *Barney Miller*. Replacement jobs in the Broadway productions of *I'm Not Rappaport* and *The Sisters Rosensweig* preceded *The Gathering*. Not having seen him in either of those roles, I was pleasantly surprised by his performance at the Cort. Twelve-year-old Max Dworin also handled himself professionally as the bar mitzvah boy, trading quips with aplomb. His Playbill bio dedicated his performance to the memory of his grandfather Leon Klinghoffer. (I assume this is the same Leon Klinghoffer who was killed by terrorists aboard the cruise ship *Achille Lauro*, five months after Reagan went to Bitburg and six years before Dworin was born.)

> **One or two good scenes do not make a play, especially one that is clumsily stuffed with sitcom jokes. *The Gathering* was very much in earnest, but it was all pretty hopeless.**

Back in the first act, when Stuart picked up the phone to talk to Pat Buchanan, he removed his yarmulke before talking. (Laugh.) Gabe yelled "anti-Semite" into the phone. (Laugh.) Gabe then said: "I shouldn't be so hard on him. I understand he had an uncle who died in the camps." Pause for two beats, in preparation for the punch line. "Fell off a tower."

Funny, yes, the biggest laugh of the evening. But is that the kind of laugh you want in a Holocaust drama?

The Adventures of Tom Sawyer

Mark Twain placed the famous fence-painting scene right near the beginning of his 1876 novel, *The Adventures of Tom Sawyer*, in chapter 2. You remember: Tom has been commanded to whitewash a fence, as Saturday afternoon punishment for some minor misdeed. He quickly maneuvers his friends into doing the work—and paying him for the privilege (half-eaten apples, old doorknobs, and such).

As the chapter draws to a close, Twain notes that Tom "had discovered a great law of human action, without knowing it—namely, that in order to make a man or a boy covet a thing, it is only necessary to make the thing difficult to attain. If he had been a great and wise philosopher, like the writer of this book, he would now have comprehended that Work consists of whatever a body is *obliged* to do, and that Play consists of whatever a body is not obliged to do."

Twain peppered *Tom Sawyer* with wry commentary; while he was convinced by his editor to market the work as a children's book, he clearly was speaking to adults as well: "Part of my plan has been to try to pleasantly remind adults of what they once were themselves, and of how they felt and thought and talked, and what queer enterprises they sometimes engaged in."

Without Twain's point of view, the whole thing was a dull and aimless Twain-wreck.

The Adventures of Tom Sawyer has remained imperishable for 126 years, and not because of its plot. In fact, Twain began his continuation of the tale—*The Adventures of Huckleberry Finn (Tom Sawyer's Comrade)*—with the following notice: "PERSONS attempting to find a motive in this narrative will be prosecuted; persons attempting to find a moral in

MINSKOFF THEATRE

UNDER THE DIRECTION OF JAMES M. NEDERLANDER AND MYRON A. MINSKOFF

JAMES M. NEDERLANDER AND JAMES L. NEDERLANDER
AND
WATT/DOBIE PRODUCTIONS
PRESENT

THE ADVENTURES OF

TOM SAWYER

BASED ON THE NOVEL BY MARK TWAIN

BOOK BY
KEN LUDWIG

MUSIC AND LYRICS BY
DON SCHLITZ

STARRING

JOSHUA PARK   JIM POULOS   KRISTEN BELL
LINDA PURL   JOHN DOSSETT   JANE CONNELL   TOM ALDREDGE   KEVIN SERGE DURAND
JOHN CHRISTOPHER JONES   TOMMY HOLLIS   RICHARD POE   MARSHALL PAILET

WITH

STEPHEN LEE ANDERSON   PATRICK BOLL   ANN WHITLOW BROWN   MICHAEL BURTON   PIERCE CRAVENS
ÉLAN   STACIA FERNANDEZ   JOE GALLAGHER   BLAKE HACKLER   JOHN HERRERA   NIKKI M. JAMES
DONNA LEE MARSHALL   ERIK J. MCCORMACK   AMY JO PHILLIPS   KATE REINDERS   ELISE SANTORA
MEKENZIE ROSEN-STONE   RIC STONEBACK   SALLY WILFERT   TOMMAR WILSON

| SCENIC DESIGN BY | COSTUME DESIGN BY | LIGHTING DESIGN BY |
| HEIDI ETTINGER | ANTHONY POWELL | KENNETH POSNER |

| SOUND DESIGN BY | HAIR DESIGN BY | ORCHESTRATIONS BY | DANCE & INCIDENTAL MUSIC BY |
| LEW MEAD | DAVID BRIAN BROWN | MICHAEL STAROBIN | DAVID KRANE |

| FIGHT DIRECTOR | ADDITIONAL CHOREOGRAPHY | ASSOCIATE CHOREOGRAPHER |
| RICK SORDELET | JODI MOCCIA | ROMMY SANDHU |

| PRODUCTION MANAGER | GENERAL MANAGEMENT | PRODUCTION SUPERVISOR |
| ARTHUR SICCARDI | DEVIN KEUDELL | BEVERLEY RANDOLPH |

| PRESS REPRESENTATIVE | MARKETING | CASTING |
| BONEAU/BRYAN-BROWN | THE MARKETING GROUP | JIM CARNAHAN CSA |

MUSICAL DIRECTION BY
PAUL GEMIGNANI

CHOREOGRAPHY BY
DAVID MARQUES

DIRECTED BY
SCOTT ELLIS

Tom Sawyer   Joshua Park
Ben Rogers   Tommar Wilson
George Bellamy   Joe Gallagher
Lyle Bellamy   Blake Hackler
Joe Harper   Erik J. McCormack
Alfred Temple   Pierce Cravens
Amy Lawrence   Ann Whitlow Brown
Lucy Harper   Mekenzie Rosen-Stone
Susie Rogers   Élan
Sabina Temple   Nikki M. James
Sally Bellamy   Stacia Fernandez
Sereny Harper   Donna Lee Marshall
Lucinda Rogers   Amy Jo Phillips
Naomi Temple   Sally Wilfert
Aunt Polly   Linda Purl
Sid Sawyer   Marshall Pailet
Doc Robinson   Stephen Lee Anderson
Reverend Sprague   Tommy Hollis
Lanyard Bellamy   Richard Poe
Gideon Temple   Ric Stoneback
Lemuel Dobbins   John Christopher Jones
Muff Potter   Tom Aldredge
Huckleberry Finn   Jim Poulos
Injun Joe   Kevin Serge Durand
Judge Thatcher   John Dossett
Becky Thatcher   Kristen Bell
Widow Douglas   Jane Connell
Pap   Stephen Lee Anderson
Swings   Patrick Boll, Michael Burton, John Herrera, Kate Reinders, Elise Santora

Time and Place: St. Petersburg, Missouri, 1844

it will be banished; persons attempting to find a plot in it will be shot. BY ORDER OF THE AUTHOR"

This voice—the voice of Mark Twain—was altogether missing from Broadway's *The Adventures of Tom Sawyer*, the final new musical of the 2000–2001 season. So were most of Twain's old jokes, swept away to make room for new old jokes by Ken Ludwig. What remained was a series of plot points, grossly tampered with. Without Twain's point of view, the whole thing was a dull and aimless Twain-wreck.

Aimless pretty much describes this show. The creators did have an aim, I suppose; they clearly wanted a shot at the market for Disney's *Beauty and the Beast*. Twain's adventures were homogenized and pasteurized and desensitized and—yes—whitewashed. Tom's pal Jim, the slave, was retired in favor of a Disneytized Missouri, where Tom goes to a happily integrated school, a first for pre–Civil War Missouri. Mr. Ludwig's Becky pries open schoolteacher Dobbins's desk to find a book of romantic poetry. Mr. Twain's Becky—back in 1876—found an anatomy book, complete with "a handsomely engraved and colored human figure, stark naked." We don't see what's inside the book, mind you; but the mere words "stark naked" are too stark, I guess, for the twenty-first-century family audiences at which the musical was aimed.

And tell me, just how old is young Tom, anyway? The author was very careful not to spell it out for us, and with good reason. If Tom was deemed to be ten, say, then many twelve-year-old readers would no doubt look at the book as kid's stuff. By keeping Tom ageless, Twain was equally able to hook eight-year-olds and nine-year-olds and elevens and twelves. Whatever age Twain intended, Tom and Huck were clearly meant to be prepubescent. Tom begins his "seduction" of Becky with the question "Do you love rats?" Becky doesn't (love rats), but she counters by offering to let Tom chew her chewing gum for a while, "but you must give it back to me."

The age of the stage Tom was never spelled out, either, but I knew we were in trouble when they started the show by pulling the leading man out of an onstage swimming hole. Not to worry; he was not "stark naked," as you'd expect in rural Missouri in the nineteenth century, but fully clad below the belly button. Tom (Joshua Park) was bare chested, though, and from where I was sitting it looked like this Tom Sawyer—Twain's prepubescent lad—had shaved his armpits. He was also taller than most of the cast, but that didn't matter much after a while. *All* of the little boys and girls save one looked old enough to buy a drink in Texas, and a glance at the Playbill bios made it clear that most of these kids had college degrees. The one exception was the boy playing Tom's half brother, Sidney. In the book, Tom is two or three years older than Sid; at the Minskoff, Tom seemed twelve or sixteen years Sid's senior. The annoyingly snooty Sid remained pretty much as Twain created him, which might be why Marshall Pailet gave the only performance with any punch to it.

> From where I was sitting it looked like this Tom Sawyer—Twain's prepubescent lad—had shaved his armpits.

Tom, Becky (Kristen Bell), and Huck (Jim Poulos) couldn't play the kids' vulnerability because they were clearly not kids. The crotchety Aunt Polly (Linda Purl), conversely, lost her crotchets and about twenty years so that she could sing a love song. Becky's father Judge Thatcher (John Dossett) was likewise rejuvenated, allowing him to flirt with Polly. The kindly Widow Douglas was transformed into a musical comedy character comedienne, solely so that musical comedy character comedienne Jane Connell could play her. In the novel, the Widow adopted Huck after he foiled a plot to murder her in chapter 30 (of 35). In the musical, the Widow saw him on the street and tried to adopt him early on, simply for some hoped-for-but-hopeless comedy relief. Musical comedy character comedian Tom Aldredge was also lost somewhere in there, as the drunkard Muff Potter. Aldredge seems always to be working, perhaps because he takes any job that comes along. A fellow named Kevin Serge Durand came off better than most, as an intense and somewhat frightening Injun Joe. At times I felt that he had simply wandered over from auditions for Inspector Javert in *Les Misérables*, but at least he was playing a character.

The adaptation was, all in all, pretty bare-bones. The show started with a clichéd musical comedy introduction to the characters called "Hey, Tom Sawyer." (My handy little notebook reveals that midway through this song I noted, "This makes *Jane Eyre* look good." By the end of the number, I had changed it to "This makes *Jane Eyre* look *very* good.")

Ludwig's one prior Broadway musical was the highly successful *Crazy for You*, which succeeded more for its Gershwin score than for its libretto. Ludwig also wrote two Broadway farces, *Lend Me a Tenor* and *Moon over Buffalo*. Both of these failed, although *Tenor* seems to be a stock and amateur favorite; personally, I found them both mirthlessly unfunny. (*Moon over Broadway*, D. A. Pennebaker's documentary about the creation of *Moon over Buffalo*, presents Ludwig as a desperate comedy writer in dire need of a joke doctor. It is highly recommended to anyone wishing to see what happens when a Broadway play goes way wrong.) Ludwig's humor, in the case of *Tom Sawyer*, was the sort in which the schoolteacher speaks fractured French all night long.

Country-music writer Don Schlitz arrived on Broadway with a Playbill bio boasting of "50+ hits including 24 Number Ones" as well as "three CMAs, two ACMs, and two Grammys." All of this translated into merely one decent song in the second act, a guitar ballad called "This Time Tomorrow." Otherwise, there wurn't much to write home to Nashville about.

Schlitz's reception wasn't simply a matter of Broadway types bashing any songwriter who didn't grow up in Shubert Alley. Consider the six new musicals of the 2000–2001 season. Five—count 'em—five came from composers making their Broadway debuts. (The other was Stephen Flaherty's problematical *Seussical*.) The only two successful scores of the year—and the only two successful musicals—came from composers far less renowned than Schlitz, arriving with absolutely no number ones or CMAs or even ACMs between them. That didn't keep Broadway from embracing David Yazbek's *The Full Monty* and Mel Brooks's *The Producers*. Ed Kleban, of *A Class Act*, had Broadway experience, certainly, but not as a composer. Paul Gordon, another decidedly non-Broadway type, garnered at least some respect for *Jane Eyre*; while that score was flawed, it was far more interesting (and far more enjoyable) than the Schlitz songs. As a lyricist, Schlitz was the kind of guy who rhymes "Robin Hood" with "old Sherwood" and "right" with "life." I have no doubt that he'll soon have some more number ones to his credit, but not from the score of *Tom Sawyer*.

> **Don Schlitz arrived on Broadway boasting of "50+ hits including 24 Number Ones" as well as "three CMAs, two ACMs, and two Grammys." All of this translated into merely one decent song.**

The whole, unimpressive shebang was under the control of director Scott Ellis. Ellis first hit the big time with the 1991 off-Broadway revue *And the World Goes 'Round—The Songs of Kander and Ebb*. This was quite a snappy little revue, featuring a top-notch cast and some of the snazziest staging since Tommy Tune came to town. While Ellis got the directing credit, it was his choreographer who got the break. The late and much-missed Tyler Gatchell, coproducer of the Kander and Ebb show, was gen-

eral manager of the upcoming *Crazy for You*. He convinced the producers to gamble on Susan Stroman, and you know what happened to her.

As for Ellis, he has been constantly active, with credits including *Steel
Pier* (with Stroman); Roundabout revivals of *Company*, *A Month in the
Country*, *1776*, and *The Rainmaker*; and New York City Opera revivals of
A Little Night Music and *110 in the Shade*. Each and every one of these pro-
ductions, I'm afraid, was hampered by noninspired direction. Ellis also did
the Roundabout revival of *She Loves Me*, which was a delight; but he dis-
appointed me with his misguided *Company* and hasn't won me back since.
I keep thinking that his next show will be better. Maybe it will, but not
Tom Sawyer.

Standing in the midst of it all, with no place to hide—literally—was
musical director Paul Gemignani. Gemignani—who worked with Ludwig and Stroman and director Mike Ockrent on *Crazy for You*—has con-
ducted more important musicals than you can shake a stick at, stuff like *A
Little Night Music* and *On the Twentieth Century* and *Sweeney Todd*. At the
end of the season, he received a special Tony Award for lifetime achievement in the theatre. His distinguished head, bobbing like a buoy in the
pit in front of the onstage swimming hole, seemed way out of place at this
kiddie musical. Oh, well, it's a living. (His Playbill bio read, in its entirety,
"Paul Gemignani dedicates his work on *Tom Sawyer* to the memory of
Mike Ockrent.")

During "Ain't Life Fine," one of those choral numbers for happy towns-
folk, I had a sudden sense of déjà vu. I was sitting in the very same seat
from which I saw *Angel*, the 1978 musicalization of Thomas Wolfe's *Look*

Homeward Angel. (Maybe not the exact same seat, but close.) As *Angel* was about to begin, arranger-conductor Wally Harper climbed over my toes to the adjoining seat. Wally and I had worked on a show the year before, a real stinker that closed out of town before they even finished orchestrating the overture. We spent most of *Angel* identifying the songs that the composer had borrowed his melodies from—quick, this one's from *Peter Pan!*—which at least kept us engaged in the show. I had no such discussion with the lady sitting next to me at *Tom Sawyer.* When she started crinkling her candy wrappers, though, I must say that the noise didn't bother me in the least.

The Adventures of Tom Sawyer opened on a Thursday night. The following Tuesday, I received a press release: Broadway's Number One Family Musical—acclaimed by John Simon in *New York* magazine as "a children's musical suitable for adults"—had reduced its weeknight orchestra price from $85 to $30. By Friday, the "special May sale" was extended to weekend performances as well. A closing notice was posted the following Tuesday, the actors collected their last paycheck Thursday, and *Tom Sawyer* packed up his whitewash on Sunday afternoon. There went $7.5 million or so down the ole swimmin' hole.

George Gershwin Alone

George Gershwin Alone presented a fellow named Hershey Felder playing, singing, and speaking the work and life of George Gershwin from the stage of the Helen Hayes Theatre. When Gershwin himself went on the road in 1934, he was canny enough *not* to go alone; he took along a conductor (Charles Previn, André's uncle), a thirty-piece band, and tenor James Melton singing cowboy ballads to boot. George, surely, would not have played and sung and talked for eighty minutes straight. (That is, he wouldn't have done it onstage; in someone's living room he could go on for hours.) To some, this might imply that Felder alone was better than Gershwin alone. At any rate, Felder's act was a lot more economical.

Felder's evening consisted of seventy minutes of "play," plus a nine-minute coda during which he played *Rhapsody in Blue*. The seventy minutes was comprised of Felder performing nine complete songs (with sections of others), separated by lame monologues that attempted to tell us everything we always wanted to know about George Gershwin. Sort of a character study without the character. Compare *George Gershwin Alone* with Terrence McNally's portrait of Maria Callas in *Master Class*; well, we don't even need to begin to make the comparison, do we?

> When George Gershwin went on the road, he was canny enough *not* to go alone; he took along a conductor, a thirty-piece band, and a tenor singing cowboy ballads.

The musical selections included "Swanee" (1919), in which Felder's Gershwin makes the startling claim that he was the first composer ever to change from the minor to major within a song; "I Got Rhythm" (1930), during which Felder enthuses about writing the song for such a big star as Ethel Merman, who in fact was unknown at the time; "Embraceable You" (1930); "But Not for Me" (1930); "The Man I Love" (1924), in the form of a commercial for Feen-a-mint, a laxative chewing gum; "Bess, You Is My Woman" (1935), in which Felder re-creates a grand "first performance" of the song (complete with lyrics) before an audience of DuBose Heyward and Ira Gershwin—who collaborated on the lyrics and by that point would have heard the music endlessly; "They Can't Take That Away from Me" (1937); a truncated version of the tone poem *An American in Paris* (1928), which Felder chronologically places way after *Porgy and Bess* although it was written seven years earlier; and "Love Is Here to Stay" (1938). All of this followed by the 1924 *Rhapsody*.

As you can see, Felder's Gershwin was all over the place; oddly enough, three of the nine songs selected for full treatment came from one relatively unimportant show, *Girl Crazy*. Why these songs, only one of which I'd consider indispensable Gershwin, as opposed to any number of others? Beats me.

The narrative sections were curious, and some of the facts were simply wrong. Felder's Gershwin told us that he got his first big break as the rehearsal pianist of *The Ziegfeld Follies of 1919*. In fact, George was already on Broadway as a composer in 1916, and his first successful musical—*La,*

La Lucille*—opened a month before the *Follies*; the *Lucille* music cover was projected on the stage left wall of the set, directly across from Felder's piano bench. Felder's Gershwin told us that he suffered his brain tumor because he was kicked in the head when he was six, this based on some farfetched comment somebody once made years after George's death. Felder's Gershwin also told us about his pal, Georgie Kaufman. I suppose he means playwright George S. Kaufman; did anyone ever call him "Georgie"? Felder's Gershwin also told us that he went broke backing *Porgy*

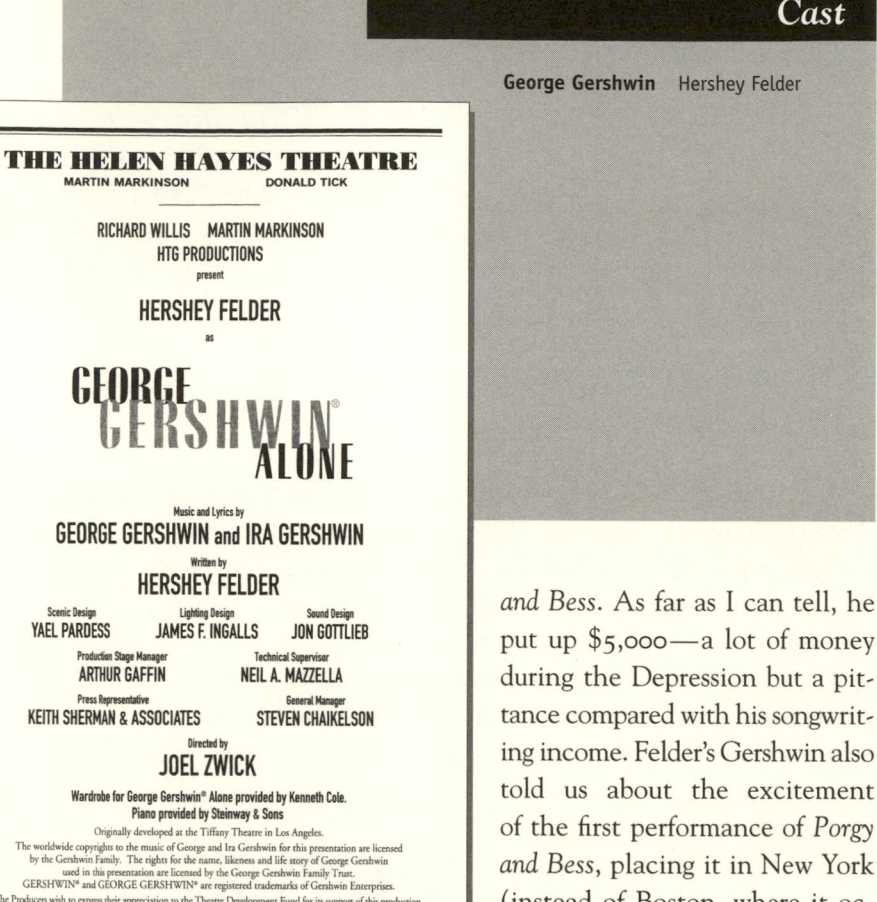

THE HELEN HAYES THEATRE
MARTIN MARKINSON   DONALD TICK

RICHARD WILLIS   MARTIN MARKINSON
HTG PRODUCTIONS
present

HERSHEY FELDER
as

GEORGE
GERSHWIN®
ALONE

Music and Lyrics by
GEORGE GERSHWIN and IRA GERSHWIN
Written by
HERSHEY FELDER

Scenic Design   Lighting Design   Sound Design
YAEL PARDESS   JAMES F. INGALLS   JON GOTTLIEB

Production Stage Manager   Technical Supervisor
ARTHUR GAFFIN   NEIL A. MAZZELLA

Press Representative   General Manager
KEITH SHERMAN & ASSOCIATES   STEVEN CHAIKELSON

Directed by
JOEL ZWICK

Wardrobe for George Gershwin® Alone provided by Kenneth Cole.
Piano provided by Steinway & Sons

Originally developed at the Tiffany Theatre in Los Angeles.
The worldwide copyrights to the music of George and Ira Gershwin for this presentation are licensed
by the Gershwin Family. The rights for the name, likeness and life story of George Gershwin
used in this presentation are licensed by the George Gershwin Family Trust.
GERSHWIN® and GEORGE GERSHWIN® are registered trademarks of Gershwin Enterprises.
The Producers wish to express their appreciation to the Theatre Development Fund for its support of this production.

and Bess. As far as I can tell, he put up $5,000—a lot of money during the Depression but a pittance compared with his songwriting income. Felder's Gershwin also told us about the excitement of the first performance of *Porgy and Bess*, placing it in New York (instead of Boston, where it occurred).

Other "true" stories were used in a misleading manner. Felder tended to take anecdotes in passing and—by spotlighting them as major portions of the narrative—blow them out of proportion. For example, Gershwin once played through a movie score in progress for Samuel Goldwyn, who was producing the film in question. Afterward, George commented that Goldwyn treated him like he was a novice, auditioning songs. (Gershwin was already suffering from the undiagnosed brain tumor that would soon end his life, so who knows what that audition sounded like.) This anecdote referred to the events of one afternoon, but Felder built it into a key complaint of Gershwin's life. Other major monologues included George complaining about his mother, and George stung by anti-Semitic remarks.

Yes, these anecdotes were based on something somebody, somewhere once remembered and told some biographer years later. But are these the

George Gershwin Alone
Opened: April 30, 2001
Closed: July 22, 2001
96 performances (and 16 previews)
Profit/Loss: Loss
George Gershwin Alone ($65 top) was scaled to a potential
gross of $316,410 at the 597-seat Helen Hayes. Weekly
grosses averaged about $75,000, with grosses remaining
consistently at this level. (Survival in such a case is
possible only when there's a tiny payroll and the producer
owns the theatre.) Total gross for the run was $1,055,351.
Attendance was about 41 percent, with the box office
grossing about 23 percent of dollar-capacity.

Critical
Scorecard

Rave	1
Favorable	2
Mixed	0
Unfavorable	2
Pan	5

important events of Gershwin's life? Is this what we should be talking about? Granted, such lapses and inaccuracies mean little to anyone other than Gershwin fans; but I don't suppose anyone other than Gershwin fans were likely to buy a ticket to *George Gershwin Alone*.

And then there was the music itself. Felder, a concert pianist, clearly knows his Gershwin, and he played Gershwin's published song arrangements fairly well. In fact, he might well have played *better* than Gershwin. As someone highly familiar with the work, though, I found strange pauses in many of the pieces. Gershwin was a distinctive piano player; modern technology has made it possible for us to hear rescued restorations of his recordings and piano rolls. Felder often hesitated over the notes, halting the rhythm; this was done for effect, surely, but it sounded pretty non-Gershwin-like. The playing of the *Rhapsody* was even odder. Not only were these pauses present; at the performance I attended, Felder seemed to be playing wrong notes (and not just a couple). He also threw in some sloppy glissandos near the end. Why not play the piece as written?

Felder had a reason for this, as it turned out. After viewing *George Gershwin Alone*, I came across an interview he had with Celia McGee in the *Daily News*. "I don't play *Rhapsody* as George would have played it," he said, "but as an answer to all his critics who didn't take him seriously." What Felder seemed to be saying is that he plays the *Rhapsody* as George would if he could play as well as Hershey Felder. Which is an interesting viewpoint, I guess.

> **Such lapses and inaccuracies mean little to anyone other than Gershwin fans; but I don't suppose anyone other than Gershwin fans was likely to buy a ticket to *George Gershwin Alone*.**

So here we had a fellow who introduced himself as George Gershwin but didn't sound like him or comport himself like him or give us much in the way of accuracy. When it came time for the *Rhapsody*—the most important part of *George Gershwin Alone*—Felder's Gershwin not only didn't sound like Gershwin; he didn't even *try* to sound like Gershwin.

Felder seemed to be saying that he plays the *Rhapsody* as George would if he could play as well as Hershey Felder.

So I simply went back home, put on my *Gershwin Plays Gershwin* CD, and spent some time with George Gershwin alone. Without Hershey Felder.

King Hedley II

Consider the response if you or I or Jon Robin Baitz or Edward Albee announced, back in 1984, that we were going to write a new play every two years for the next twenty years and have them all produced on Broadway. Then, add in that the plays would be well received; and that they would win two Pulitzers, six Critics Circle Awards, one Tony, and five additional Tony nominations among them. And add in that they would all deal with African-American culture, utilizing almost exclusively African-American casts and directors.

Not very likely, I'd say.

August Wilson has done just that. He embarked on a ten-play cycle about the black experience in America, with each play set in a different decade. At present, he has covered all but the first and last decades of the twentieth century. The fifty-six-year-old playwright started his first major play, *Jitney*, in 1972. That work—set in a taxi station in 1971—was produced in 1982 at the Allegheny Repertory Theatre in Pittsburgh. (A revised version finally reached New York in April 2000, when it was mounted off-Broadway by the Second Stage Theatre. It won Wilson his sixth Drama Critics Circle Award for Best Play.)

> Consider the response if you or I announced that we were going to write a new play every two years for the next twenty years and have them all produced on Broadway.

Wilson first received national acclaim with *Ma Rainey's Black Bottom*. This play was set in 1927 in Chicago (the only one of the plays in the cycle that doesn't take place in Pittsburgh). *Ma Rainey* was selected for a reading at the O'Neill Theatre Center. Lloyd Richards, dean of the Yale

Stool Pigeon   Stephen McKinley
  Henderson
King   Brian Stokes Mitchell
Ruby   Leslie Uggams
Mister   Monté Russell
Tonya   Viola Davis
Elmore   Charles Brown

Setting: The Hill District, Pittsburgh,
  Pennsylvania, 1985

VIRGINIA THEATRE
A JUJAMCYN THEATRE

JAMES H. BINGER   ROCCO LANDESMAN
CHAIRMAN   PRESIDENT

PAUL LIBIN   JACK VIERTEL
PRODUCING DIRECTOR   CREATIVE DIRECTOR

Sageworks   Benjamin Mordecai   Jujamcyn Theaters
52nd Street Productions   Spring Sirkin   Peggy Hill
and Manhattan Theatre Club
in association with
Kardana-Swinsky Productions

present

Brian Stokes Mitchell
in
AUGUST WILSON'S
KING HEDLEY II
starring
Leslie Uggams
with

Charles Brown   Viola Davis
Stephen McKinley Henderson   Monté Russell

Set Design   Costume Design   Lighting Design
David Gallo   Toni-Leslie James   Donald Holder

Sound Design   Waltz Choreography   Fight Director
Rob Milburn   Dianne McIntyre   David S. Leong

Production Stage Manager   Technical Supervision   Casting
Diane DiVita   Unitech   Barry Moss C.S.A.

General Manager   Public Relations
Roger Alan Gindi   Barlow·Hartman

Directed by
Marion McClinton

This production premiered at the Pittsburgh Public Theatre in December 1999,
and at Seattle Repertory Theatre in February 2000, and has also been presented by
Huntington Theatre Company, Mark Taper Forum, and Goodman Theatre.

The producers wish to thank the Theatre Development Fund for its support of this production.

Manhattan Theatre Club's Education Programs for King Hedley II are supported by AT&T.

School of Drama, saw it and mounted a full production at the Yale Repertory Theatre. (Richards, famously, had directed Lorraine Hansberry's groundbreaking *Raisin in the Sun* in 1959.) Yale's production transferred to Broadway in 1984, winning the Critics Circle Award and a Tony nomination. Wilson has been a Broadway regular, and an unlikely one, ever since. (He wrote at least five earlier plays, but only *Jitney* has resurfaced.)

Wilson's greatest success came with *Fences* (set in 1957). Arriving on Broadway—via Yale—in 1987, it earned Wilson his first Pulitzer, his Tony, and his second Critics Circle Award. *Joe Turner's Come and Gone* (set in 1911) followed in 1988, winning another Critics Circle Award and another Tony nomination. *The Piano Lesson* (set in 1937) arrived in 1990, winning another Pulitzer and another Critics Circle Award; Wilson won an Emmy, as well, for his 1995 television adaptation of the play. *Two Trains Running* (set in 1969) arrived in 1992, adding yet another Tony nomination. *Seven Guitars* (set in 1948) arrived on Broadway in 1996, winning another Critics Circle Award and Tony nomination.

This record is about as impressive as any modern dramatist can hope to achieve; those folks at the Drama Critics Circle sure love his work. Only one of the shows has been a commercial hit: *Fences*. The others have been hard sells on Broadway, struggling along for a while before closing at a loss. *Fences* boasted the presence of a major star, James Earl Jones, but I'd ascribe its success to its involving story of a father-son relationship. Wilson has never attempted to make his plays universal; he has clearly, and purposefully, been writing about African-Americans. In his other plays, I've always felt that I was watching a slice of African-American culture; in *Fences*, I simply felt like I was watching plain, ordinary, everyday Americans (which is to say, people like me). Maybe that's why it's the only Wilson play to have been embraced by a mass, Broadway audience. Yes, *Fences* included memorable performances by Jones, Mary Alice, and Courtney Vance; but other Wilson plays have been every bit as rich and memorable.

Wilson's work has its devoted fans, but it has left others cold. His language and imagery can be a lot of work to follow, and some theatregoers —after several tries—are no longer interested in investing their concentration in another installment. I, myself, am neither here nor there. *Ma Rainey* impressed me for the strength of the main characters. I felt that they had not simply walked on from the wings; they lived full lives—real lives—before coming to the theatre. Charles S. Dutton, who played Levee, the trumpet player, was especially good—and he had especially good material to work with.

Fences, as indicated, was mesmerizing. *Joe Turner* seemed more specialized, and not all that interesting; *The Piano Lesson*, which received almost universal acclaim, lost me somewhere along the way. *Two Trains Running* kept my attention, but just barely. And then came *Seven Guitars*, which seemed to me to go on and on and on. I was ready to leave after three guitars, although I stayed in my seat (and was rewarded by some fine performances). But I absorbed very little, which seriously compromised my enjoyment of *King Hedley II*. Because *Hedley*, it turned out, was a sequel to *Seven Guitars*. You didn't need to know *Seven Guitars* in order to understand *Hedley*, but it certainly would have helped. The majority of the audience—theatre critics excepted—presumably had never seen *Seven Guitars*. Maybe they should have included a plot synopsis in the program.

> **Viola Davis was absolutely breathtaking. She has now given two exceptional performances, with two well-earned Tony nominations. Why is it that she only gets to Broadway in August Wilson plays?**

King Hedley II spent eight years in jail for the murder of someone named Pernell, whose offense seems to have been that he called Hedley "Champ." Hedley is the son of Ruby and another fellow called King Hedley, who was from Jamaica (or Haiti). Ruby ran off to East Saint Louis to pursue a singing career with someone called Walter Kelly, leaving Hedley II with someone called Louise (which causes Hedley II—in *Hedley II*—to resent Ruby). Hedley I murdered a fellow called Floyd Barton back in the last act of *Seven Guitars*, although I think that I dozed through the murder. Hedley II, thus, has followed in the footsteps of his fabled father by murdering Pernell. The only thing is, Hedley *wasn't* Hedley's father; his father was really a fellow named Leroy, who was killed by Elmore (during *Seven Guitars*). That provides the climax of *King Hedley II*, which ends with Ruby accidentally shooting Hedley II with a silver derringer that Elmore sold Mister who gave it to Ruby (for reasons unknown). There's also some chatter about someone called Red Carter, a drummer who introduced Ruby to Walter Kelly and who appears to have been Mister's father, who ran off with someone called Edna Stewart. There's also a fellow named Stool Pigeon, who walks around chanting, "God's a bad motherf—er," who in *Seven Guitars* was called Canewell and won a Tony Award. And let's not forget old Aunt Ester, an offstage character who dies offstage during the first act at the age of 366, and whose cat is reincarnated when its grave is doused with the blood of the dying Hedley II. Old Aunt Ester is likely to turn up in the next play of Wilson's cycle, and I simply can't wait.

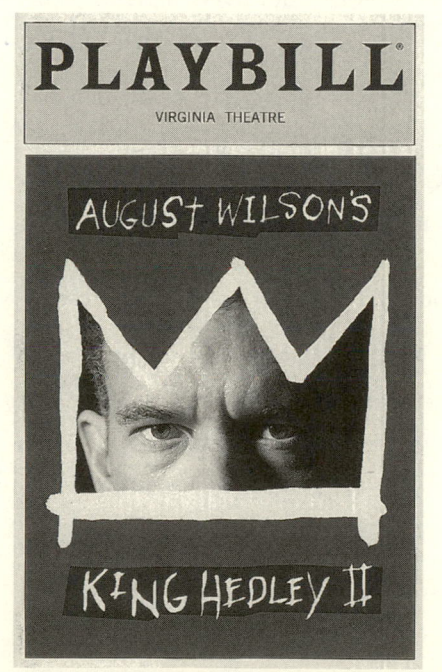

Let me clarify that I enjoyed *King Hedley*, more than any Wilson play since *Fences*. The language engrossed me in a way that it hadn't in the previous plays; the sheer poetry of Wilson's writing held my interest and attention for three long hours. The characters were usually interesting, and sometimes profound. Several monologues were exceptional; one, in particular, was cited in most of the reviews—even by critics who didn't like the play. This is not common, mind you; praising a *speech*? Hedley's wife, Tonya, is carrying his baby but is planning to get rid of it. "I ain't raising no kid to have somebody shoot him," she says. "To have his friends shoot him. To have the police shoot him." This, apparently, approaches the heart of Wilson's play. "It used to be," says Hedley, "you got killed over something. Now you get killed over nothing." (Mary Bogumil, in her 1999 book *Understanding August Wilson*, quotes the playwright as saying that *King Hedley II* will "look at what caused the breakdown in the black family to the point where kids started shooting one another.")

Tonya was played by an actress named Viola Davis, who was ab-

I suppose that if I'd entered the theatre fresh from reading *Seven Guitars*, I'd have enjoyed the play as much as the three critics who gave *Hedley* rave reviews.

solutely breathtaking. While the name wasn't familiar to me, the moment Davis walked on I remembered her for her phenomenal performance in *Seven Guitars*. Davis is a Juilliard actress; she has now given two exceptional performances on Broadway, with two well-earned Tony nominations (and the award for *Hedley*). Why is it, I wonder, that she only gets to Broadway in August Wilson plays?

King Hedley II was also helped along by an actor named Charles Brown, best remembered for the Negro Ensemble Company's *A Soldier's Play* and *Home*. (The latter of these transferred to the Cort, earning Brown his first Tony nomination.) Brown played Wilson's conman Elmore, who came in like a whirlwind after an hour or so. Mr. Wilson's words, in Mr. Brown's hands, proved spellbinding. As I was sitting in the Virginia struggling with the plot, I consciously decided that the magical words and these two magical performances more than made up for *Hedley*'s lapses. So I just sat back and let Wilson and Davis and Brown entertain me.

The play was overstocked with flavorful speeches, in fact. The aforementioned Stool Pigeon, who stockpiles old newspapers, spouted on at length. Being the resident madman, he spoke the truth. "The story's been written," he told us as the evening began, "all that's left now is the playing out." Ruby, the mother, had long reminiscences, mostly about her days as a band singer. And then there was King Hedley himself. He talked and talked and talked and talked, and therein came one of the problems of the evening. Brian Stokes Mitchell has come a long way since his years as a

King Hedley II
Opened: May 1, 2001
Closed: July 1, 2001
72 performances (and 24 previews)
Profit/Loss: Loss
King Hedley II ($70 top) was scaled to a potential gross of
    $563,337 at the 1,259-seat Virginia. Weekly grosses
    averaged about $207,000, building to $245,000 just
    before the Tony Awards but soon falling below $160,000.
    Total gross for the run was $2,479,599. Attendance was
    about 57 percent, with the box office grossing about 39
    percent of dollar-capacity.

TONY AWARD NOMINATIONS
Best Play: August Wilson
Best Performance by a Leading Actor: Brian Stokes Mitchell
Best Performance by a Leading Actress: Leslie Uggams
Best Performance by a Featured Actor: Charles Brown
Best Performance by a Featured Actress: Viola Davis
    (WINNER)
Best Direction of a Play: Marion McClinton

DRAMA DESK AWARDS
Outstanding Featured Actor: Charles Brown (WINNER)
Outstanding Featured Actress: Viola Davis (WINNER)

Critical Scorecard

Rave	3
Favorable	2
Mixed	0
Unfavorable	4
Pan	1

supporting player on one of those TV medical series of the 1980s. (Oddly enough, he played the foil to Gregory Harrison, who has also been storming the Broadway theatre—most recently in *Follies*—with far less success than Mitchell.) Mitchell is favored by a robust baritone, a pleasant stage demeanor, and a comedic sense, all of which he put to use in his Tony Award–winning performance in the 1999 revival of *Kiss Me, Kate*. These assets didn't help *Hedley* much, though. Mitchell stood onstage, with a scowl and a zigzag scar running along his ear, and spoke the words clearly and loudly. But that wasn't enough.

Perhaps this was a problem in the writing; Hedley was a mixed-up lad (and with good reason). Stokes did not seem centered on the stage, though; he seemed almost weightless. James Earl Jones (of *Fences*) and Charles Dutton (of *Ma Rainey* and *The Piano Lesson*) gave performances that were firmly anchored. This has nothing to do with physical bulk; Jason Robards (in just about anything) or Kevin Spacey (in *The Iceman Cometh*), for example, were similarly ever-present. Jones's and Dutton's and Robards's and Spacey's characterizations stayed with the audience throughout the plays, even when the actors themselves were offstage.

Mitchell accomplished this himself, to some extent, in *Ragtime*. His Hedley, though, wandered in and out of the evening.

King Hedley II played five regional engagements prior to its pre-Broadway tryout at the Kennedy Center. Dutton had been expected to join Hedley for Washington and New York, but he disappeared from the picture in January 2001. Mitchell—just out of *Kiss Me, Kate*—was a last-minute replacement. He did a fairly impressive job under the circumstances, the circumstances being that this was an impossibly difficult role for a musical comedy actor who had apparently never appeared in a drama.

Call me old-fashioned; but if a playwright is going to favor me with hours' worth of colorful exposition, I want to at least be able to understand the plot. If the playwright wants to be oblique, that's fine, too. But Wilson wasn't being oblique; he was spelling things out at length. I suppose that if I'd entered the theatre fresh from reading *Seven Guitars*, I'd have enjoyed the play as much as—well, as much as the three critics who gave *Hedley* rave reviews. My overall reaction was merely favorable, thanks to Wilson's poetry and the performances of Ms. Davis and Mr. Brown.

42nd Street

The big, brassy, bountiful Broadway musical died a cruel death in the mid-1960s. Ineffective shows, aging creators, a changing public, and rising costs combined to bring an era to an end. Top-dollar Broadway musicals started to become smaller and smaller. The full-bodied ensemble, back in the 1950s, was typically built on four eights: eight male singers, eight female singers, eight male dancers, eight female dancers. This started to diminish, until they might hire only twelve or sixteen altogether. (The 1975 musical *A Chorus Line* was built around an audition to select four "boys" and four "girls.") Increased labor and material costs took their toll, as shows became less and less lavish. Exceptions, like the 1971 production of *Follies* and the 1973 revival of *Irene*, had enormous losses despite lengthy runs. By the middle of the decade, the big Broadway musical was but a memory.

In 1978, Michael Stewart and Mark Bramble were writing one of those shows that make you want to pawn your typewriter and move to the farm. *The Grand Tour* had the trappings of a theatre party special—a score by Jerry Herman, the most overtly Jewish hero since *Fiddler on the Roof*, and a bona fide ticket-selling star in Joel Grey. But it was a show without purpose, and the handwriting was on the wall long before they began their tryout in San Francisco.

Escaping from the pressures of *The Grand Tour* one night, Stewart and Bramble went to the movies. In the days before VCRs and videocassette rentals and cable TV, the only way you could see an old movie was on television—in the middle of the night, chopped up with commercials—or at a "revival house." Back then, there was a movie theatre in the basement of Carnegie Hall, and that's where Stewart and Bramble went to see the 1933 movie musical *42nd Street*.

"I wish we were working on *this* instead," said one to the other.

The idea immediately took root, reinforced (I suppose) by every hour spent on *The Grand Tour*. Why not do a big, brassy, bountiful Broadway musical? The kind of show nobody did anymore—the biggest, brassiest, most bountiful, most expensive Broadway musical ever.

Stewart and Bramble went about securing the rights to *42nd Street*. Not the easiest thing to arrange, mind you; it took more than a year to locate the heirs to the author of the original novel. They broached the subject with Herman, who had also collaborated with Stewart on *Hello, Dolly!*—at the time, the longest-running musical comedy in history. (Actually, they called Herman the night they saw the film, as soon as they got home.) Herman gave them a sage piece of advice: Use the songs from the movie. So they got the music rights, too, supplementing the songs in the film with others by songwriters Harry Warren and Al Dubin. Director-choreographer Gower Champion—who had worked with Stewart on *Bye Bye Birdie*, *Carnival*, and *Dolly!*—quickly hopped on board.

And then it came time to find a producer who would give them the outsize production they envisioned. David Merrick wanted the show, but Stewart and Champion were unhappy with their treatment on *Mack & Mabel* in 1974; when things got bad, Merrick reacted by publicly humiliating them. Still, they set up a meeting.

> **Stewart and Bramble insisted on a fiscally burdensome sixteen girls. Merrick said, "Sixteen? I wouldn't do it with less than twenty-four."**

Stewart and Bramble insisted on a fiscally burdensome sixteen girls. Merrick said, "Sixteen? I don't think so." (Pause, for effect.) "I wouldn't do it with less than twenty-four."

How can you turn down such an offer, even if it is from the devil in a black mustache? Merrick, at that point in his career, was independent enough—and eccentric enough—to pour his own money into the biggest, brassiest, most bountiful Broadway musical ever.

Stewart and Bramble and Champion and Merrick's *42nd Street* opened on August 25, 1980. Champion died that afternoon, capping this larger-than-life extravaganza about cheers and tears on Broadway with its own larger-than-death aura. The show ran eight and a half years, closing on January 8, 1989, after 3,486 performances, in third place on the long-run

Cast (in order of appearance)

FORD CENTER FOR THE PERFORMING ARTS ⓕ
AN SFX THEATRICAL GROUP VENUE

Dodger Theatricals
Joop van den Ende and Stage Holding
present

Michael Cumpsty in Christine Ebersole

42ND STREET

Book by
Michael Stewart & Mark Bramble

Music by
Harry Warren

Lyrics by
Al Dubin

Based on the novel by Bradford Ropes

Original Direction and Dances by
Gower Champion

also starring
Mary Testa   Jonathan Freeman
David Elder

Michael Arnold   Mylinda Hull
Michael McCarty   Richard Muenz
Allen Fitzpatrick   Beth Leavel

Billy Stritch
and
Kate Levering

with

Brad Aspel   Kelli Barclay   Becky Berstler   Randy Bobish   Chris Clay
Michael Clowers   Maryam Myika Day   Alexander de Jong   Amy Dolan   Isabelle Flachsmann
Melissa Giattino   Jennifer Jones   Dontee Kiehn   Renée Klapmeyer   Jessica Kostival
Keirsten Kupiec   Todd Lattimore   Melissa Rae Mahon   Michael Malone
Brian J. Marcum   Jennifer Marquardt   Meredith Patterson   Darin Phelps
Wendy Rosoff   Megan Schenck   Kelly Sheehan   Tamlyn Brooke Shusterman
Megan Sikora   Jennifer Stetor   Erin Stoddard   Yasuko Tamaki
Jonathan Taylor   Jerry Tellier   Elisa Van Duyne   Erika Vaughn   Luke Walrath
Mike Warshaw   Merrill West   Shonn Wiley   Catherine Wreford

Scenery Design
Douglas W. Schmidt

Costume Design
Roger Kirk

Lighting Design
Paul Gallo

Sound Design
Peter Fitzgerald

Production Stage Manager
Frank Hartenstein

Casting
Jay Binder

Wigs & Hair Design
David H. Lawrence

Musical Direction
Todd Ellison

Musical Adaptation, Arrangements
& Additional Orchestrations
Donald Johnston

Orchestrations
Philip J. Lang

Music Coordinator
John Miller

Executive Producer
Dodger Management Group

Technical Supervisor
Peter Fulbright

Marketing Consultant
Margery Singer

Press Representative
Boneau/Bryan-Brown

Musical Staging and New Choreography by
Randy Skinner

Directed by
Mark Bramble

The producers wish to express their appreciation to Theatre Development Fund for its support of this production.

Andy Lee   Michael Arnold
Maggie Jones   Mary Testa
Bert Barry   Jonathan Freeman
Mac   Allen Fitzpatrick
Phyllis   Catherine Wreford
Lorraine   Megan Sikora
Diane   Tamlyn Brooke Shusterman
Annie   Mylinda Hull
Ethel   Amy Dolan
Billy Lawlor   David Elder
Peggy Sawyer   Kate Levering
Oscar   Billy Stritch
Julian Marsh   Michael Cumpsty
Dorothy Brock   Christine Ebersole
Abner Dillon   Michael McCarty
Pat Denning   Richard Muenz
Waiters   Brad Aspel, Mike Warshaw, Shonn Wiley
Thugs   Allen Fitzpatrick, Jerry Tellier
Doctor   Allen Fitzpatrick
Ensemble   Brad Aspel, Becky Berstler, Randy Bobish, Chris Clay, Michael Clowers, Maryan Myika Day, Alexander deJong, Amy Dolan, Isabelle Flachsmann, Jennifer Jones, Dontee Kiehn, Renée Klapmeyer, Jessica Kostival, Keirsten Kupiec, Todd Lattimore, Melissa Rae Mahon, Michael Malone, Jennifer Marquardt, Meredith Patterson, Darin Phelps, Wendy Rosoff, Megan Schenck, Kelly Sheehan, Tamlyn Brooke Shusterman, Megan Sikora, Jennifer Stetor, Erin Stoddard, Yasuko Tamaki, Jonathan Taylor, Jerry Tellier, Elisa Van Duyne, Erika Vaughn, Mike Warshaw, Merrill West, Shonn Wiley, Catherine Wreford
Swings   Kelli Barclay, Melissa Giattino, Brian J. Marcum, Luke Walrath

**Original Broadway Revival Cast
Album:**   Q Records 92953

musical list. (It has since been knocked down to seventh by the four Andrew Lloyd Webber–Cameron Mackintosh blockbusters.)

42nd Street was the largest spectacle Broadway had seen in years. After
seven months at the Winter Garden, the show shuffled off to the Majestic: Merrick's favorite theatre, with more than one hundred additional
seats and a larger potential gross. Meanwhile, *Cats*—a super-extrava-
ganza of a different stripe—took root at the Winter Garden. *Cats* begat
Les Miz begat *Phantom* begat *Saigon* begat *Beauty and the Beast* begat *The
Lion King*. Soon, a large segment of the Broadway industry was concen-
trating on extravaganza-like, family-themed musicals that catered to
nontheatregoing tourists and could run for years and years and years.

In 1997, two state-of-the-extravaganza-art theatres opened right
smack dab on 42nd Street. Bramble instantly realized that *42nd Street* on
42nd Street had a ring to it and set about getting the show back on the
boards. (Mike Stewart died in 1987.) While Bramble was searching for a
producer willing to mount a suitably lavish Broadway production, Joop
van den Ende—the Dutch showman—was planning a *42nd Street* of his
own. Bramble, who had directed productions of the show in London,
Japan, and Australia, signed on; he took along Randy Skinner, Champion's 1980 dance assistant, who had restaged the choreography on
numerous occasions. Van den Ende—not coincidentally—is a partner in
Dodger Theatricals, the Broadway producing and management concern.
42nd Street opened in Amsterdam in September 2000, and one thing led
to another. When the Trevor Nunn–Susan Stroman *Oklahoma!* canceled
its December 2000 booking at the Ford Center, Michael David of the
Dodgers snapped it up. And there you had it, *42nd Street* on 42nd Street.

I admired the 1980 production for its exuberance, its style, and the
power of all those tap dancers on the stage in front of you. The show contained one of the most effective opening moments of any musical you've
seen. You heard the thundering of what sounded like hundreds of tap
shoes; the curtain rose to knee height, allowing you to see all those toes
tapping; and then came a magical pause, just you and the sound of those
feet. This pause—and its sheer unexpectedness—literally stopped the
show before it started. What a wonderful idea, teasing the audience into
exhilaration before they even knew what had hit them.

This was Gower's 1980 opening. And it was accidental. During tech
rehearsals at the Kennedy Center Opera House, they had just started a
run-through when Gower called for everyone to stop. The stage manager
heard the command over his headphones, and relayed it to the curtain-

man. The kids onstage didn't hear it, and just kept tapping—resulting in a magical musical theatre moment. In 2001, they added a fillip to it; this time the tap shoes were in candy-bright colors, making for an even warmer image. This touch was indicative of what would follow. (Bramble

also added mirrors upstage for the opening moment, so that the unsuspecting audience saw an astounding 152 feet a-tapping.) Gower's opening number was in muted shades, trying to re-create the look of a thirties black-and-white film. The new *42nd Street* was friendlier and brighter, trying to re-create the dream of a thirties musical comedy.

I was impressed by the show in 1980, finding it satisfactory entertainment; in 2001, I actually enjoyed it. There were numerous small—and some significant—changes throughout the evening. Bramble and Skinner were working from Champion's original production, but alterations were made in the book, direction, choreography, and even the song list. This is not all that uncommon in a musical; anyone who directs multiple companies of a musical knows that you're likely to come up with better ways of doing things with each successive rehearsal period. If you're convinced that these improvements work, and if you also happen to be the author, there's no reason that you shouldn't write them into the script.

But the main difference came in the tone of the production. In 1980, I felt like I was watching two distinct shows. The spectacle show, with thirty-eight girls and boys tap-tap-tapping away, was spectacular (and remained so in 2001). Under Gower's direction, though, the story part of the evening seemed to belong in a different theatre. Jerry Orbach (as Julian Marsh) and Tammy Grimes (as Dorothy Brock) were the adults, more mature than the cast—not only in age—and more somber as well. The evening switched gears, constantly, from high to low and back.

In 2001, the actors all seemed to be playing the same show. Julian

Marsh wasn't some untouchable deity, out of reach of the chorus; he seemed to be a lonely guy at the top, secretly longing to be invited along to the kids' potluck suppers. Bramble's revised version also indicated that this big-time director might end up romantically involved with Peggy Sawyer. In 1980, one never suspected that this might happen—although the director (Gower) did indeed have an offstage romance with Peggy (Wanda Richert).

Contemplating this difference, it occurred to me that this "wall" was common in Gower's later work. The same thing happened in *Mack & Mabel*; when Bob Preston was onstage, you got a very different show than when Gower had the girls careening down an enormous slide into the orchestra pit. And Bernadette Peters, the much younger leading lady, seemed a very different *Mabel* in her book scenes than in her musical numbers. This also existed, to varying degrees, in *Sugar*, *Irene*, and *The Happy Time*. Perhaps Gower was more comfortable with songs than story. Or maybe, by that point of his career, he was simply not interested in the nonmusical moments.

It should be remembered, too, that Gower never had the opportunity to finish his work on *42nd Street*. Musicals are typically fixed and polished and refined during their tryout tours and previews (and even after the opening). In the case of *42nd Street*, Gower was struggling with the dances all through the Washington tryout, and—unbeknownst to the others— he was literally dying. He would steal valuable time from rehearsals to rush off and get blood transfusions. Did Gower have time to do everything he wanted? Did he have the time (and energy) to concentrate on tightening the book scenes and working with the actors on line interpretation? No. And he simultaneously had Merrick battling him and torturing him and threatening to fire him.

Bramble and Stewart had observed in 1980 that by the final scene, the only characters the audience seemed to care about were Julian and Peggy. Could the two be romantically linked? It didn't happen in the movie, and wasn't possible onstage at that point. While directing the Amsterdam production in 2000, Bramble remembered this idea and experimented with it. By giving the audience just a hint of a Julian-Peggy romance, the former wall disappeared—and resulted in a far more involving plot.

Bramble, with twenty years of experience on multiple companies of the show, also changed the design concept. The 1980 production looked, physically, like a David Merrick musical; while Merrick used many different designers over the years, there was a similar visual feeling to many of his musicals (especially those designed by Oliver Smith and Robin Wagner). A typical Merrick musical looked like—well, like *The Producers*. The new *42nd Street*—a lavish valentine to old-fashioned musical comedy—looked like it was designed, specifically, to look spectacular on the stage of the Ford Center. Doug Schmidt did a wonderful job, throwing little surprises at us along the way (and some big ones, too, like a Busby Berkeley overhead mirror). Costume designer Roger Kirk, too, provided a rainbow palette of colors in his ensemble costumes. His gowns for Christine Ebersole were especially eye-catching.

As was Ms. Ebersole's performance. Dorothy Brock is a woman scorned, a megastar whose spotlight has passed her by. Ebersole was absolutely furious about it; she shot daggers—very funny daggers—at everyone in range. The daggers mostly missed, which made her Dorothy even more enraged. Her delivery was as crisp as a Granny Smith in late October, and if body language could kill—well, just watch out. Michael Cumpsty, a dramatic performer who gave strong performances in *Racing Demon* and *Copenhagen*, was an unlikely Julian Marsh. While no match for Jerry Orbach, the consumate musical theatre performer who created the role, he was more than adequate (although not too comfortable up there). Kate Levering—en route from Susan Stroman's *Music Man* to Stroman's *Thou Shalt Not*—made a strong Peggy Sawyer, although a somewhat frosty one; David Elder danced circles around the stage (and lit it up) as Billy Lawlor; and

> In 1997, two state-of-the-extravaganza-art theatres opened right smack dab on 42nd Street. Bramble instantly realized that *42nd Street* on 42nd Street had a ring to it.

Mary Testa got her fair share of laughs as Maggie Jones. Michael Arnold (as the dance director of the show within the show) and Mylinda Hull (as the wisecracking Anytime Annie) served as sparkplugs. Choreographer Skinner's dancers were, all in all, worth their weight in gold sequins, rousing the audience to fever pitch on several occasions.

The revival of *42nd Street* came to town with a special marketing edge: Few people expected it to be any good. All season long, the revival everybody looked forward to was *Follies*. Potential casting was discussed at length, with all sorts of names flying here and about, long before anything was set. Tickets were hard to come by; more than a few people subscribed to Roundabout solely to get guaranteed *Follies* seats. Sondheim fans flew in from all over the country to ensure that they'd see the first Broadway production of this fabled show since its ignominious closing in 1972.

(People fly to New York to see Broadway shows all the time, of course; but for *Follies* they scheduled special trips.) When *Follies* began previews in March, word quickly spread: It wasn't any good. The season's first revival, *The Rocky Horror Show*, was only so-so; and the upcoming *Bells Are Ringing* had just been slain—critically speaking—out of town. *42nd Street* started previewing, and the first reports were that it was lots of fun. Suddenly, the overlooked revival became the show to look forward to. This in itself is not enough to make you a hit; but it helps to have people on your side, and suddenly *42nd Street* had people on its side. (A familiar refrain at the time was "I didn't even plan to see *42nd Street* again, but what I've heard makes me want to go.")

> Gower Champion's opening number was in muted shades, trying to re-create the look of a thirties black-and-white film. The new *42nd Street* was friendlier and brighter, trying to re-create the dream of a thirties musical comedy.

42nd Street was helped by the new musicals, too. *The Full Monty* opened in October to highly enthusiastic (though not ecstatic) reviews and settled down to strong (though not sellout) business. *The Producers* opened in April to ecstatic reviews and blockbuster business. By the time *42nd Street* opened, *Full Monty* was no longer a hot ticket; and *The Producers*, being impossible to get, provided no competition. The season's other new musicals—*Seussical*, *Jane Eyre*, *A Class Act*, and *The Adventures of Tom Sawyer*—were all limping along to early closings. *42nd Street* was not unanimously loved by the critics; the *New York Times* gave it a deflatingly bad review. But the general critical consensus was far better than that for any of the season's other musicals or musical revivals (except *The Full Monty* and *The Producers*).

This left *42nd Street*, the last show of the season, in a highly favorable position. Adding to this was the probability that the show would win the best revival Tony Award. (The competing shows all received decidedly worse reviews and did negligible business.) The producers—the *42nd Street* producers, that is—could also look forward to a boost from the upcoming Tony Awards show. It has been well demonstrated that an effective excerpt on the telecast—broadcast to a concentrated audience of theatre fans across the country—can translate into an enormous upswing in ticket sales. And what shows off better on the small screen than a stageful of attractive, exuberant tap dancers? The combination of reviews, word of mouth, two Tony Awards, and TV exposure pushed *42nd Street* near the capacity mark by July.

42nd Street
Opened: May 2, 2001
Still playing May 28, 2001
29 performances (and 31 previews)
Profit/Loss: To Be Determined
42nd Street ($90 top) was scaled to a potential gross of
    $1,009,891 at the 1,839-seat Ford Center. Weekly grosses
    averaged about $541,000, previewing in the $400,000s
    but quickly building over $800,000 in June. Total gross
    for the partial season was $4,059,109. Attendance was
    about 75 percent, with the box office grossing about 66
    percent of dollar-capacity.

TONY AWARD NOMINATIONS
Best Revival of a Musical (WINNER)
Best Performance by a Leading Actress: Christine Ebersole
    (WINNER)
Best Performance by a Featured Actress: Kate Levering
Best Performance by a Featured Actress: Mary Testa
Best Direction of a Musical: Mark Bramble
Best Choreography: Randy Skinner
Best Scenic Design: Douglas W. Schmidt
Best Costume Design: Roger Kirk
Best Lighting Design: Paul Gallo

DRAMA DESK AWARDS
Outstanding Revival of a Musical (WINNER)

Critical
Scorecard

Rave	5
Favorable	3
Mixed	0
Unfavorable	0
Pan	2

There were those who complained about the change Bramble and
Skinner made to the climax of Champion's act 2 ballet. Originally, Peggy
and Billy got caught in a shower of gangster bullets, and Billy fell dead in
Peggy's arms. All I can say is, I always hated that part of the show; it
seemed a retread from dozens of other pseudo-ballets, stale and extraneous. (Apparently it was an unfinished moment; Gower ran out of time
and couldn't think of anything else to do. The gangster shooting the lead
dancer seems to have been borrowed from Richard Rodgers and George
Balanchine's ballet "Slaughter on Tenth Avenue," from the 1936 musical
On Your Toes.)

I—for one—was glad to see this last-minute murder go, especially because of what took its place. This time, a pickpocket was shot—not Billy.
He comforts Peggy on the almost bare stage. As the song picked up—
"The big parade goes on and on, it's a rhapsody of laughter and tears"—
the stage suddenly sprang to life. The back wall of the stage, specifically.
Actors appeared, dancing, on top of the wall. The wall then started to un-
fold; it turns out this was not a wall but a staircase, eleven feet high. As

the steps descended and the dancers filled them, more and more kids entered over the top. The Ford Center stage is about fifty feet deep, far larger than other Broadway theatres. This allowed Bramble and Skinner and designer Doug Schmidt to build a grand finale, unlike anything you've ever seen on a Broadway stage.

Much better than simply shooting the tap-dancing tenor, if you ask me.

Hair

The trouble with the Encores! concert version of *Hair* can be boiled down to one word: "choreography." Not the choreography per se, by former Encores! artistic director Kathleen Marshall; but the concept of choreography itself.

The world of *Hair*, the self-described American Tribal Love-Rock Musical, existed on the streets of the East (and West) Village back in the Vietnam War years. The authors called their cast of characters not a chorus nor an ensemble but a tribe. A tribe of hippies, of dropouts, of highly individual individuals united by certain passions (peace, flowers, freedom, happiness) and certain hates (war and any sort of authority figures). While this tribe does many things together in the course of the evening, the one thing that the tribe members do not do—and cannot do—are synchronized dance steps.

The Encores! *Hair* began with the cast ranged across the upstage scaffolding, then wending their way down and around Rob Fisher's band as they sang "Aquarius." (In the original Broadway version, the cast—I mean, the tribe—made their entrance from the rear of the house in bare feet, stepping over the tops of the seats and the heads of the theatregoers and immediately obliterating the fourth wall.) As the Encores! actors reached downstage, they started to dance. Not move around to the music, but dance as if they'd rehearsed the steps in a rehearsal hall with mirrors. The evening immediately got off on the wrong foot—feet, actually—and never recovered.

Berger (Tom Plotkin) came out and did his opening monologue, and it was just about as flat as could be. Berger is the resident wild man of the group, and he is supposed to appear to be slightly dangerous. A puppy dog after we get to know him, but to the audience he is supposed to embody the danger of all those wild, drug-crazed hippies. His long hair, his dirty clothes, his larger-than-life mode of expression—this is supposed to make the audience *uncomfortable*. "Because I'm different, you think I'm subversive," someone sings a little further on, and that's the whole point of *Hair*; these kids are different but they're definitely *not* subversive. These are your kids, folks, your kids without haircuts. You are letting your government send your own kids off to Vietnam to get killed, and the most decent and heroic member of the tribe—a fellow who is simply looking for love

This tribe does many things together in the course of the evening, but the one thing that the tribe members do not do —and cannot do—are synchronized dance steps.

and the meaning of life—gets drafted, has his hair cut off, and turns up at the end of the evening in a military coffin.

At the top of the show, though, Berger *needs* to make the audience nervous. Nervous that he might jump down from the stage and slobber all over them, perhaps, but in any case nervous and uncomfortable. At Encores!, Berger was merely an actor (and I blame the production, not the actor). Yes, he had long hair—or frizzy hair, anyway; none of the boys had particularly long hair—but he wasn't much of a threat, and the language of his opening monologue was awfully tame by modern standards. At one point, Berger threatened to remove his pants. Plotkin, at this point, revealed some bright white underpants. Now these were not only white; they were brand-new, white-out-of-the-package. And a blasé theatregoer might well have thought—what?? Did hippies even wear underwear? I, myself, never bothered to check this out; but if they did wear underwear, I don't suppose they kept it bleached and pressed and "Rinso-white," to quote a phrase from the lyricists. (Rinso was a laundry bleach at the time.) Those pristinely clean underpants aptly describe what happened to *Hair* at Encores!

After the plodding monologue, Plotkin went into his opening number, "Donna." As he sang, six dancers spread out evenly along the apron and danced. They twirled and spun and did the twist, frug-ing in a frenzy as if they were still on *Hullabaloo*. The tribe, at Encores!, was staged as a herd; at every possible moment throughout the evening, everybody got into the act, generically. Those six dancers continually trotted out to do more and more choreography, and more damage to the aesthetics of the piece.

The response to this first big number was tepid, except for some

Claude   Luther Creek
Berger   Tom Plotkin
Woof   Kevin Cahoon
Hud   Michael McElroy
Sheila   Idina Menzel
Jeanie   Miriam Shor
Dionne   Brandi Chavonne Massey
Crissy   Jessica-Snow Wilson
Mother   Sheri Sanders, Kathy Deitch, Eric Millegan
Father   Kevin Cahoon, Gavin Creel, Miriam Shor
Principal   Kevin Cahoon, Gavin Creel, Miriam Shor
Tourist Couple   Jesse Tyler Ferguson, Billy Hartung
General Grant   Jesse Tyler Ferguson
Abraham Lincoln   Rosalind Brown
Buddhadalirama   Miriam Shor
The Tribe   Rosalind Brown, Bryant Carroll, E. Alyssa Claar, Gavin Creel, Kathy Deitch, Jessica Ferraro, Jesse Tyler Ferguson, Stephanie Fittro, Billy Hartung, Todd Hunter, Eric Millegan, Sean Jeremy Palmer, Sheri Sanders, Carolyn Saxon, Michael Seelbach, Yuka Takara

---

CITY CENTER
Judith E. Daykin, President & Executive Director

CITY CENTER ENCORES!

Artistic Director	Musical Director	Director-in-Residence
Jack Viertel	Rob Fisher	Kathleen Marshall

HAIR

Book and Lyrics By	Music By
Gerome Ragni & James Rado	Galt MacDermot

Produced for the Broadway stage by Michael Butler
Originally Produced by the New York Shakespeare Festival

Starring

Kevin Cahoon   Luther Creek   Jesse Tyler Ferguson
Brandi Chavonne Massey   Michael McElroy   Idina Menzel
Tom Plotkin   Miriam Shor   Jessica-Snow Wilson

Featuring

Rosalind Brown   Bryant Carroll   E. Alyssa Claar   Gavin Creel   Kathy Deitch
Jessica Ferraro   Stephanie Fittro   Billy Hartung   Todd Hunter   Eric Millegan
Sean Jeremy Palmer   Sheri Sanders   Carolyn Saxon   Michael Seelbach   Yuka Takara

Musical Director
Rob Fisher

Scenic Consultant	Costume Consultant	Lighting	Sound
John Lee Beatty	Martin Pakledinaz	Ken Billington	Scott Lehrer

Production Stage Manager	Musical Coordinator
Bonnie L. Becker	Seymour Red Press

Casting	Associate Choreographer
Jay Binder	Joey Pizzi

Directed and Choreographed By
Kathleen Marshall

Major sponsorship for *City Center Encores!* is provided by a grant from
AOL Time Warner, Inc.

The development of *Encores!* is assisted by seed support from The New York Times Company Foundation
Hair is presented by arrangement with Tams-Witmark Music Library, Inc.
560 Lexington Avenue, New York, New York 10022

City Center 55th Street Theater Foundation, Inc. gratefully acknowledges the significant support it receives from the
New York City Department of Cultural Affairs including support through the Cultural Challenge Program

Baldwin Piano, Official Piano of City Center

---

whooping from way up in the balcony. Ah-ha, I thought; Encores! finally selected a show that could attract younger audiences and sell some of those faraway seats beneath the eaves of the City Center. But from the main floor and the mezzanine, little enthusiasm was apparent. Poor Mr. Plotkin is a modern-day professional, one of the few bright lights in *Footloose* (and one of the many wasted talents in *Seussical*). As Berger, he provided no threat, and it was instantly clear that it was going to be a long night.

Because Berger *needs* to be a madman. Gerry Ragni wrote the role for himself—think "Puck on acid"—and continued to play it offstage for the rest of his life. For many years thereafter, you'd see Ragni roaming the theatre district, often turning up to cadge a ticket at opening nights or final previews. (Not that *Hair* didn't make him extremely wealthy.) Ragni stood out in any crowd, thanks to his "snaggy, shaggy, ratty, matty"

Medusa cut. He died of cancer in 1991, by which point the theatrical world of *Hair* was long gone.

After Berger's big opening, *Hair* continued with fragmentary songs about drugs and sex and race—which, in 1968, were outspoken enough to keep the audience off balance. "Sodomy," for example, was filled with five-dollar sex words that many in the audience could only vaguely identify. (By 2001, these terms were in the junior high school curriculum.) To the Encores! audience, these songs—and the accompanying action—seemed quaint. A fellow named Luther Creek came on as Claude Hooper Bukowski, the Polish boy from Queens with the accent from "Manchester, England." (Why Manchester, England? Because the boy was emulating the Beatles, who had arrived on our shores in 1964 and in some ways upended society. Audiences in 1968 were well aware of this, but did the Encores! audience pick up on it?)

Claude's introductory song also suffered from those dancers, with their Carnaby Street turns and flounces, but Creek was good enough to earn our attention. (A graduate of *Rent*, Creek was a holdover from a 1993 production of *Hair* that coauthor James Rado directed.) The show, though, didn't really get under way until Creek led the company in the rousing "I Got Life." Finally, they picked up a little steam, but it soon dissipated thanks to a particularly undernourished cast. *Hair* has always been hard to cast in a traditional manner; the show is best performed by eccentric talents, and eccentric talents are not necessarily likely to arrive at auditions bearing Equity cards.

There wasn't another winning moment until the appearance of the girl playing Jeanie, the very pregnant tribe member in love with Claude. Jeanie leads the "Air" trio; this song—about carbon dioxide and other poisons—got an especially big reaction (the president of the United States had recently signed legislation allowing more arsenic in our drinking water). This girl had such a refreshing personality that everything momentarily picked up. At intermission I dug through the Playbill to find that she was Miriam Shor. That name might not mean anything to you unless you saw her in *Hedwig and the Angry Itch*, where she created the role of Yitzak. She was extremely good there, although who knew whether she was man or woman (or other)? It turns out Shor is a fine performer, and she was one of the few delights at City Center.

Kevin Cahoon (as Woof) and Jesse Tyler Ferguson (as the Tourist Lady who sings "My Conviction")—both of whom have given enjoyable performances elsewhere—perked up *Hair* as well, but the rest of the cast made little impact. Plotkin, the Berger, didn't have much luck with his characterization; neither did *Rent* star Idina Menzel, as Sheila, the NYU undergrad who believes in love. Menzel sang well, but she might as well have been in a recording studio. She seemed strangely oblivious of her surroundings and the other characters onstage.

The key to *Hair*'s original success was the score; tuneful, enjoyable, and in some cases exceedingly pretty.

Director-choreographer Kathleen Marshall, who had been riding high in 1999–2000 (with *Kiss Me, Kate*; *Saturday Night*; and *Wonderful Town*), had a rough time of it in 2000–2001 (with *Seussical*, *Follies*, and *Hair*). But that's just the way these things go. You're up one minute, down the next; just ask Susan Stroman, who had to go through *Big* (1996) and *Steel Pier* (1997) before finally making *Contact* (2000). People tend to blame choreographers for all sorts of transgressions, but I ask you: What could the choreographer of *Seussical* have done to make the show better? Would good dances have made it a hit? And what about *Follies*? There were many things wrong—with the concept, the production, the sets, and the casting. What's a poor choreographer to do?

Watching *Hair* at Encores!, more than one audience member wondered what made the show such a big hit in 1968. And it was a hit, an enormous one with multiple companies worldwide, the most successful show between *Fiddler on the Roof* (in 1964) and *A Chorus Line* (1975). *Hair* ran 1,750 performances; when it closed, it ranked seventh on the all-time long-running musical list (with *Oklahoma!* and *South Pacific* in fifth and sixth place). Not bad for a profane, antigovernment musical about sex and drugs and all sorts of other items that was sure to offend a significant portion of the theatregoing audience.

The nudity made it a hit, some say, but I don't think so. Yes, most of the cast was up there onstage naked at the end of the first act. During the "Be-In" number, a drop flew in from the flies. The tribe untied it and spread it on the deck. As Claude started his ballad "Where Do I Go?"—one of the loveliest tunes in the show—the cast crawled under slits located throughout the drop, which now became a full-stage blanket. While Claude was singing, they skimmied out of their shirts and jeans—and underwear, if any—under cover of darkness and the drop. Twelve measures from the end of the song—when the cast started to sing "Peace, flowers, freedom, happiness"—the naked actors emerged from the slits in the drop and stood up, arms open wide. (Nudity was optional, although it was a popular moment with the actors.) This was done in low-level light, although much brighter than the corresponding climax in this season's *The Full Monty*. What you saw, though, was merely twenty or so people in their early twenties standing naked on stage in low-level light. Not a nude accentuated by a spotlight, or in-your-face body parts or simulated sex; simply living statues, haphazardly arranged and lit. (For the record: There was no nudity at City Center.)

The 1968 *Hair* had more tangles—on the road, especially—due to its antiwar stance, typified in the song "Don't Put It Down." ("Crazy for the red, white and blue," went the lyric.) This was sung by four scruffy-looking boys, who accompanied the number by using a real, live, genuine American flag as a mere prop; this in the middle of the Vietnam War, when this same flag was regularly used to drape coffins of the boys overseas. *Hair* was certainly against the draft, encouraging young men to burn

their draft cards. I don't suppose many audience members went out and did so, though. *Hair* was also in favor of drugs, although I suppose that any audience members who left the theatre and immediately indulged were simply doing what they were already doing. Did *Hair* encourage sexual freedom? Maybe so, in the case of some younger theatregoers.

The key to *Hair*'s success, it seems to me, was the melodic and surprisingly listener-friendly score. Audiences were well aware that they were headed for a so-called rock show. The nonrock fans among the audience expected that the music would be loud enough to blast them out of the theatre, which it was. They did not, however, expect to find the music tuneful, enjoyable, and even—in some cases—exceedingly pretty. "Aquarius," "Easy to Be Hard," "Frank Mills," "Good Morning Starshine," "Let the Sunshine In," "Walking in Space," "What a Piece of Work Is Man," "Where Do I Go?"—this is quite a collection, not to mention some lively list songs like "Hair" and "I Got Life."

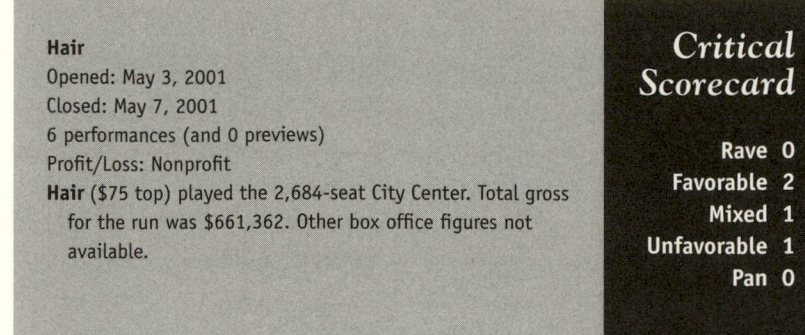

Hair
Opened: May 3, 2001
Closed: May 7, 2001
6 performances (and 0 previews)
Profit/Loss: Nonprofit
Hair ($75 top) played the 2,684-seat City Center. Total gross
for the run was $661,362. Other box office figures not
available.

*Critical
Scorecard*

Rave 0
Favorable 2
Mixed 1
Unfavorable 1
Pan 0

These songs are pretty good even today, when the age of Aquarius has morphed into the age of Geritol. On opening night at City Center, Mac-Dermot was onstage at the keyboard (playing opposite Encores! music director Rob Fisher), and Rado came onstage for curtain calls; they were seventy-two and sixty-seven, respectively. Suffice it to say, *Hair* was the last musical to have multiple song hits on the charts.

The inner strength of *Hair* has always been in its cast. The 1968 tribe included Rado and Ragni, giving definitive performances in the leading roles; Lynn Kellogg as Sheila; Shelley Plimpton as Crissy, the teenaged waif; Ronald Dyson, leading off the proceedings with "Aquarius" in his impossibly sweet high tenor; the young and unknown Melba Moore doing a phenomenal job with most of the heavy singing; and the young and unknown Diane Keaton playing numerous small roles.

Hair had an even more dynamic cast when it was revived at the Biltmore in October 1977. This was just nine and a half years after it first opened there, and a mere five years since the original production closed in the summer of 1972. Pretty quick, and—as it turned out—much too soon. The show suffered from ineffective performances in the leading roles. (Ragni, then thirty-five, kept hinting that maybe he should take over as Berger, resulting in a series of firings and an ultimate hole in the center of the production.) Otherwise, the principals included Ellen Foley as Sheila; Cleavant Derricks as Hud; Annie Golden as Jeanie; and Kristin Vigard as Crissy. Also on hand were Loretta Devine (doing the heavy singing), Charlaine Woodard (doing the heavy clowning), Byron Utley, and Peter Gallagher.

The cast also included, for a while, yours truly. I was managing the show, a rather thankless task as it was a struggle from start to finish. Upon arriving backstage one Wednesday afternoon, the stage manager said:

"Good. You're on today." We were so overwhelmed by Ragni- and Rado-ordered firings and illnesses and slipped disks, that there simply weren't enough bodies to go around. I was drafted to play Hubert, the husband of the Tourist Lady who turns out not to be a lady, as well as General Grant in the second-act hallucination sequence. I did seven performances, and let me say: I was good. For years thereafter, every time I saw Ragni on the street, he told me that I was the best Hubert they ever had. (No wonder, given that I was surely the most out-of-place person ever to appear on Broadway in *Hair*.)

It was a wonderful experience for a nonperformer, actually, and I recommend it highly. You get to stand there onstage, surveying the faces of the first few rows of theatregoers; the dark shadow of the rest of the house; the warm red glow of the exit lights at the back of the auditorium. You also learn how you can—with a mere sideways glance at the right moment—get your own, personal roar out of hundreds and hundreds of people. (Director Tom O'Horgan didn't tell me to stop, so I kept doing it.) The only trouble I had, actually, was being assaulted by Derricks—who went on to star in *Dreamgirls*—whose character thought I was the funniest thing he had ever seen and proceeded to tighten my tie with my neck still in it; and being attacked by Devine—who also went on to star in *Dreamgirls*—who every night tried to remove my trousers.

Twenty-four years later, there were several press reports about the Encores! production transferring to Broadway, citing the great reviews. What great reviews? I wondered. There were some good ones, specifically a highly favorable almost-rave from Ben Brantley in the *Times*. But the other reviews were less enthusiastic, and there weren't very many of them; few critics even bothered to report on *Hair*. (Compare this reaction with the seven raves out of seven accorded the 2000 Encores! production of *Wonderful Town*, which also tried to arrange a transfer.) The Weisslers (of *Chicago*) and the Richard Frankel group (of *The Producers*) were apparently hotly trying to outnegotiate each other, but by mid-June the transfer was dead. Which was probably for the best.

If I found the concert version of *Hair* somewhat less than full-bodied, I think that it was nevertheless a brave and necessary choice for the folks at City Center Encores! I can understand that a significant number of subscribers might not have been too pleased; *Hair*, a somewhat vulgar, in-your-face show with a rocklike score, is precisely the sort of musical that some folks go to Encores! to avoid.

But the number of shows suitable for the Encores! format is not unlimited. Yes, there are a lot of dusty, old, long-lost musicals in the record books; but many of them belong where they are. Encores! can keep mining the Rodgers and Hart and Porter and Gershwin archives—you won't get a complaint from me—but they will inevitably start running out of good Rodgers and Hart and Porter and Gershwin shows. Better they should save some of those titles to do two or three or five years from now. Encores! needs to start turning to other types of Broadway musicals, and *Hair*—being an unquestionably groundbreaking, record-breaking blockbuster

If the concert version of *Hair* was somewhat less than full-bodied, it was nevertheless a brave and necessary choice for the folks at City Center Encores!

with a rich score—was a good place to start. They also, presumably, will try their hand at some earlier musicals. Operetta, anybody? This, too, might not be to the liking of some subscribers; but Encores!, going into its ninth season, can't keep doing precisely what they're doing. Otherwise, we'll start seeing revivals of Encores! greatest hits, and that's not something any of us should look forward to.

Curtain Calls

Honorable Mention

for noteworthy contributions to the season

There follows a highly personal list of people whose contributions, one way or another, made the season of theatregoing brighter.

Bells Are Ringing
Faith Prince

Betrayal
Juliette Binoche
Liev Schreiber
John Slattery
David Leveaux (director)
Rob Howell (as scenic and costume designer)

Blast
Andy Smart (trumpeter)
James Mason (director)

Bloomer Girl
Jubilant Sykes
Everett Bradley
Rob Fisher (musical director)

A Class Act
Lonny Price (as actor and director)
Randy Graff

A Connecticut Yankee
Judith Blazer
Seán Martin Hingston

The Dinner Party
Len Cariou
Penny Fuller
Veanne Cox

Follies
Blythe Danner
Polly Bergen
Eric Stern (musical director)

42nd Street
Christine Ebersole
Kate Levering
Mary Testa
David Elder
Mark Bramble (director)
Randy Skinner (choreographer)
Douglas W. Schmidt (scenic designer)
Roger Kirk (costume designer)
Todd Ellison (musical director)

The Full Monty
Patrick Wilson
John Ellison Conlee
Jason Danieley
Kathleen Freeman
André De Shields

David Yazbek (as composer and
  lyricist)
Terrence McNally (librettist)
Jack O'Brien (director)
Harold Wheeler (orchestrator)
Ted Sperling (musical director)
Kimberley Grigsby (conductor)

The Gathering
Hal Linden

Gore Vidal's The Best Man
Charles Durning
Elizabeth Ashley
Christine Ebersole
Jonathan Hadary

Hair
Luther Creek
Miriam Shor

The Invention of Love
Richard Easton
Robert Sean Leonard
Tom Stoppard (author)
Jack O'Brien (director)
Bob Crowley (scenic designer)
Brian MacDevitt (lighting designer)

Jane Eyre
Marla Schaffel
James Barbour
Mary Stout
John Caird (as director)
Scott Schwartz (codirector)
John Napier (scenic designer)
Jules Fisher and Peggy Eisenhauer
  (lighting designers)

Judgment at Nuremberg
Maximilian Schell
George Grizzard
Michael Hayden
Michael Mastro

King Hedley II
Viola Davis
Charles Brown
August Wilson (author)
Marion McClinton (director)

The Man Who Came to Dinner
Byron Jennings
Lewis J. Stadlen

One Flew over the Cuckoo's Nest
Gary Sinise
Ross Lehman

The Producers
Nathan Lane
Matthew Broderick
Roger Bart
Gary Beach
Cady Huffman
Brad Oscar
Mel Brooks (as composer and
  lyricist)
Mel Brooks and Thomas Meehan
  (librettists)
Susan Stroman (as director and
  choreographer)
Robin Wagner (scenic designer)
William Ivey Long (costume
  designer)
Doug Besterman (orchestrator)
Patrick S. Brady (musical director)

Proof
Mary-Louise Parker
Larry Bryggman
Ben Shenkman
David Auburn (author)
Daniel Sullivan (director)
John Lee Beatty (scenic designer)

The Rocky Horror Show
Alice Ripley
Dick Cavett

Christopher Ashley (director)
David Rockwell (designer)

The Search for Signs of Intelligent Life in the Universe
Lily Tomlin
Jane Wagner (as author and director)

Seussical
Kevin Chamberlin
Janine LaManna
Anthony Blair Hall
Stephen Flaherty (composer)
Lynn Ahrens (lyricist)
Doug Besterman (orchestrator)
David Holcenberg (musical director)

Stones in His Pockets
Seán Campion
Conleth Hill
Marie Jones (author)
Ian McElhinney (director)

The Tale of the Allergist's Wife
Linda Lavin
Shirl Bernheim
Charles Busch (author)
Lynne Meadow (director)
Santo Loquasto (scenic designer)

Tony Wrap-Up
(and Other Awards)

TONY AWARDS

The 2000–2001 season's Tony Award nominations are listed below, with asterisks denoting the winners. Overlooked people who—for various reasons—might have been expected to receive nominations are also mentioned.

Best Play

The Invention of Love (Author: Tom Stoppard)
King Hedley II (Author: August Wilson)
*Proof** (Author: David Auburn)
The Tale of the Allergist's Wife (Author: Charles Busch)

Overlooked

The Dinner Party (Author: Neil Simon)
Stones in His Pockets (Author: Marie Jones)

Proof seemed the obvious winner—especially with its Pulitzer Prize in hand—until *The Invention of Love* took the Drama Critics Circle Award for Best Play. (As a consolation, the Drama Critics gave *Proof* the award for Best American Play.) The Tony voters favored *Proof* over *Invention of Love* (as did I), with neither *Hedley* nor *Allergist* having a chance.

Best Musical

A Class Act
The Full Monty
Jane Eyre
*The Producers**

Overlooked

Seussical

The Producers was the biggest hit in generations, which was enough to give the show a sweep in all eligible categories, for a record-setting twelve awards. Enough said.

Best Revival of a Play

Betrayal
Gore Vidal's The Best Man
One Flew over the Cuckoo's Nest*
The Search for Signs of Intelligent Life in the Universe

Overlooked

The Man Who Came to Dinner

This category had no clear-cut winner, as all the nominees received somewhat mixed reviews. *Cuckoo's Nest* was the only nominee still running on Tony Sunday, which helped them win the award.

Best Revival of a Musical

Bells Are Ringing
Follies
42nd Street*
The Rocky Horror Show

42nd Street was pretty clearly the best of the bunch: the only one of the shows to actually get good reviews, and the only one to attract significant audiences.

Best Book of a Musical

Linda Kline and Lonny Price, *A Class Act*
Terrence McNally, *The Full Monty*
John Caird, *Jane Eyre*
Mel Brooks and Thomas Meehan, *The Producers**

Again, *The Producers* was the all-around Best Musical, and the book was a major asset. No chance for anyone else.

Best Original Score (Music and Lyrics) Written for the Theatre

Edward Kleban (Music and Lyrics), *A Class Act*
David Yazbek (Music and Lyrics), *The Full Monty*
Paul Gordon (Music), Paul Gordon and John Caird (Lyrics), *Jane Eyre*
Mel Brooks (Music and Lyrics), *The Producers**

Overlooked

Stephen Flaherty (Music) and Lynn Ahrens (Lyrics), *Seussical*

The score was the weakest asset of *The Producers*, perhaps, but the songs worked well in the theatre, which placed Brooks way ahead of the competition. (From his acceptance speech: "I'd like to thank Stephen Sondheim for not writing a show this year.")

Best Performance by a Leading Actor in a Play

Seán Campion, *Stones in His Pockets*
Richard Easton, *The Invention of Love**
Conleth Hill, *Stones in His Pockets*
Brian Stokes Mitchell, *King Hedley II*
Gary Sinise, *One Flew over the Cuckoo's Nest*

Overlooked

Len Cariou, *The Dinner Party*
Alan Cumming, *Design for Living*
Charles Durning, *Gore Vidal's The Best Man*
George Grizzard, *Judgment at Nuremberg*
Nathan Lane, *The Man Who Came to Dinner*
Hal Linden, *The Gathering*
Tony Roberts, *The Tale of the Allergist's Wife*
Maximillian Schell, *Judgment at Nuremberg*
Liev Schreiber, *Betrayal*

Sinise and Hill gave suitably flashy performances, but the voters went with Easton, a veteran character actor who gave a sturdy and sympathetic performance.

Best Performance by a Leading Actress in a Play

Juliette Binoche, *Betrayal*
Linda Lavin, *The Tale of the Allergist's Wife*
Mary-Louise Parker, *Proof**
Jean Smart, *The Man Who Came to Dinner*
Leslie Uggams, *King Hedley II*

Overlooked

Jennifer Ehle, *Design for Living*

Parker well deserved the award for her striking performance in *Proof*, although Linda Lavin could easily have taken it for her hysterical portrayal of the title character in *The Allergist's Wife*. Lavin's frequent missed performances might have worked against her; few things annoy a

Tony voter more than showing up at a performance when the star doesn't.

Best Performance by a Leading Actor in a Musical

Matthew Broderick, *The Producers*
Kevin Chamberlin, *Seussical*
Tom Hewitt, *The Rocky Horror Show*
Nathan Lane, *The Producers**
Patrick Wilson, *The Full Monty*

Overlooked

James Barbour, *Jane Eyre*
Michael Cumpsty, *42nd Street*
Lonny Price, *A Class Act*

This, again, was a foregone conclusion. Lane magnanimously offered to share his award with Broderick, but thanks to his Bialystock in *The Producers* he was clearly "The King of Broadway."

Best Performance by a Leading Actress in a Musical

Blythe Danner, *Follies*
Christine Ebersole, *42nd Street**
Randy Graff, *A Class Act*
Faith Prince, *Bells Are Ringing*
Marla Schaffel, *Jane Eyre*

Overlooked

Judith Ivey, *Follies*

This one was a tight call. Ebersole gave a wonderful comic performance, but some felt she was not in a "leading" role. (Her character was onstage only ten minutes in the second act.) Prince labored admirably, trying to carry a misguided production on her (poorly costumed) shoulders, while newcomer Schaffel did extremely well in a long and difficult role. Schaffel won the Drama Desk Award, throwing the Tony race up for grabs, but Ebersole prevailed.

Best Performance by a Featured Actor in a Play

Charles Brown, *King Hedley II*
Larry Bryggman, *Proof*
Michael Hayden, *Judgment at Nuremberg*
Robert Sean Leonard, *The Invention of Love**
Ben Shenkman, *Proof*

Overlooked

Jonathan Hadary, *Gore Vidal's The Best Man*
Lewis J. Stadlen, *The Man Who Came to Dinner*

This was an especially tough category this year. Brown, Bryggman, Leonard, and Shenkman were equally deserving. The category designation made the difference: Leonard and Bryggman could just as well have been placed in the Leading Actor category, in which case it would have been a very different race.

Best Performance by a Featured Actress in a Play

Viola Davis, *King Hedley II**
Johanna Day, *Proof*
Penny Fuller, *The Dinner Party*
Marthe Keller, *Judgment at Nuremberg*
Michele Lee, *The Tale of the Allergist's Wife*

Overlooked

Elizabeth Ashley, *Gore Vidal's The Best Man*
Veanne Cox, *The Dinner Party*

The relatively unknown Davis was so exceptionally good that she was favored, despite some worthy competitors (including three veteran actresses with major starring credits).

Best Performance by a Featured Actor in a Musical

Roger Bart, *The Producers*
Gary Beach, *The Producers**
John Ellison Conlee, *The Full Monty*
André De Shields, *The Full Monty*
Brad Oscar, *The Producers*

Overlooked

David Elder, *42nd Street*
Jarrod Emick, *The Rocky Horror Show*

This was a tough category, as both *The Full Monty* and *The Producers* contained five major male roles. Anything can happen when two or three people from the same show are nominated and split the vote, but Beach—the flashiest of them all—was able to pull it off.

Best Performance by a Featured Actress in a Musical

Polly Bergen, *Follies*
Kathleen Freeman, *The Full Monty*
Cady Huffman, *The Producers**
Kate Levering, *42nd Street*
Mary Testa, *42nd Street*

Overlooked

Janine LaManna, *Seussical*
Alice Ripley, *The Rocky Horror Show*
Emily Skinner, *The Full Monty*
Mary Stout, *Jane Eyre*

This was also a tough category this year, with at least eight performers deserving a nomination. Huffman did a fine job, but popular favorites Bergen or Freeman might easily have won as feisty old survivors (especially had they not been competing against each other). It was impossible to fight the *Producers* juggernaut, though.

Best Direction of a Play

Marion McClinton, *King Hedley II*
Ian McElhinney, *Stones in His Pockets*
Jack O'Brien, *The Invention of Love*
Daniel Sullivan, *Proof**

Overlooked

Terry Kinney, *One Flew over the Cuckoo's Nest*
David Leveaux, *Betrayal*
Joe Mantello, *Design for Living*
Lynne Meadow, *The Tale of the Allergist's Wife*
Jerry Zaks, *The Man Who Came to Dinner*

As in the Best Play category, the race was between O'Brien and Sullivan. O'Brien did a superb job with a difficult play and might well have won (especially since he did a similarly good job on *The Full Monty*). Sullivan, though, brought out every possible value in the exceptional *Proof* and was thus rewarded.

Best Direction of a Musical

Christopher Ashley, *The Rocky Horror Show*
Mark Bramble, *42nd Street*
Jack O'Brien, *The Full Monty*
Susan Stroman, *The Producers**

Overlooked

Lonny Price, *A Class Act*
Matthew Warchus, *Follies*

The Producers was an avalanche of laughter in all departments, which means that the director made good choices all around (and made everything work, too).

Best Choreography

Jerry Mitchell, *The Full Monty*
Jim Moore, George Pinney, and John Vanderkolff, *Blast*
Randy Skinner, *42nd Street*
Susan Stroman, *The Producers**

Overlooked

Kathleen Marshall, *Follies*

Stroman put the comedy back in musical comedy choreography, taking her second consecutive award in this category (after *Contact*).

Best Scenic Design

Bob Crowley, *The Invention of Love*
Heidi Ettinger, *The Adventures of Tom Sawyer*
Douglas W. Schmidt, *42nd Street*
Robin Wagner, *The Producers**

Overlooked

John Napier, *Jane Eyre*
David Rockwell, *The Rocky Horror Show*

Wagner's scenery perfectly mirrored Mel Brooks's insanities, resulting in a surefire win (despite wonderfully evocative work from Crowley for *The Invention of Love*).

Best Costume Design

Theoni V. Aldredge, *Follies*
Roger Kirk, *42nd Street*
William Ivey Long, *The Producers**
David C. Woolard, *The Rocky Horror Show*

Long—who just might have the best sense of humor (in his work) of any Broadway designer—was perfect casting for *The Producers*, and he outdid himself.

Best Lighting Design

Jules Fisher and Peggy Eisenhauer, *Jane Eyre*
Paul Gallo, *42nd Street*
Peter Kaczorowski, *The Producers**
Kenneth Posner, *The Adventures of Tom Sawyer*

Kaczorowski did a thoroughly professional job on *The Producers* and was swept along with the rest of the show's creative staff. Fisher and Eisenhauer's work on Jane Eyre might well have been the "best" of the year, but voters stuck with *The Producers*.

Best Orchestrations

Doug Besterman, *The Producers**
Larry Hochman, *A Class Act*
Jonathan Tunick, *Follies*
Harold Wheeler, *The Full Monty*

The orchestrator of a hit like *The Producers* is guaranteed to get votes of people who aren't quite sure which orchestrations are best. Besterman earned the award anyway, giving *The Producers* the wild and wacky sound called for by the composer.

SPECIAL TONY AWARDS

For a special theatrical event

Blast

For lifetime achievement in the theatre

Paul Gemignani, musical director

For excellence in the theatre

Betty Corwin and the Theatre on Film and Tape Archive at the New York
   Public Library for the Performing Arts at Lincoln Center
New Dramatists
Theatre World

Regional Theatre

Victory Gardens Theater, Chicago, Illinois

PULITZER PRIZE FOR DRAMA

Edward Albee, *The Play About the Baby*
David Auburn, *Proof**
Kenneth Lonergan, *The Waverly Gallery*

NEW YORK DRAMA CRITICS CIRCLE AWARDS

Best Play

The Invention of Love (Author: Tom Stoppard)

Best American Play

Proof (Author: David Auburn)

Best Musical

The Producers

Best Revival

[No award was given]

DRAMA DESK AWARDS

Outstanding Play

Proof (Author: David Auburn) (Tony Award winner)

Outstanding Musical

The Producers (Tony Award winner)

Outstanding Musical Revue

Forbidden Broadway 2001: A Spoof Odyssey (off-Broadway)

Outstanding Revival of a Play

Gore Vidal's The Best Man

Outstanding Revival of a Musical

42nd Street (Tony Award winner)

Outstanding Actor in a Play

Richard Easton, *The Invention of Love* (Tony Award winner)

Outstanding Actress in a Play

Mary-Louise Parker, *Proof* (Tony Award winner)

Outstanding Actor in a Musical

Nathan Lane, *The Producers* (Tony Award winner)

Outstanding Actress in a Musical

Marla Schaffel, *Jane Eyre*

Outstanding Featured Actor in a Play

Charles Brown, *King Hedley II*

Outstanding Featured Actress in a Play

Viola Davis, *King Hedley II* (Tony Award winner)

Outstanding Featured Actor in a Musical

Gary Beach, *The Producers* (Tony Award winner)

Outstanding Featured Actress in a Musical

Cady Huffman, *The Producers* (Tony Award winner)

Outstanding Director of a Play

Jack O'Brien, *The Invention of Love*

Outstanding Director of a Musical

Susan Stroman, *The Producers* (Tony Award winner)

Outstanding Choreography

Susan Stroman, *The Producers* (Tony Award winner)

Outstanding Book of a Musical

Mel Brooks and Thomas Meehan, *The Producers* (Tony Award winner)

Outstanding Music

David Yazbek, *The Full Monty*

Outstanding Lyrics

Mel Brooks, *The Producers* (Tony Award winner)

Outstanding Orchestrations

Doug Besterman, *The Producers* (Tony Award winner)

Outstanding Set Design of a Play

Bob Crowley, *The Invention of Love*

Outstanding Set Design of a Musical

Robin Wagner, *The Producers* (Tony Award winner)

Outstanding Costume Design

William Ivey Long, *The Producers* (Tony Award winner)

Outstanding Lighting Design

Paul Anderson, *Mnemonic* (off-Broadway)

Outstanding Sound Design

Christopher Shutt, *Mnemonic* (off-Broadway)

Outstanding Solo Performance

Pamela Gien, *The Syringa Tree* (off-Broadway)

Unique Theatrical Experience

Mnemonic (off-Broadway)

Special Awards

Seán Campion and Conleth Hill, for their performances in *Stones in His Pockets*

Reba McEntire for her performance in *Annie Get Your Gun* (Broadway replacement)

The casts of *Cobb* (Michael Cullen, Clark Jackson, Matthew Mabe, Michael Sabatino) and *Tabletop* (Rob Bartlett, Harvey Blanks, Jack Koenig, Dean Nolen, Elizabeth Hanly Rice, Jeremy Webb) for Outstanding Ensemble Performance (both off-Broadway)

Holdovers

As the 2000–2001 season began on May 29, 2000, the following shows were playing on Broadway.

Aida   Musical. Opened March 23, 2000, at the Palace. Music by Elton John; lyrics by Tim Rice; book by Linda Woolverton and Robert Falls & David Henry Hwang; directed by Robert Falls; choreographed by Wayne Cilento. 2000 Tony Awards: Score; Leading Actress (Heather Headley); Scenic Design (Bob Crowley); Lighting Design (Natasha Katz). Still playing May 28, 2001. To date: 492 performances (and 27 previews). Profit/loss: to be determined.

Annie Get Your Gun   Musical revival. Opened March 4, 1999, at the Marquis. Music and lyrics by Irving Berlin; book by Herbert and Dorothy Fields (revised by Peter Stone); directed and choreographed by Graciela Daniele. 1999 Tony Awards: Revival; Leading Actress (Bernadette Peters). Closed September 1, 2001, after 1,046 performances (and 35 previews). Total gross for the run was $82,148,713. Attendance was about 82 percent, with the box offices grossing about 77 percent of dollar-capacity.

Beauty and the Beast   Musical. Opened April 18, 1994, at the Palace; closed September 5, 1999. Reopened November 12, 1999, at the Lunt-Fontanne. Music by Alan Menken; lyrics by Howard Ashman and Tim Rice; book by Linda Woolverton; directed by Robert Jess Roth; choreographed by Matt West. 1994 Tony Award: Costume Design (Ann Hould-Ward). Still playing May 28, 2001. To date: 2,887 performances (and 46 previews). Profit/loss: profit.

Cabaret   Musical revival. Opened March 19, 1998, at the Kit Kat Klub (Henry Miller's Theatre); transferred November 14, 1998, to Studio 54. Music by John Kander; lyrics by Fred Ebb; book by Joe Masteroff; directed by Sam Mendes and Rob Marshall; choreographed by Rob Marshall. 1998 Tony

Awards: Musical Revival; Leading Actress (Natasha Richardson); Leading Actor (Alan Cumming); Featured Actor (Ron Rifkin). Still playing May 28, 2001. To date: 1,288 performances (and 37 previews). Profit/loss: profit.

Cats   Musical. Opened October 7, 1982, at the Winter Garden. Music by Andrew Lloyd Webber; lyrics by T. S. Eliot; directed by Trevor Nunn; choreographed by Gillian Lynne. 1983 Tony Awards: Musical; Score; Book; Direction; Featured Actress (Betty Buckley); Costume Design (John Napier); and Lighting Design (David Hersey). Closed: September 10, 2000, after 7,485 performances (and 16 previews). Profit/loss: profit.

Chicago   Musical revival. Opened November 14, 1996, at the Richard Rodgers; transferred February 12, 1997, to the Shubert. Music by John Kander; lyrics by Fred Ebb; book by Fred Ebb and Bob Fosse (adaptation by David Thompson); directed by Walter Bobbie; choreographed by Ann Reinking in the style of Bob Fosse. 1997 Tony Awards: Musical Revival; Director; Choreographer; Leading Actress (Bebe Neuwirth); Leading Actor (James Naughton); Lighting Design (Ken Billington). Still playing May 28, 2001. To date: 1,890 performances (and 22 previews). Profit/loss: profit.

Contact   Musical. "Written" by John Weidman; directed and choreographed by Susan Stroman. Opened March 30, 2000, at the Vivian Beaumont. 2000 Tony Awards: Best Musical; Choreographer; Featured Actor (Boyd Gaines); Featured Actress (Karen Ziemba). Still playing May 28, 2001. To date: 485 performances (and 31 previews). Profit/loss: nonprofit [profit].

Copenhagen   Play. By Michael Frayn; directed by Michael Blakemore. 2000 Tony Awards: Play; Director; Featured Actress (Blair Brown). Opened April 11, 2000, at the Royale. Closed January 21, 2001, after 326 performances (and 21 previews). Total gross for the run was $11,570,839. Attendance was about 71 percent, with the box office grossing about 56 percent of dollar-capacity. Profit/loss: profit.

Dame Edna: The Royal Tour   Play. Opened October 17, 1999, at the Booth. Devised and written by Barry Humphries. 2000 Special Tony Award for a Live Theatrical Event. Closed July 2, 2000, after 297 performances (and 39 previews). Total gross for the run was $9,815,693. Attendance was about 79 percent, with the box office grossing about percent of 75 dollar-capacity. Profit/loss: profit.

Dirty Blonde   Play. By Claudia Shear; conceived by Claudia Shear and James Lapine; directed by James Lapine. Opened May 1, 2000, at the Helen Hayes. Closed March 4, 2001, after 353 perfomances (and 20 previews). Total gross for the run was $7,925,422. Attendance was about 74 percent, with the box office grossing about 60 percent of dollar-capacity. Profit/loss: profit.

Footloose   Musical. Opened October 22, 1998, at the Richard Rodgers. Music by Tom Snow (and others); lyrics by Dean Pitchford (and others); book by Dean Pitchford and Walter Bobbie; directed by Walter Bobbie; choreographed by A. C. Ciulla. Closed July 2, 2000, after 709 performances (and 18 previews). Total gross for the run was $37,134,917. Attendance was about 80 percent, with the box office grossing about 63 percent of dollar-capacity. Profit/loss: loss.

Fosse   Musical revue. Opened January 14, 1999, at the Broadhurst. Conceived by Richard Maltby Jr., Chet Walker, and Ann Reinking; choreography by Bob Fosse; directed by Richard Maltby Jr.; choreography recreated by Chet Walker; codirected and cochoreographed by Ann Reinking. 1999 Tony Awards: Musical; Orchestrations (Ralph Burns and Doug Besterman); Lighting Design (Andrew Bridge). Closed August 25, 2001, after 1,093 performances (and 21 previews). Total gross for the run was $68,997,054. Attendance was about 88 percent, with the box office grossing about 78 percent of dollar-capacity. Profit/loss: profit.

The Green Bird   Play with music. By Carlo Gozzi; translated by Albert Bermel and Ted Emery; original music by Elliot Goldenthal. Opened April 18, 2000, at the Cort. Closed June 4, 2000, after 56 performances (and 15 previews). Total gross for the run was $1,787,997. Attendance was about 50 percent, with the box office grossing about 39 percent of dollar-capacity. Profit/loss: loss.

Jekyll & Hyde   Musical. Opened April 28, 1997, at the Plymouth. Music by Frank Wildhorn; book and lyrics by Leslie Bricusse; directed by Robin Phillips; choreographed by Joey Pizzi. Closed January 7, 2001, after 1,543 performances (and 45 previews). Total gross for the run was $78,056,883. Attendance was about 83 percent, with the box office grossing about 75 percent of dollar-capacity. Profit/loss: loss.

Jesus Christ Superstar   Musical revival. Music by Andrew Lloyd Webber; lyrics by Tim Rice; directed by Gale Edwards; choreographed by Anthony Van Laast. Opened April 16, 2000, at the Ford Center. Closed September 3, 2000, after 161 performances (and 28 previews). Total gross for the run was $11,284,435. Attendance was about 73 percent, with the box office grossing about 53 percent of dollar-capacity. Profit/loss: loss.

Kiss Me, Kate   Musical revival. Opened November 18, 1999, at the Martin Beck. Music and lyrics by Cole Porter; book by Sam and Bella Spewack; directed by Michael Blakemore; choreographed by Kathleen Marshall. 2000 Tony Awards: Revival; Leading Actor (Brian Stokes Mitchell); Director (Michael Blakemore); Costume Design (Martin Pakledinaz); Orchestrations (Don Sebesky). Closed December 31, 2001, after 883 performances (and 28 previews). Total gross for the run was $65,051,743. Attendance was about 84 percent, with the box office grossing about 74 percent of dollar-capacity. Profit/loss: profit.

The Lion King   Musical. Opened November 13, 1997, at the New Amsterdam. Music by Elton John and others; lyrics by Tim Rice and others; book by Roger Allers and Irene Mecchia; directed by Julie Taymor; choreographed by Garth Fagan. 1998 Tony Awards: Musical; Director; Choreographer; Scenic Design (Richard Hudson); Costume Design (Taymor); and Lighting Design (Donald Holder). Drama Critics Circle Award for Best Musical. Still playing May 28, 2001. To date: 1,478 performances (and 33 previews). Profit/loss: profit.

Les Misérables   Musical. Opened March 12, 1987, at the Broadway; moved October 16, 1990, to the Imperial. By Alain Boublil and Claude-Michel Schönberg; music by Claude-Michel Schönberg; lyrics by Herbert Kretzmer; adapted and directed by Trevor Nunn and John Caird. 1987 Tony Awards: Musical; Score; Book; Featured Actor (Michael Maguire); Featured Actress (Frances Ruffelle). Still playing May 28, 2001. To date: 5,855 performances. Profit/loss: profit.

Miss Saigon   Musical. Opened April 11, 1991, at the Broadway. Music by Claude-Michel Schönberg; lyrics by Richard Maltby Jr. and Alain Boublil; book by Alain Boublil and Claude-Michel Schönberg; directed by Nicholas Hytner; choreographed by Bob Avian. 1991 Tony Awards: Leading Actor (Jonathan Pryce); Leading Actress (Lea Salonga); Featured Actor (Hinton Battle). Closed January 28, 2001, after 4,097 performances (and 19 previews). Total gross for the run was $285,843,972. Profit/loss: profit.

A Moon for the Misbegotten   Play revival. Opened March 19, 2000, at the Walter Kerr. By Eugene O'Neill; directed by Daniel Sullivan. 2000 Tony Award: Featured Actor (Roy Dotrice). Closed July 2, 2000, after 120 performances (and 15 previews). Total gross for the run was $5,354,179. Attendance was about 81 percent, with the box office grossing about 71 percent of dollar-capacity. Profit/loss: profit.

Much Ado About Everything   Written and directed by Jackie Mason. Opened December 30, 1999, at the Golden. Closed July 30, 2000, after 186 performances (and 33 previews). Total gross for the run was $5,303,427. Attendance was about 85 percent, with the box office grossing about 75 percent of dollar-capacity. Profit/loss: profit.

The Music Man   Musical revival. Book, music, and lyrics by Meredith Willson; directed and choreographed by Susan Stroman. Opened April 27, 2000, at the Neil Simon. Closed December 30, 2001, after 699 performances (and 22 previews). Total gross for the run was $45,976,995. Attendance was about 77 percent, with the box office grossing abut 72 percent of dollar-capacity. Profit/loss: loss.

The Phantom of the Opera   Musical. Opened January 26, 1988, at the Majestic. Music by Andrew Lloyd Webber; lyrics by Charles Hart; book and additional lyrics by Richard Stilgoe; directed by Harold Prince; choreographed by Gillian Lynne. 1988 Tony Awards: Musical; Director; Scenic Design (Maria Bjornson); Lighting Design (Andrew Bridge); Leading Actor (Michael Crawford); and Featured Actress (Judy Kaye). Still playing May 28, 2001. To date: 5,566 performances (and 16 previews). Profit/loss: profit.

The Real Thing   Play revival. Opened April 17, 2000, at the Ethel Barrymore. By Tom Stoppard; directed by David Leveaux. 2000 Tony Awards: Revival; Leading Actor (Stephen Dillane); Leading Actress (Jennifer Ehle). Closed August 13, 2000, after 136 performances (and 24 previews). Total gross for the run was $5,645,810. Attendance was about 68 percent, with the box office grossing about 58 percent of dollar-capacity. Profit/loss: profit.

Rent   Musical. Opened April 29, 1996, at the Nederlander. Book, music, and lyrics by Jonathan Larson; directed by Michael Greif; choreographed by Marlies Yearby. 1996 Tony Awards: Musical; Score; Book; Featured Actor (Wilson Jermaine Heredia). Drama Critics Circle Award for Best Musical. Pulitzer Prize for Drama. Still playing May 28, 2001. To date: 2,121 performances (and 16 previews). Profit/loss: profit.

The Ride Down Mt. Morgan   Play. By Arthur Miller; directed by David Esbjornson. Opened April 9, 2000, at the Ambassador. Closed July 23, 2000, after 121 performances (and 23 previews). Total gross for the run $3,948,515. Attendance was about 62 percent, with the box office grossing about 43 percent of dollar-capacity. Profit/loss: loss.

Riverdance   Musical revue. Opened March 16, 2000, at the Gershwin. Music and lyrics by Bill Whelan; directed by John McColgan. Closed August 26, 2001, after 605 performances (and 13 previews). Total gross for the run was $45,553,810. Attendance was about 75 percent, with the box office grossing about 60 percent of dollar-capacity. Profit/loss: loss.

Saturday Night Fever   Musical. Opened October 21, 1999, at the Minskoff. Music and lyrics by the Bee Gees and others; book by Nan Knighton; directed and choreographed by Arlene Phillips. Closed December 30, 2000, after 501 performances (and 27 previews). Total gross for the run was $37,585,638. Attendance was about 76 percent, with the box office grossing about 65 percent of dollar-capacity. Profit/loss: loss.

Swing!   Musical revue. Opened December 9, 1999, at the St. James. Directed and choreographed by Lynne Taylor-Corbett; production supervised by Jerry Zaks. Closed January 14, 2001, after 461 performances (and 43 previews). Total gross for the run was $24,623,691. Attendance was about 61 percent, with the box office grossing about 50 percent of dollar-capacity. Profit/loss: loss.

Taller Than a Dwarf   Play. Opened April 24, 2000, at the Longacre. By Elaine May; directed by Alan Arkin. Closed June 11, 2000, after 56 performances (and 37 previews). Total gross for the run was $2,557,061. Attendance was about 65 percent, with the box office grossing about 50 percent of dollar-capacity. Profit/loss: loss.

True West   Play revival. Opened March 9, 2000, at the Circle in the Square. By Sam Shepard; directed by Matthew Warchus. Closed July 29, 2000, after 154 performances (and 21 previews). Total gross for the run was $5,035,352. Attendance was about 86 percent, with the box office grossing about 77 percent of dollar-capacity. Profit/loss: profit.

Uncle Vanya   Play revival. By Anton Chekhov; translated by Mike Poulton; directed by Michael Mayer. Opened April 30, 2000, at the Brooks Atkinson. Closed June 11, 2000, after 41 performances (and 29 previews). Total gross for the run was $2,098,735. Attendance was about 80 percent, with the box office grossing about 57 percent of dollar-capacity. Profit/loss: nonprofit [loss].

The Wild Party   Musical. Opened April 13, 2000, at the Virginia. Music and lyrics by Michael John LaChiusa; book by Michael John LaChiusa and George C. Wolfe; directed by George C. Wolfe; choreographed by Joey McKneely. Closed June 11, 2000, after 68 performances (and 36 previews). Total gross for the run was $3,919,522. Attendance was about 63 percent, with the box office grossing about 43 percent of dollar-capacity Profit/loss: loss.

Shows That Never Reached Town

Every season, numerous productions are announced for Broadway that for any number of reasons never arrive. Many of these are typically more wishful than realistic; others succumb to financial woes or tryout blues. The following shows were announced to arrive on Broadway during the 2000–2001 season. Some, though not all, are still likely prospects.

Brighton Beach Memoirs   Revival of the 1983 play. By Neil Simon. Produced by Emanuel Azenberg. Initial plans were to mount both *Brighton Beach Memoirs* and *Broadway Bound* (1986), two parts of Simon's trilogy, with Linda Lavin in the lead. When Lavin signed on for the Broadway transfer of *The Tale of the Allergist's Wife*, plans were revised to mount only *Brighton Beach Memoirs* (without Lavin). Plans for a spring opening were canceled in September 2000, influenced, presumably, by the unexpected decision to take Simon's *The Dinner Party* to Broadway.

It's Good to Be Alive   (formerly titled *Ostrovsky*) Musical comedy, about a star of the Yiddish Theatre on lower Second Avenue. Music by Cy Coleman; book by Avery Corman; lyrics by Coleman and Corman; directed by Gene Saks; choreographed by Pat Birch. Alan King was mentioned to star. Initially announced for spring 2000, then announced for fall 2000.

Little Women   Musical, based on the novel by Louisa May Alcott. Music by Jason Howland; lyrics by Mindi Dickstein; book by Allan Knee; directed by Nick Corley; choreographed by Jennifer Paulson Lee. With Rita Gardner, Kerry O'Malley, and Mary Gordon Murray. Plans to begin previews October 31, 2000, at the Ambassador were canceled, due in part to the replacement of original songwriters by Kim Oler and Alison Hubbard. The show played a February 2001 workshop at Duke University.

Mack & Mabel   Revival of the 1974 musical, based on the November 2000 concert version at Reprise! (the Los Angeles equivalent of Encores!). Music and lyrics by Jerry Herman; book by Michael Stewart, revised by Francine Pascal; directed by Arthur Allan Seidelman; choreographed by Dan Siretta; silent film staging by Bill Irwin. With Douglas Sills, Jane Krakowski, and Donna McKechnie. An April 23, 2001, opening was postponed due to unavailability of a theatre, with the date rescheduled to November 2001 and, later, to January 10, 2002.

The Magician   (formerly titled *Blackstone*) Musical about magician Harry Blackstone. Music by Grant Sturiale; lyrics by Judd Woldin; book by Ivan Menchell; directed by Leslie Reidell; choreographed by Patricia Birch. Broadway previews were announced for August 2000.

The Night They Raided Minsky's   Musical comedy based on the legendary burlesque producer. Music by Charles Strouse; lyrics by Susan Birkenhead; book by Evan Hunter. Plans for a fall 2000 Broadway opening (following a July tryout at the Ahmanson Theatre in Los Angeles) were canceled, due in part to the death of director Mike Ockrent and the withdrawal of choreographer Susan Stroman. A developmental reading of the musical was held in May 2001, under the direction of Jerry Zaks.

Oklahoma!   Revival of the 1943 musical comedy. Music by Richard Rodgers; book and lyrics by Oscar Hammerstein 2nd; directed by Trevor Nunn; choreographed by Susan Stroman; produced by Cameron Mackintosh. The 1998 Royal National Theatre revival was initially scheduled for a fall 1999 Broadway opening but was postponed in February when American Actors' Equity rejected Mackintosh's request to import the London cast. In April 2000 the show was announced for a December 7, 2000, opening at the Ford Center (with an American cast). The show was once again postponed in July 2000 because of scheduling conflicts. In May 2001 it announced a new opening date of March 21, 2002, at the Gershwin.

The Rhythm Club   Musical about two composers of swing music in Hamburg, Germany, in the 1930s. Music by Matthew Sklar; book and lyrics by Chad Beguelin; directed by Eric D. Schaeffer; choreographed by Jodi Moccia. With Jeremy Kushnier, Lauren Ward, and Tim Martin Gleason. Played a September 2000 tryout at the Signature Theatre in Arlington, Virginia. A March 22, 2001, opening at the Virginia was announced, following a Chicago break-in. When Chicago was canceled, the Broadway opening was rescheduled to February 15; this, in turn, was postponed due to financing problems.

Tallulah   One-woman play about Tallulah Bankhead. By Sandra Ryan Heyward; directed by Michael Lessac; produced by SFX Theatrical Group and James M.

Nederlander. With Kathleen Turner. A pre-Broadway tour began in Minneapolis on October 3, 2000, prior to an announced April 2001 Broadway opening. In December, the Broadway engagement was postponed until the fall, due to unavailability of a theatre. The tour closed March 18, 2001, in Stamford, Connecticut. In May 2001, it was announced that *Tallulah* would not reopen.

Thoroughly Modern Millie   Musical adapted from the 1967 motion picture. Additional music by Jeanine Tesori; additional lyrics by Dick Scanlan; book by Richard Morris; directed by Michael Mayer; choreographed by Rob Ashford. With Sutton Foster, Tonya Pinkins, Pat Carroll, and Jim Stanek. Played an October 2000 tryout at the La Jolla Playhouse in San Diego. A spring 2001 opening was postponed due to unavailability of a theatre, and a November 15, 2001, opening "at a Nederlander Theatre" was announced. In July 2001, this, too, was canceled, and the opening was pushed back to April 18, 2002, at the Marquis.

A Thousand Clowns   Revival of the 1962 comedy. By Herb Gardner; directed by John Rando. With Tom Selleck. An April 2001 opening was postponed due to unavailability of a theatre, but the play opened on July 11, 2001, at the Longacre.

The Visit   A musical, based on the play by Friedrich Dürrenmatt. Music by John Kander; lyrics by Fred Ebb; book by Terrence McNally; directed by Frank Galati; choreographed by Ann Reinking. With Angela Lansbury and Philip Bosco. Plans for a March 15, 2001, opening at the Broadway were changed to a mid-April opening, and then canceled after Lansbury withdrew. A tryout at the Goodman Theatre in Chicago opened October 1, 2001, starring Chita Rivera and John McMartin.

Long-Run Leaders

The following shows, separated into plays and musicals, have run more than 1,000 performances on Broadway. The productions are listed in order of their all-time ranking. Because yesterday's record-breaking run might pale in comparison to a moderate hit of today, an additional column indicates productions that were at one time among the top ten, showing the highest level achieved.

The assumption that shows are running longer today than ever before holds true—but only for musicals. Six of the ten longest-running musicals opened since 1979, with at least one other likely to work its way into the top ten. One musical—the revival of *Cabaret*—broke the thousand-performance mark during the 2000–2001 season. However, all but three of the twenty-six plays to exceed 1,000 performances opened prior to 1980. The last play to exceed 1,000 performances opened in 1983, and it climbed only to fourteenth place on the list; at season's close, the longest-running current plays, *The Dinner Party* and *Proof*, had barely reached the 250 performance mark.

Performance totals are current through May 27, 2001. Shows marked with an asterisk were still running at press time.

Musicals				
All-time Ranking	Title	Opening Date	Number of Performances	Highest Ranking
1	Cats	October 7, 1982	7,485	1
2	A Chorus Line	July 25, 1975	6,137	1
3	* Les Misérables	March 12, 1987	5,855*	3*
4	Oh! Calcutta!! (revival)	September 24, 1976	5,852	2
5	*The Phantom of the Opera	January 26, 1988	5,566*	5*
6	Miss Saigon	April 11, 1991	4,097	6

(*continued*)

All-time Ranking	Title	Opening Date	Number of Performances	Highest Ranking
7	42nd Street	August 25, 1980	3,486	3
8	Grease	February 14, 1972	3,388	1
9	Fiddler on the Roof	September 22, 1964	3,242	1
10	*Beauty and the Beast	April 18, 1994	2,887*	10*
11	Hello, Dolly!	January 16, 1964	2,844	1
12	My Fair Lady	March 15, 1956	2,717	1
13	Annie	April 21, 1977	2,377	7
14	Man of La Mancha	November 22, 1965	2,328	4
15	Oklahoma!	March 31, 1943	2,212	1
16	* Rent	April 29, 1996	2,121*	
17	Smokey Joe's Café	March 2, 1995	2,036	
18	Pippin	October 23, 1972	1,944	7
19	South Pacific	April 7, 1949	1,925	2
20	The Magic Show	May 28, 1974	1,920	9
21	* Chicago (revival)	November 14, 1996	1,890*	
22	Dancin'	March 27, 1978	1,774	
23	La Cage Aux Folles	August 21, 1983	1,761	
24	Hair	April 29, 1968	1,750	7
25	The Wiz	January 5, 1975	1,672	
26	Crazy for You	February 19, 1992	1,622	
27	Ain't Misbehavin'	May 8, 1978	1,604	
28	The Best Little Whorehouse in Texas	April 17, 1978	1,584	
29	Evita	September 25, 1979	1,567	
30	Jekyll & Hyde	April 28, 1997	1,543	
31	Dreamgirls	December 20, 1981	1,521	
32	Mame	May 24, 1966	1,508	7
33	Grease! (revival)	May 11, 1994	1,503	
34	*The Lion King	November 13, 1997	1,478*	
35	The Sound of Music	November 16, 1959	1,443	4
36	Me and My Girl	August 10, 1986	1,420	
37	How To Succeed in Business without Really Trying	October 14, 1961	1,417	5
38	Hellzapoppin'	November 22, 1938	1,404	1
39	The Music Man	December 19, 1957	1,375	5
40	Funny Girl	March 26, 1964	1,348	9
41	*Cabaret (revival)	March 19, 1998	1,288*	
42	Promises, Promises	December 1, 1968	1,281	
43	The King and I	March 29, 1951	1,246	4

All-time Ranking	Title	Opening Date	Number of Performances	Highest Ranking
44	1776	March 16, 1969	1,217	
45	Sugar Babies	October 8, 1979	1,208	
46	Guys and Dolls	November 24, 1950	1,200	4
47	Cabaret	November 20, 1966	1,165	
48	Annie Get Your Gun	May 16, 1946	1,147	3
49	Guys and Dolls (revival)	April 14, 1992	1,143	
50	Bring in 'Da Noise, Bring in 'Da Funk	April 25, 1996	1,130	
51	Pins and Needles	November 27, 1937	1,108	1
52	They're Playing Our Song	February 11, 1979	1,082	
53	Kiss Me, Kate	December 30, 1948	1,070	5
54	Don't Bother Me, I Can't Cope	April 19, 1972	1,065	
55	The Pajama Game	May 13, 1954	1,063	9
56	Shenandoah	January 7, 1975	1,050	
57	Damn Yankees	May 5, 1955	1,019	10
58	Grand Hotel	November 12, 1989	1,018	
59	Big River	April 25, 1985	1,005	

Plays

All-time Ranking	Title	Opening Date	Number of Performances	Highest Ranking
1	Life with Father	November 8, 1939	3,224	1
2	Tobacco Road	December 4, 1933	3,182	1
3	Abie's Irish Rose	May 23, 1922	2,327	1
4	Deathtrap	February 26, 1978	1,792	4
5	Gemini	May 21, 1977	1,788	4
6	Harvey	November 1, 1944	1,775	4
7	Born Yesterday	February 4, 1946	1,642	5
8	Mary, Mary	March 8, 1961	1,572	6
9	The Voice of the Turtle	December 8, 1943	1,557	4
10	Barefoot in the Park	October 23, 1963	1,530	8
11	Same Time, Next Year	March 13, 1975	1,453	10
12	Arsenic and Old Lace	January 10, 1941	1,444	4

(continued)

All-time Ranking	Title	Opening Date	Number of Performances	Highest Ranking
13	Mummenschanz	March 30, 1977	1,326	
14	Brighton Beach Memoirs	March 27, 1983	1,299	
15	Angel Street	December 5, 1941	1,295	5
15	Lightnin'	August 26, 1918	1,291	1
16	Cactus Flower	December 8, 1965	1,234	
17	Sleuth	November 12, 1970	1,222	
18	Torch Song Trilogy	June 10, 1982	1,222	
19	Equus	October 24, 1974	1,209	
20	Amadeus	December 17, 1980	1,181	
21	Mister Roberts	February 18, 1948	1,157	10
22	The Seven Year Itch	November 20, 1952	1,141	
23	Butterflies Are Free	October 21, 1969	1,128	
24	Plaza Suite	February 14, 1968	1,097	
25	Teahouse of the August Moon	October 15, 1953	1,027	
26	Never Too Late	November 27, 1962	1,007	

The Season's Toll

The following people, who worked on Broadway or made an important contribution to the legitimate theatre, died between May 29, 2000, and May 27, 2001.

Steve Allen, 78; died October 30, 2000, of a heart attack, in Los Angeles. Influential talk show host and originator of the *Tonight Show* in 1953. A prolific songwriter, Allen wrote the score for the musical *Sophie* (based on the life of Sophie Tucker), which ran for eight performances in 1963.

Jean-Pierre Aumont, 90; died January 30, 2001, in Saint-Tropez. French film actor who starred opposite Vivien Leigh in the 1963 Broadway musical *Tovarich*.

Lyn Austin, 78; died October 29, 2000, in a traffic accident in Manhattan. Innovative producer and founder of the experimental Music-Theater Group in 1970. Prior to that, she coproduced *Copper and Brass*, Elaine May and Terrence McNally's *Adaptation/Next*, and Arthur Kopit's *Indians*.

Thomas Babe, 59; died December 6, 2000, of lung cancer, in Stamford, Connecticut. Playwright whose credits included *Kid Champion*, *A Prayer for My Daughter*, and *Fathers and Sons*, written while he was playwright-in-residence at Joseph Papp's New York Shakespeare Festival.

Sandy Baron, 64; died January 21, 2001, of emphysema, in Los Angeles. Stand-up comic whose Broadway credits included the original production of *One Flew Over the Cuckoo's Nest*, *Tchin-Tchin*, and as star replacement in *Lenny*.

Jonathan Bixby, 41; died April 29, 2001, of colon cancer, in Manhattan. Co-founder of the Drama Dept. and costume designer whose credits included *As Bees in Honey Drown*, *June Moon*, and *Urinetown*.

Gary Bonasorte, 45; died November 9, 2000, of lymphoma, in Manhattan. Off-Broadway playwright and cofounder of the Rattlestick Theater Company.

Victor Borge, 91; died December 23, 2000, in Greenwich, Connecticut. Danish-born pianist and satirist of classical music whose *Comedy in Music* opened in 1953 for 849 performances (more than two years), the longest-running solo show in Broadway history. Borge and *Comedy in Music* made two return visits to Broadway, in 1964 and 1977.

John Bury, 75; died November 12, 2000, of heart disease, in Gloucestershire, England. Innovative British set designer whose Broadway credits included *Oh, What a Lovely War!*, *The Rothschilds*, and *Amadeus* (for which he won scenic and lighting Tony Awards).

Vincent Canby, 76; died October 15, 2000, of cancer, in Manhattan. Critic for the *New York Times* who covered films from 1965 to 1993 before moving to the drama pages.

Arthur Cantor, 81; died April 8, 2001, of a heart attack, in Manhattan. Producer whose credits included *The Tenth Man, A Thousand Clowns*, the 1975 Maggie Smith revival of *Private Lives*, and *On Golden Pond*.

Mary Colquhoun, 61; died September 10, 2000, of ovarian cancer, in Manhattan. Casting director of many Broadway and off-Broadway productions.

Frances Ann Dougherty, 82; died April 25, 2001, in East Hampton, New York. Producer of the National Repertory Theatre, with Broadway credits including the 1964 productions of *The Seagull* (starring and directed by Eva Le Gallienne) and *The Crucible*.

Val Dufour, 73; died July 27, 2000, in Manhattan. Actor who appeared in *High Button Shoes, South Pacific, Picnic*, and *Stalag 17*. He was also an Emmy Award–winning soap opera star.

David Dukes, 55; died October 9, 2000, of a heart attack, on location in Spanaway, Washington. Broadway credits included major roles in the 1971 revival of *School for Wives, Bent*, Arthur Miller's *Broken Glass*, and star replacement stints in *Amadeus* and *M. Butterfly*.

Eldon Elder, 79; died December 11, 2000, of heart failure, in Manhattan. Set designer whose credits included *Time Out for Ginger, The Girl in Pink Tights*, and the Mel Brooks musical *Shinbone Alley*. He was also the first resident designer at the New York Shakespeare Festival, for which he designed the Delacorte Theatre.

Julius J. Epstein, 91; died December 30, 2000, in Los Angeles. Screenwriter of many films, including *Casablanca* (written with his twin brother, Philip), as well as the 1944 Broadway comedy *Chicken Every Sunday*. He also collaborated with Stephen Sondheim on *Saturday Night*, a 1955 musical that had its New York debut during the 1999–2000 season.

Don Ettlinger, 86; died August 7, 2000, in Nyack, New York. Librettist of the musical *Ambassador*. Best known as a writer for films (*Rebecca of Sunnybrook Farm*) and television.

Lucille Fletcher, 88; died August 31, 2000, in Langhorne, Pennsylvania. Author of the 1972 thriller *Night Watch*, as well as the radio play and screenplay *Sorry, Wrong Number*.

Stan Freeman, 80; died January 13, 2001, of emphysema, in Hollywood. Songwriter, nightclub performer, and longtime accompanist for Marlene Dietrich, he was cocomposer-lyricist for the Broadway musicals *I Had a Ball* and *Lovely Ladies, Kind Gentlemen*.

Peter Gennaro, 80; died September 28, 2000. Broadway choreographer whose many credits included *Seventh Heaven*, *West Side Story* (as cochoreographer), *Fiorello!*, *The Unsinkable Molly Brown*, and *Annie*. His early work as a dancer included important spots in the Jerome Robbins–Bob Fosse musicals *The Pajama Game* (in the "Steam Heat" number) and *Bells Are Ringing*.

José Greco, 82; died December 31, 2000, of heart failure, in Lancaster, Pennsylvania. World-renowned flamenco dancer who brought his company to the Shubert Theatre in 1951 for a two-month Broadway engagement. (A lawsuit was instituted in June 2001 claiming that death was caused by an infection Greco developed after breaking a toe in a scuffle with Amtrak police.)

Otis L. Guernsey Jr., 82; died May 2, 2001, of pancreatic cancer, in Woodstock, Vermont. Theatre critic who spent almost twenty years at the *Herald Tribune* and served as editor of the *Best Plays* series for thirty-six years.

Sir Alec Guinness, 86; died August 5, 2000, of prostate cancer, in West Sussex, England. The legendary great film actor also made occasional stage appearances, including Broadway engagements in T. S. Eliot's *The Cocktail Party*, *Ross* (as Lawrence of Arabia), and his Tony Award–winning performance as Dylan Thomas in *Dylan*. Film credits included *The Bridge over the River Kwai*, *Great Expectations*, *Kind Hearts and Coronets*, *The Man in the White Suit*, and *Star Wars* (which made him really famous).

William Hammerstein, 82; died March 9, 2001, in Washington, Connecticut, of complications from a stroke. Producer-director and the eldest son of Oscar Hammerstein 2nd. His producing credits included Neil Simon's first play, *Come Blow Your Horn*, and Garson Kanin's *A Gift of Time*. Directing credits included the 1979 revival of *Oklahoma!* He also won a special Tony Award in 1957 for his work establishing the City Center Light Opera Company.

David M. Haskell, 52; died August 30, 2000, of brain cancer, in Woodland Hills, California. Actor whose credits included the original production (and film version) of *Godspell*.

David Heneker, 94; died January 30, 2001, in Wales. British songwriter whose many credits included two musicals—*Irma La Douce* and *Half a Sixpence*—that were hits in both London and New York.

Jerry Jarrett, 82; died May 16, 2001, in Manhattan. Actor whose major credit was a replacement stint as Tevye in the original production of *Fiddler on the Roof*. He also appeared in Irving Berlin's *This Is the Army* and the comedy *At War with the Army*.

Maria Karnilova, 80; died April 20, 2001, in Manhattan, of cancer. Ballerina turned musical comedy star, best known for her Tony Award–winning performance as Golde in *Fiddler in the Roof*. Other credits included *Stars in Your Eyes* (in which she was in the chorus with Jerome Robbins), *Call Me Mister* (in which she met and married her husband of fifty years, George S. Irving), *Gypsy* (as stripper Tessie Tura), and *Zorbá*.

Pat Kauffman, 76; died November 24, 2000, in Manhattan. Tireless founder of Entertainment for the Blind, an organization that arranged for and distributed hundreds of thousands of complimentary tickets to visually impaired theatregoers.

Harvey J. Klaris, 61; died January 12, 2001, of heart failure, in Manhattan. Producer whose credits included *Nine*, *Cloud Nine*, and *The Tap Dance Kid*.

Werner Klemperer, 80; died December 6, 2000, of cancer, in Manhattan. Character actor best known for the role of Colonel Klink on the sitcom *Hogan's Heroes*, for which he won two Emmy Awards. Son of conductor Otto Klemperer, his Broadway credits included the 1988 revival of *Cabaret* and the 1995 revival of *Uncle Vanya*.

Jack Kroll, 74; died June 8, 2000, of colon cancer, in Manhattan. Theatre critic for *Newsweek* for thirty-five years.

Ring Lardner Jr., 85; died October 31, 2000, of cancer, in Manhattan. Screenwriter, son of the famous humorist-playwright, and last surviving member of the blacklisted "Hollywood Ten." His credits included the Oscar-winning screenplays for *Woman of the Year* and *M*A*S*H* and the book for the Bert Lahr musical *Foxy*.

Stephanie Lawrence, 50; died November 4, 2000, in London. British star of such musicals as *Evita, Starlight Express, Marilyn*, and *Blood Brothers*, in which she also appeared on Broadway.

Joseph Leon, 82; died March 25, 2001, in Bradenton, Florida. Character actor whose credits included *Pipe Dream, The Beauty Part*, and *Social Security*. He starred in Arnold Wesker's *The Merchant*, taking over when Zero Mostel died during the tryout.

Warner LeRoy, 65; died February 22, 2001, of lymphoma, in Manhattan. Flamboyant restaurateur and son of Hollywood royalty (director Mervyn LeRoy and Warner Bros. daughter Doris Warner). LeRoy's off-Broadway producing credits included Tennessee Williams's *Garden District* (1958), which included the one-act *Suddenly Last Summer*; Maxwell Anderson's final play, *The Golden Six* (1958); and *Between Two Thieves* (1960), which LeRoy also wrote and directed.

John Lindsay, 79; died December 20, 2000, of complications from pneumonia and Parkinson's disease, in Hilton Head, South Carolina. Mayor of New York City during its "Fun City" years from 1965 through 1973. Lindsay served as chairman of Lincoln Center Theater from 1984 to 1991 and remained as chairman emeritus at the time of his death.

Kert Lundell, 64; died September 11, 2000, of lung cancer, in Manhattan. Set designer whose credits included *The Investigation*, Neil Simon's *The Sunshine Boys*, and Gower Champion's *Rockabye Hamlet*.

Michael Maggio, 49; died August 19, 2000, of complications from posttransplant lymphoma, in Chicago. Director whose New York credits included the 1989 New York Shakespeare Festival production of *Titus Andronicus*, the musical version of *Wings*, and the drama *My Thing of Love*. He directed numerous plays at the Goodman Theatre, for which he served as associate director.

Nancy Marchand, 72; died June 18, 2000, of cancer, in Stratford, Connecticut. Award-winning stage and television actress whose credits included *And Miss Reardon Drinks a Little*, the 1980 revival of *Morning's at Seven*, *The Cocktail Hour*, and *The End of the Day*. Television credits included prominent roles on *Lou Grant* (for which she won four Emmy Awards) and *The Sopranos*.

Walter Matthau, 79; died July 1, 2000, of cardiac arrest, in Santa Monica, California. Stage and screen actor. Broadway credits included *A Shot in the Dark* and *The Odd Couple* (both of which earned him Tony Awards). Film credits included *The Fortune Cookie* (for which he won an Oscar) and *The Odd Couple*.

Frances Mercer, 85; died November 12, 2000, in Los Angeles. Singer who appeared in Kern and Hammerstein's *Very Warm for May* and Cole Porter's *Something for the Boys*.

Michael Meyer, 79; died August 3, 2000, in London. Author of authoritative biographies of both Ibsen and Strindberg and translator of more than thirty plays by the two Scandinavians.

Jason Miller, 62; died May 13, 2001, of a heart attack, in Scranton, Pennsylvania. Actor turned playwright, best known for his Pulitzer Prize–winning *That Championship Season* (his only play to reach Broadway) and his starring role in the film *The Exorcist*.

Loften Mitchell, 82; died May 14, 2001, in Queens, New York. Playwright whose credits included librettos for the musicals *Bubbling Brown Sugar* and *Ballad for Bimshire*.

Ruth Mitchell, 81; died November 3, 2000, after a long illness, in Manhattan. One of Broadway's top stage managers, she worked extensively with director-choreographer Jerome Robbins (on shows like *West Side Story* and *Gypsy*) and producer-director Harold Prince (on shows like *A Funny Thing Happened on the Way to the Forum* and *Fiddler on the Roof*). Beginning in 1966, she served as associate producer for musicals produced by Prince.

Robert Montgomery Jr., 77; died September 2, 2000, of lung cancer, in Sag Harbor, New York. Entertainment lawyer, well known in the theatre for his post as trustee of the Cole Porter Musical and Literary Property Trusts.

Richard Mulligan, 67; died September 26, 2000, of cancer, in Los Angeles. Actor whose stage credits included leading roles in *The Mating Dance*, *Special Occasions*, and Herb Gardner's *Thieves*. Television credits included Emmy Award–winning performances in the sitcoms *Soap* and *Empty Nest*.

N. Richard Nash, 87; died December 11, 2000, in Manhattan. Playwright whose credits included *The Rainmaker* (which was revived during the 1999–2000 season) and the musicals *Wildcat*, *110 in the Shade*, and *The Happy Time*.

Portia Nelson, 80; died March 6, 2001, in Manhattan. Cabaret singer, actress, and songwriter, her theatre credits included acting in *The Golden Apple* and writing music and lyrics for the 1955 Broadway revue *Almost Crazy*.

Harold Nicholas, 79; died on July 3, 2000, of heart failure, in Manhattan. Younger half of the famed tap-dancing act the Nicholas Brothers (with his brother Fayard). They appeared on Broadway in *The Ziegfeld Follies of 1936*, *Babes in Arms*, and *St. Louis Woman* (in which he introduced "Come Rain or Come Shine").

Helen L. Nickerson, age unreported; died September 2, 2000, of a stroke, in Manhattan. Longtime assistant to (and eventually general manager for) David Merrick.

Jack O'Brian, 86; died November 5, 2000, in Manhattan. Newspaper columnist and radio commentator for almost sixty years specializing in Broadway (and TV) news and gossip.

Harold Pierson, 66; died August 1, 2000, of a heart attack, in Manhattan. Dancer and choreographer. Dancing credits included *Golden Boy*, *Sweet Charity*, and *Purlie*.

Josephine Premice, 74; died April 13, 2001, of emphysema, in Manhattan. Musical comedy actress with a distinctively squeaky voice. Her credits included *Jamaica* and *A Hand Is on the Gate* (both of which earned her Tony Award nominations) and *Bubbling Brown Sugar*.

Eugenia Rawls, 87; died November 8, 2000, of pneumonia, in Denver. Veteran actress whose stage career spanned more than fifty years, beginning in the original 1934 production of Lillian Hellman's *The Children's Hour*. Wife of Denver showman Donald R. Seawell, Rawls was a close friend and biographer of Tallulah Bankhead (who played her mother in *The Little Foxes*).

Beah Richards, 74; died September 14, 2000, of emphysema, in Vicksburg, Mississippi. Character actress whose Broadway credits included *The Miracle Worker*, *Purlie Victorious*, James Baldwin's *The Amen Corner*, and Mike Nichols's 1967 revival of *The Little Foxes*. She received two Emmy Awards (including one in 2000) and an Oscar nomination for her role as Sidney Poitier's mother in *Guess Who's Coming to Dinner*.

Jason Robards, 78; died December 26, 2000, of cancer, in Bridgeport, Connecticut. One of the great American actors of modern times, with a special affinity for the work of Eugene O'Neill. Broadway credits included three O'Neill plays

(*Long Day's Journey into Night*, *A Moon for the Misbegotten*, and *The Iceman Cometh*), Arthur Miller's *After the Fall*, and *A Thousand Clowns*. Screen credits included *All the President's Men* and *Julia*, for which he won Oscars in successive years.

Francis Ruivivar, 40; died May 23, 2001, of leukemia, in Las Vegas. Musical theatre actor whose credits included *Shogun—The Musical* and *Passion*; also served as replacement in the role of The Engineer in the Broadway production of *Miss Saigon*.

Sir Harry Secombe, 79; died April 11, 2001, of cancer, in Guildford, England. Beloved British comedian who sprang to fame on the 1950s British radio program *The Goon Show* (with Peter Sellers and Spike Milligan). Stage credits included the British musical hit *Pickwick*, in which he also starred on Broadway, and *The Four Musketeers*.

Max Showalter, 83; died July 30, 2000, in Middletown, Conn. Stage and screen actor whose credits included Kern and Hammerstein's *Very Warm for May* and Irving Berlin's *This Is the Army*; also served as replacement in *Hello, Dolly!* and *The Grass Harp*. He was also a composer, with one Broadway musical—*Harrigan 'n' Hart*—to his credit.

Ann Sothern, 92; died March 15, 2001, in Ketchum, Idaho. Comedienne best known for her film work and as star of two hit 1950 sitcoms. Under her real name, Harriette Lake, she starred in Rodgers and Hart's *America's Sweetheart* and took over the female lead in the original production of George and Ira Gershwin's *Of Thee I Sing*.

Beatrice Straight, 86; died April 7, 2001, in North Ridge, California. Actress whose stage credits included *The Innocents*, Arthur Miller's *The Crucible* (for which she won a featured actress Tony Award), and Edward Albee's *Everything in the Garden*. She also won a featured actress Oscar for *Network*.

Mildred Traube, 90; died July 21, 2000, in Manhattan. Longtime head of the Society of Stage Directors and Choreographers, as well as widow of *Angel Street* producer Shepard Traube.

Peter Turgeon, 80; died October 6, 2000, in Stony Brook, New York. Actor whose credits included *A Thurber Carnival* and *Little Me*.

Gwen Verdon, 75; died October 17, 2000, in Woodstock, Vermont. One of Broadway's most beloved musical comedy stars, the redheaded dancer-singer-comedienne starred in five musicals choreographed by Bob Fosse (whom she married in 1960). She won Tony Awards for each of her four Broadway musicals in the 1950s. Credits included *Can-Can, Damn Yankees, New Girl in Town, Redhead, Sweet Charity,* and *Chicago.*

Ray Walston, 86; died January 1, 2001, in Beverly Hills. Character man best known for his Tony Award–winning role in *Damn Yankees* and his Emmy-winning role as the title character in the sitcom *My Favorite Martian.* Walston also played Luther Billis in the Chicago and London companies of *South Pacific,* recreating the role on the screen as well.

Mary K. Wells, 79; died August 14, 2000, of an infection of the colon, in Manhattan. Actress whose credits included *Any Wednesday,* Edward Albee's *Everything in the Garden,* and the 1969 revival of *Three Men on a Horse.* She was also an actor and writer on TV soap operas.

Edward Winter, 63; died March 8, 2001, of Parkinson's disease, in Woodland Hills, California. Actor whose Broadway credits included *Cabaret* and *Promises! Promises!* (for both of which he received Tony nominations).

Jim Wise, 81; died November 13, 2000, in Manhattan. Composer of the 1968 off-Broadway hit *Dames at Sea.*

Freddy Wittop, 89; died February 2, 2001, in Atlantis, Florida. Costume designer whose credits included *Hello, Dolly!, Carnival, I Do! I Do!,* and other musicals. He also had a separate career as a "Spanish" dancer, under the name Federico Rey.

Mary Hunter Wolf, 95; died November 3, 2000, in Hamden, Connecticut. One of Broadway's first female directors whose credits included *Carib Song, Ballet Ballads,* and Jean-Paul Sartre's *The Respectful Prostitute.*

G. Wood, 80; died July 24, 2000, of heart failure, in Manhattan. Composer and actor whose composing credits included the off-Broadway musical *F. Jasmine Adams* (based on *The Member of the Wedding*) and off-Broadway revues, including *Shoestring '57, Put It in Writing,* and Julius Monk's *Baker's Dozen.*

Richard Woods, 77; died January 16, 2001, in Englewood, New Jersey. Character actor whose Broadway credits included *Sail Away, Coco, Deathtrap,* and numerous productions with the APA-Phoenix Theatre Company.

Index

Page numbers in **boldface** indicate extended discussion of 2000–2001 shows. All people, titles, and organizations mentioned in the text have been indexed. For reference purposes, selected people who are billed on the theatre program title pages but not specifically discussed in the text have also been included.